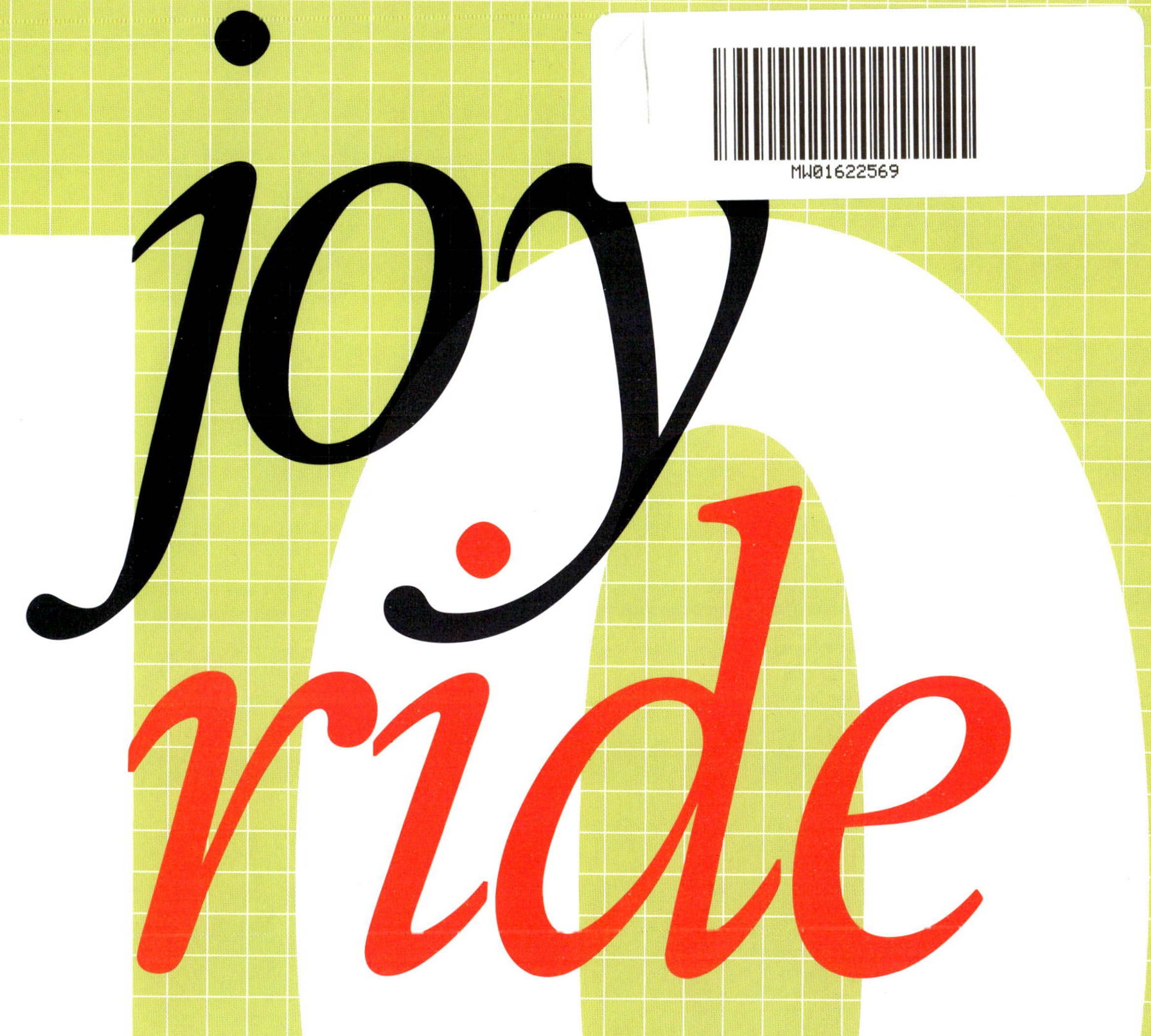

joy ride

10 YEARS OF THE WOODWARD DREAM CRUISE

BY THE DETROIT FREE PRESS

Detroit Free Press
600 W. Fort St.
Detroit, MI 48226
www.freep.com

Manufactured by Quad/Graphics, West Allis, Wis., United States of America.

Other recent books by the Free Press:

Men at Work
Life After Baseball
Life Lessons
Portraits of War
Razor Sharp: Drew Sharp
Hang 10
Time Frames
The Detroit Almanac
HeartSmart Kids Cookbook
State of Glory
The Corner
PC@Home
Fishing Michigan
Hockey Gods
Motoons: Mike Thompson
Ernie Harwell: Stories From My Life in Baseball
Corner to Copa
Century of Champions
Believe!
Stanleytown

➤ To order any of these titles, please call 800-245-5082 or visit **www.freep.com/bookstore**

➤ To subscribe to the Free Press, call 800-395-3300.

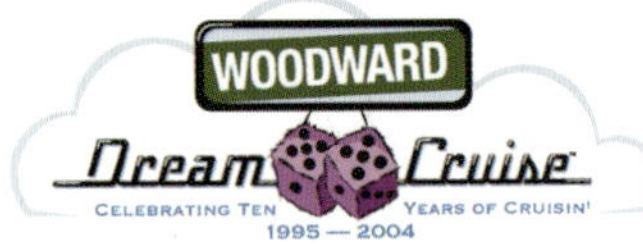

Editor: Tina Croley

Designer: Mauricio Gutierrez

Photo editors: Todd Cross, Kathy Kieliszewski

Photo technicians: Rose Ann McKean, Jessica Trevino, Kathryn Trudeau

Writer: Bill Laitner

Copy editors: Sherita Wyche Bryant, Holly Griffin

Project coordinator: Dave Robinson

Illustrations: Rick Nease

Graphics: Kofi Myler

Research: Shelley Lavey

Cover photo: Kirthmon F. Dozier

Special thanks:
Caron A. Hall, Woodward Dream Cruise executive director
Nancy Andrews, Free Press director of photography
Steve Dorsey, Free Press design and graphics director
Thom Fladung, Free Press managing editor
Carole Leigh Hutton, Free Press publisher and editor
Dale Parry, Free Press deputy managing editor
Mark Phelan, Free Press auto critic
Ron Recinto, Free Press assistant metro editor
Steve Spalding, Free Press assistant business editor

CONTENTS

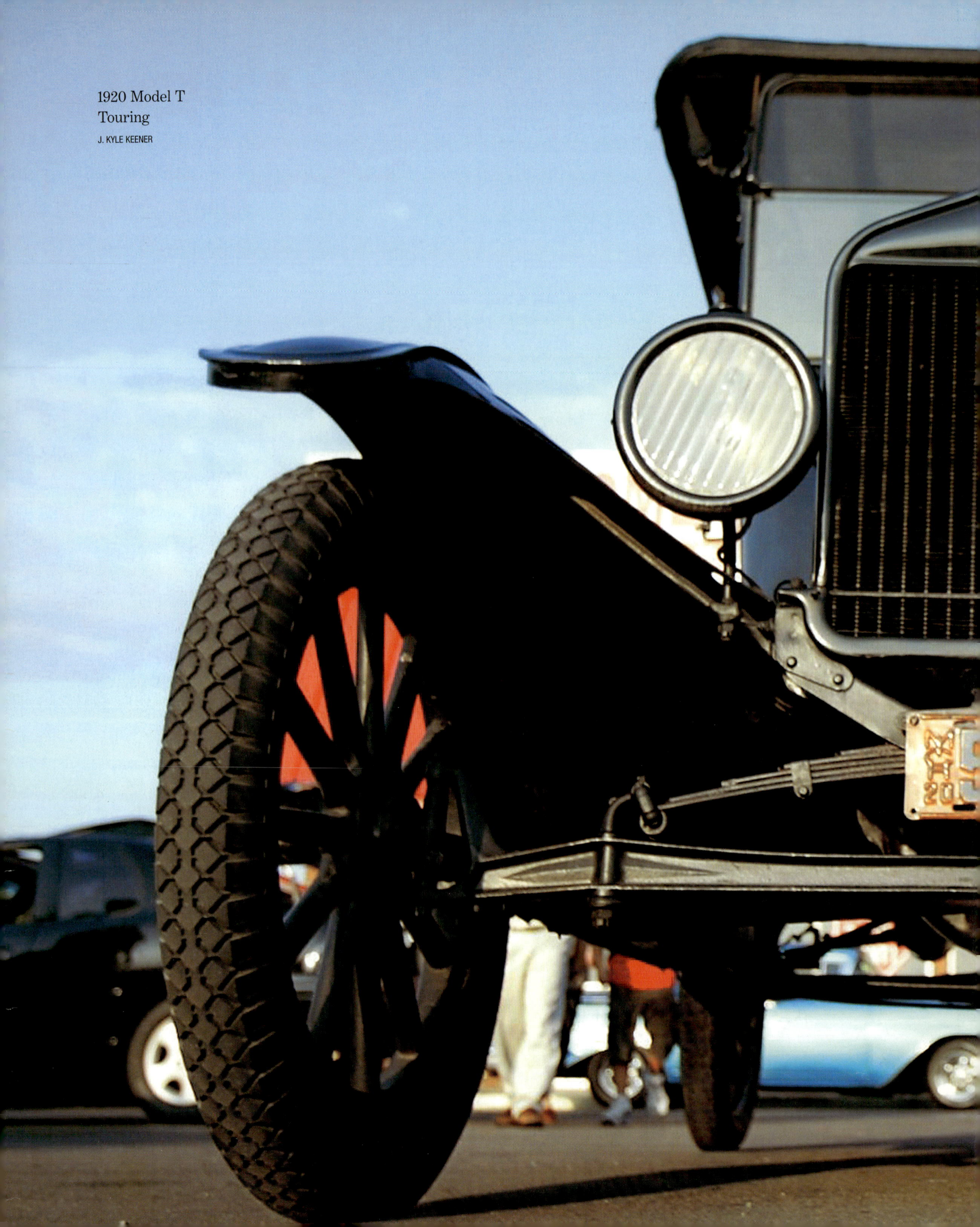

1920 Model T
Touring

J. KYLE KEENER

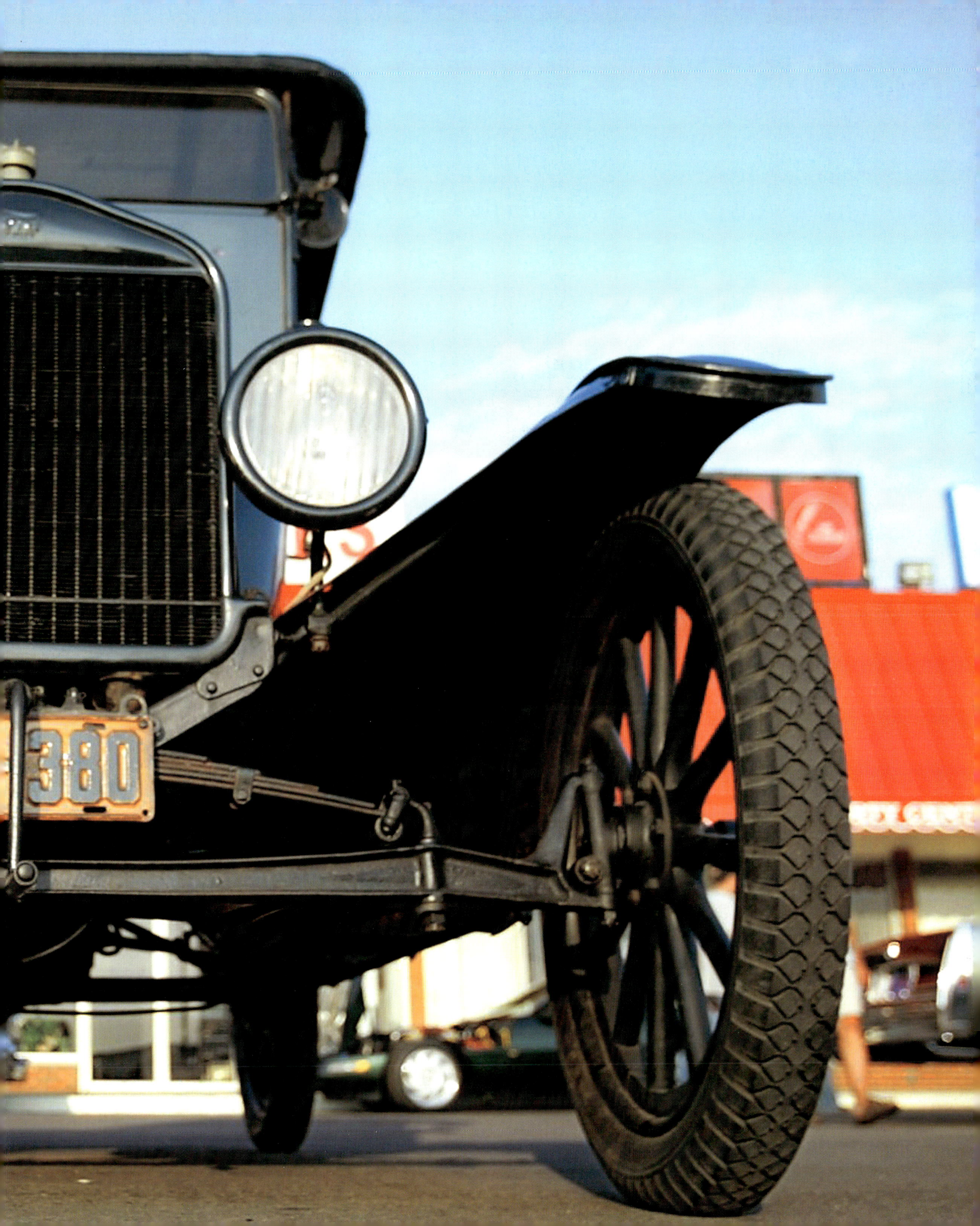
380

By BILL LAITNER

They call it the greatest one-day car event in the world. Hearing that, across the nation and around the globe, auto enthusiasts nod their heads. They know there are other mega- and multiday events involving the automobile. They know about Hot August Nights in Reno, Nev., and the Route 66 Rendezvous in San Bernardino, Calif. Those events and others elsewhere rack up hefty attendance numbers by drawing crowds day

DREAM

after day, often pulling in the same repeat visitors.

But car nuts also know this: Nowhere is there, on a single day, a single event that draws as many people from all over the world of cars and car craziness as the Woodward Dream Cruise, which runs from northern Detroit through its suburbs to downtown Pontiac.

From its earliest days as a fund-raiser for a children's soccer field, the Dream Cruise has grown beyond anyone's wildest dreams. Now, it's rolling toward its 10th year and bound to set another record.

Organizers say only the massive power outage of 2003, which blacked out much of Michigan and the nation until hours before the curtain lifted on Dream Cruise IX, followed by the first heavy rains in the history of the event kept crowds from breaking the 2002 record of 1.7 million attendees.

Months before the 10th anniversary Dream Cruise, Web site hits and sales of membership kits were already over previous tabs. Organizers say the cruise-o-meter is rapidly heading toward 2 million.

Of course, the point isn't how big it is. It's *why* so many come.

WHAT IS IT THAT BRINGS auto fans, their friends, relatives and travelers to cruise Woodward, to park and lift hoods, take photos and mostly just stand in awe and delight at the curbsides of America's quintessential cruising boulevard?

That's easy. They come to watch and show off tens of thousands of classic cars, from the auto industry's earliest days to an era of unbridled horsepower when America's imagination and technical prowess knew no bounds.

More than any other event and any other place, Woodward and its Dream Cruise mark Detroit's and America's place in history as the motoring and industrial centers of the world. But, there's something else that's special about the Dream Cruise: It's not packaged and produced.

The Woodward Dream Cruise is by and for regular folks.

Real car nuts started it and keep it going, even in the face of increasingly hyped marketing efforts by auto manufacturers — who've descended in hordes after seeing how popular the Dream Cruise is.

Yet, nothing commercial on the Woodward strip can dim the plain-spoken love of automobilia by those who drive hundreds, sometimes thousands, of miles to attend. Hot-rod groups and car club members will tell you: No advertising or flashy new-car display can cool the ardor that Dream Cruise fans have for this parade of history and horsepower.

The Dream Cruise, from its start, has been a nonprofit, grassroots event. Anybody can show up, and anybody can show a car — just by driving on Woodward. That makes the cruise a far cry from custom-car shows and stuffy collector events, with their steep entry fees and fussy judges. Instead, the Dream Cruise is a circus with no tickets.

Hence, the vast range of attendees, from aging gearheads with weekend grease under their fingernails and their ladies in poodle skirts and bobby socks, to a scattering of abortion opponents whose oversize posters displayed on an old school bus one year almost provoked fisticuffs. Most of all, the Dream Cruise provides a long-needed arena for countless collectors of classic cars.

"There are people who've had these old cars in their garages for 16 years, and only after the Dream Cruise happened, did they decide to finish restoring that car and get it out onto Woodward to cruise," said the Rev. Doug Jones, pastor of Pontiac's Welcome Baptist Church and Pontiac's delegate to Woodward Dream Cruise Inc., the nonprofit group that puts on the event. > > >

CRUISE

DREAM CRUISE

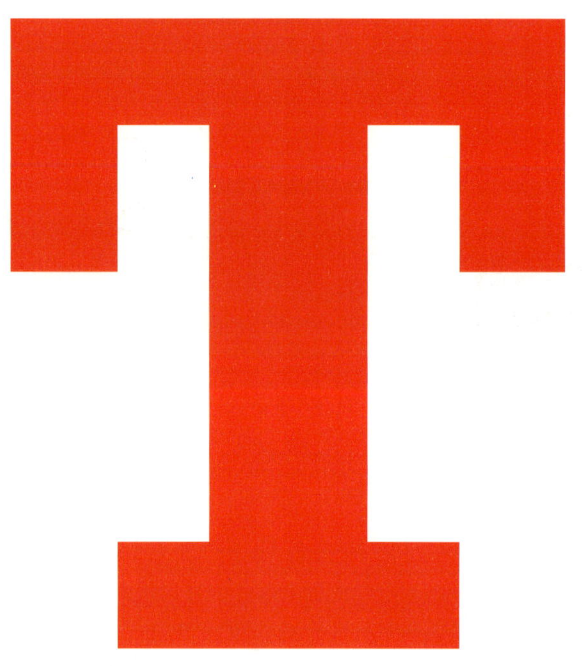

he irony of the Dream Cruise is as big as the event, but unspoken. Yes, the Dream Cruise showcases the grand past of American horsepower and technology — but in the very era when American cars rapidly lost market share to foreign models.

The Dream Cruise coincided with a burst of popular interest by car buyers and auto designers in retro designs of muscle cars and hot rods. Domestic auto makers Car hustled, reviving those old car looks, the feeling of neck-jerking acceleration, and even some of their names.

To southeast Michigan, the benefit is even more tangible. The average Dream Cruise fan spends at least $60 while visiting the event and the region, sometimes from thousands of miles away, and sometimes staying a week or more after bringing in a classic car on a trailer.

Multiplied by the 1.7 million who attended in the event's biggest year — 2002 — the result is an economic boost of well over $100 million to southeast Michigan, say Oakland County's economic development gurus.

That doesn't mean everyone loves the cruise. While restaurants are packed, art galleries and veterinarians close for the day. Many business owners on Woodward complain that patrons stay away throughout the week leading up to the Dream Cruise.

"But that's a small price for them to pay to have the Woodward corridor receive all this attention and to have people see it from all over the area," says Jean Chamberlain of Royal Oak, a longtime member of the Dream Cruise board and longtime promoter of Woodward Avenue.

WITH THE PRICE OF GASOLINE climbing and with today's teens more inclined to tweak computers than camshafts, some prognosticators have said the Dream Cruise can't go on. They've said it will peter out.

Maybe they've been out of town on the third Saturday in August. Judging by the crowds, this thing has wheels — and it isn't stopping anytime soon.

In recent years, the number of classic cars cruising at a given moment has diminished. Their engines get overheated, their brakes get fried, and so their owners park and watch others cruise by, then rejoin the crowd as men, women and machines cool down.

Cruise officials have struggled to keep non-classics off the course. But that debate is as hot as the radiators. Just what constitutes a cruise-worthy vehicle?

Should it be cars made only before 1970, or some other year? That wouldn't please Anthony Ewing of Belleville.

"Someone's dream vehicle may be a 2002 Cadillac Escalade. If they want to participate, they should be allowed to," Ewing says.

His dream car? A Lamborghini Diablo, any year.

"If I ever get one, you better believe that I will drive it in any event with the word 'dream' in it," he says.

The future of the Dream Cruise could lie in a word that sounds, to baby boomers at least, like an old stereo term: *tuners*.

Tuner cars are less about sheer horsepower and more about style: designer wheels, low-profile tires, oversize brakes, high-performance shocks and much more.

Interiors may have recherche suede and, always, audio systems that can be heard a county away.

It may well be that, even as the '57 Chevys and old Ford coupes fade into history, the tuner cars of today will be the Dream Cruise stable of tomorrow.

If so, the world's biggest one-day car event could have a lot more mileage ahead of it. ■

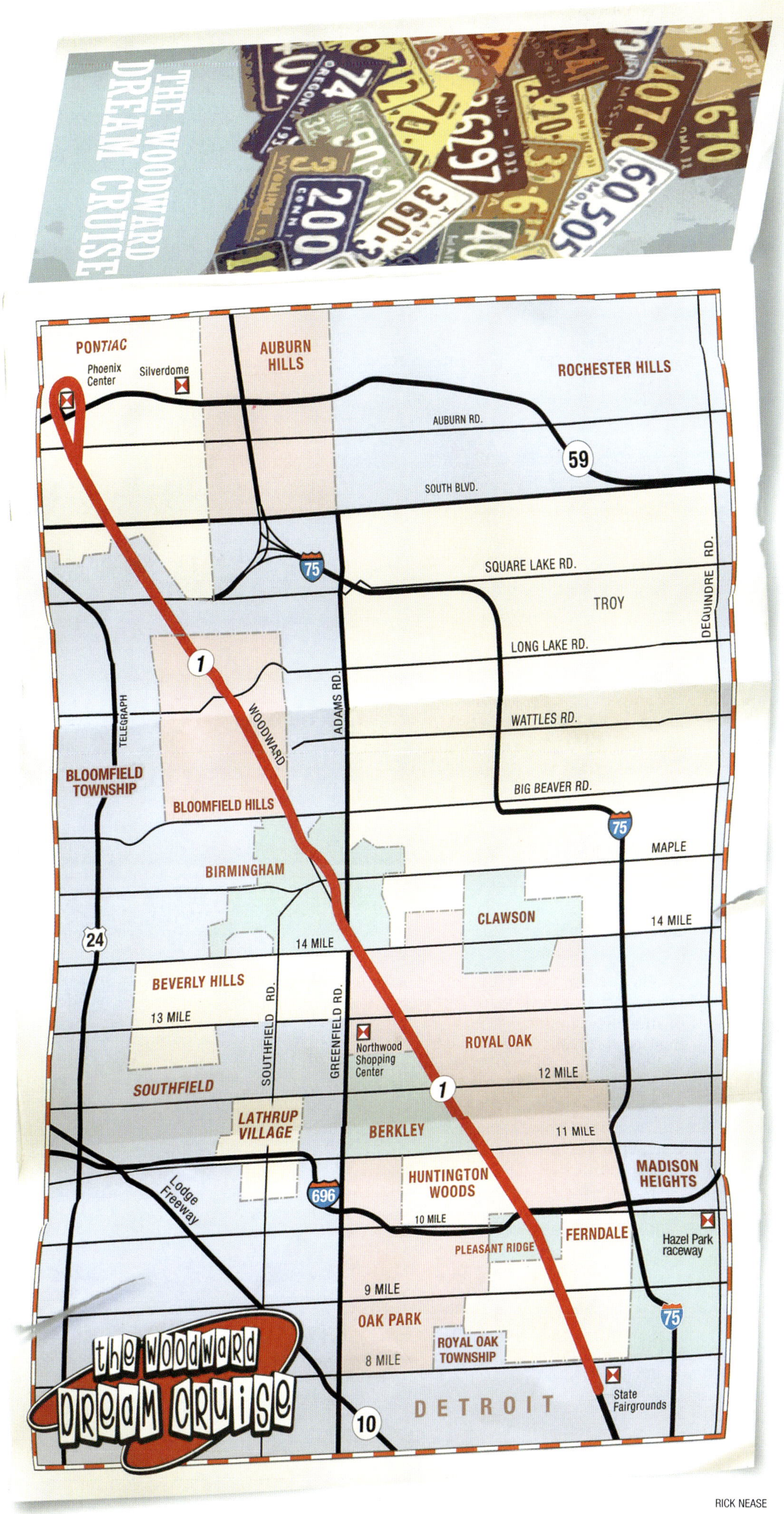

RICK NEASE

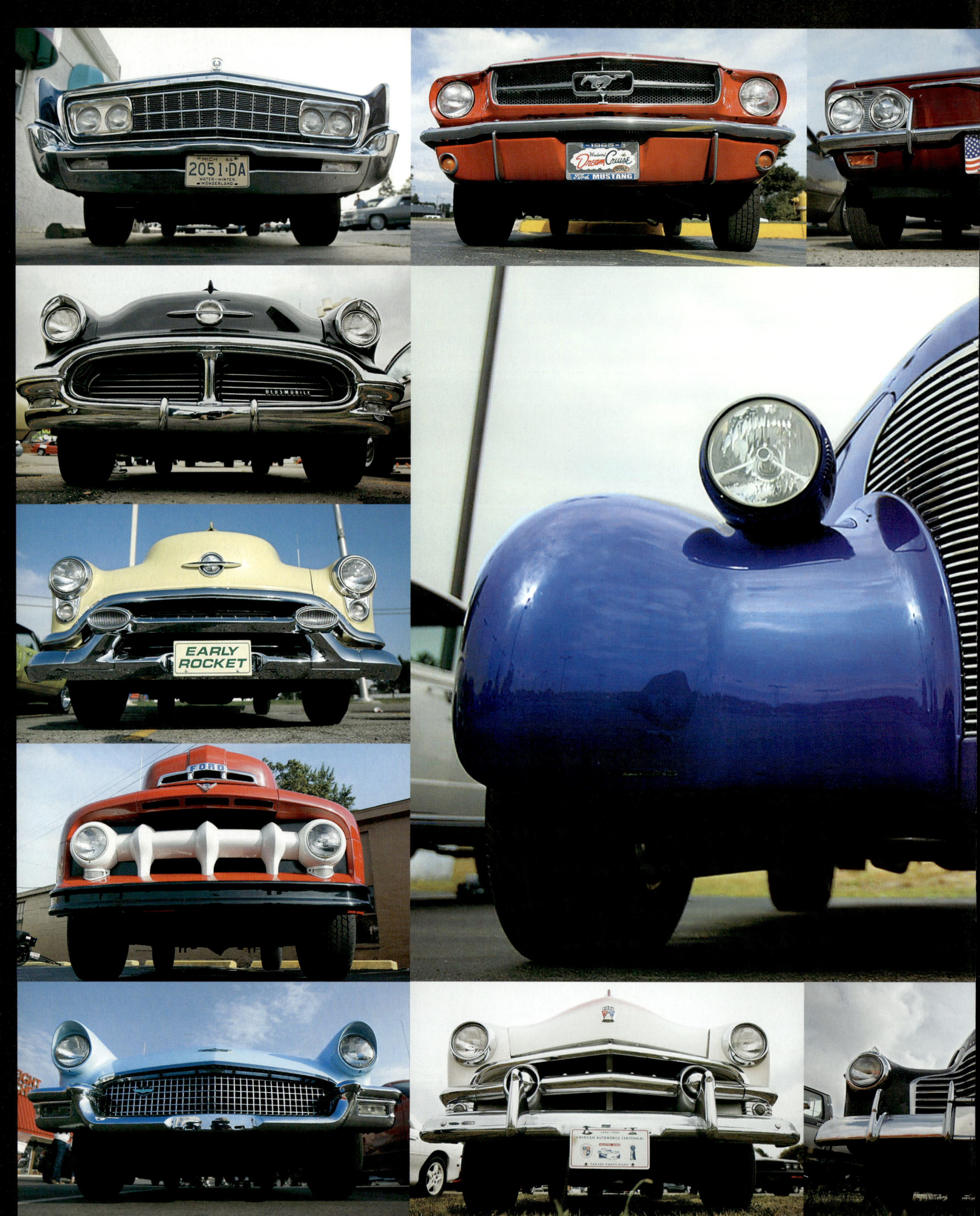
MICH 66
2051·DA
WATER-WINTER WONDERLAND
Dream Cruise
Ford MUSTANG
OLDSMOBILE
EARLY
ROCKET
FORD
AMERICAN AUTOMOBILE CENTENNIAL

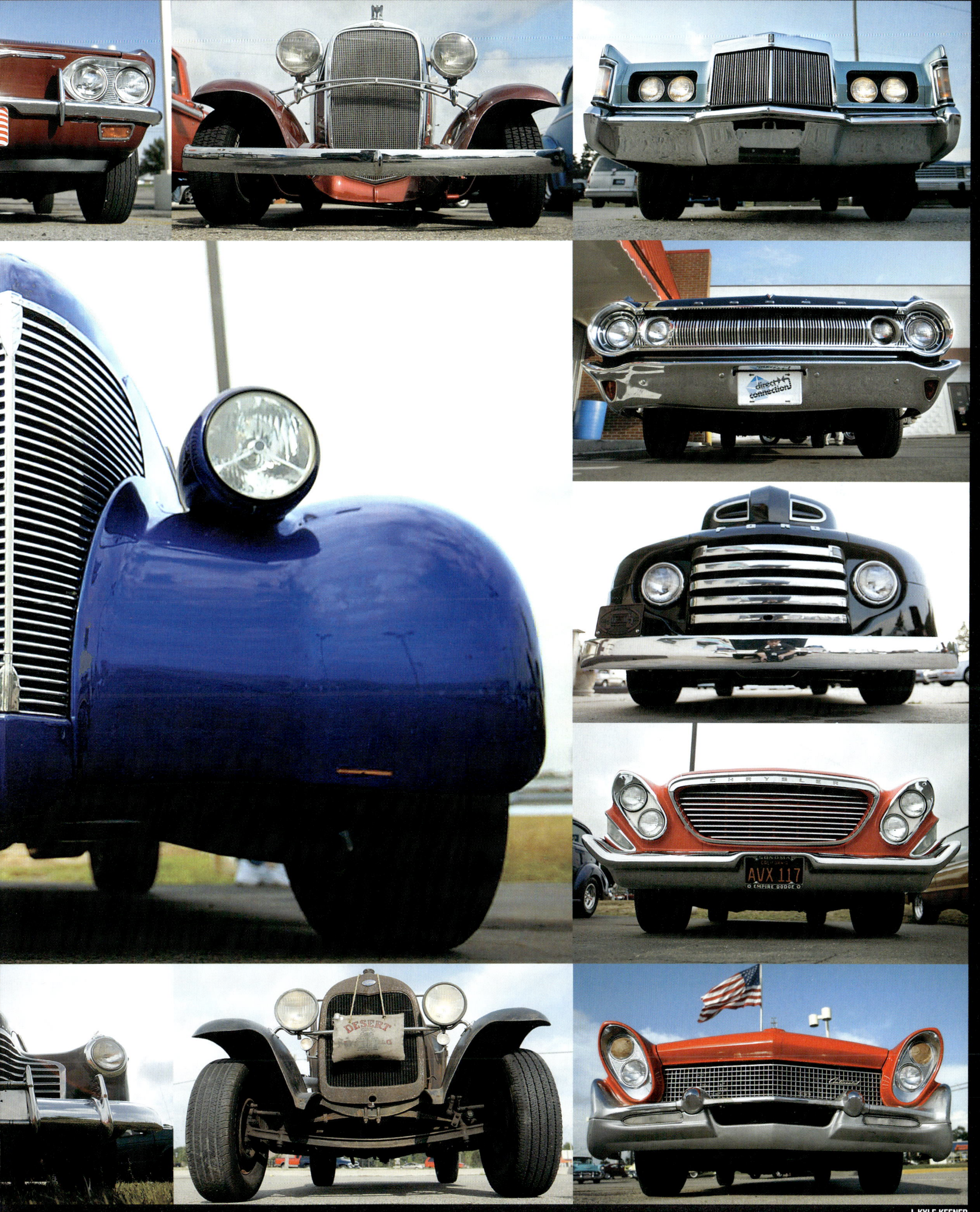

J. KYLE KEENER

DREAM CRUISE

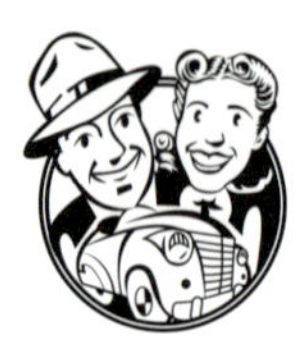

Date: Aug. 19

Attendance: More than 400,000, although fewer than 25,000 were expected.

Special moment: Six host cities — Ferndale, Pleasant Ridge, Berkley, Huntington Woods, Royal Oak and Birmingham — came together along Woodward.

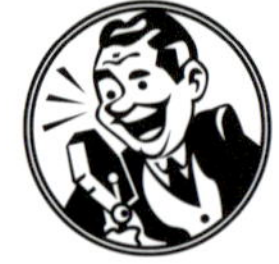

Elvis connection: Pleasant Ridge's exclusive Dream Cruise Hawaiian shirt, which turns into an annual sellout. A subliminal salute to "Blue Hawaii"?

Souvenir of choice: The dash plaque from the first Dream Cruise. To get it, cruisers drove to each city to collect puzzle pieces, then assembled them into that year's Dream Cruise logo — a blazing sun behind a generic sports car. But, organizers admit, the car looks a lot like a vintage Corvette.

1995

THE FIRST WOODWARD DREAM CRUISE DIDN'T START IN AN AD AGENCY. It wasn't birthed by PR professionals, or even by classic-car freaks.

Nope, it was a fund-raiser for a kids soccer field, led by a plumber.

In 1994, Ferndale resident Nelson House, then 54, volunteered to head the soccer fund. To bring in bucks, House dreamed up a mile-long car show, to be held in Ferndale, right on Woodward Avenue.

Word spread. Soon, the spigot House opened became a torrent, as people called from all over metro Detroit, clamoring to enter classics in the show. And Ferndale officials realized they were on to something big.

Although Woodward may be America's premier cruising highway, the Michigan Department of Transportation said no to closing it. So Dream Cruise pioneers moved Ferndale's car show to east 9 Mile, then suggested Woodward for linking it to other cities on Woodward. Besides Ferndale, the first cities to sign on were Pleasant Ridge, Royal Oak, Huntington Woods, Berkley and Birmingham.

"We were expecting maybe 25,000 people at most, up and down the whole six cities," said Caron Hall, an original Dream Cruise planner.

"We got 10 times that."

PAGE 14: AT THE STARTING LINE in his trophy-winning 1935 Ford hot rod truck, Gary Selke of Livonia cruised Woodward Avenue in early July 1995, much as he did 30 years ago. The Ford Motor Co. engineer said he wasn't going to miss the inaugural Dream Cruise on Aug. 19.

Organizers of the event — which rolled through Huntington Woods, Ferndale, Pleasant Ridge, Royal Oak, Berkley and Birmingham — expected as many as 10,000 cars to show up to celebrate the strip's glory days.

Woodward's heyday lasted about a decade, bracketed by the birth of the Big Three's muscle cars in 1964 and the gas shortages of 1973. Back then, Car and Driver magazine dubbed the strip "the street-racing capital of the world." GEORGE WALDMAN

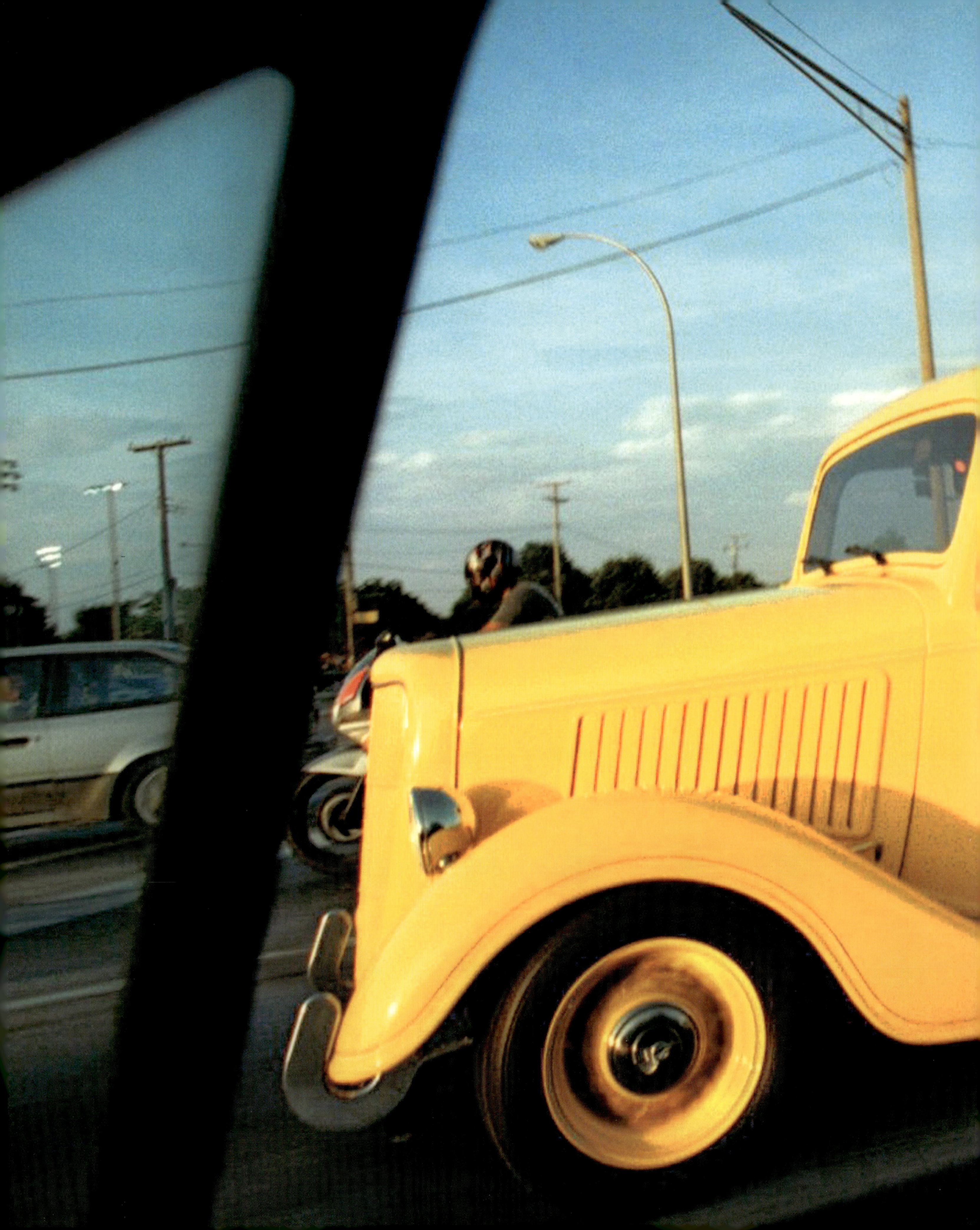

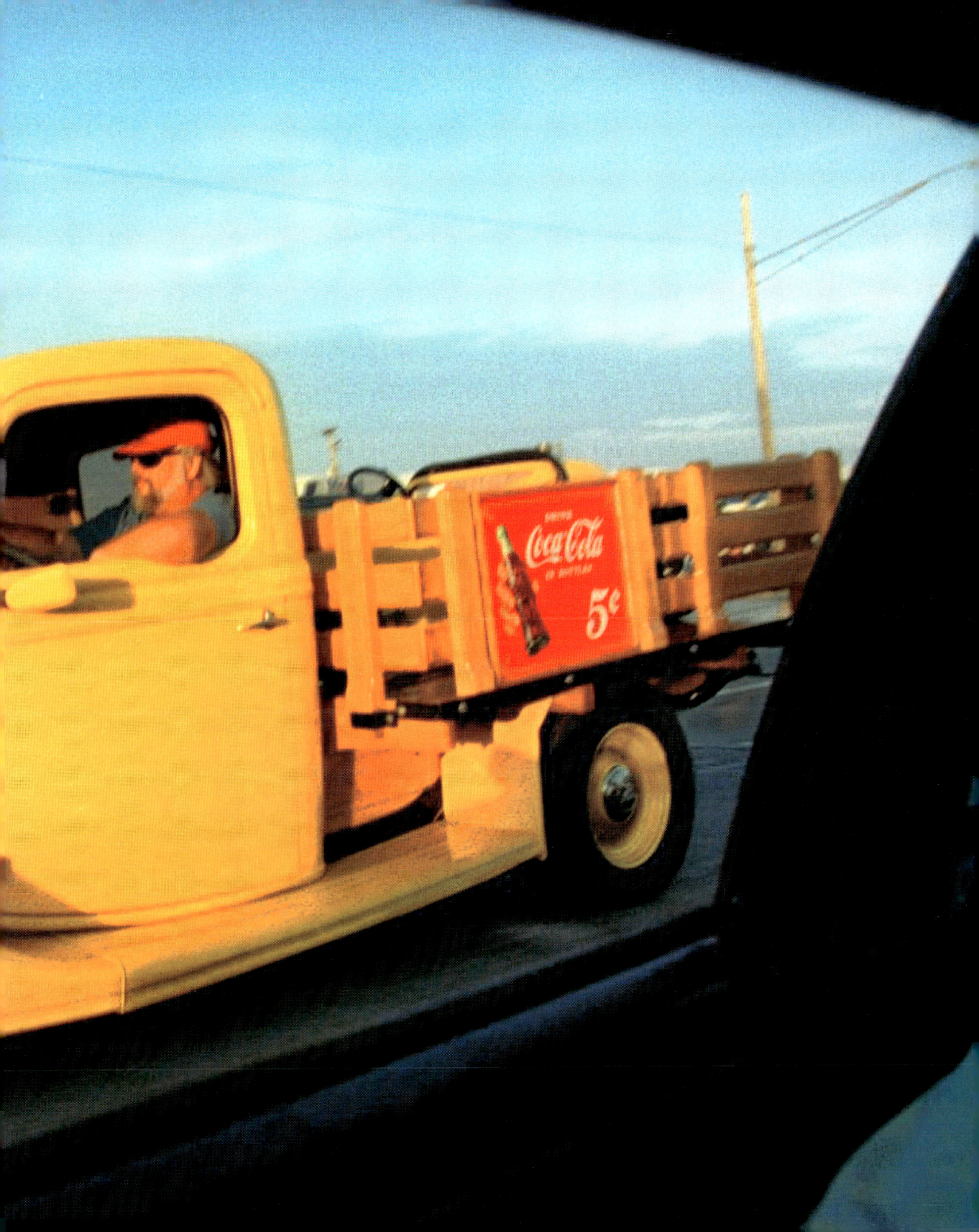
Coca-Cola
5¢

Date: Aug. 17

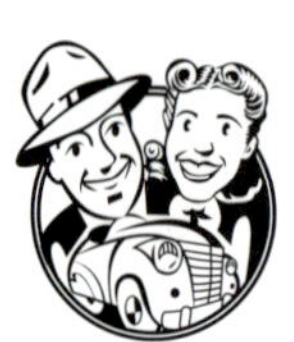

Attendance: More than 600,000, including Elvis — or some approximation thereof — who performed twice in Ferndale and once in Birmingham's Shain Park.

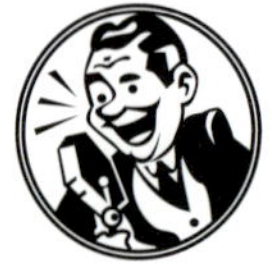

On the radio: WOMC-FM (104.3) aired wall-to-wall coverage of cruise day for the first time.

1996

IF YOUR MILL'S RUNNIN' FINE, DON'T CHANGE THE ENGINE timing.

Same with the Dream Cruise, planners realized. So they stuck with their first year's timing — the third Saturday in August — for the second cruise and every one since.

In 1996, the Dream Cruise attendance increased to more than 600,000 people.

That day, "If you were working in a charity tent or something, and went out to look around, you couldn't believe it," said Marsha Mellert, Ferndale's recreation director.

"There were all these people with smiles on their faces, all these hoods up, and you could barely move," she said.

The cruisers were still pretty much all in muscle cars and hot rods. Yet to come were the Ferraris, Model A's and baby cement mixers.

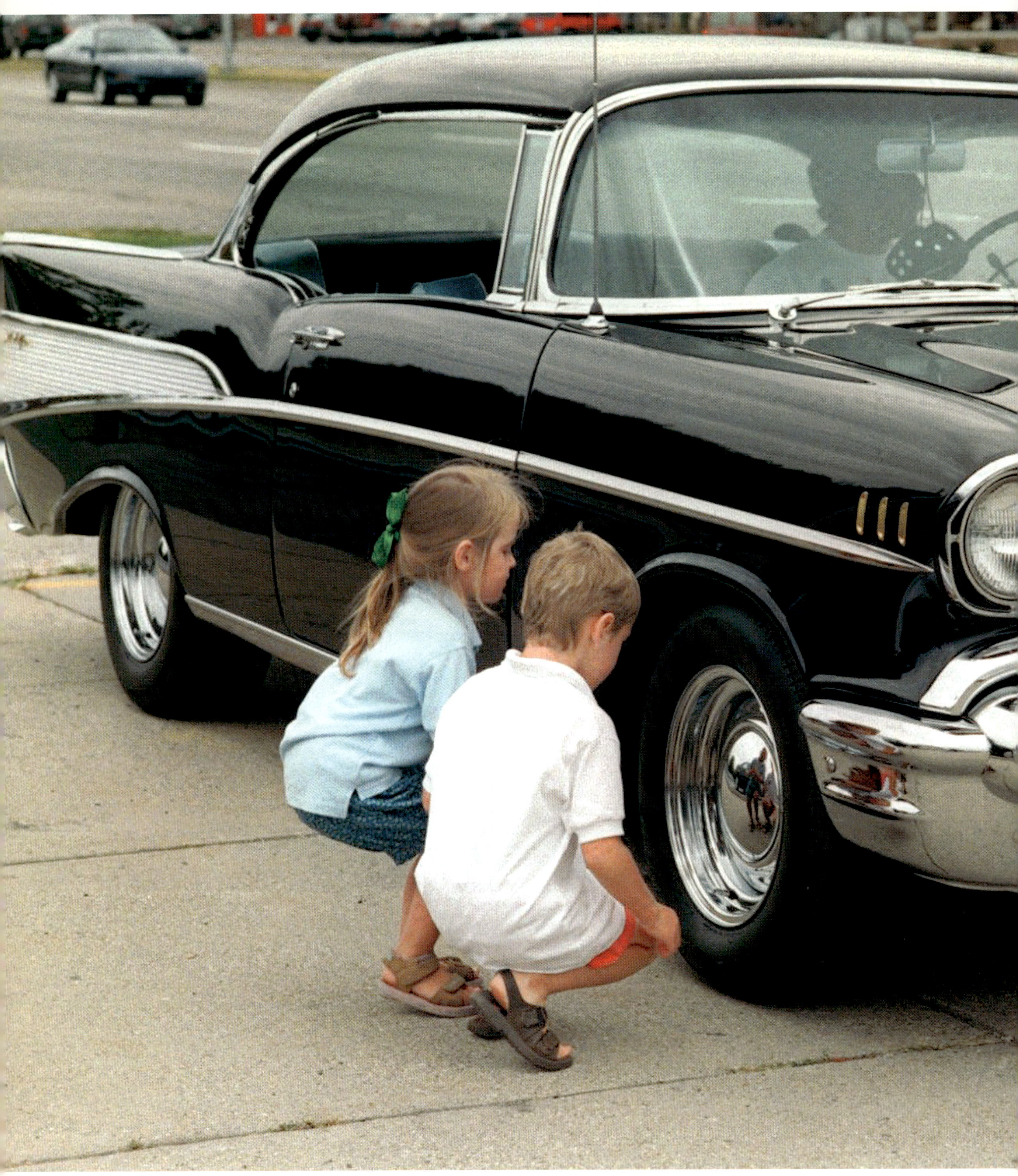

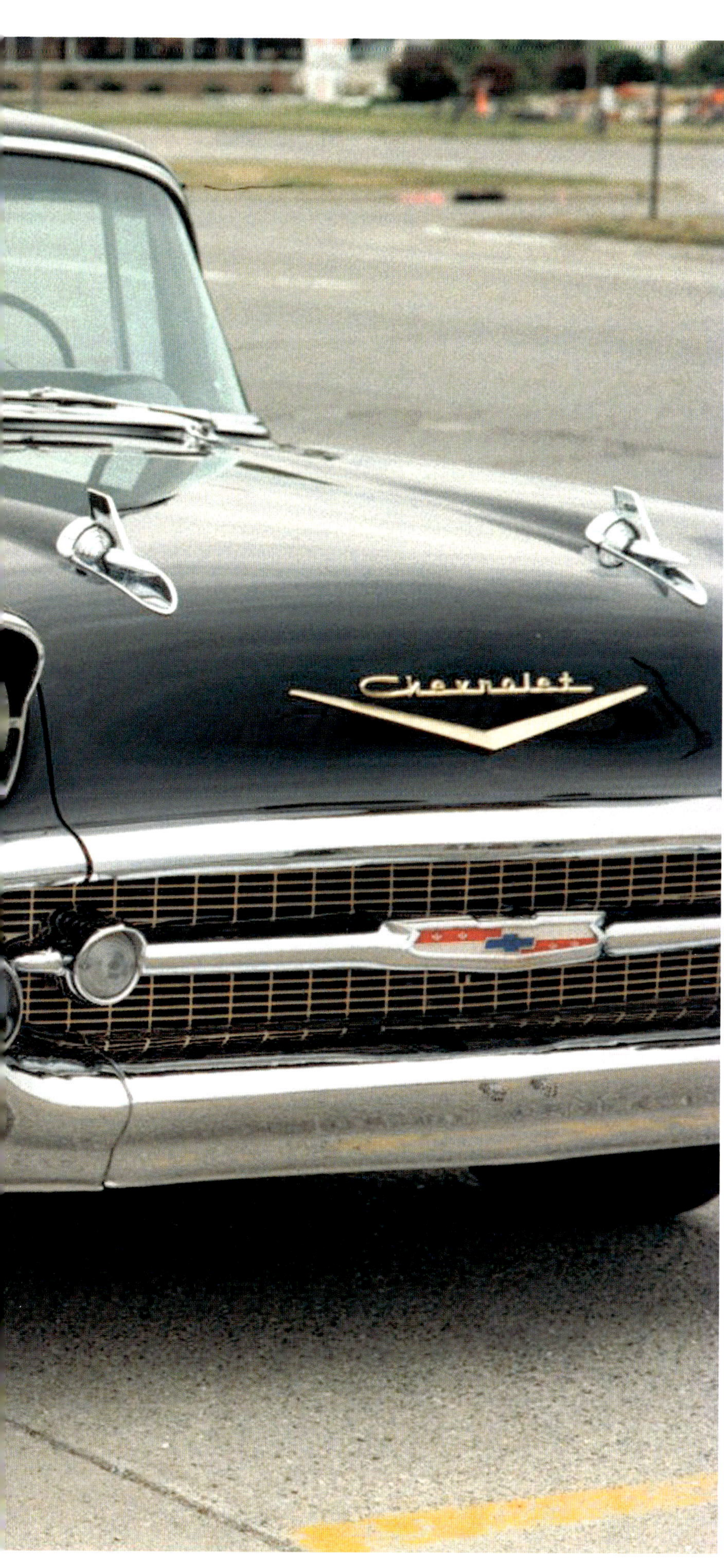

YOUNG AND OLD were drawn to the cruise. Geoffrey Laporte, 5, and 3-year-old Lindsey Laporte checked out Don Putter's wheels — a '57 Chevy Bel Air. Later in the day, Putter became one of thousands who rolled down memory lane in a classic.

PAGE 20: EVERYONE WAS GOING CAR CRAZY. Enthusiasts like these looking at customized street rods and the others who weren't scooting up and down the avenue gathered along parts of it to check out vintage vehicles. Stores peddled Dream Cruise paraphernalia and car-related goodies on sidewalks and in parking lots. The Birmingham Post Office offered to cancel mail with a Dream Cruise stamp. "I've heard from people from all over the country" asking about the cruise, said Steve Gillette, Royal Oak public works supervisor. Some of them even showed up to cruise — there were more than 600,000 people in 40,000 to 60,000 cars. About 15,000 of them came from Canada, Illinois, Wisconsin, Ohio, Florida and Minnesota. The huge party celebrating our great love of the automobile — deemed the nation's premier car event by Chevrolet — had already become an international affair.

WILLIAM ARCHIE

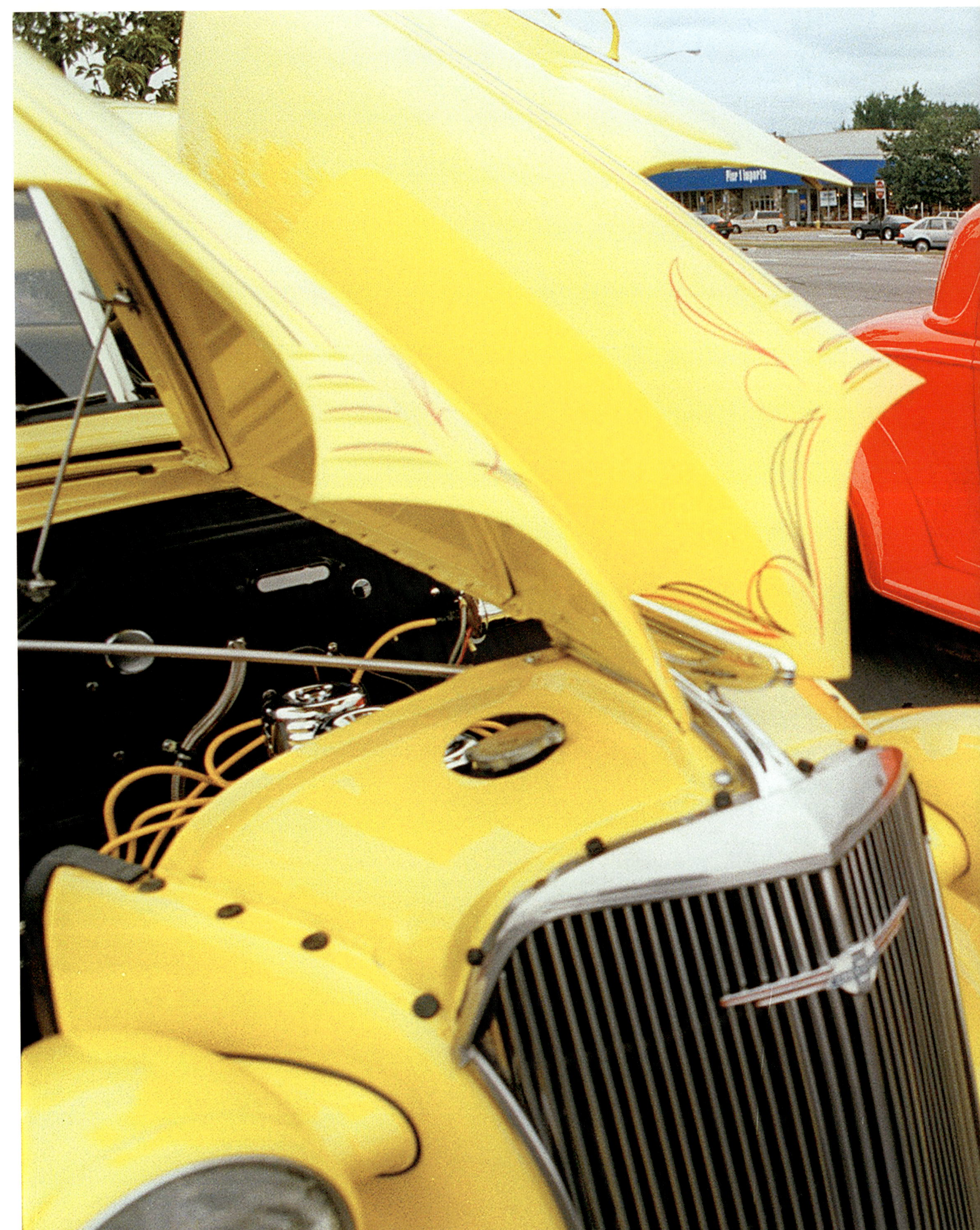

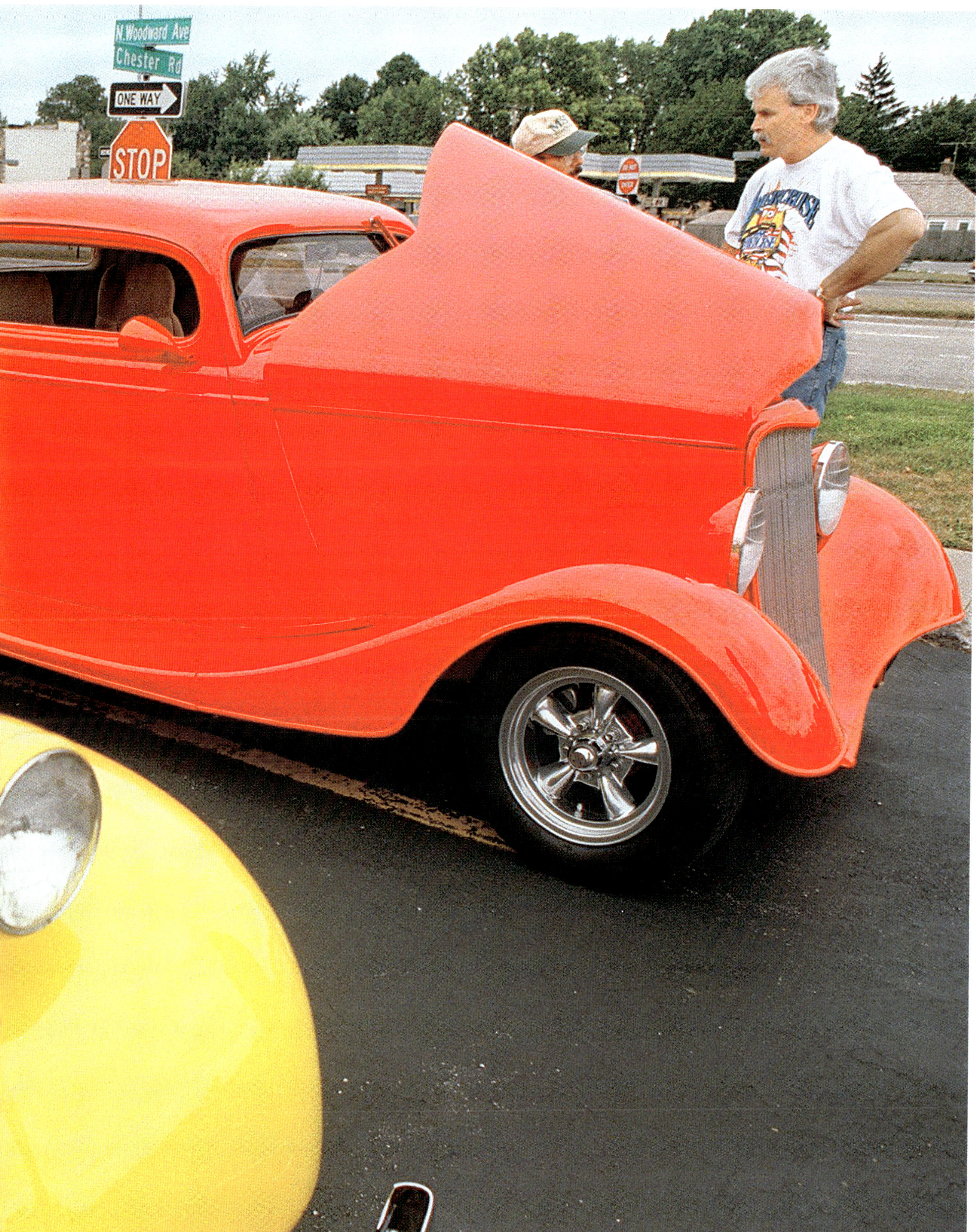

WILLIAM ARCHIE

Date: Aug. 16

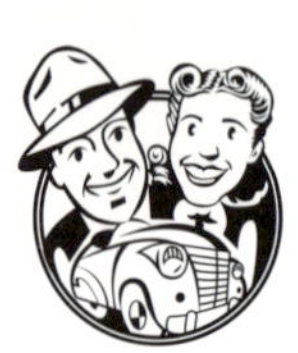

Attendance: 750,000, including Elvis, sighted in Huntington Woods.

Special moment: A big welcome to Pontiac, which joined the cruise. The route extended from Birmingham north to Pontiac, where cruisers made the loop and headed back on Woodward.

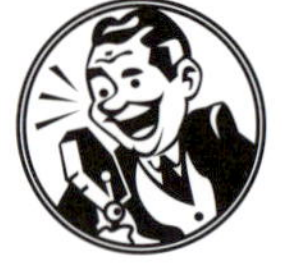

On television: Sponsor WXYZ-TV (Channel 7) aired a live special from the cruise for the first time.

1997

FROM ALL OVER THE COUNTRY, PEOPLE OF ALL AGES showed up at Dream Cruise III.

One of the big draws? The free admission, of course. The funds raised by sales of T-shirts, coffee mugs and collectibles went to defraying the cities' costs for the event, and to benefiting scores of charities that run the sidewalk sales stands.

A year earlier, planners from the six original cities had formed a nonprofit board — Woodward Dream Cruise Inc. They'd registered the event name. And they'd forged close ties to Ferndale-based radio station WOMC-FM (104.3), nicknamed Oldies 104.3.

In the early cruises, car collectors around metro Detroit heard of the Dream Cruise through 'OMC — in advance or live. Many spun their steering wheels toward Woodward. Some were drawn by memories of muscle-car music — maybe a gearhead anthem like "Dead Man's Curve."

And who from that era can forget the song that Pontiac built: "Little GTO"? In fact, it was in 1997 that the City of Pontiac officially joined the nonprofit board of the Dream Cruise.

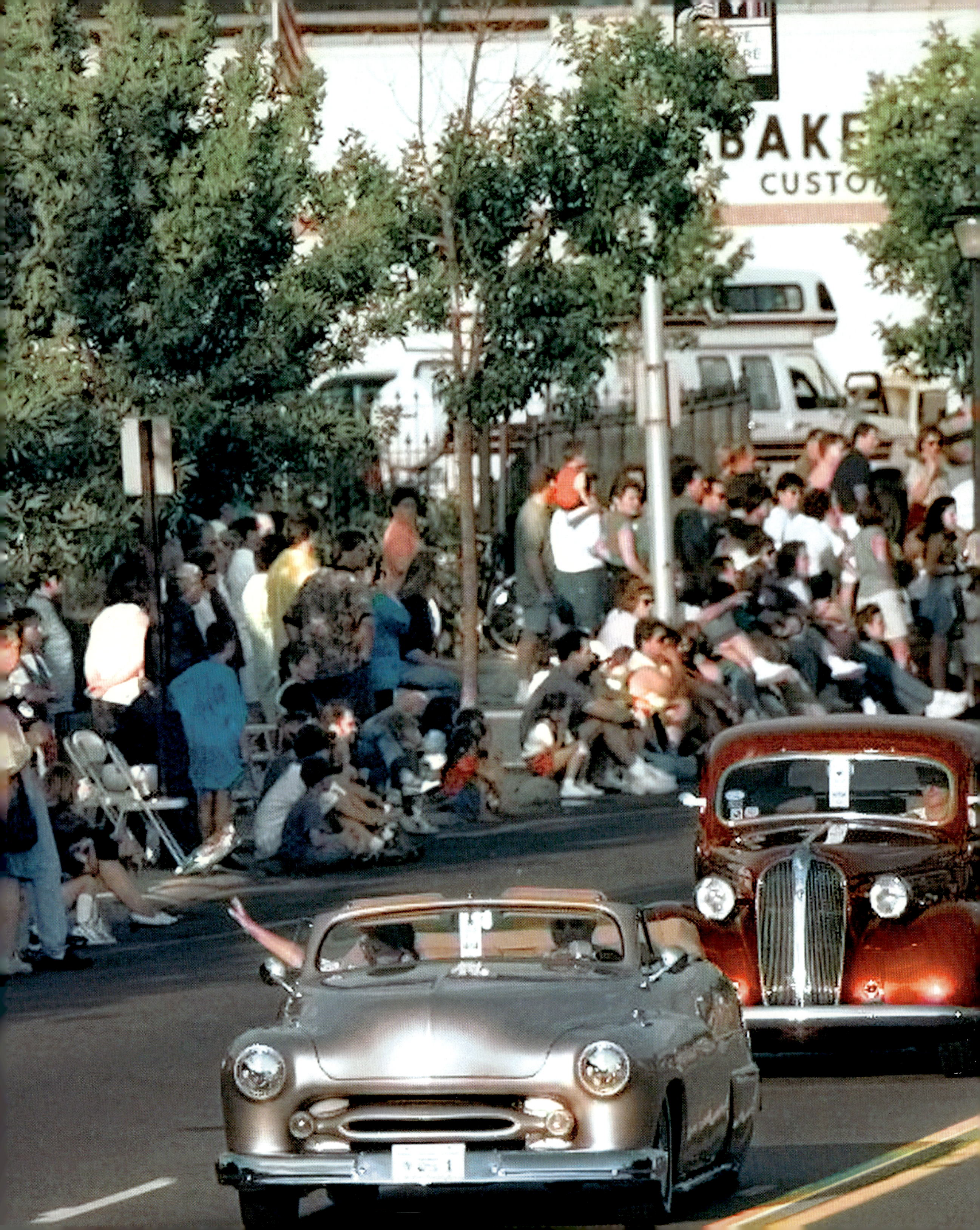
BAKE
CUSTO

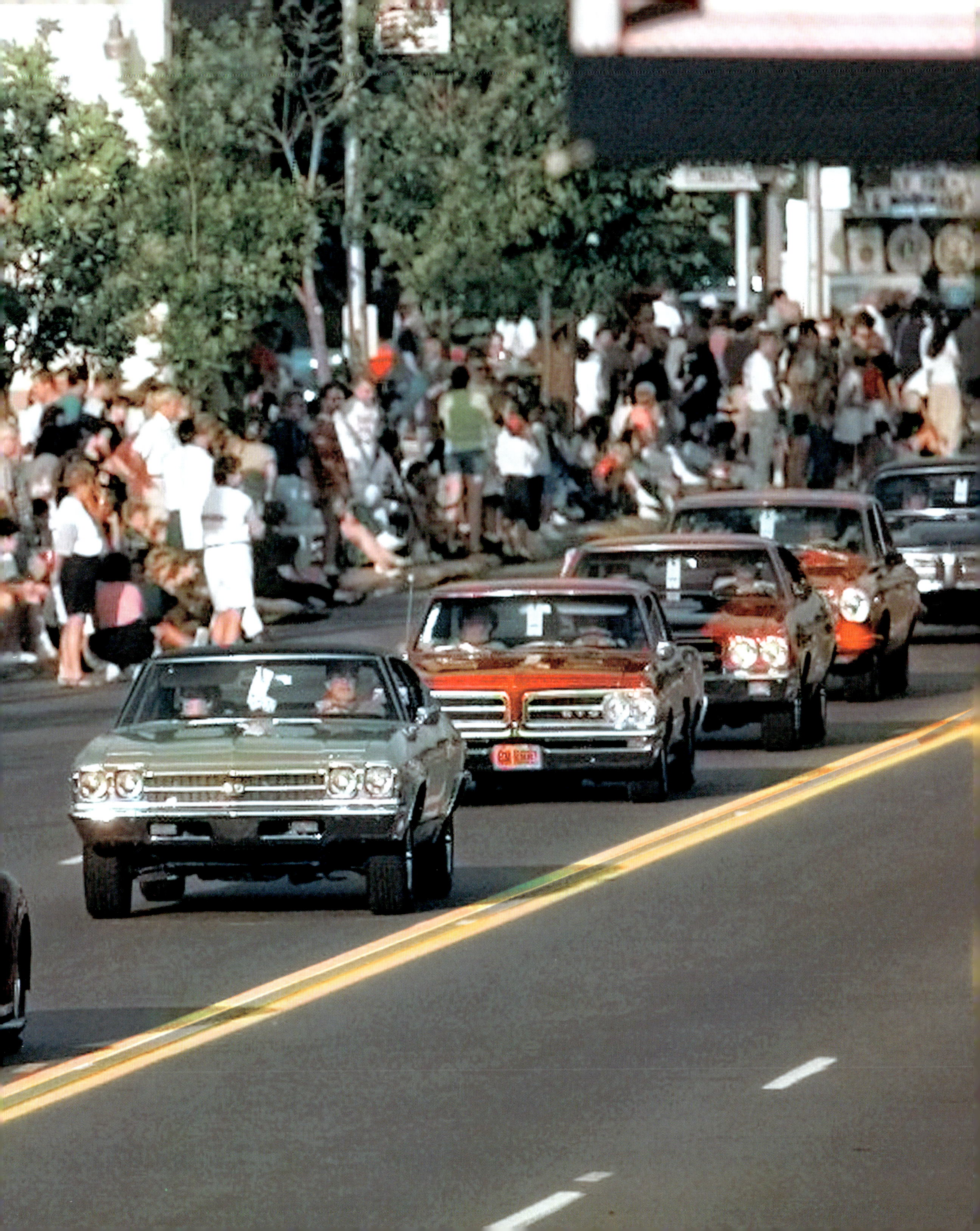

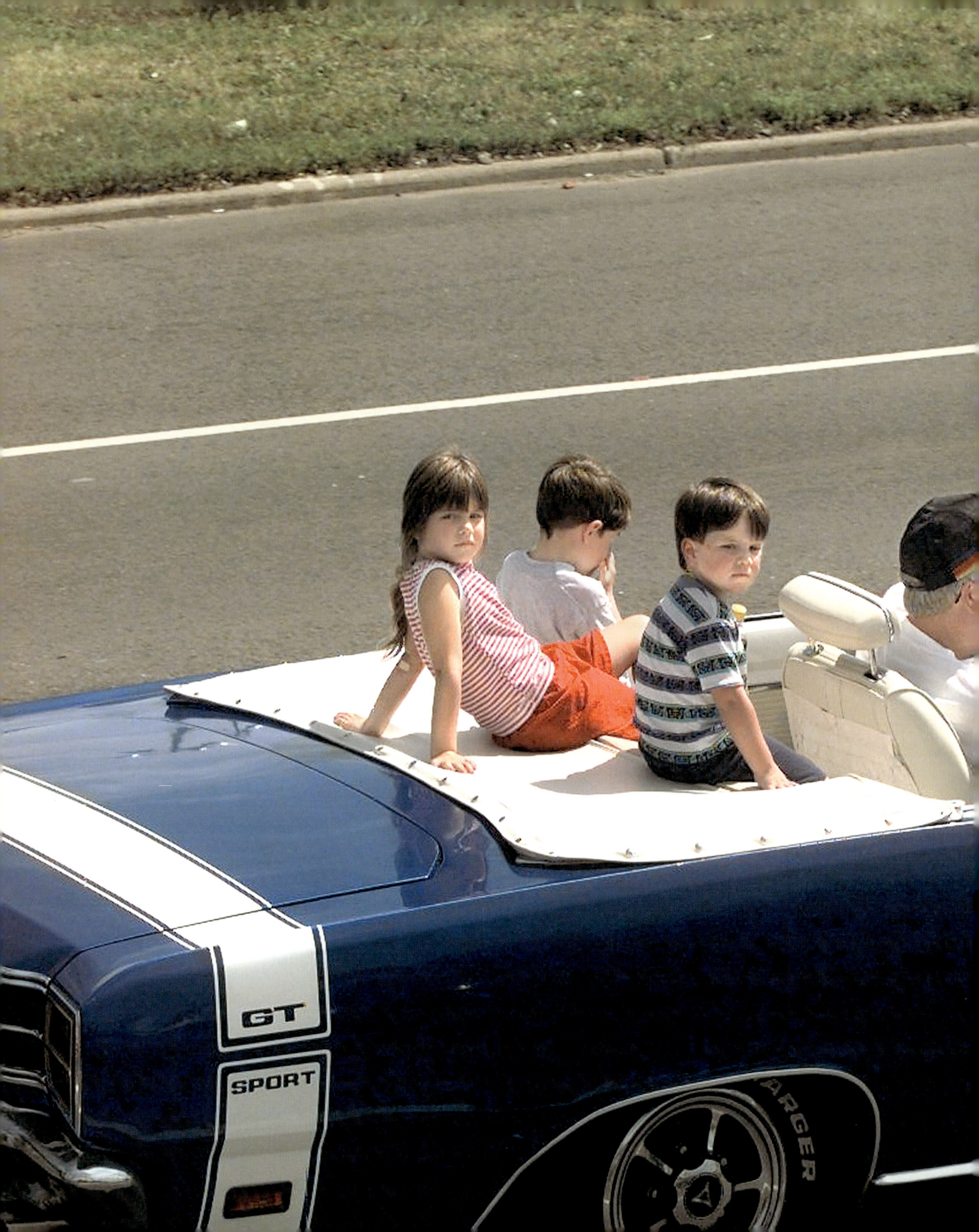
GT
SPORT

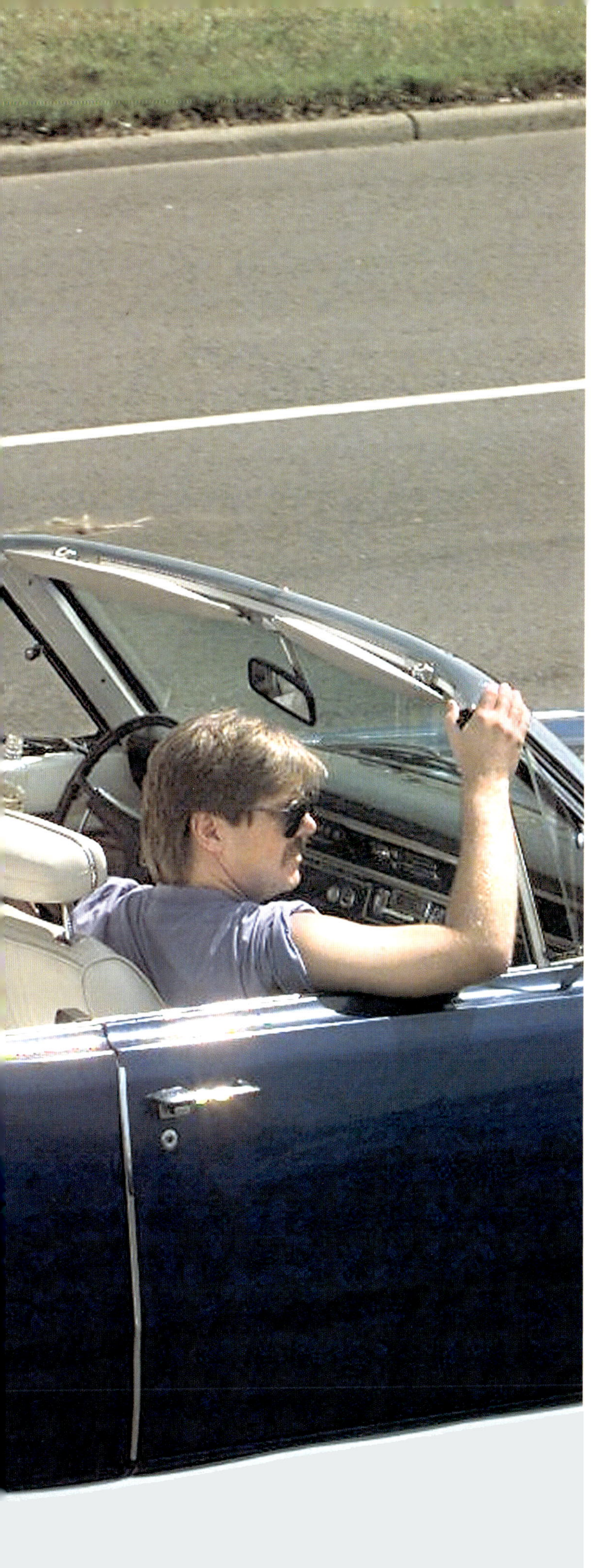

THEY WERE CRUISING and playing the radio, with no particular place to go: seeing and being seen, reliving memories of those teenage years, sharing them with the kids and having fun. The official six-city cruise route from Ferndale, through Pleasant Ridge, Huntington Woods, Berkley, Royal Oak and Birmingham extended to Pontiac in 1997.

PAGE 24: CAR BUFFS JAMMED the avenue, trying again to recreate the Woodward of the '50s and '60s, when muscle machines and other classic cars ruled the road. The drive down memory lane wasn't without rules, though. The year before, residents along Woodward had complained of traffic, drunken people and cars driving across their lawns. So this year, cruisers were warned: no alcohol, no drag racing, no tire-squealing "burn-outs" and no forgetting that all traffic rules would be strictly enforced.

Left: RICHARD LEE; Previous page: NICO TOUTENHOOFD

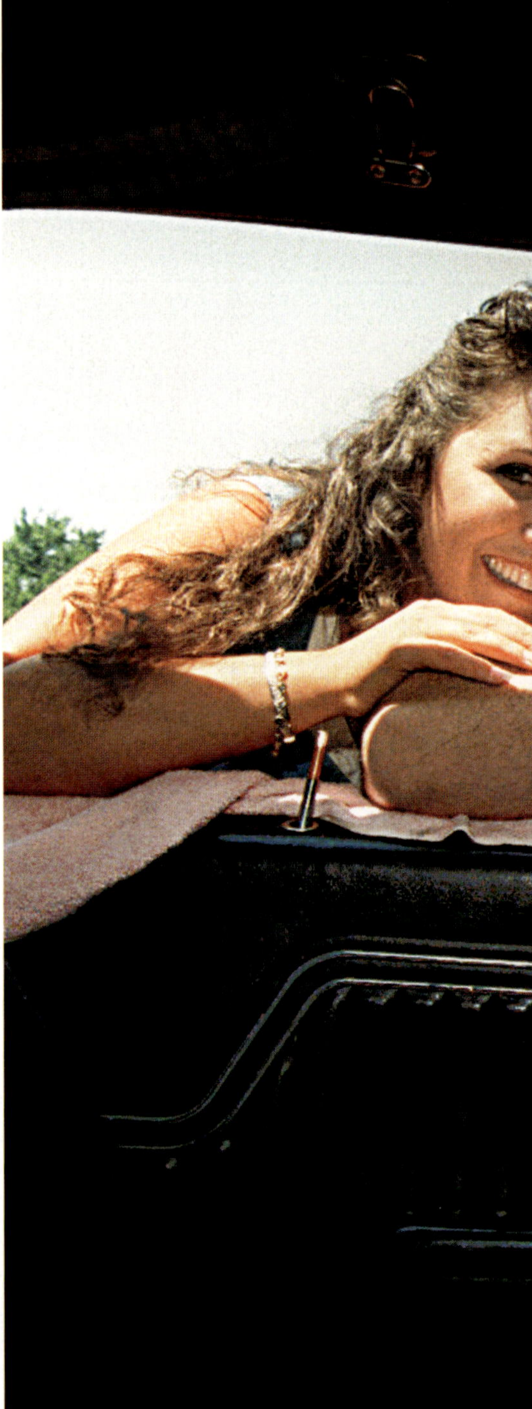

DREAMS COME TRUE. Francie Giordano can testify to that. More than 20 years ago, before anyone had even thought of the Dream Cruise, Giordano was a teenager who traveled along Woodward with her friends. She'd see Don Baldino, right, in his roadster and secretly, her heart would flutter. "He is sooooo cute!" she'd tell her friends. But she never said a word to Don, a fellow Royal Oak native. She was way too shy. Fast forward to the cruise of '96, when they laid eyes on each other again and a romance blossomed. This year, they talked marriage. Don no longer had that car — he drove a Chevelle in '97 — but now when he cruised Woodward, it was with Francie at his side.

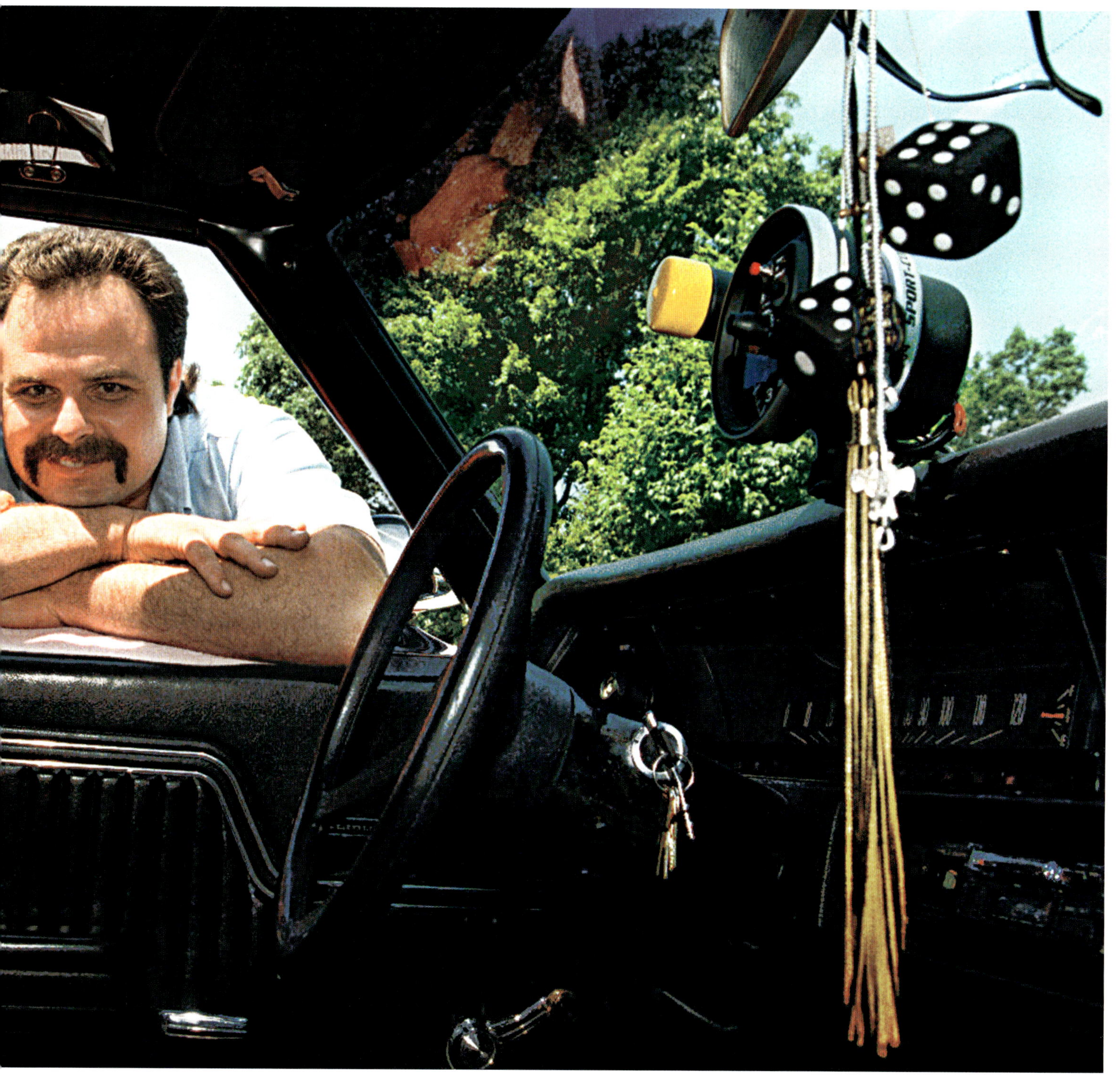

KIRTHMON F. DOZIER

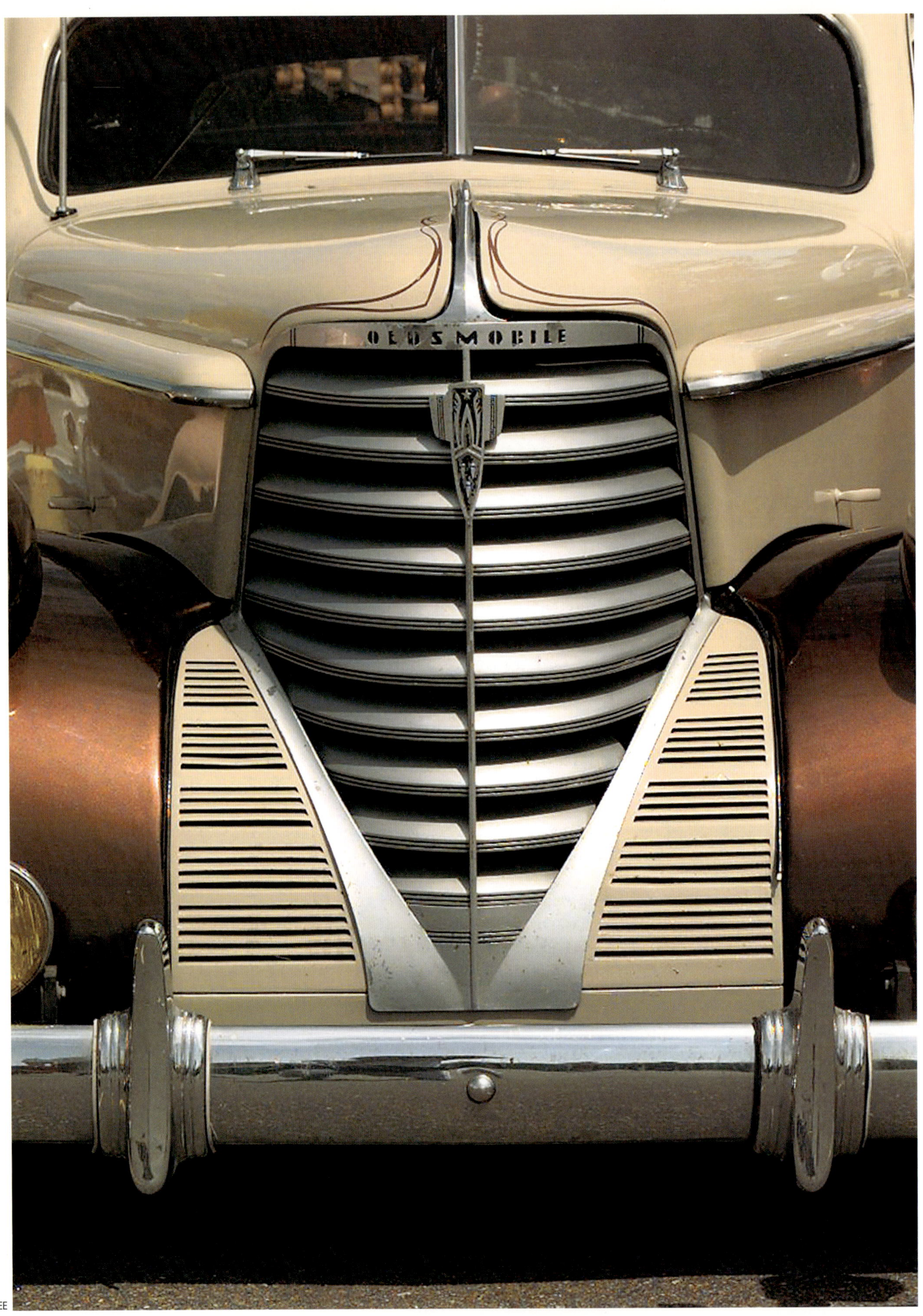

RICHARD LEE

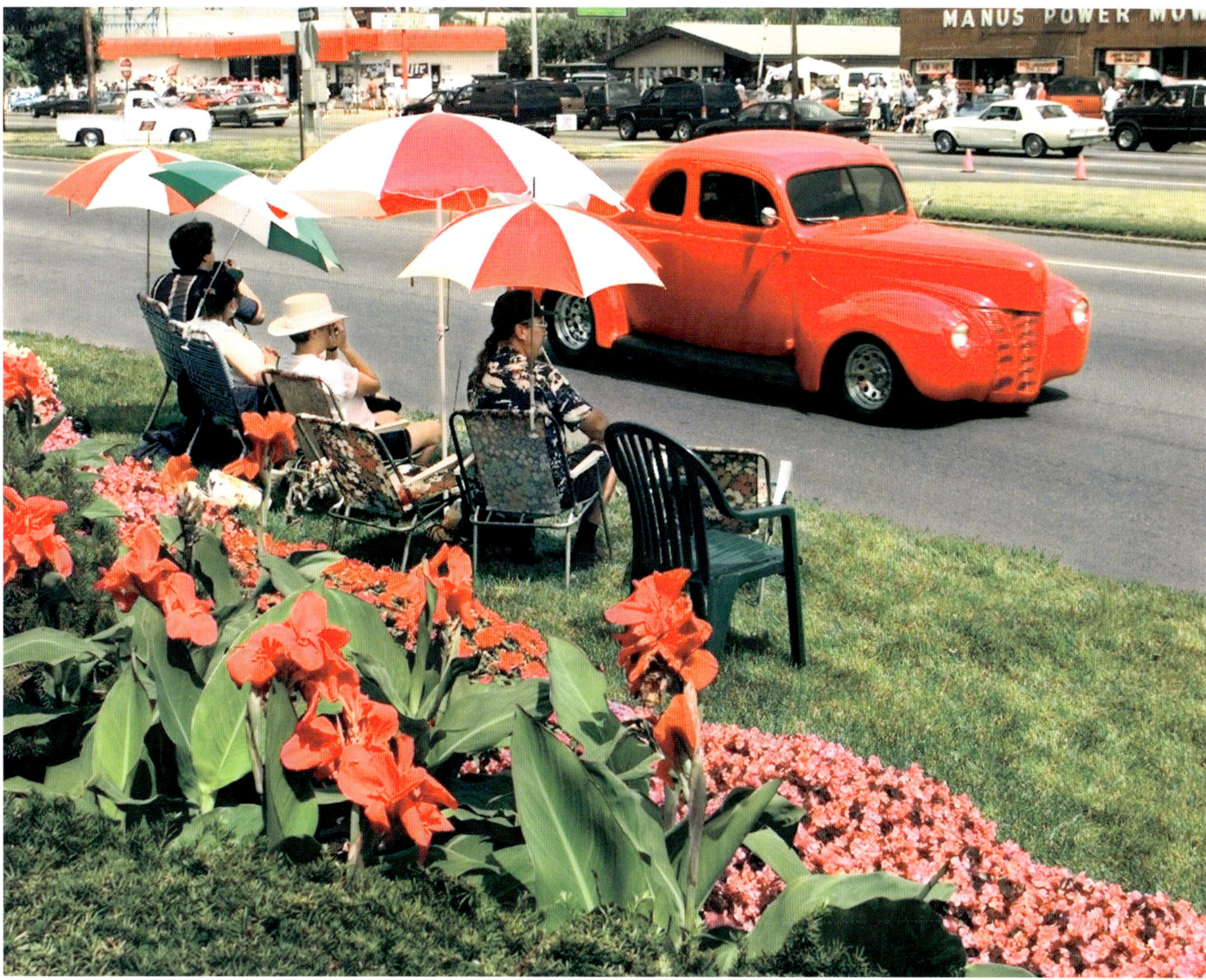

Above: RICHARD LEE; Next page: NICO TOUTENHOOFD

ABOVE: COME RAIN OR SHINE, people love the Dream Cruise. These onlookers were glad for bursts of rain that made a muggy day more tolerable. Hundreds camped out along the side of the road to get a good look. Others remembered the good old days while perched in tree branches or on van roofs and car hoods. "We used to cruise just like this," a woman from Pontiac said. "Sometimes, we would race, and other times, we'd just go get something to eat." Others came to the cruise to fantasize: "I'll never be able to own any of these, so the next best thing is to come out here and get a good look at them," car lover John Evers said. "There's nothing like an impromptu race."

LEFT: THEY SURE DON'T MAKE 'EM like this anymore. Just look at the grill on this vintage Oldsmobile, parked at the Northwood Shopping Center at 13 and Woodward in Royal Oak. Back in the day, the Northwood area was the main pit stop for cruisers. It still holds an attraction for a lot of people. The night before the '96 cruise, Woodward was so tied up with reminiscing cruisers and spectators that in '97, Royal Oak police decided to close the street at the city's border. Other cities embraced the excitement: Berkley held a classic car parade, showed a 1957 movie outdoors and invited people to dance in the street.

PAGE 32: ON DESIGNATED CRUISE DAY, 750,000 people came out. Many spent hours tied up in traffic on and around Woodward. "You might as well call it a sit," Ron Reale of Warren joked after the event. But no one complained about bad behavior — cruisers are a fairly calm crowd. Police reported few arrests. Despite the good behavior and community enthusiasm, it was uncertain whether there'd be a fourth Dream Cruise. Because of its size and congestion, the event was developing a list of detractors that included police and merchants along the strip. "This is a time bomb waiting to go off, and there's going to be a lot of finger-pointing when it does," said David Pinche, then public safety director for Bloomfield Hills, which was sandwiched between the six cities in the cruise but didn't participate. Cruise and city officials and members of the community met later in the year to decide the cruise's future.

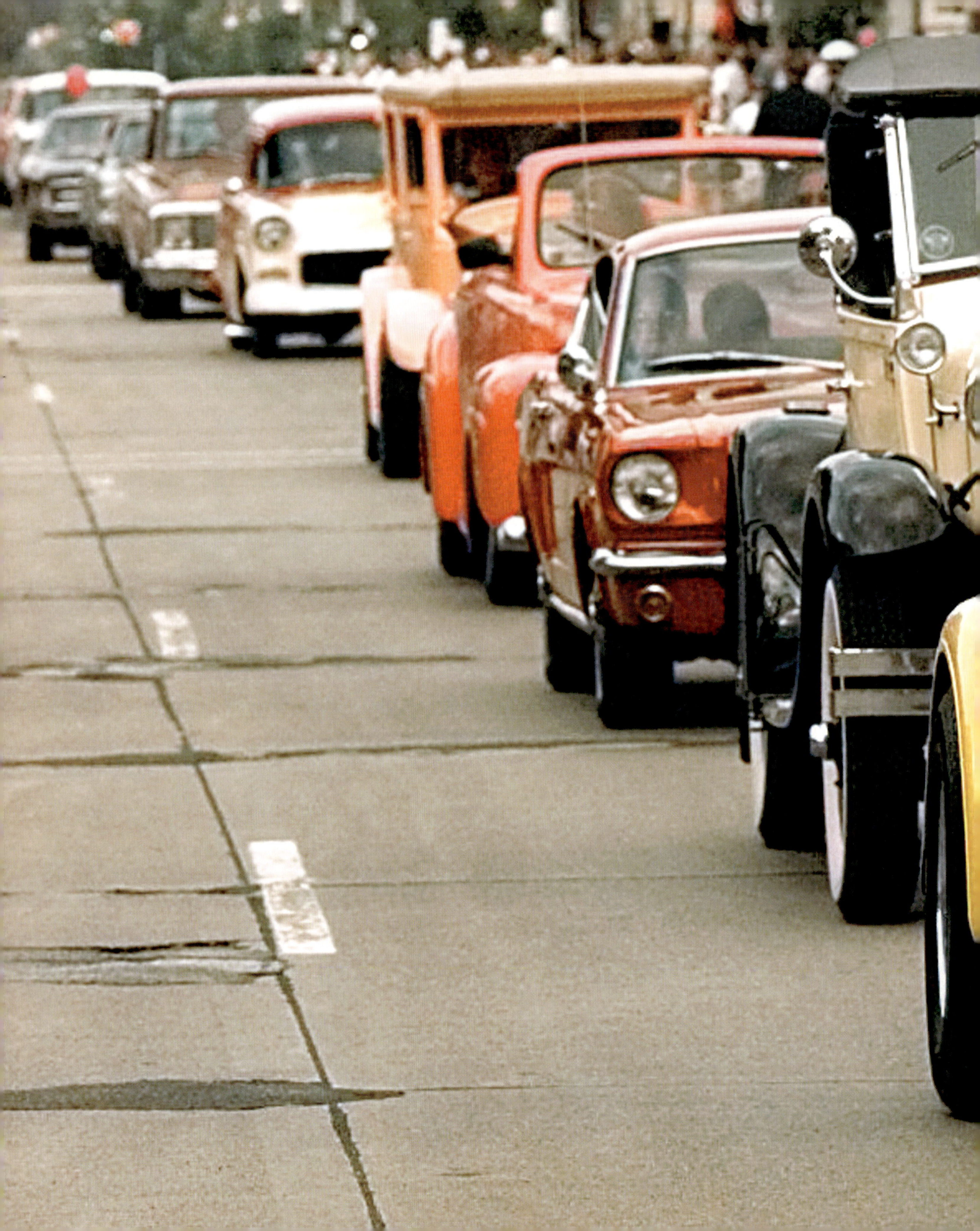

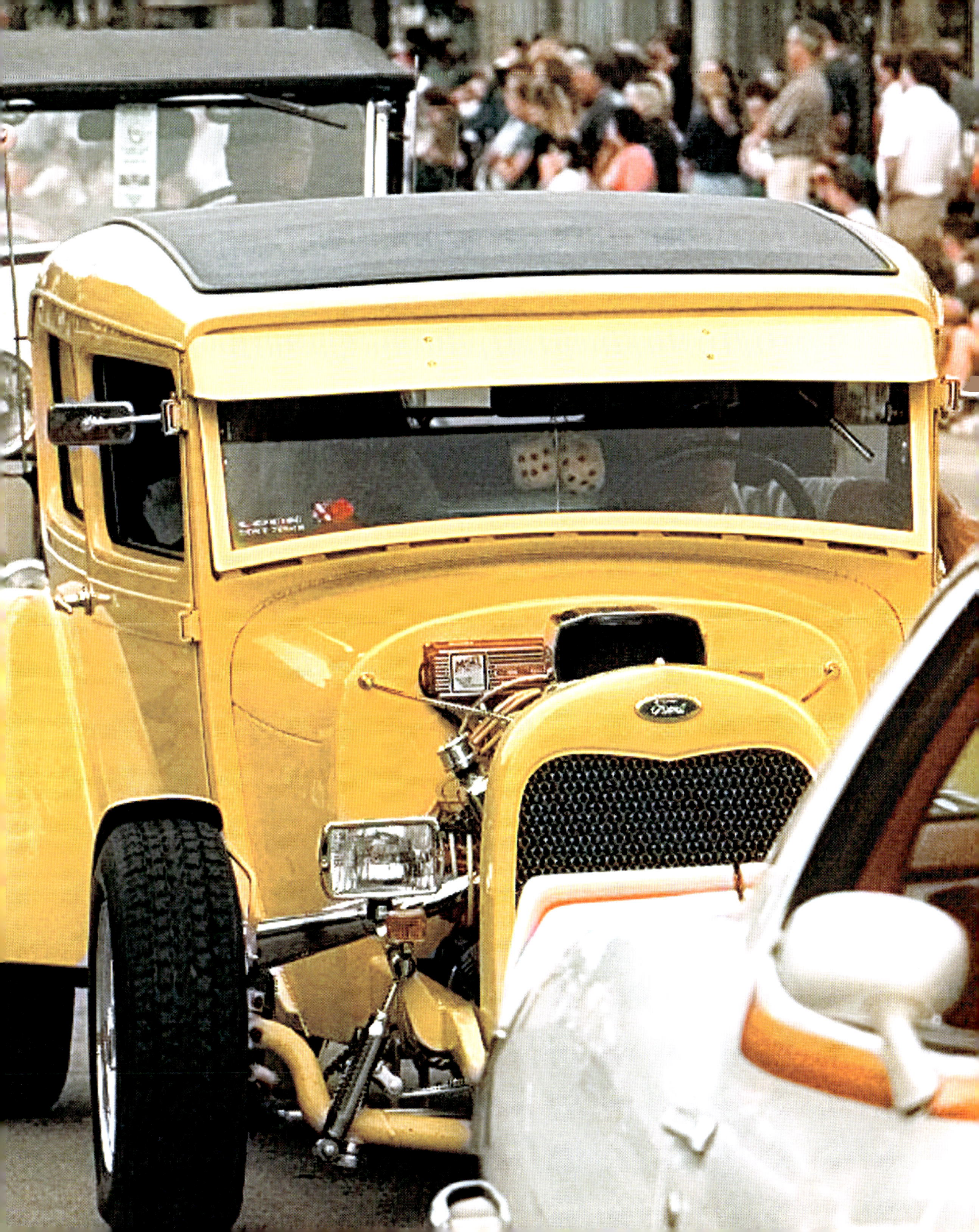

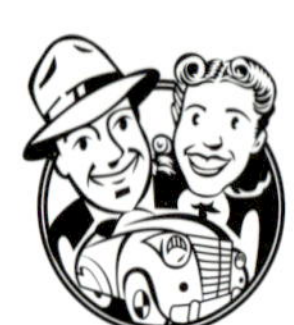

Date: Aug. 15

Attendance: 1.1 million

Historic moment: Woodward Avenue was designated as an Automobile National Heritage Area by the National Park Service.

Debate of the day: Just what is a classic, and who should be allowed in the Cruise? Here's how the Woodward Dream Cruise Committee defined it: "Any car that creates a feeling of nostalgia stimulates a memory and fulfills a fantasy."

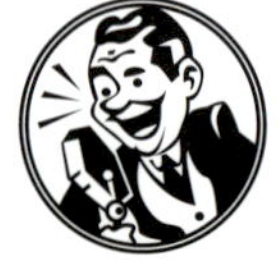

Food first: A drive-in food lane is added, reminiscent of the eats from Woodward legends like the Totem Pole.

1998

BY ITS FOURTH INCARNATION, THE DREAM CRUISE TOOK on truly gargantuan proportions — like the engines in those Mustang GT 500s, Hemi-equipped Dodges and 496-ci Chevelles.

Everyone ogled the cars, but many baby boomers recalled the legendary days of cruising during the heyday of the "Woodward strip."

Vintage cruisers say the strip started at the bygone Hedge's Wigwam restaurant in Pleasant Ridge — just south of 10 Mile Road, now the I-696 service drive. From there, cruisers drove — and, shhhh! sometimes drag-raced illegally — north about 11 miles to the long-gone Ted's drive-in, on the south side of Square Lake in Bloomfield Township. They'd park, check out the scene, grab a bite and head south again.

One of the old-time Woodward cruisers admits he got a few speeding tickets as a teen. Original Dream Cruise supporter Larry Payne cruised Woodward in the early 1960s in his black '57 Chevy, purchased "almost new" for $1,400. Then he devoted his Duggan's pub in Royal Oak to the cruising era — where you can still get burgers made with recipes from the old Woodward pit stops.

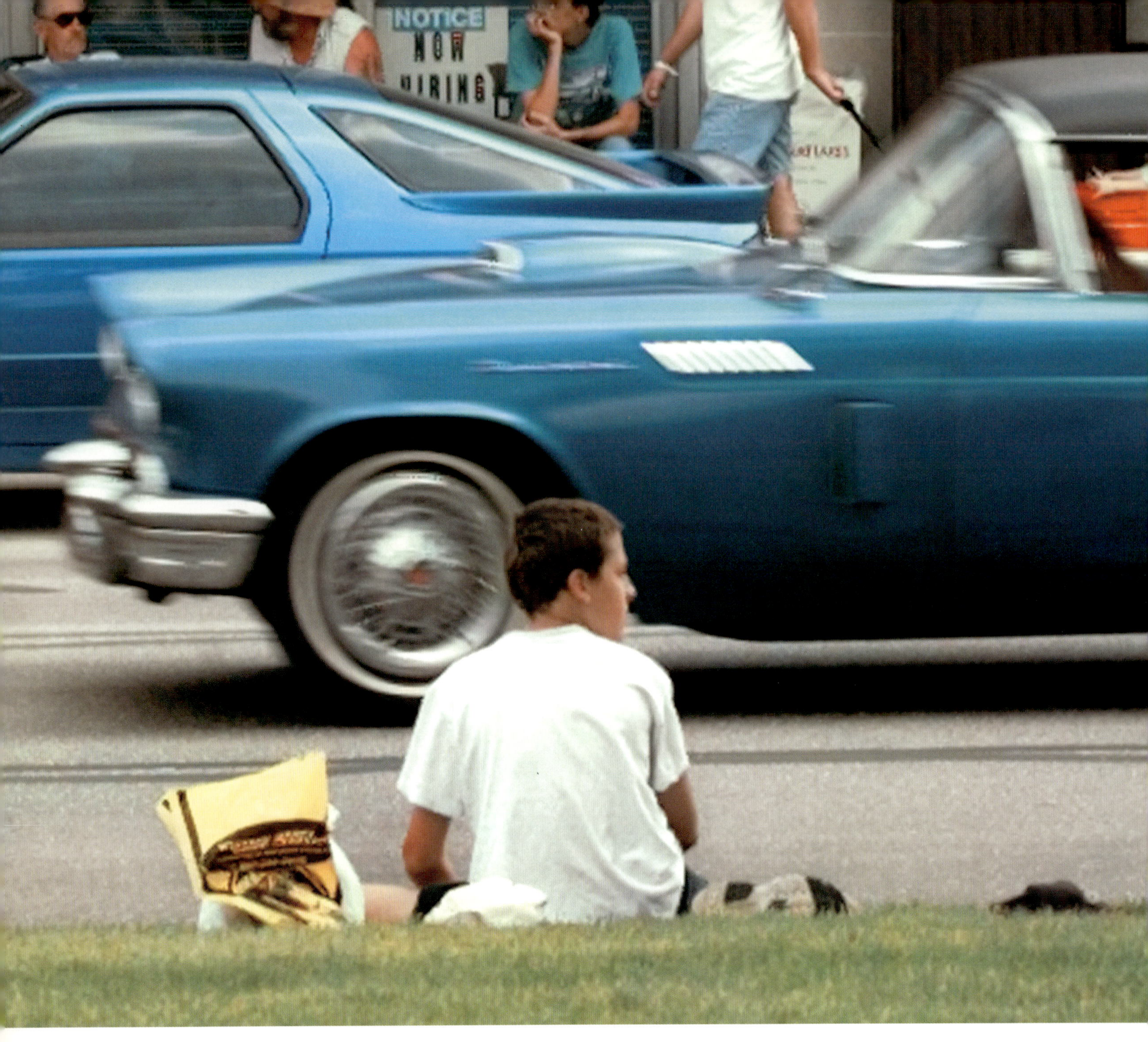

NINTEEN NINETY-EIGHT

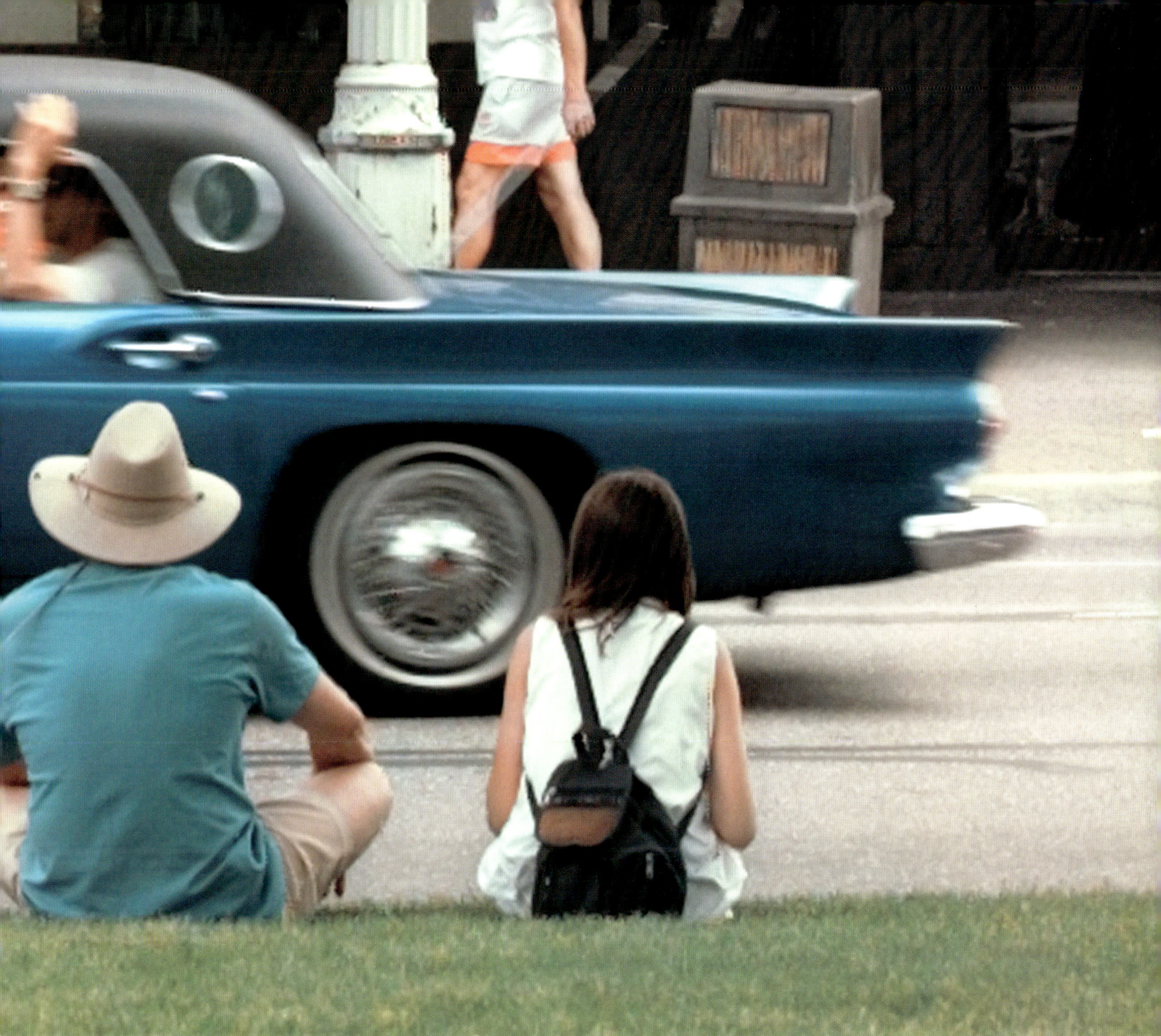

KIRTHMON F. DOZIER

THE CRUISE HAS BECOME a family affair. Jeff Kuykendall, left, his father, Les Kuykendall, and sister Sara Kuykendall snagged front-row seats for the rolling classic-car show that is the Dream Cruise. With more than 1 million attendees, the fourth annual event was the largest cruise to date and was billed as the biggest single-day car event in the world.

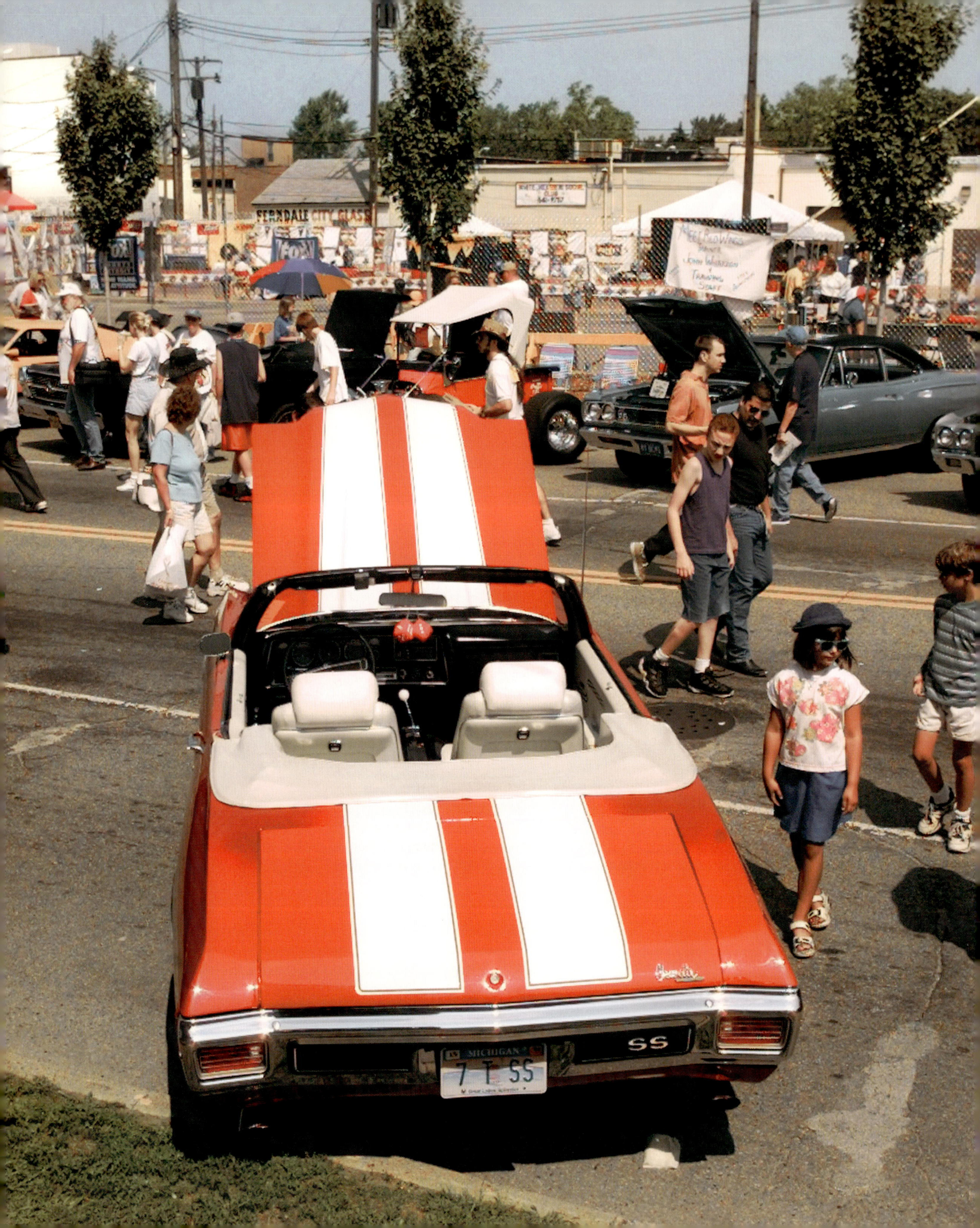
FERNDALE CITY GLASS
FOX
SS
MICHIGAN
7 T SS

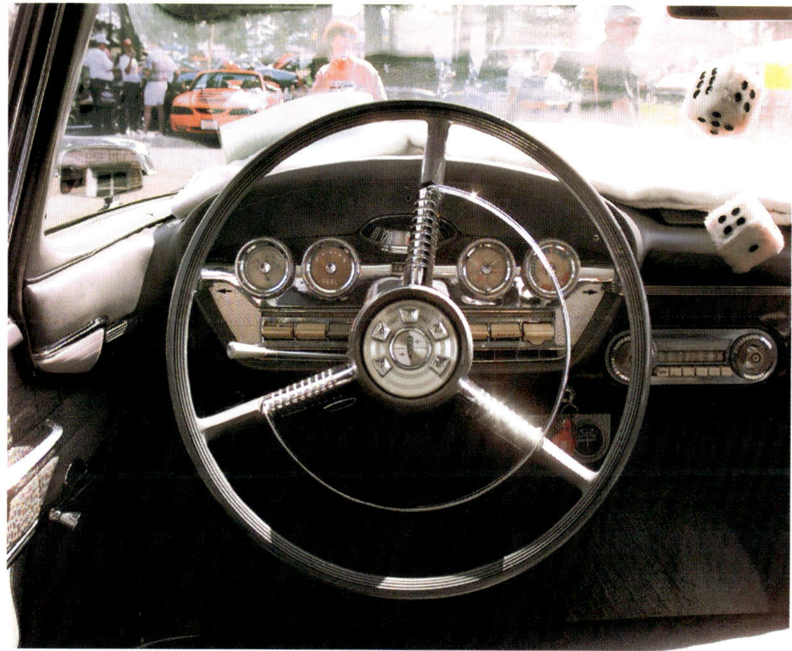

Above and left: KIRTHMON F. DOZIER

ABOVE: WHEEL APPEAL: An insider's view of a 1958 Edsel at the Michigan State Fairgrounds in Detroit.

LEFT: CAR AFICIONADOS got an up-close look at the classics in Ferndale.

WITH A LOVING TOUCH, Paul Jones of Melvindale polished his '58 Edsel, which still had all of its original parts. Jones had owned the car since 1985.

KIRTHMON F. DOZIER

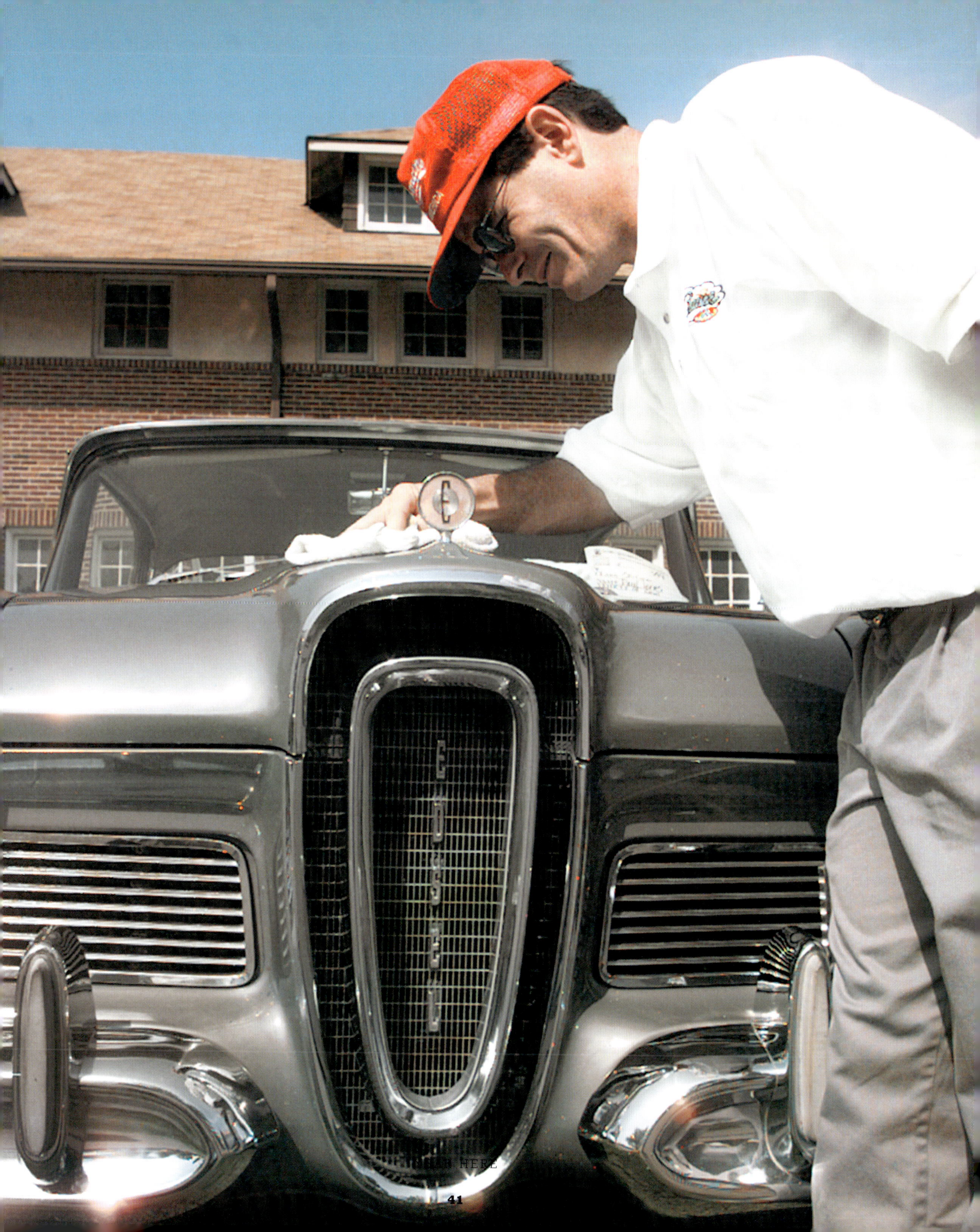
EDSEL

IT WAS PROBABLY THE BEST SEAT in the house. It was also an illegal one. But for a while, at least, Susan and James Brewer of Eastpointe got to enjoy the dreamlike weather and watch the cruise from their very own island on Woodward. On either side of them, the party was in full swing. Besides the cars zooming by, there were side streets with food and game booths, parked cars with popped hoods and thousands of other cruise-crazy spectators. About 1 million people turned out for the event. Others came along for the ride, but weren't counted. For the first time, the cool views of the cruise could be seen from the comfort of home or anywhere else in the world, via computer. Webcams broadcast the event live and sent aerial shots of Woodward in Birmingham and Royal Oak. Internet users could zoom in on whatever they wanted to see in a 180-degree radius and never have to bother with traffic or crowds. The idea came from a guy who lived about 2 blocks west of Woodward.

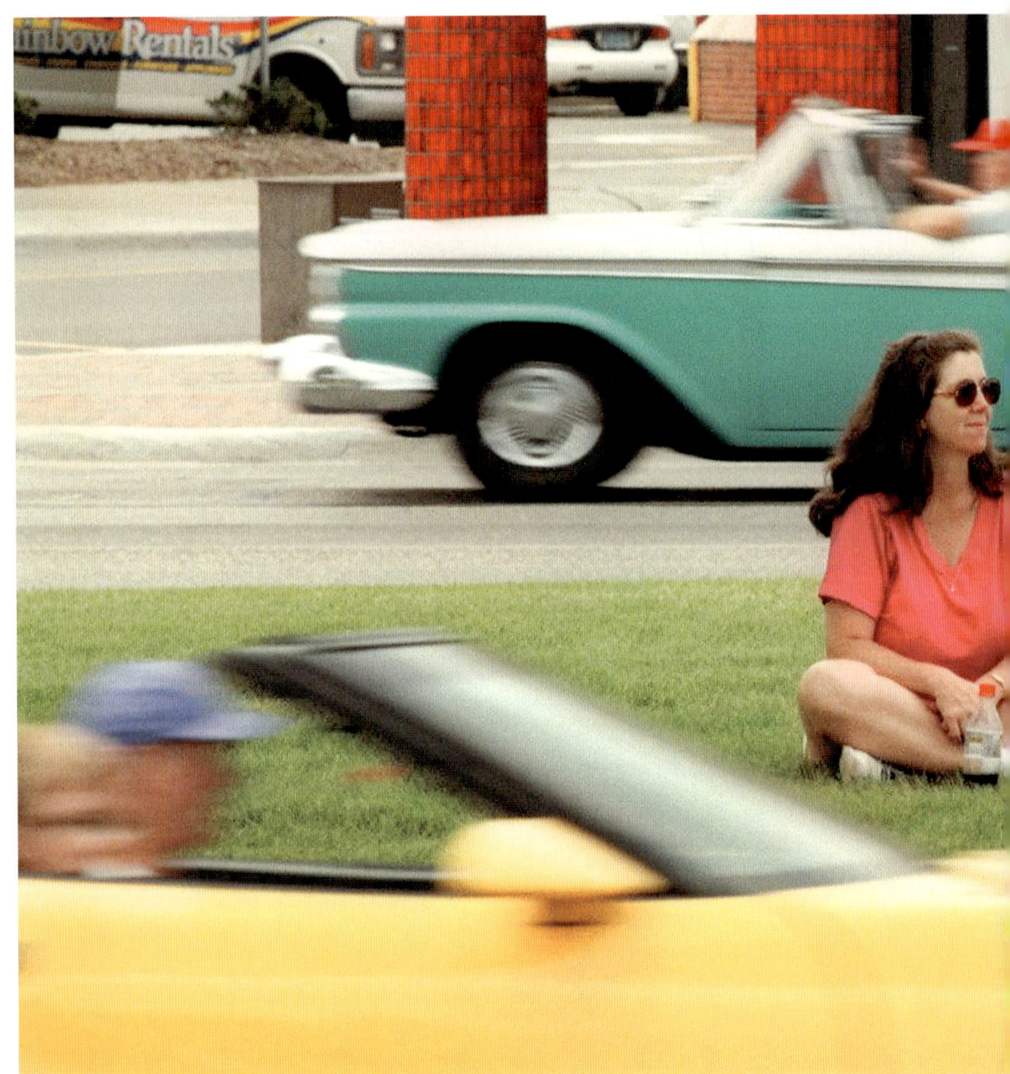

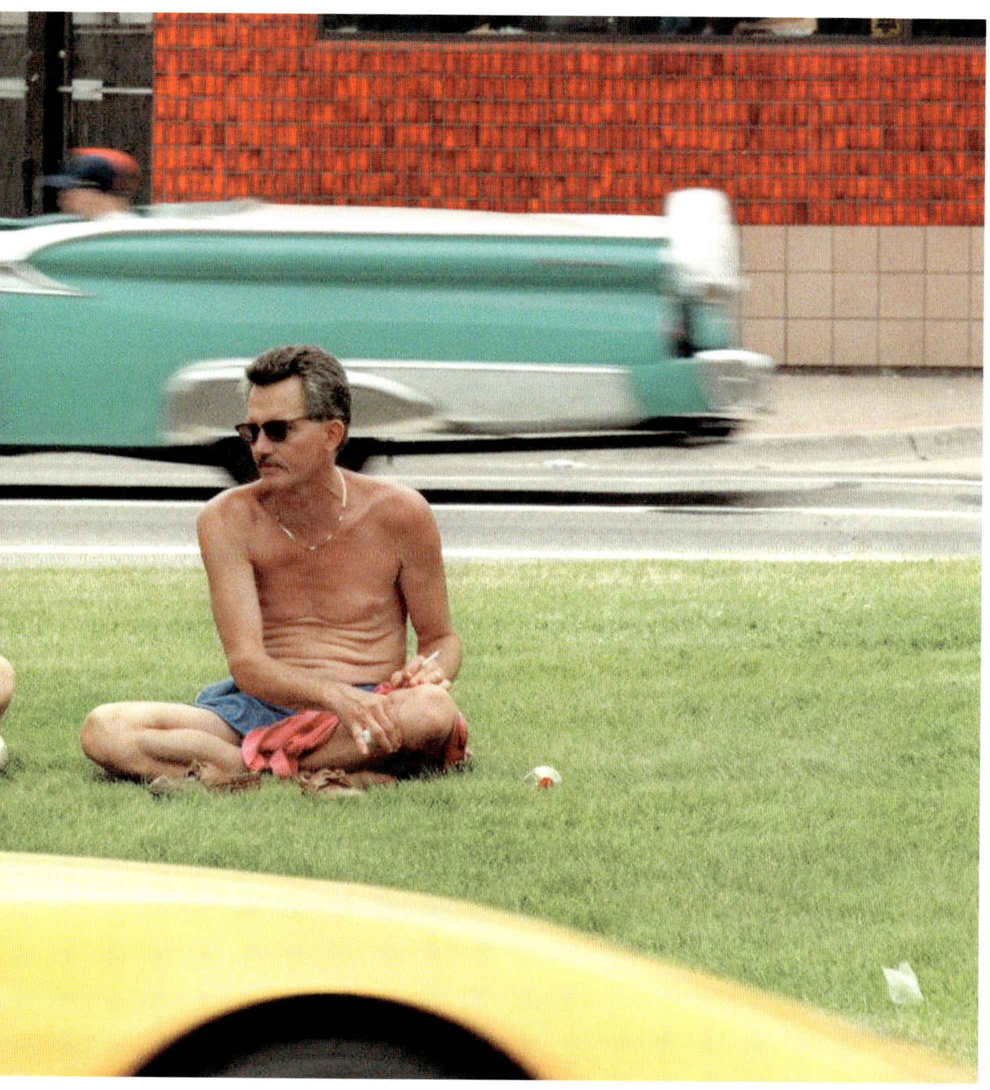

KIRTHMON F. DOZIER

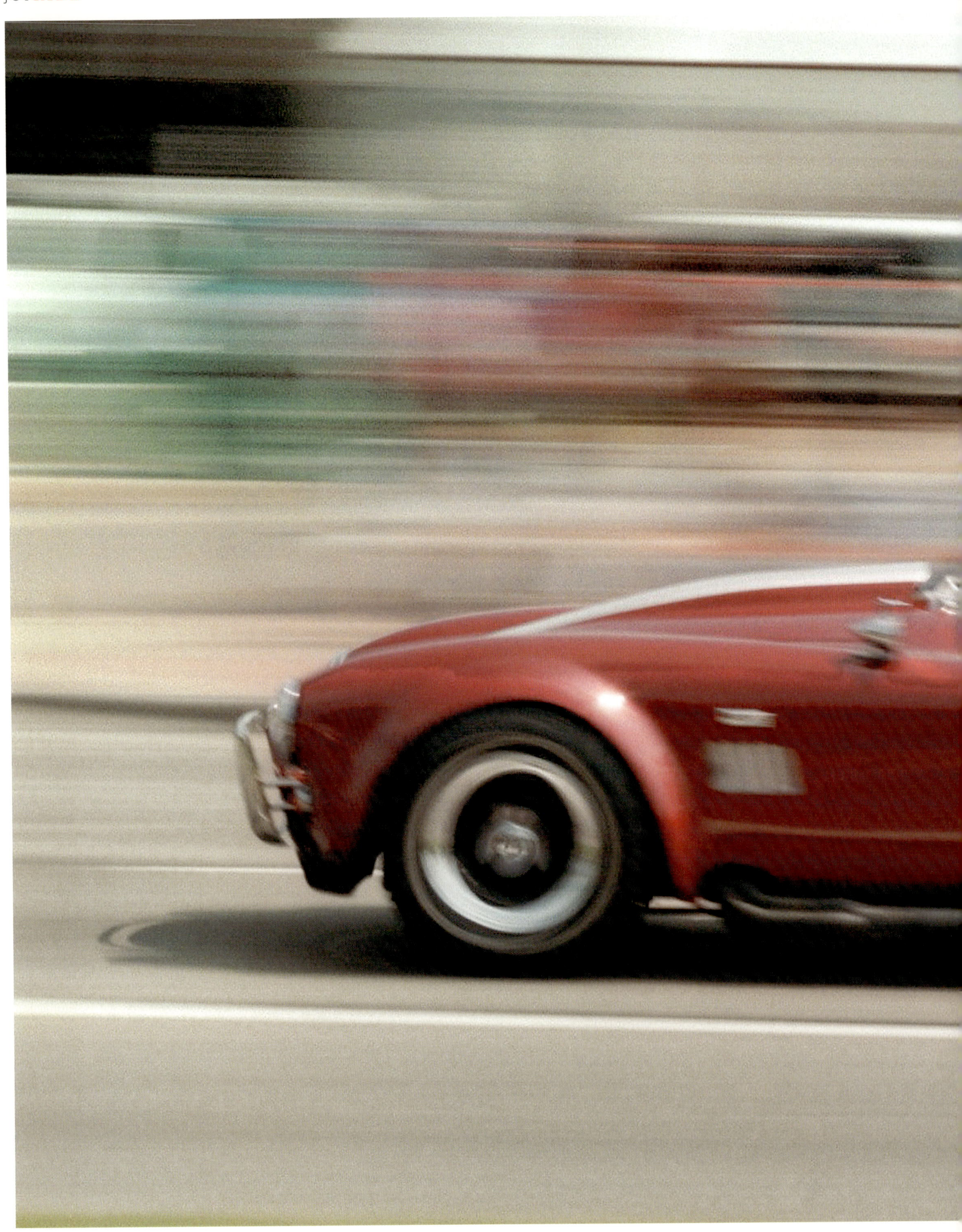

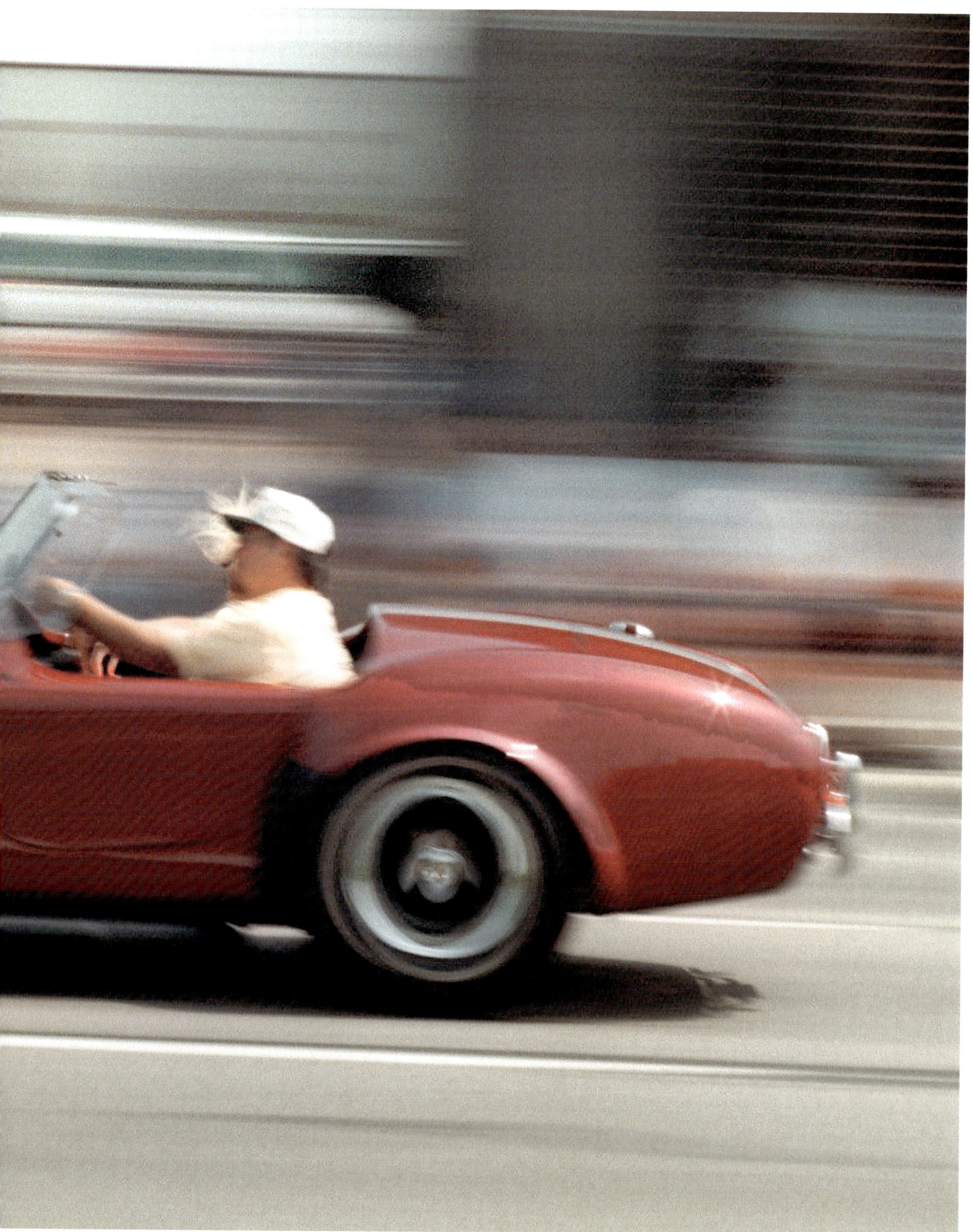

KIRTHMON F. DOZIER

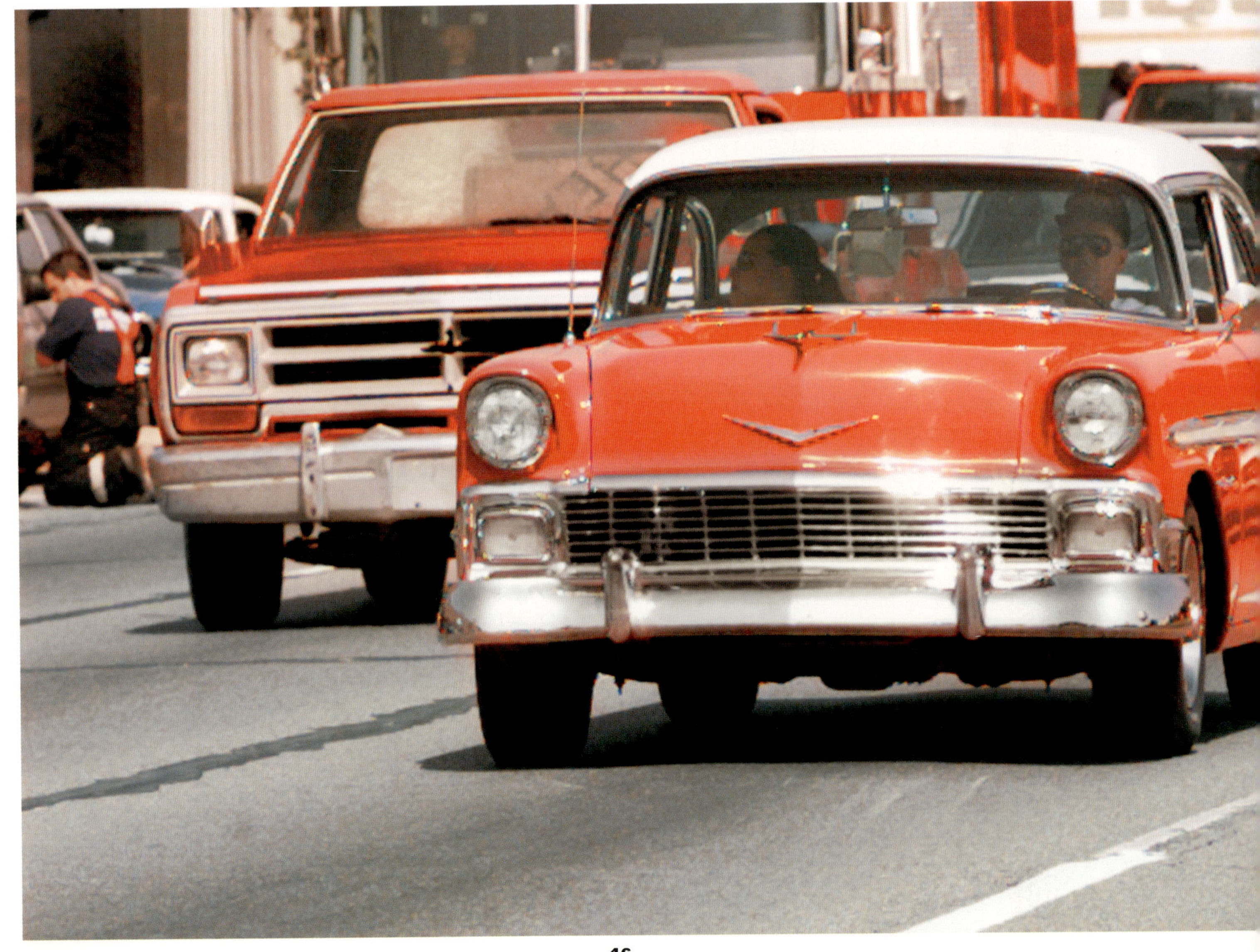

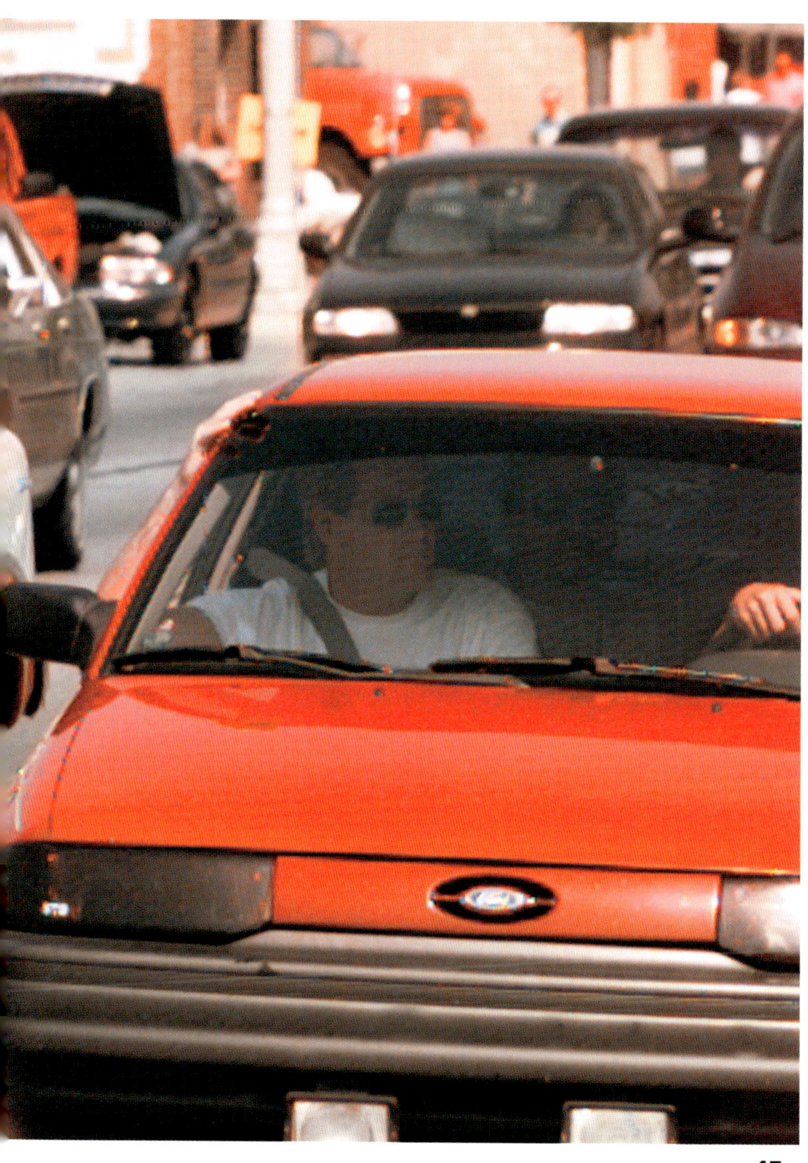

AS ERAS CLASHED, the large number of non-classic cars intermingled in the cruise became the subject of debate. "Right now, the Dream Cruise is nothing more than a traffic jam with all the late-model cars mixing in," Larry Payne, owner of Duggan's Irish Pub in Royal Oak, said at the time. The pub on Woodward has become a popular hangout during the Dream Cruise. In an attempt to ban the minivan before the 1999 cruise, Payne and others lobbied the cruise committee to create a parade that would require classic-car owners to register. Those who did not have a registration sticker would not be allowed to drive down the strip.

PAGE 48: IT'S TRUE LOVE. With his children at his side, Davie Love looked over his 1940 Buick, which was displayed at the Michigan State Fairgrounds. The little Loves are, from left, Malcolm, 2; Davie, 4, and Desiree, 6.

Left and next page: KIRTHMON F. DOZIER

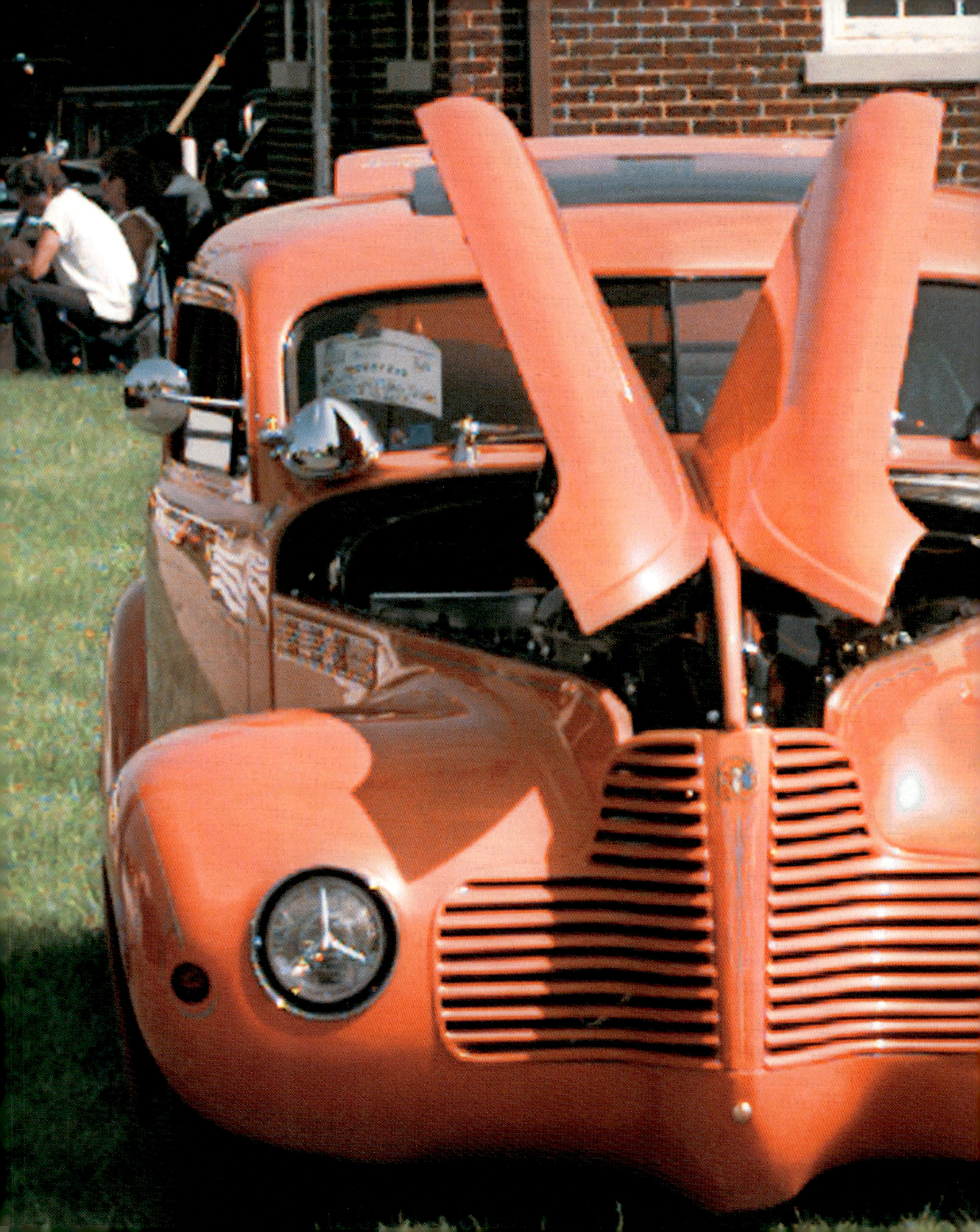

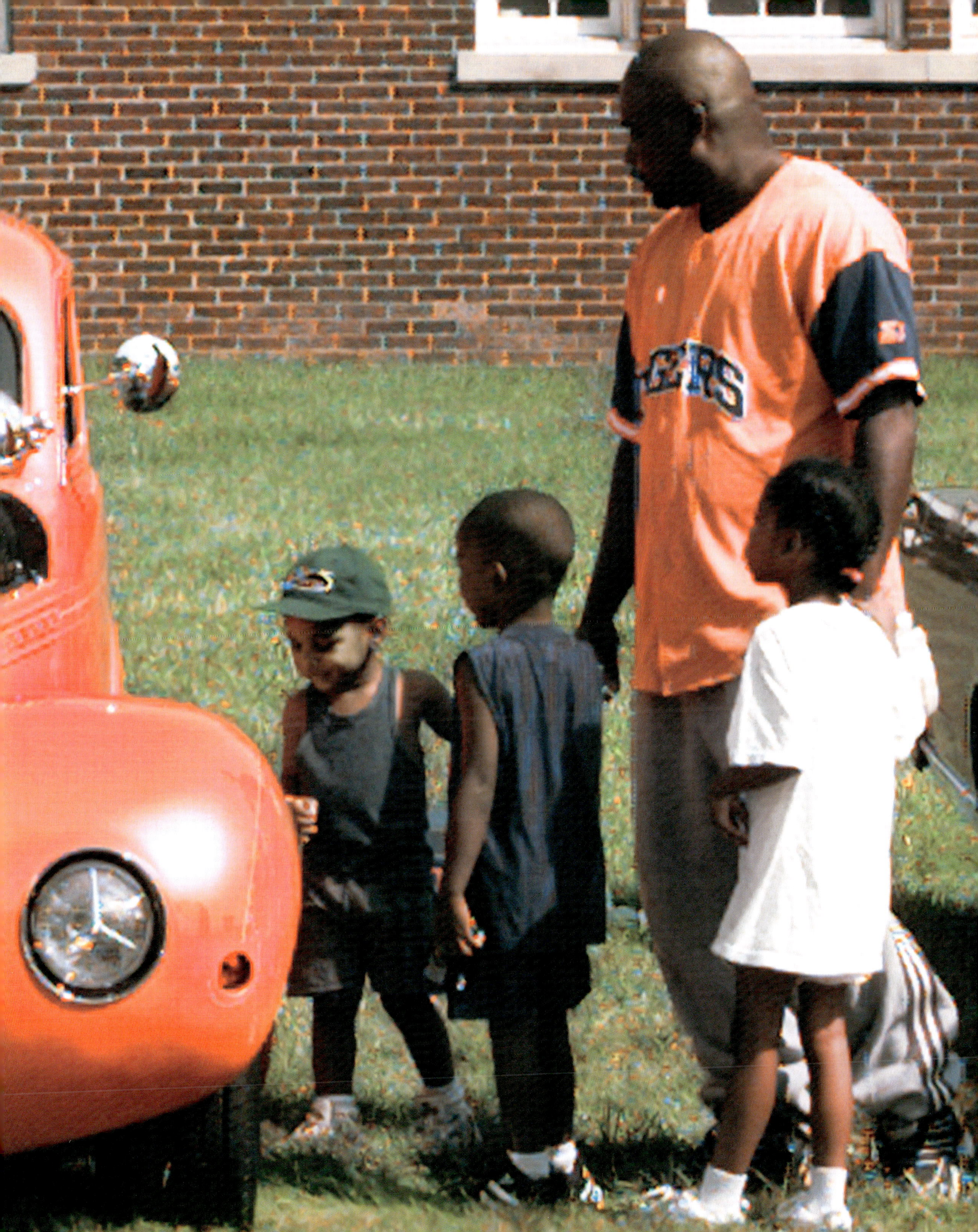

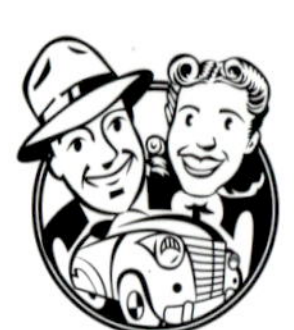

Date: Aug. 21

Attendance: 1.5 million, with 30,000 vintage and classic cars.

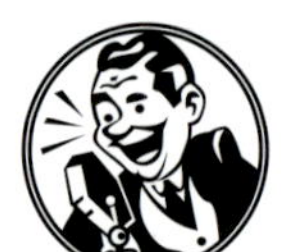

Special moment: Cruisers in classic cars got the curb lanes, which gave spectators an even better view.

More options on wheels: SMART buses began ferrying cruise fans for free, up and down Woodward. For motorists tired of the congestion, bus-riding became a great way to see the Dream Cruise.

1999

VA-ROOOM! ALTHOUGH THE DREAM CRUISE SPEAKS loudly about Detroit's Motor City heritage of horsepower, much of Woodward's cruise lore is suburban.

That's because cruisers could really "open it up" when they took a car past the vigilant police of Detroit into what, in the 1950s and '60s, was relatively unpopulated suburbia. So, cruising memories were mostly made in the 'burbs — where the Dream Cruise is.

But in 1999, auto supplier Eaton Corp. became the event's chief sponsor. That cemented a key tie not to the past, but to the present-day auto industry.

This year also was the year that Dream Cruise organizers introduced cruising lanes, using special signs to tell motorists that the two right-hand lanes of Woodward in each direction were reserved for classic cars. The goal was to "cut down on all the people who insist on cruising in their SUVs and minivans," said Bruce Henderlight, then chief of the Berkley Police Department, while letting legitimate classics take center stage.

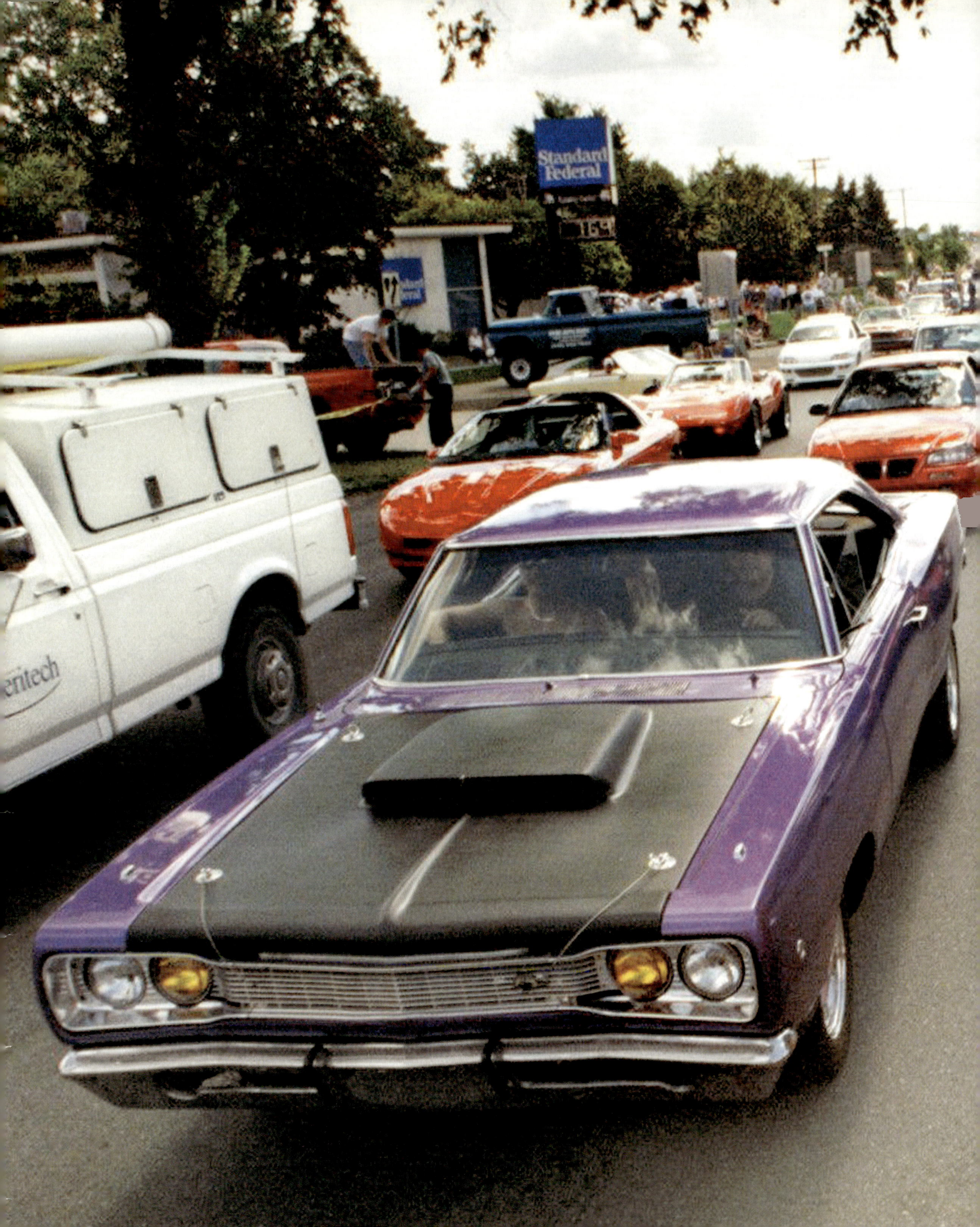
Standard Federal

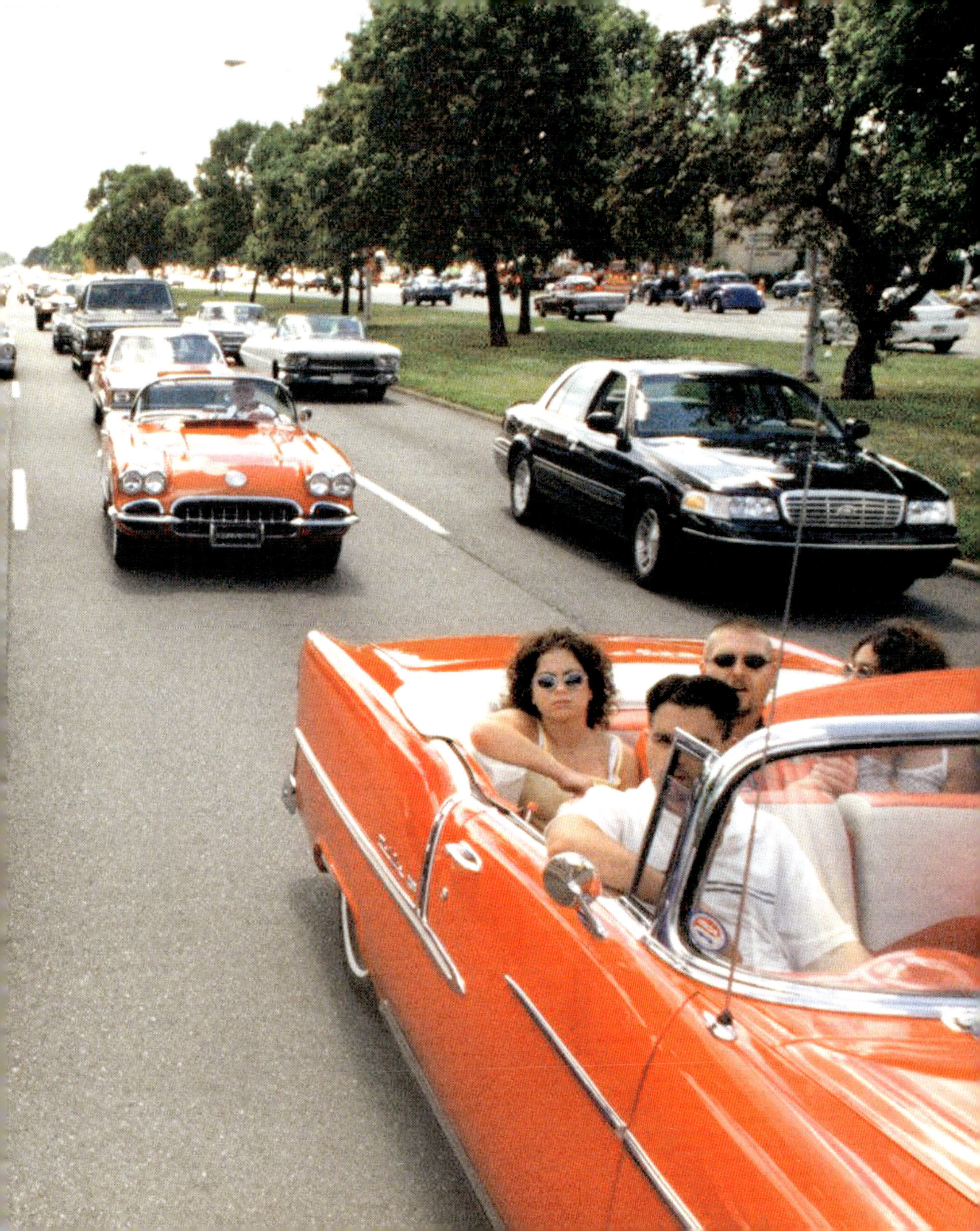

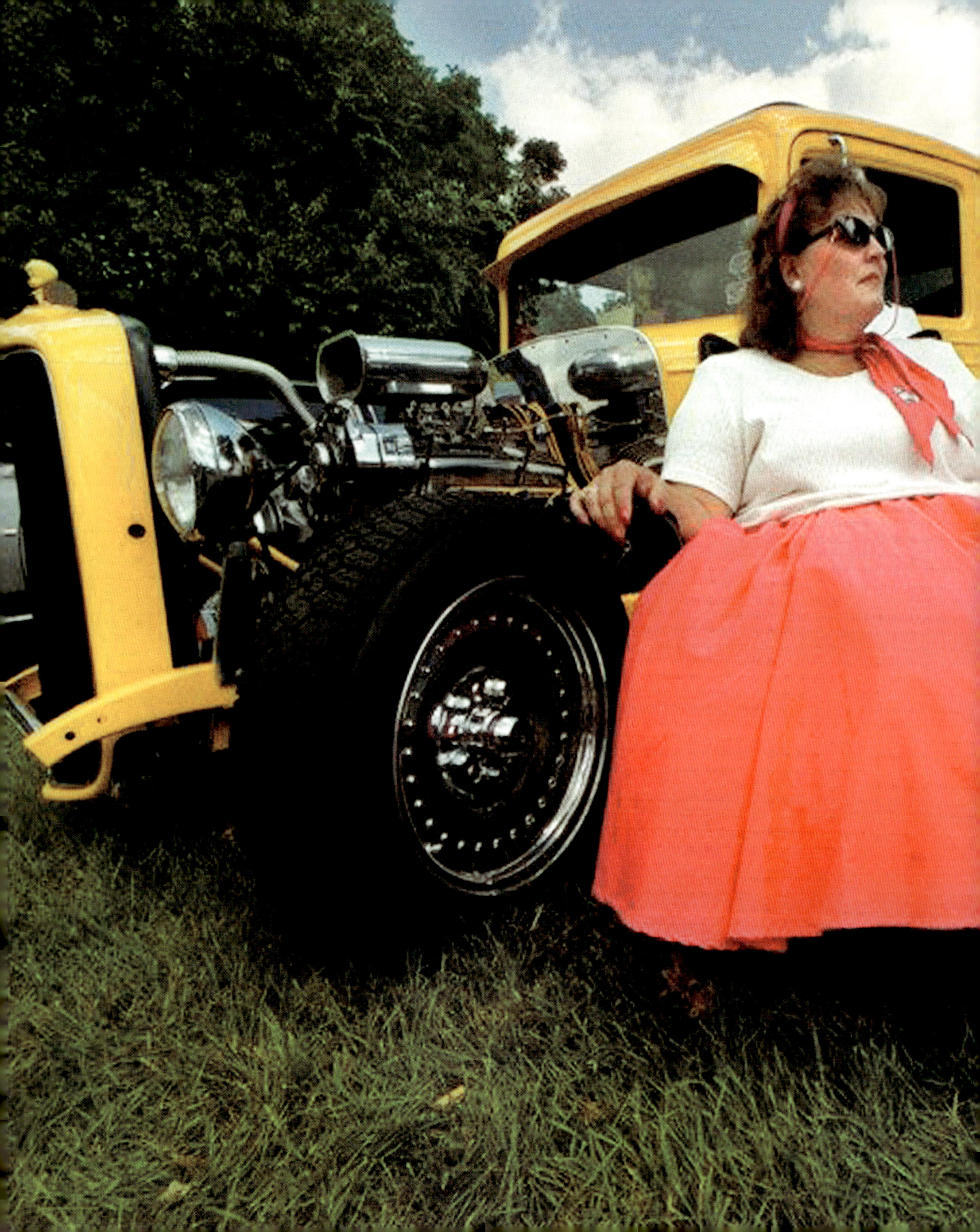

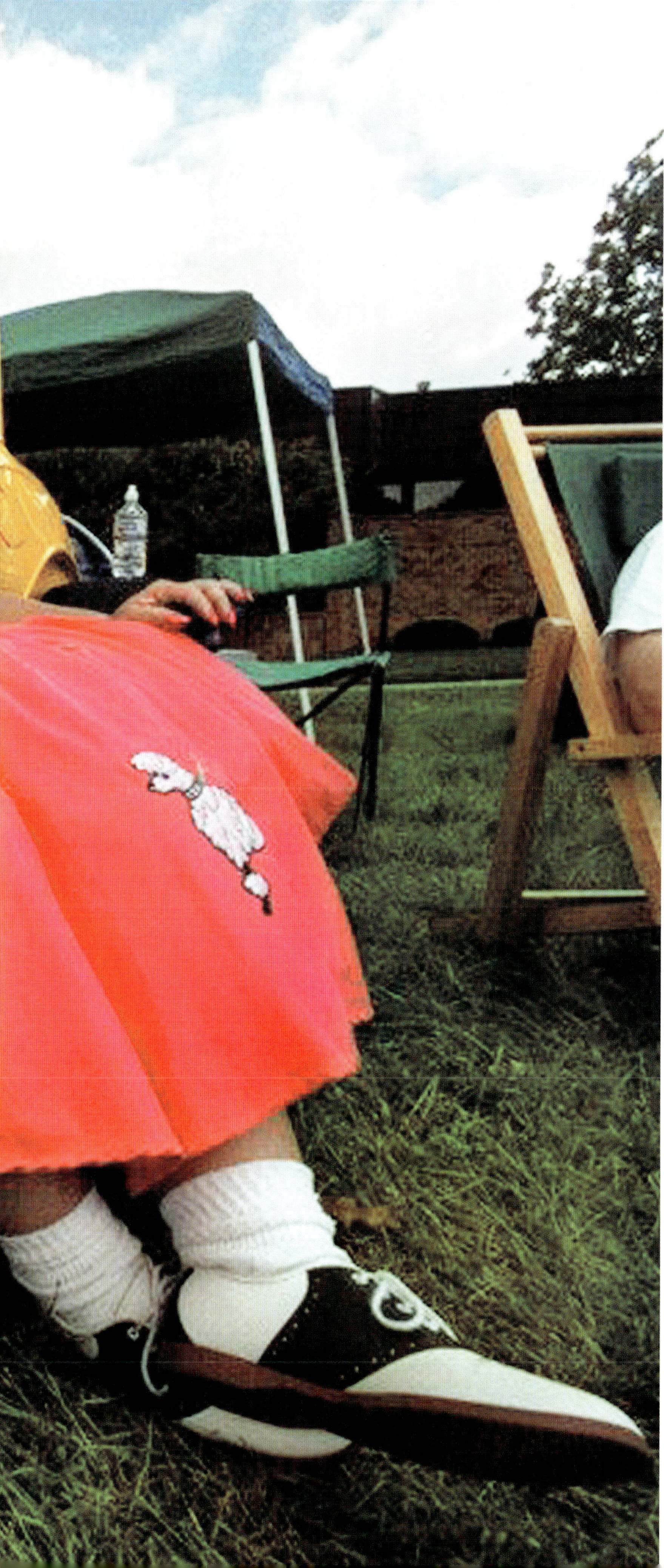

SOME PEOPLE COME TO CRUISE. Some like to watch the cars go by. People like Sheryl Rese of Dearborn did both. Rese looked laid-back, but don't let that fool you. This car lover was serious about jumping around in time. She was in her poodle skirt and saddle shoes, but she also had a 1932 Chevy coupe that would've been considered old even back in the '50s. Baby boomers loved the cruise because it let them recall a type of youthful culture that no one had ever seen before. It's often imitated, but has never been duplicated.

Left: M.J. AVILA; Previous page: ANDREW JOHNSTON

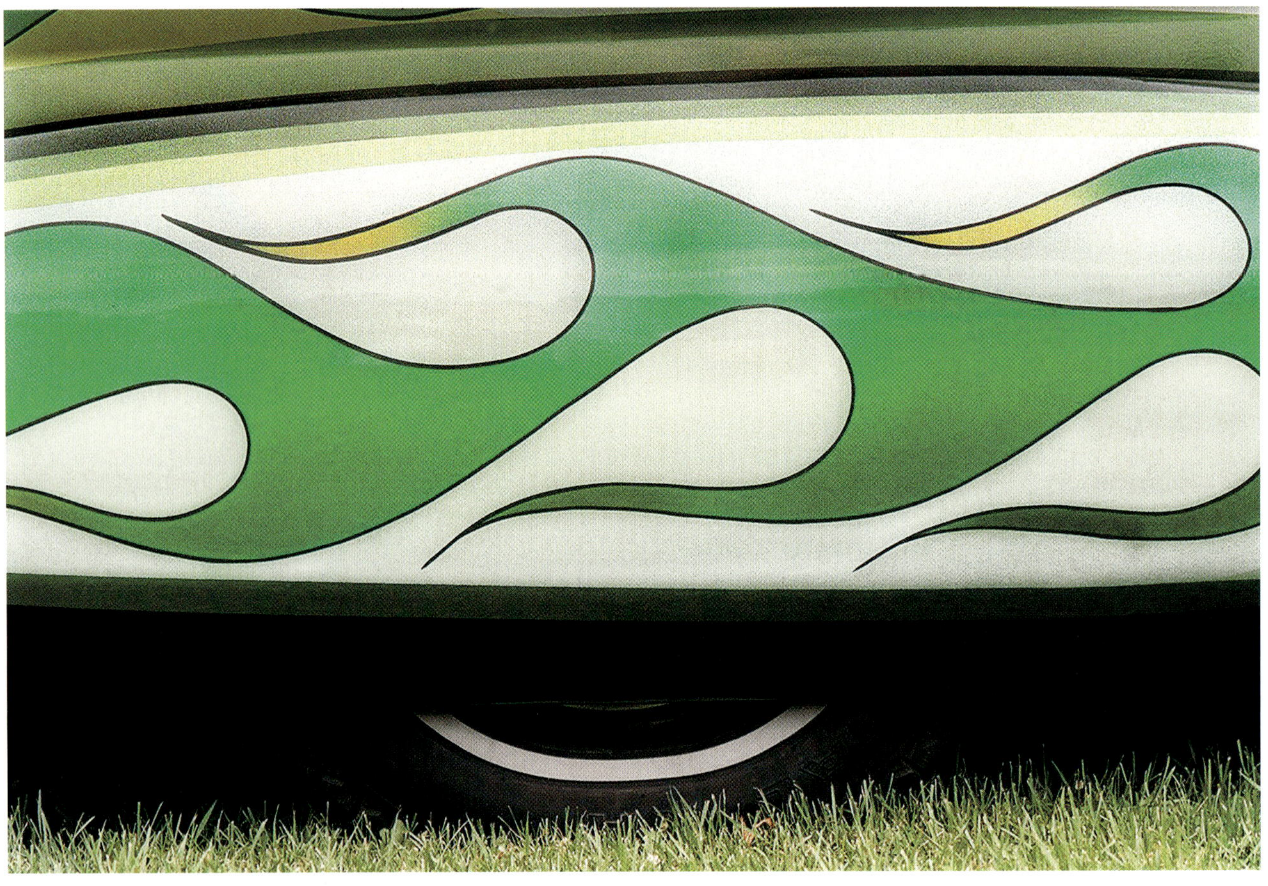

NINETEEN NINETY-NINE

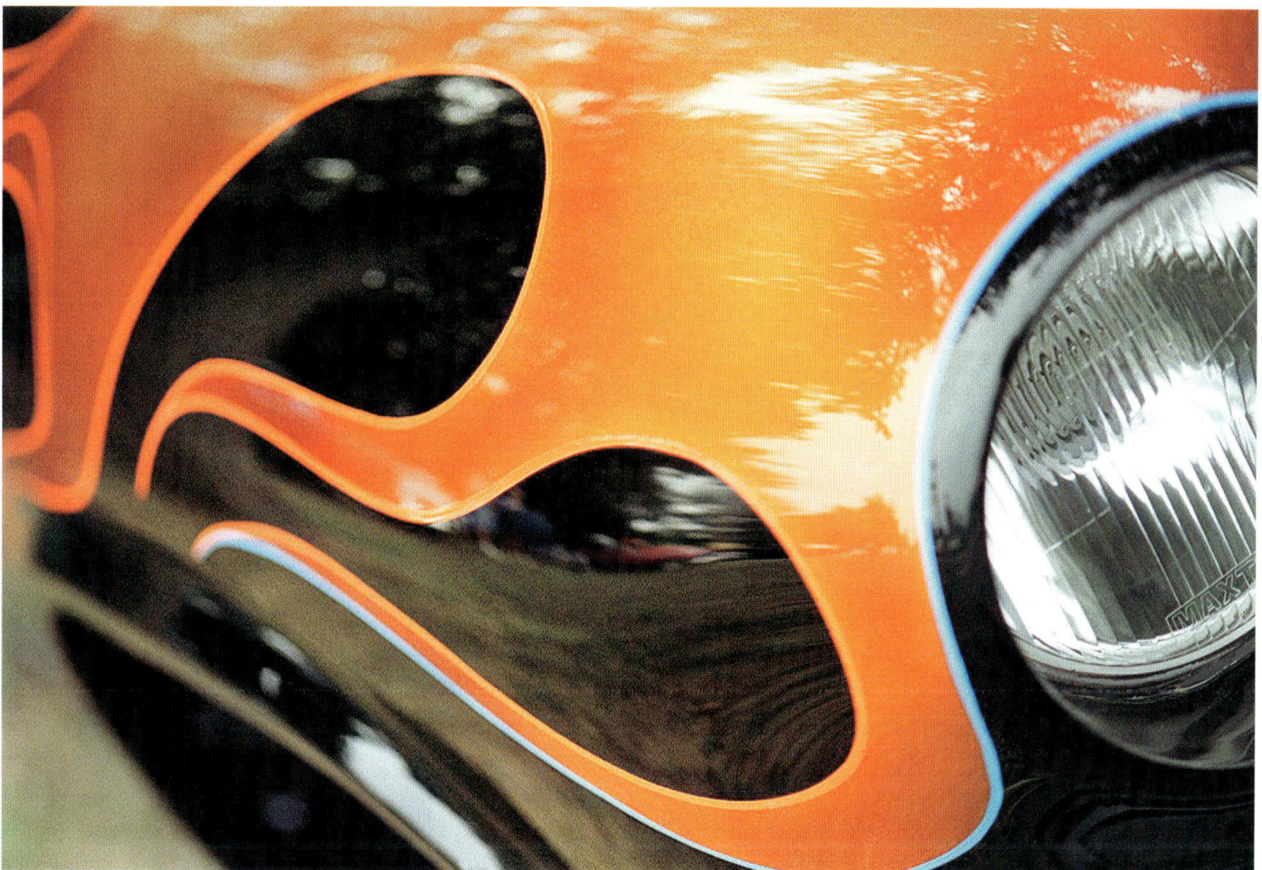

Left and above: ALLAN BARNES/Special to the Free Press

DETAILS MAKE ALL THE DIFFERENCE when it comes to old cars. There was a time when things like these were considered frivolous, a sign of rebellion. What really mattered, some thought, was the engine — torque and supercharges. Still, some people liked to stand out from the crowd. "Back then, people didn't have as much money to spend," said former Detroiter (Yosemite) Sam Radoff, said to be one of the best at painting flames on cars. So they added decorations to make their car a little different, a little cooler. And these days, people who come to the cruise looking for entertainment are glad for it. Some things cruise-watchers saw this year: from left, the metal panels, or bubble skirt, fitted across the wheel of this 1970 Ford Custom 500 to make it look sexy and low to the ground and the front of this 1950 Mercury painted with flames and pinstripes intended to enhance its contours. The Ford and the Mercury are examples of Yosemite Sam's handiwork.

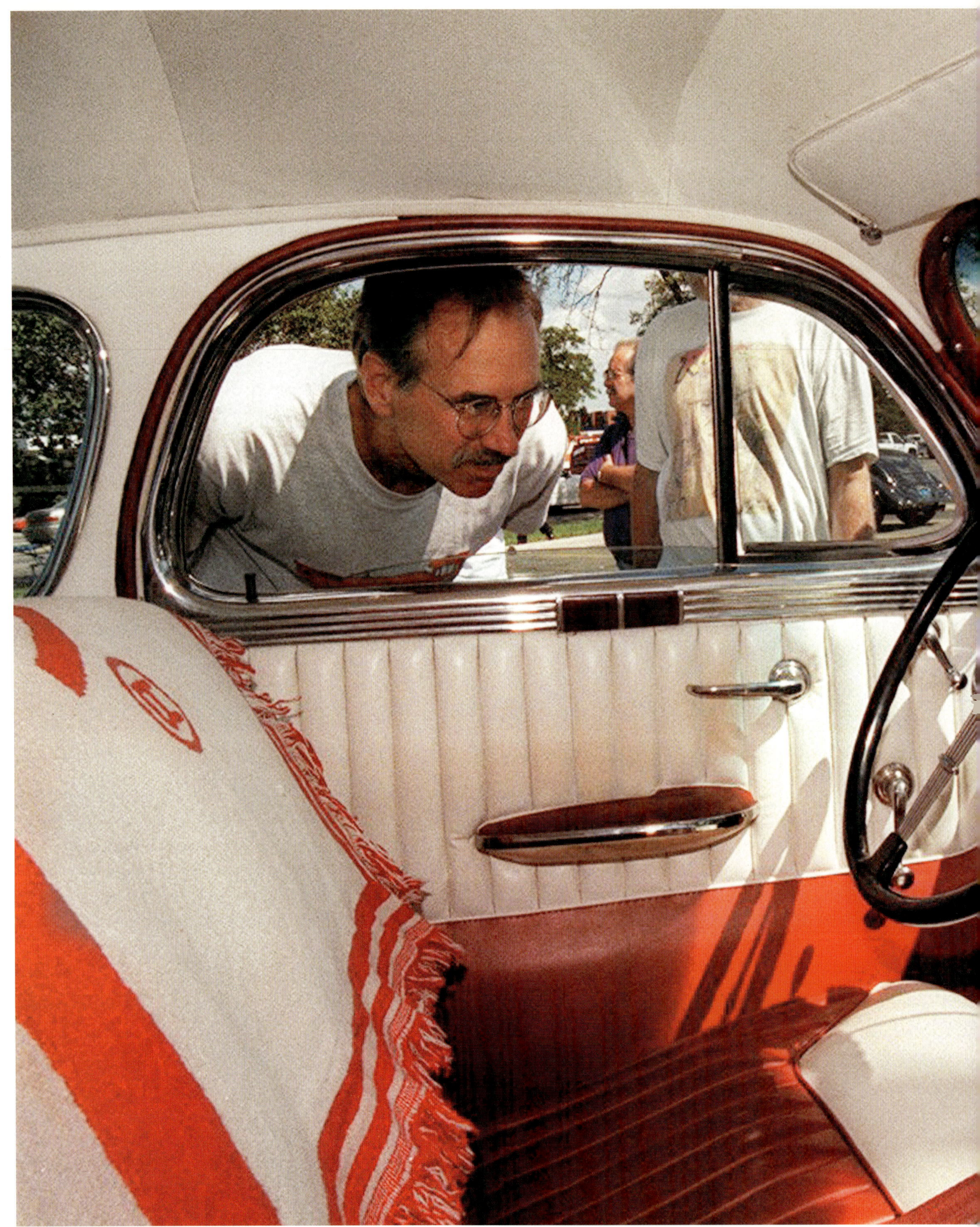

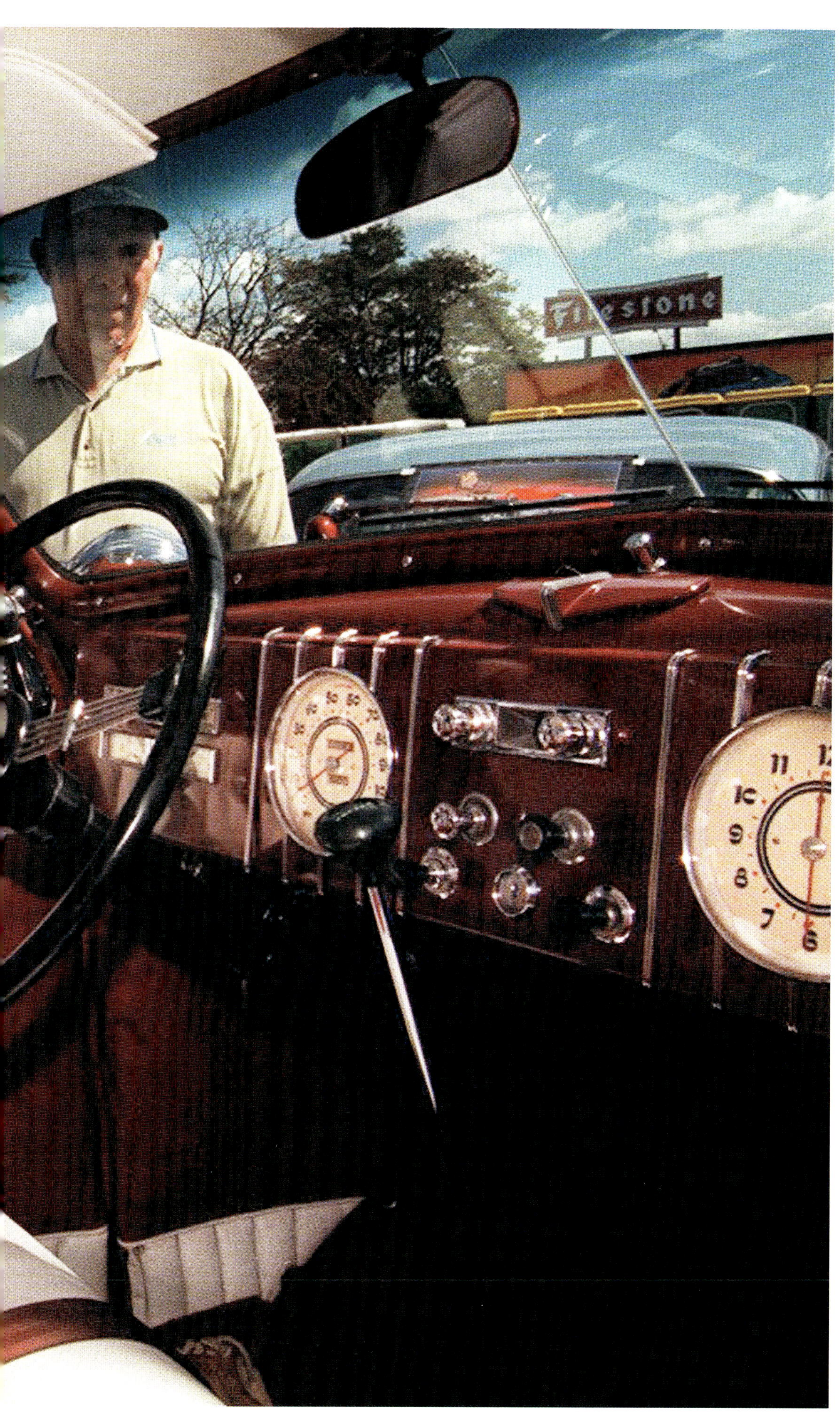

MAN, CHECK IT OUT! Alan Penney couldn't resist taking a peek inside this 1937 LaSalle parked on a lot off Woodward near 13 Mile. There's a lot to admire about this car, from the nice, smooth seats and the massive steering wheel to the old-style gearshift, speedometer and clock. Penney, who lived in Royal Oak, was among the cruise fans who gathered early to start gawking, making sure they wouldn't miss any car like one this roaming up and down Woodward. This year's cruise ran from 8 Mile in Ferndale through downtown Pontiac. Cities along the route — with the exception of Bloomfield Hills and Bloomfield Township, holdouts in hosting the cruise and participating in cruise-related activities — sponsored bands and other entertainment.

WILLIAM ARCHIE

"LOOK AT THOSE FINS! It's so elegant," Barb Schultz said after seeing a Cadillac like this one, a 1959 Eldorado. This model, owned by the Cadillac Motor Car Division, sat gleaming in Royal Oak's Memorial Park, ready to bring a chorus of ooooohs and ahhhhhs from crowds of admirers.

Right: PATRICIA BECK; Next page: M.J. AVILA

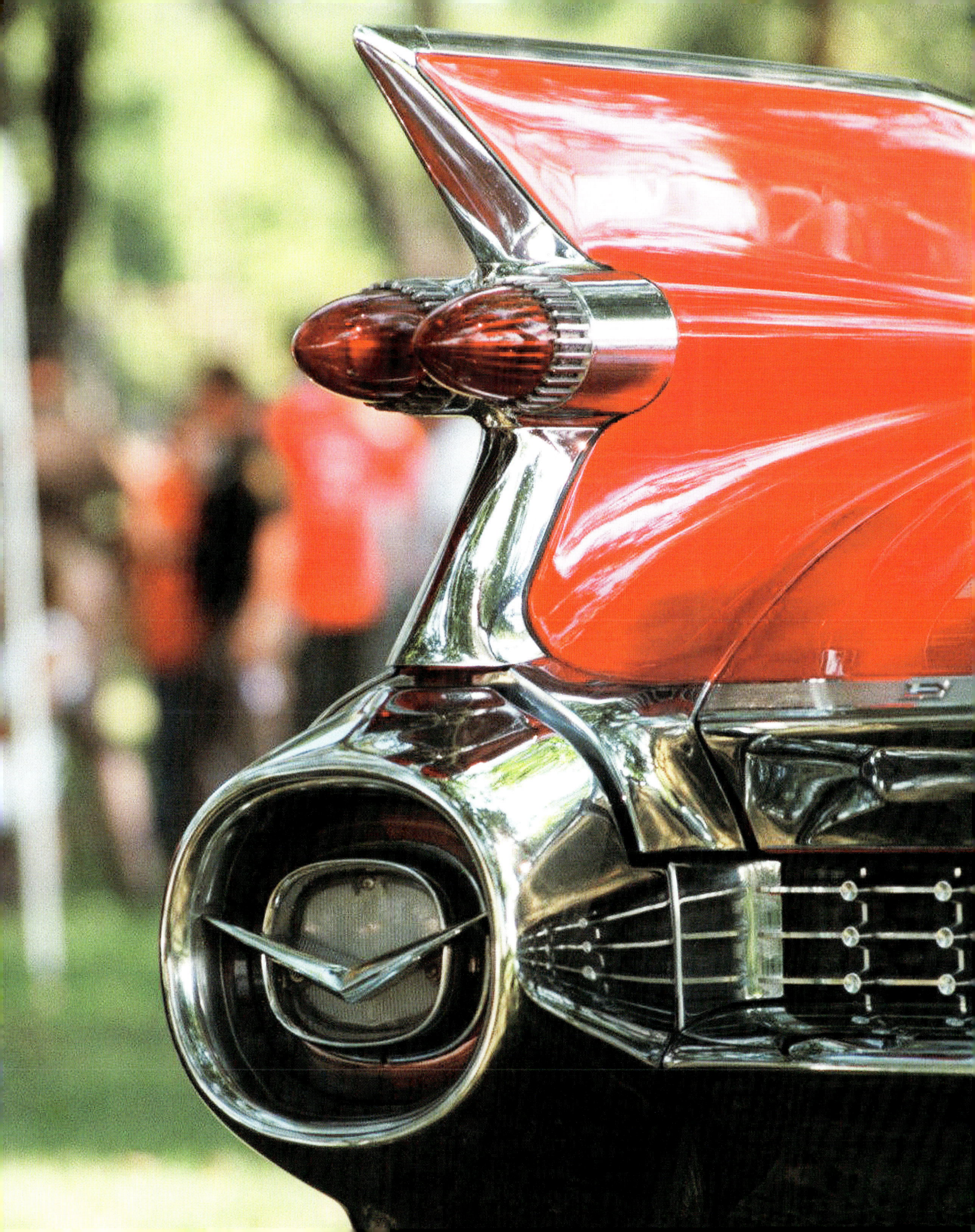

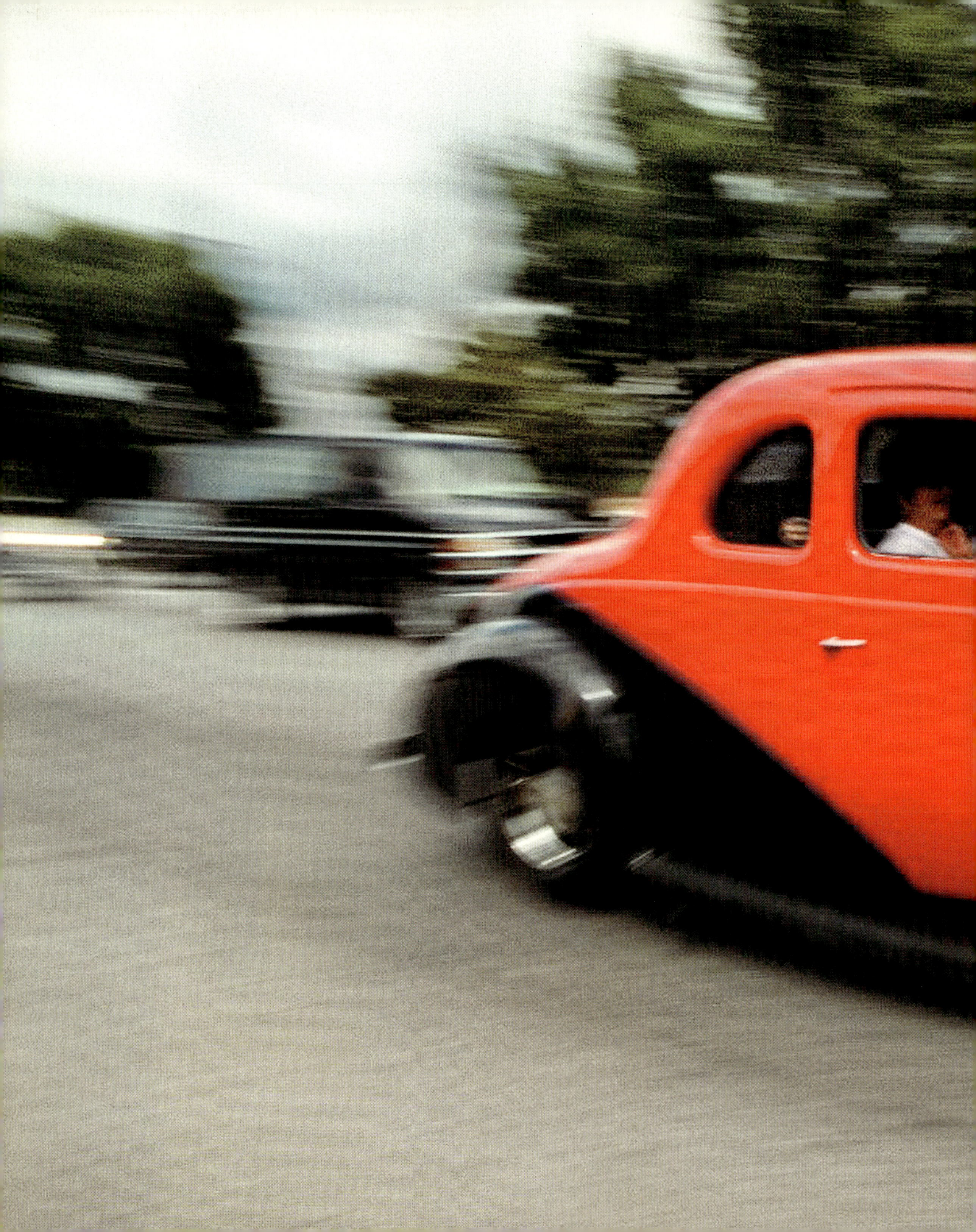

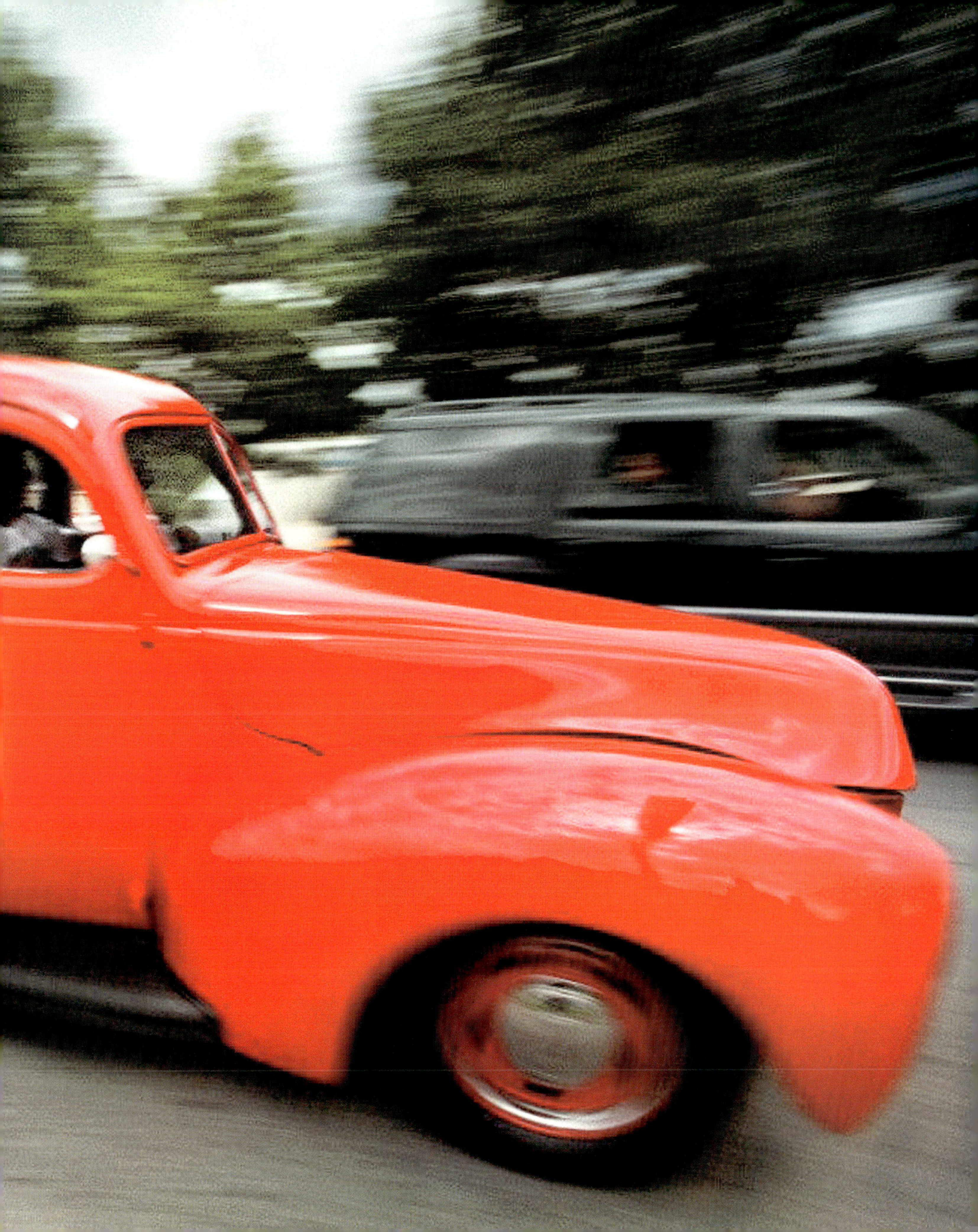

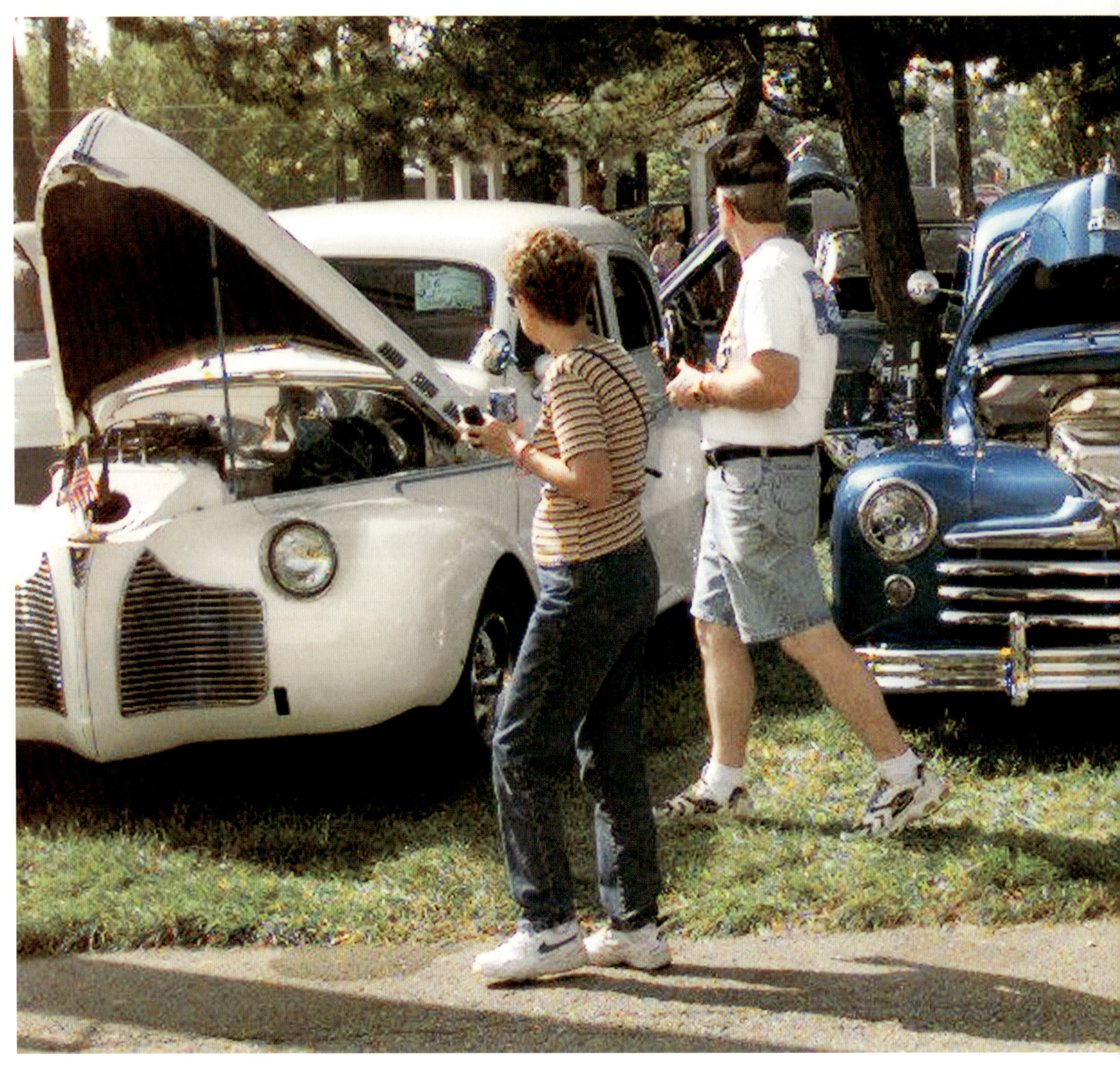

NINETEEN NINETY-NINE

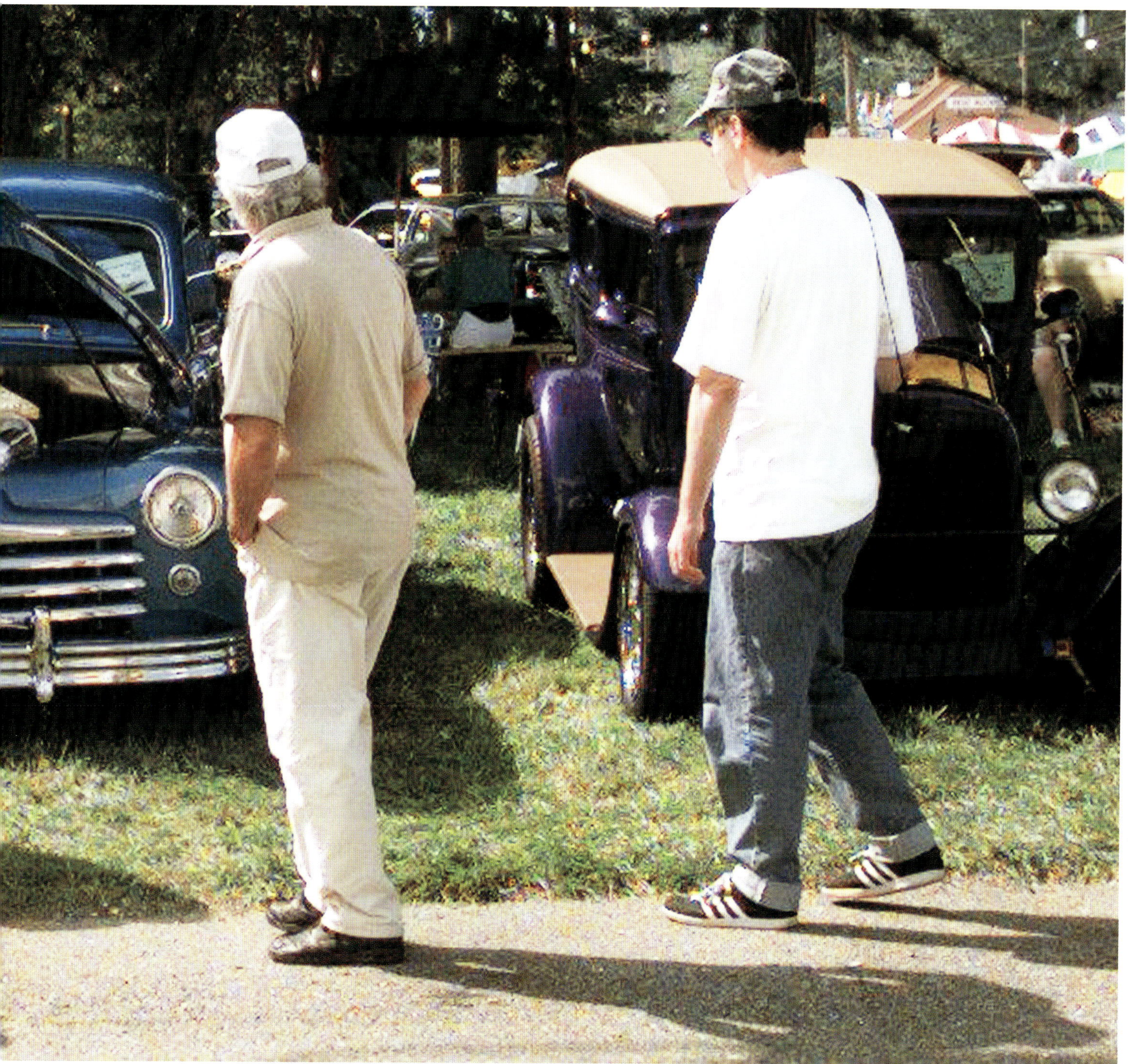

KIRTHMON F. DOZIER

AFTER BEING ON THE ROAD, some drivers parked their prized possessions at the Michigan State Fairgrounds so people from the metro area and elsewhere could get a closer look. This year's cruise crowd included 58 car-crazy Australians who came from halfway around the world just to be "in the land where it all began," said David Clee, who lived about 100 miles south of Sydney and was president of the Pontiac Car Club of Australia. "I'm sure that all of us are going to be in awe," said member Stuart Griffiths, who couldn't wait to experience the Dream Cruise and see Woodward in person, not just on the Internet. The group of farmers, nurses, police officers and mechanics traveled about 10,000 miles, at a cost of $4,000 each, to attend the cruise. They arrived in Los Angeles, drove across the United States — cruising through Vegas, Denver and Chicago — before finally arriving in Pontiac, right before the big show. Some brought relatives along for a family vacation and a chance to get a decent tan (August is a winter month in Australia). As for the cars — including Griffiths' 1974 Firebird and '68 Pontiac, Clee's '67 Firebird coupe and 1980 Trans-Am and some others that date to 1926 — it just wasn't possible to bring them along, Griffiths said.

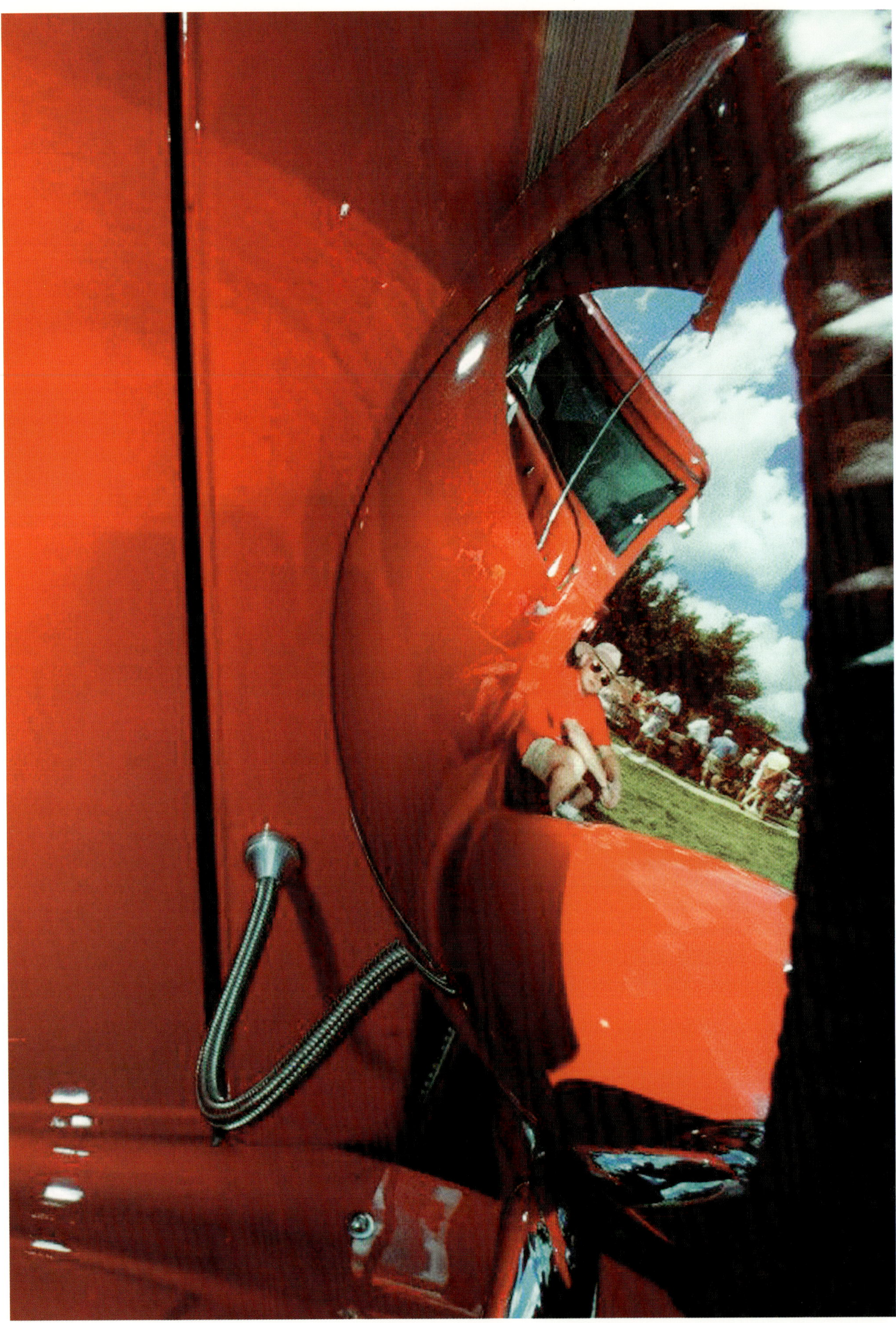

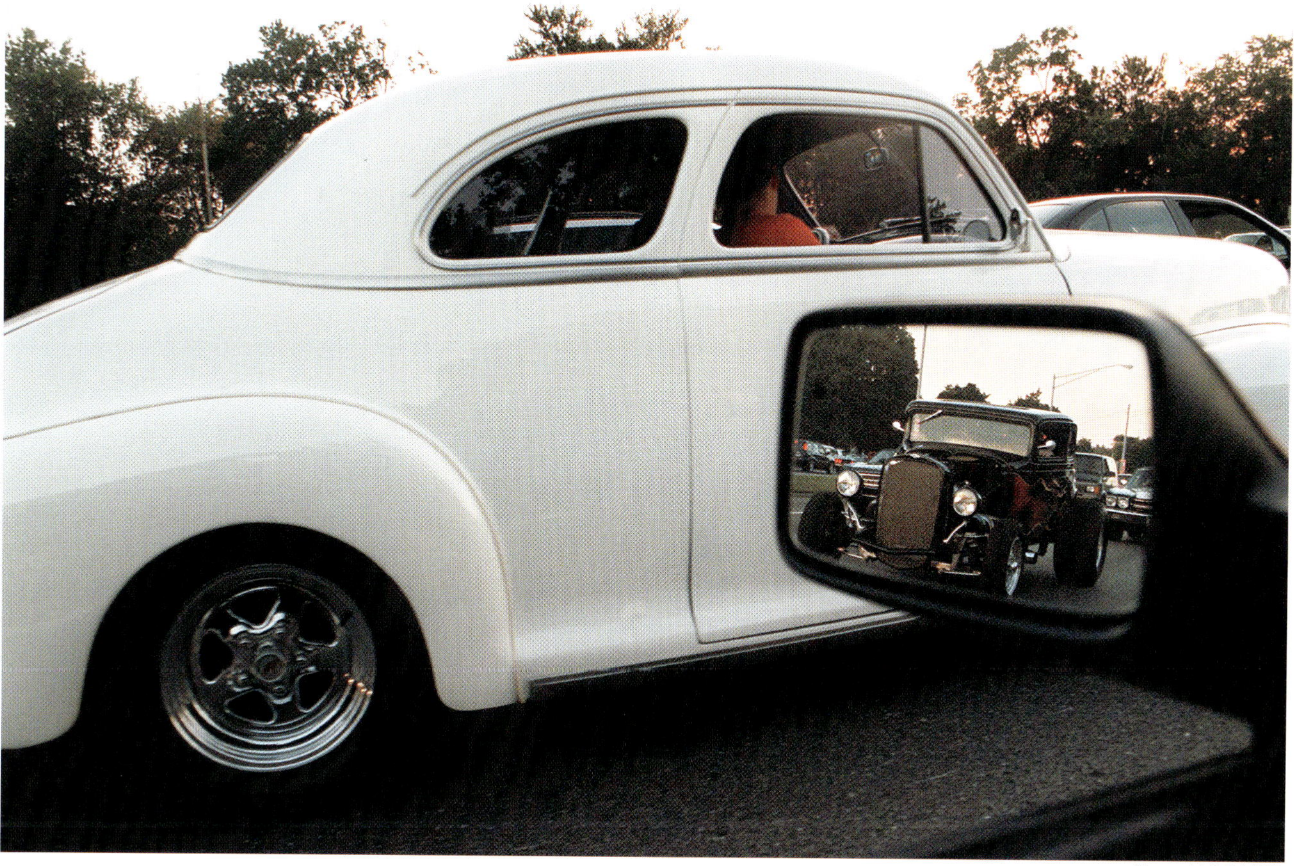

Above and left: M.J. AVILA

THERE ARE LOTS OF VIEWS on classic cars, both on the road and off. This year, the debate over what separates the real deal from a cream puff pretender seemed especially contentious. This is what the Classic Car Club of America said about the issue: True classics were built only from 1925 to 1948. That would include the '48 Chevy above and the older car behind it. The description also embraces the 1931 Ford Model A that a reflective headlight, left, shows Donald Kern of Harrison Township sitting on. Anything 25 years or older is a historic vehicle, the club says. Dream Cruise aficionados were even pickier: Some said that if the car wasn't from the '50s or '60s, it didn't belong at the event. "The Model A never cruised Woodward," car collector Dan Hosler of Waterford said. Cruise official Jean Chamberlain was a bit more diplomatic: "What we consider classic is usually the '50s and '60s cars," she said. "However, the guy who bought a Corvette last year thinks he's got a classic. And we've got muscle cars and hot rods and Vipers and a lot of new stuff." So what *is* a classic? "The unique cars coming out of Detroit since the '30s," she said.

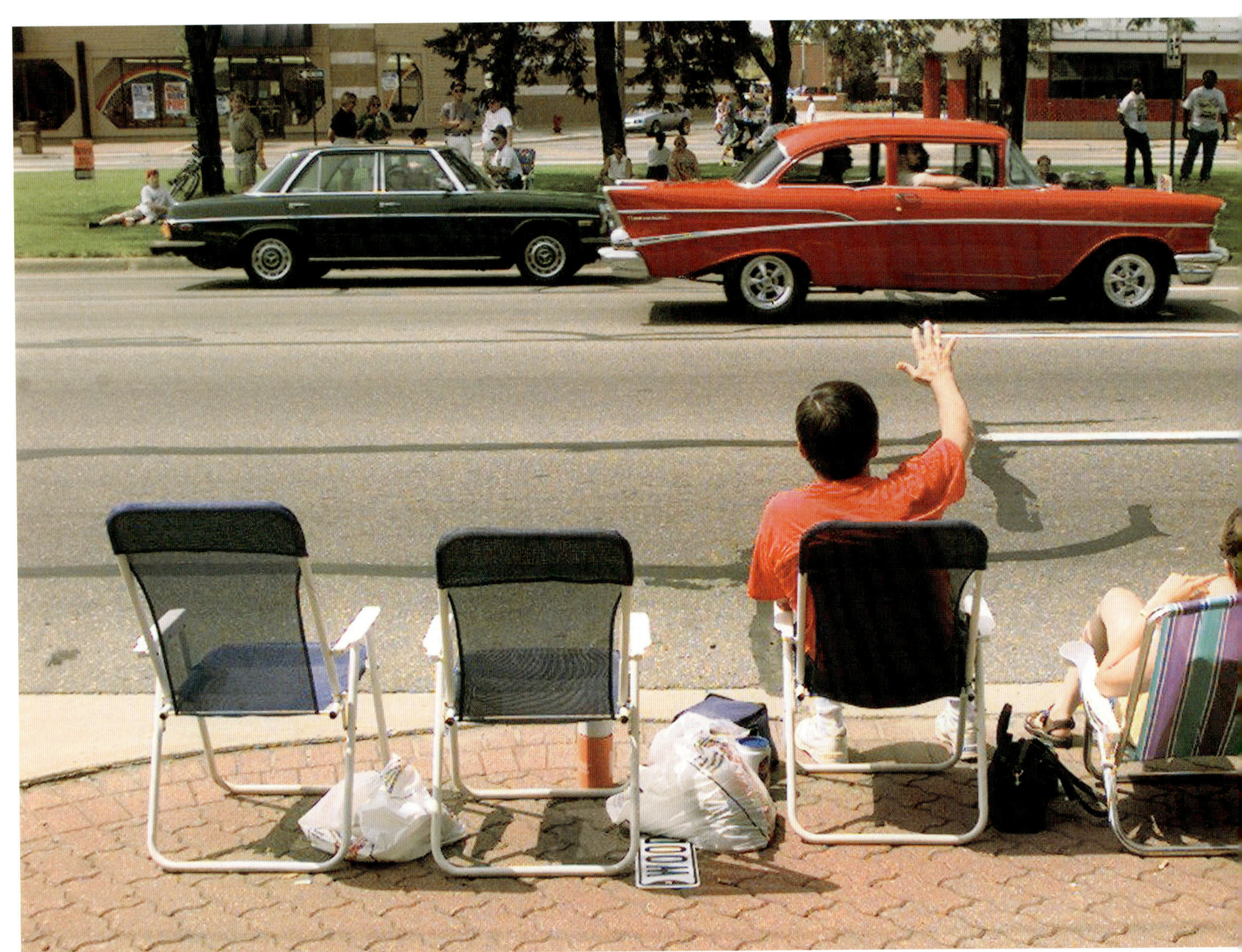

NINETEEN NINETY-NINE

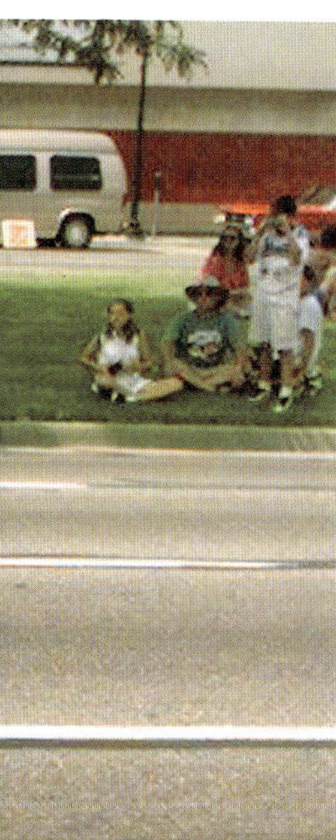

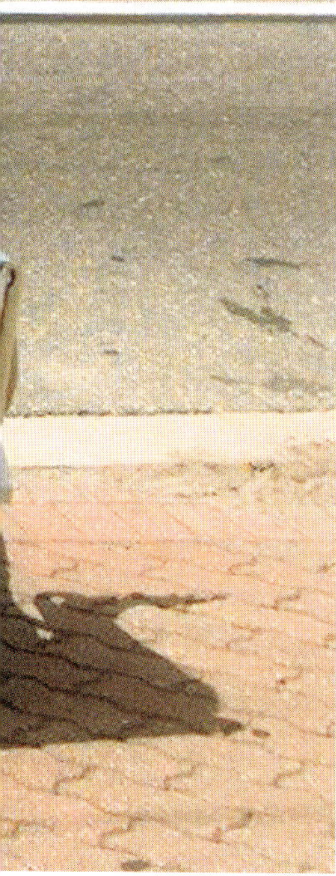

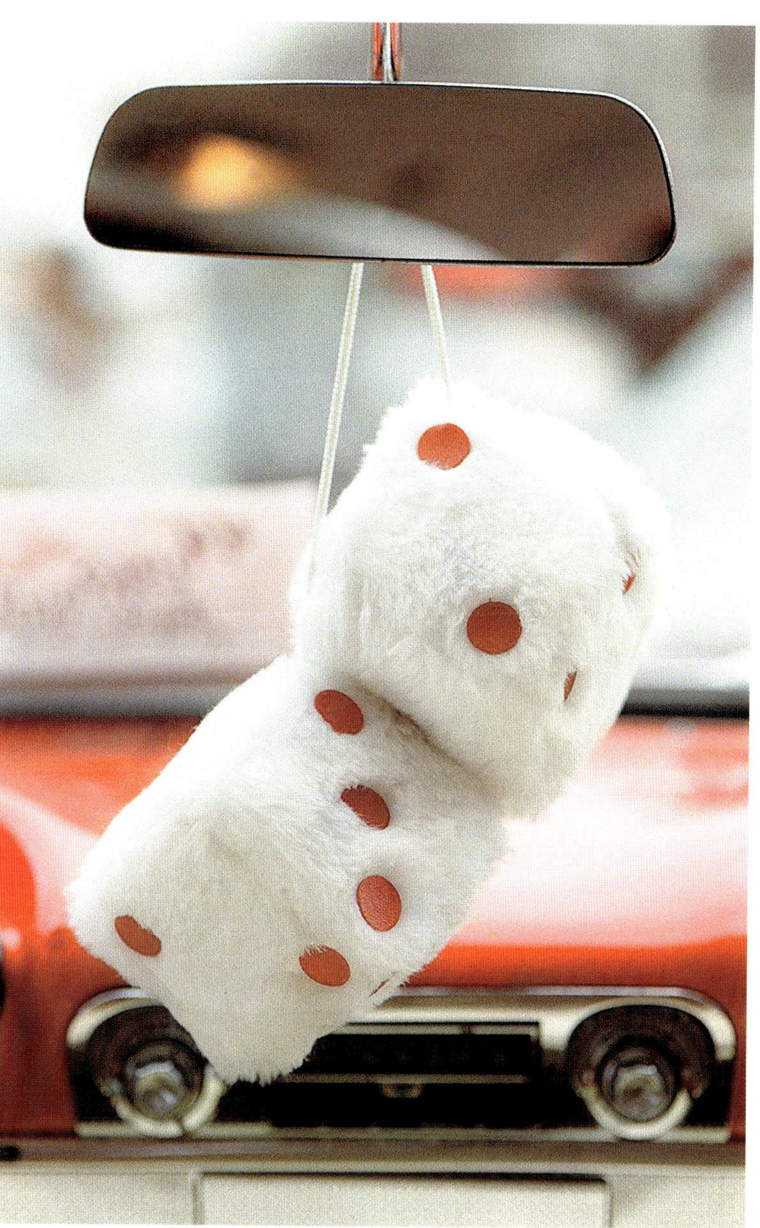

Left: KIRTHMON F. DOZIER; Above: ALLAN BARNES/Special to the Free Press

FEELING LUCKY? Before the days of widespread gambling, a pair of fuzzy dice — a staple in hot-rod magazines of the late '40s and early '50s — had a slightly illicit image. Now they're so tame, the Art Van furniture store sold them. Another must-have for this year's cars was "Cruisin Songs from the Motor City," a CD featuring 14 songs with a car theme. The local artists stuck to the original versions of tunes such as "Route 66," "Low Rider," "Mustang Sally" and "Little Red Corvette," but made occasional variations. On "No Money Down," John Sinclair sang: "I'm gonna cruise down Woodward Avenue/All the way to 8 Mile Road." A portion of sales from Dream Cruise T-shirts, street signs, collectors items and other merchandise benefitted 75 charities.

FAR LEFT: Thanks to a new (voluntary) traffic-control plan reserving the two outside lanes for classic cars, the view wasn't obstructed by late-model automobiles. Classic car watchers and drivers praised the move, saying traffic congestion was lighter than it had been in years. "This isn't about zipping up and down Woodward," said James Berger, 23, of Troy, who drove a 1958 Corvette. What's important is that the people watching get a good look at the cars, he said.

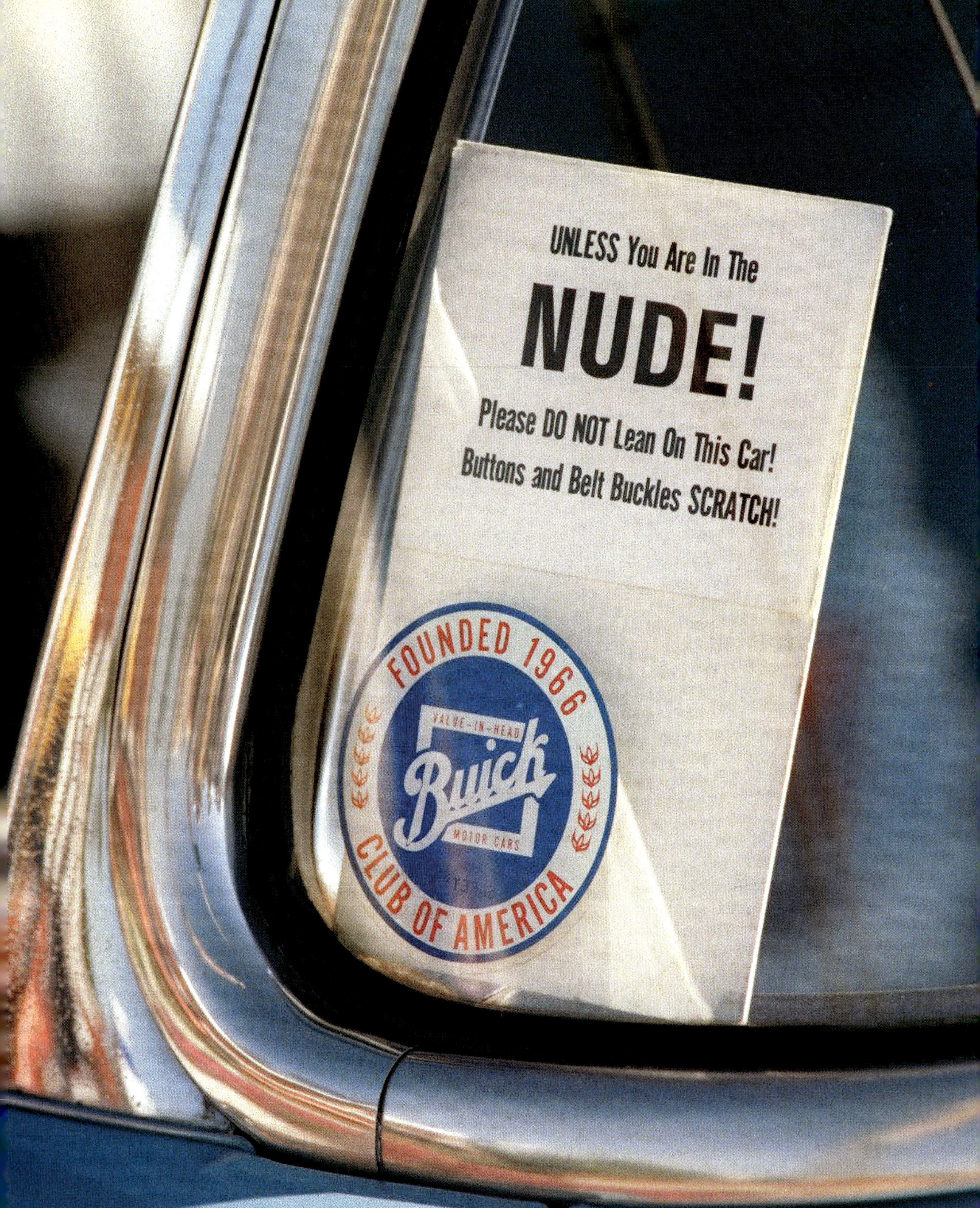
UNLESS You Are In The
NUDE!
Please DO NOT Lean On This Car!
Buttons and Belt Buckles SCRATCH!
FOUNDED 1966
VALVE-IN-HEAD
Buick
MOTOR CARS
CLUB OF AMERICA

IT'S NOT JUST ABOUT THE CAR, as the sign in the window of this Buick would have you believe. It's about protecting a memory, too. Younger people may have trouble understanding all this passion for a car, Greg Arendt, 43, of Clinton Township said. They see automobiles as a means of getting from one place to another, and having a car isn't as big of a deal as it once was. Back in the day, a car was instant entertainment and people cruised for fun. "When you talk about the good old days, this is it," said Nick Spiroff, of Milford. "We'd drive around, hang out, meet girls. ... If you found someone to race, all the better." Woodward's mystique began in the '60s with an ad showing the Pontiac GTO — now the icon of the muscle-car world. The car was stopped at a turnaround median, heading in the direction of Woodward, presumably to cruise and race. It sparked excitement among teens looking for something to do. And almost instantly, they started using cars for cruising, racing and socializing. The cruising spirit continued strong until around the '70s, when residents in the communities along Woodward and police joined up to start a state-sponsored campaign to thwart cruising. "Police just started stopping everyone and really hassled anyone cruising down Woodward at night," said Jim Wangers, author of "The Glory Days: When Horsepower and Passion Ruled Detroit" (Bentley Books, $24.95). Higher gas prices proved to be the ultimate killjoy.

Left: ANDREW JOHNSTON; Next page: M.J. AVILA

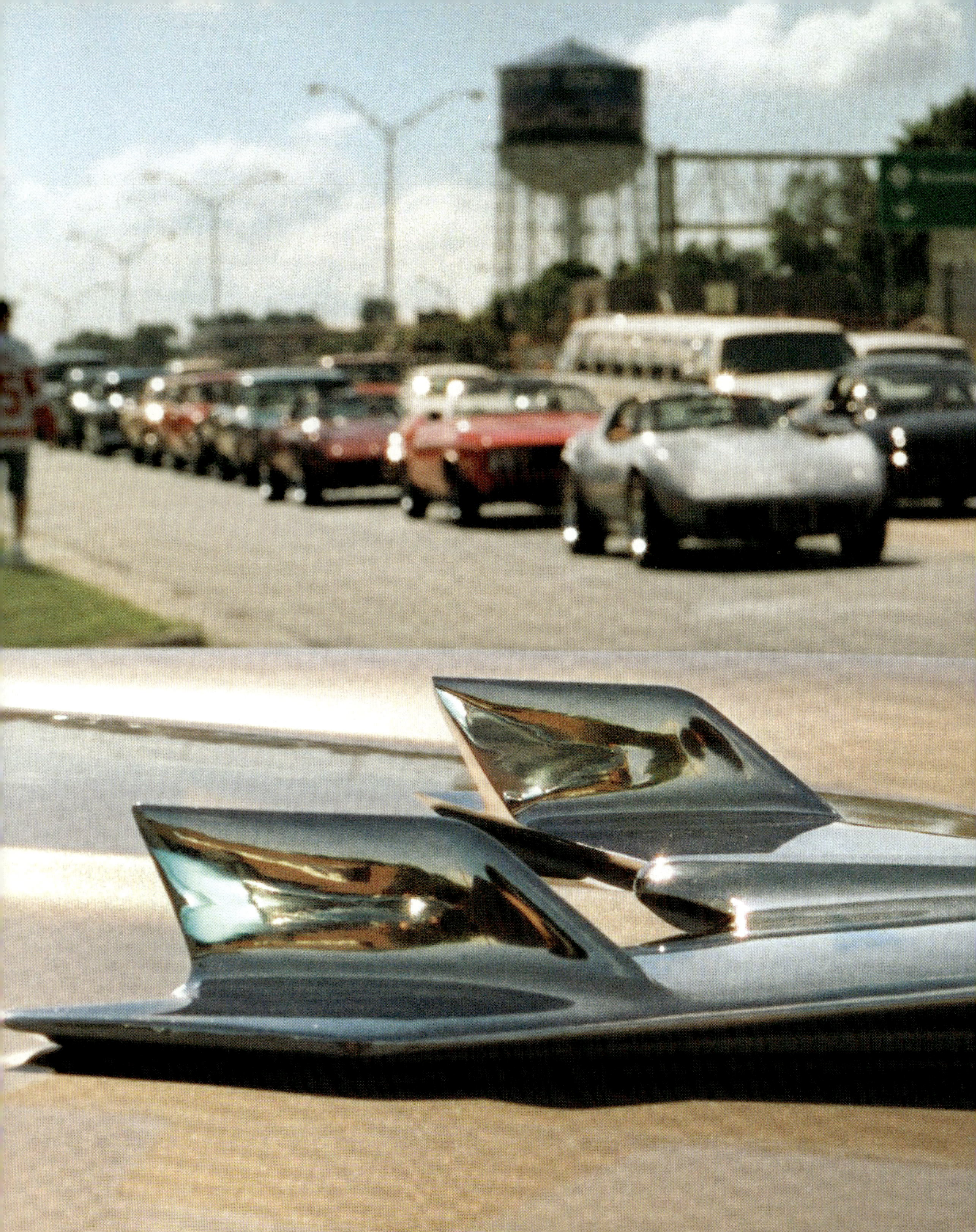

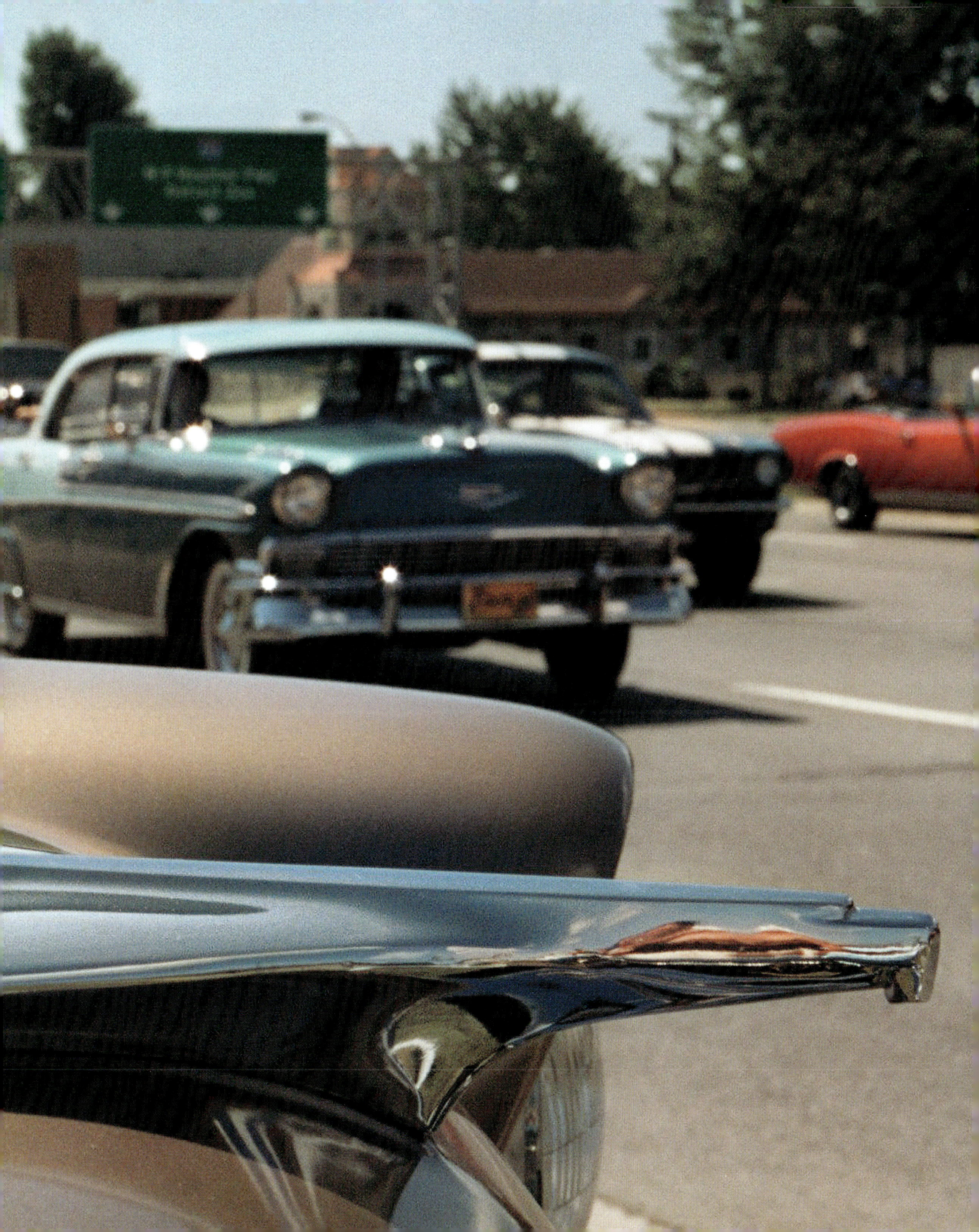

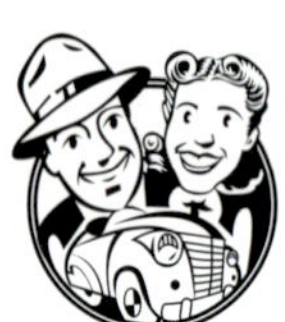

Date: Aug. 19

Attendance: 1.3 million

Special moment: Just call it Dream Cruise Part II. On Sunday, a much smaller crowd gathered along Woodward Avenue in parking lots. "Every year this gets bigger and better," said Lee Meredith, 48, owner of Metro Car Company Inc. in Detroit, a Saturday and Sunday fan. "Nobody wants to go back home."

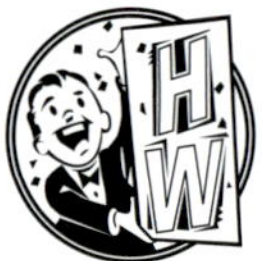

Small but important moment: Huntington Woods staged a mini-cruise for kids — all the fun done on a smaller scale.

Making history: Photos, video and a narrative history of the Cruise became part of the Library of Congress permanent collection in Washington, D.C.

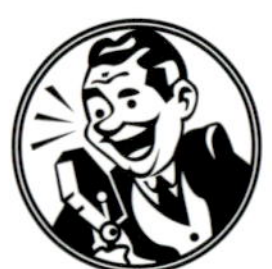

Summer sounds: Mitch Ryder played Ferndale, and Pontiac boasted the Contours, Marvelettes, Chubby Checker and Bowser.

2000

FOR THE SIXTH DREAM CRUISE, THE INTERNATIONAL audience flowers, as inquiries stream from around the globe into www.woodwarddreamcruise.com.

Cruise publicist Linda Ashley says she was stunned when a Turkish television station asked her for advice on where to set up their cameras.

This cruise lured a lot more than classics.

Fans gazed at the propellers under Aqua Car and oogled the official Wienermobile from Oscar Mayer.

And they wondered out loud about their favorites: "Hey, where's that Volkswagen bug with the two front ends and no rear? That thing had two steering wheels!" (Answer: The two-headed Beetle rolled in 1997 but not again until 2002.)

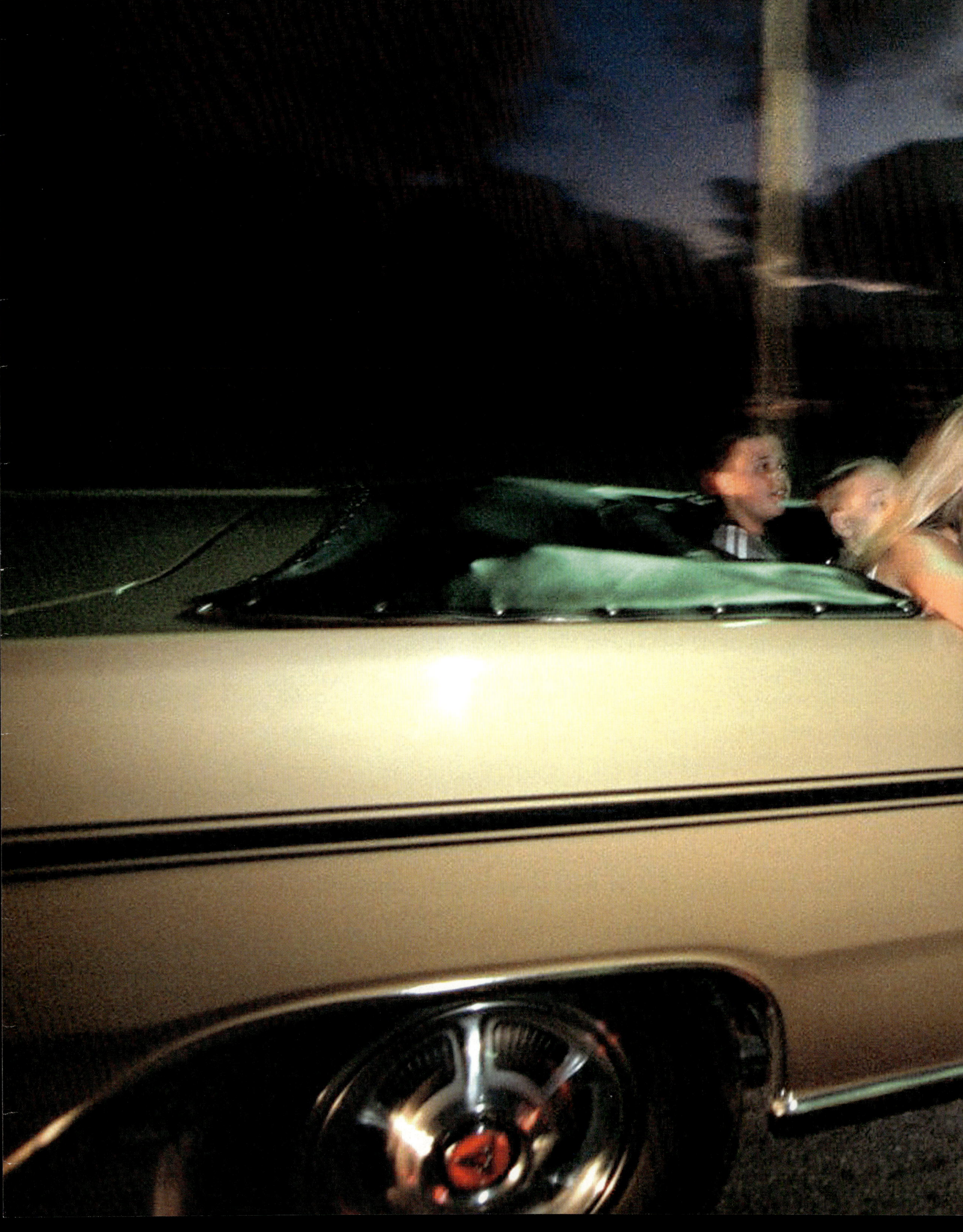

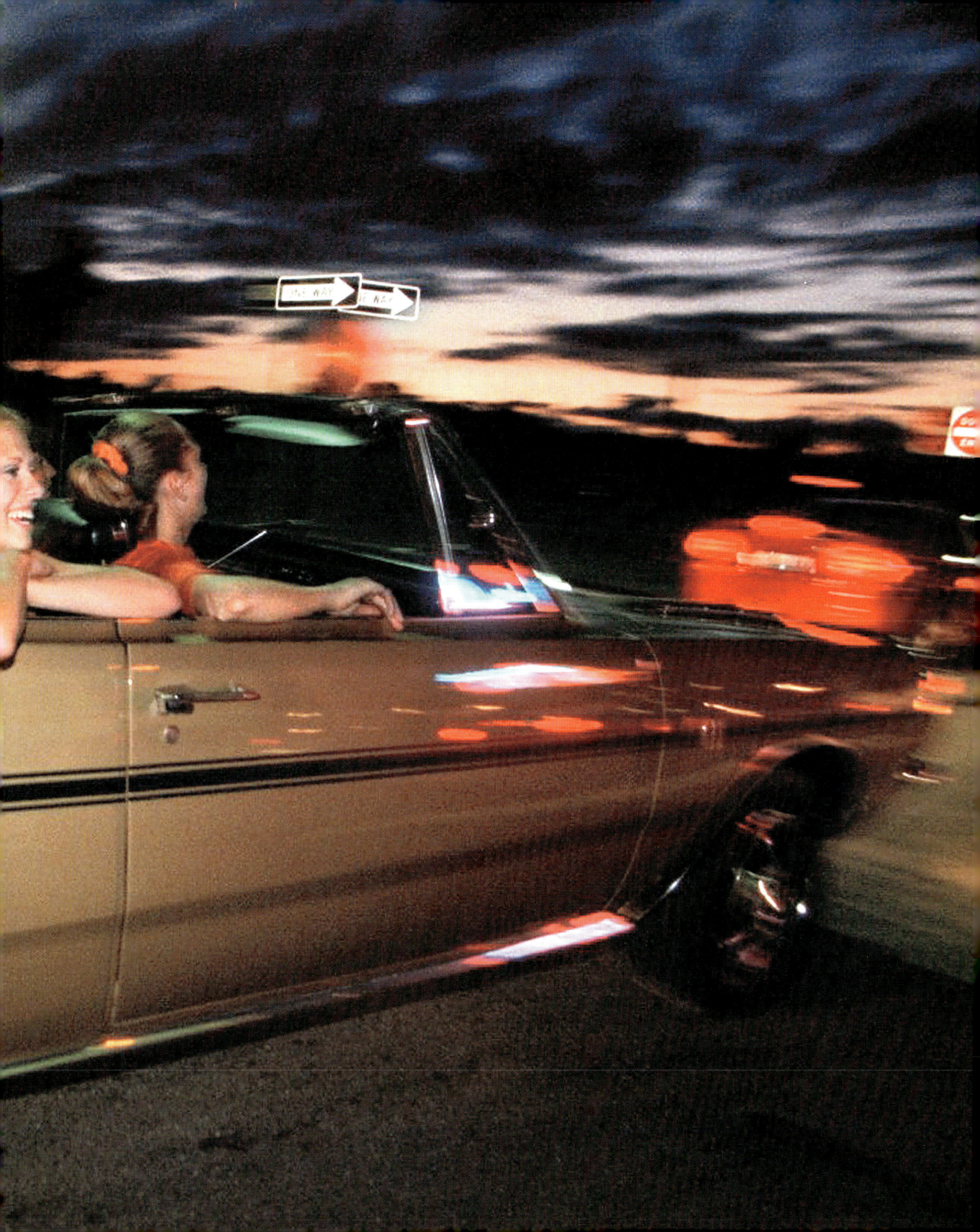
ONE WAY

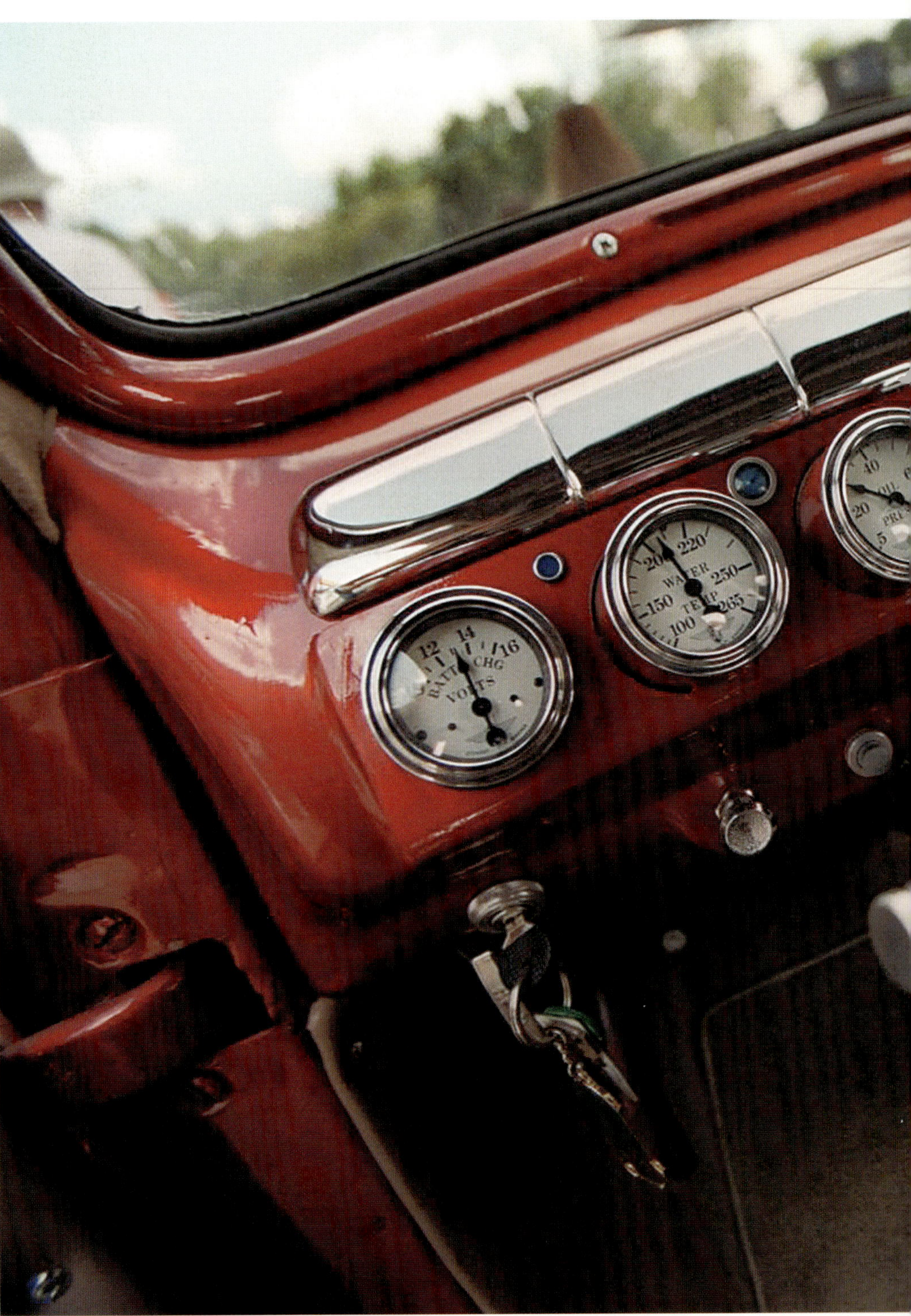

THE DASHBOARD of a well-cared-for 1947 Ford coupe gleamed on Woodward at 13 Mile in Royal Oak during the cruise. The sixth annual event started at 8 a.m. Saturday. Under partly cloudy skies, thousands staked out prime grassy spots to display their cars while spectators, taking advantage of relatively light traffic, went from city to city looking for concerts, games and eats. By mid-afternoon, Woodward resembled one massive party stretching from 10 Mile to 14 Mile roads.

PAGE 76: EARLY-BIRD REVELERS cruised northbound Woodward Avenue in Royal Oak as the sun set on the eve of the 2000 Dream Cruise. Thousands of car buffs hit the road before Saturday's event, turning miles of Woodward into a creeping parking lot of vintage automobilia. This year's pre-cruise crowd began accumulating at midweek and even forced Royal Oak police to shut parts of the nearly impassible strip Wednesday night.

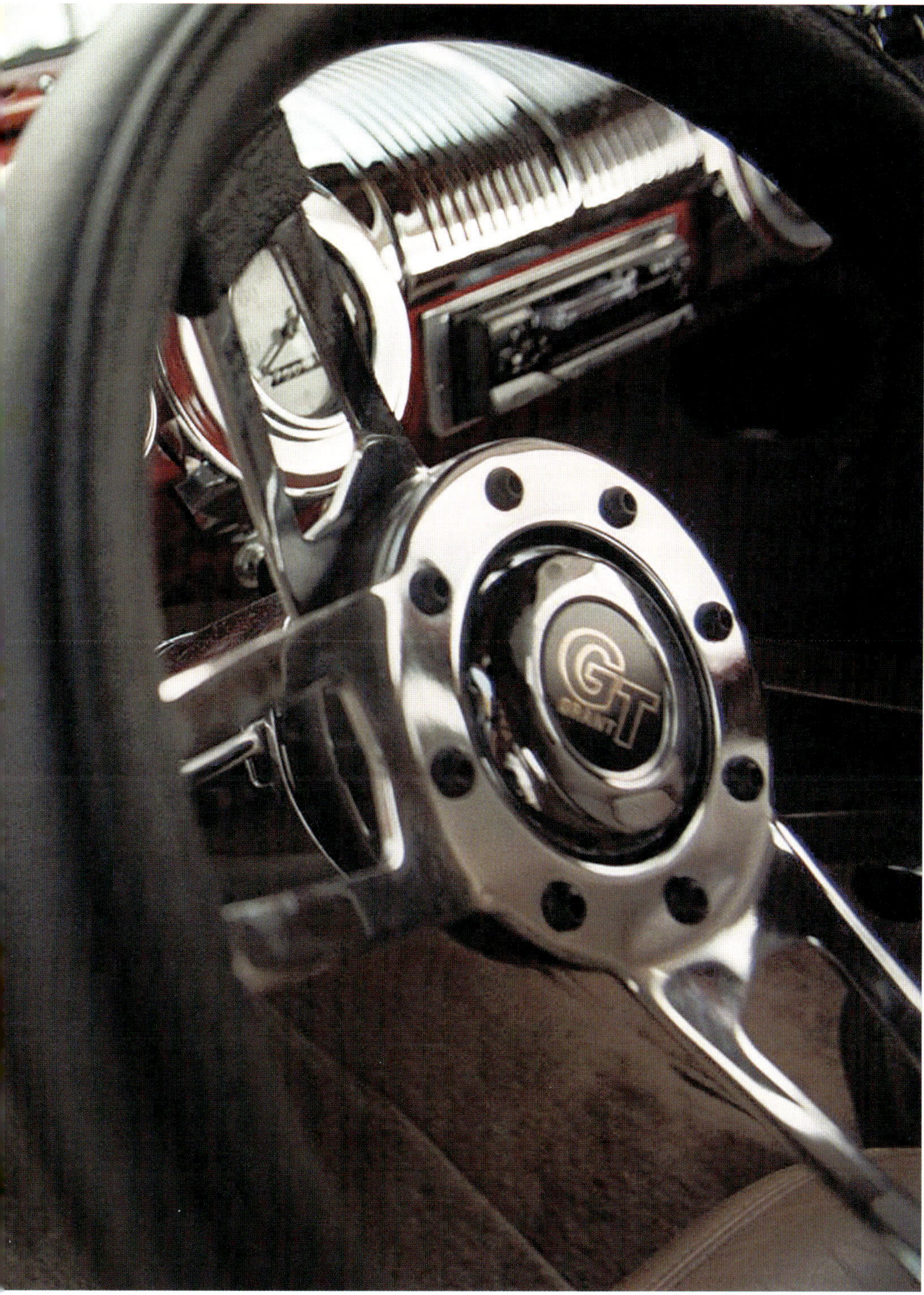

Previous page and above: TOM PIDGEON/Special to the Free Press

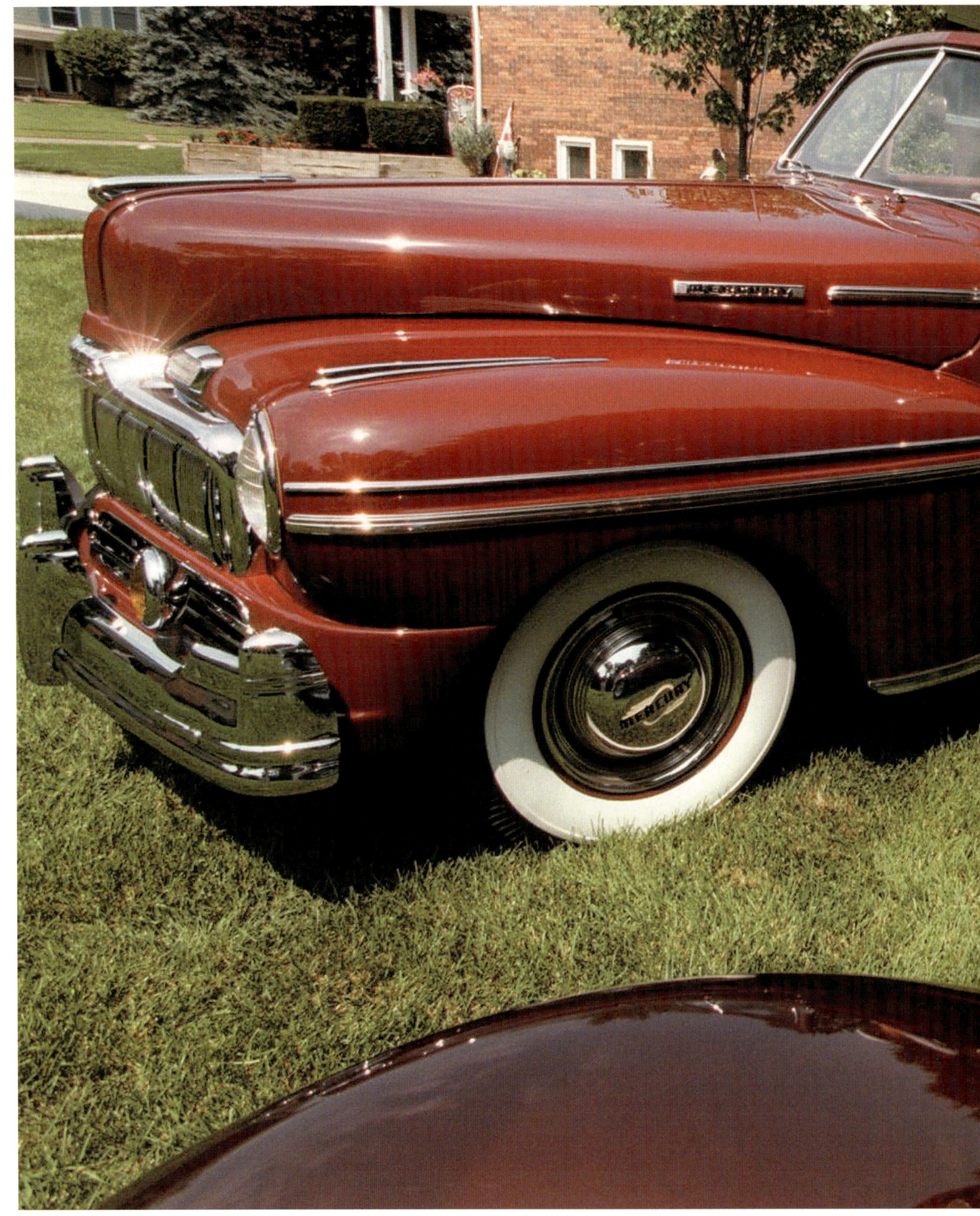
MERCURY

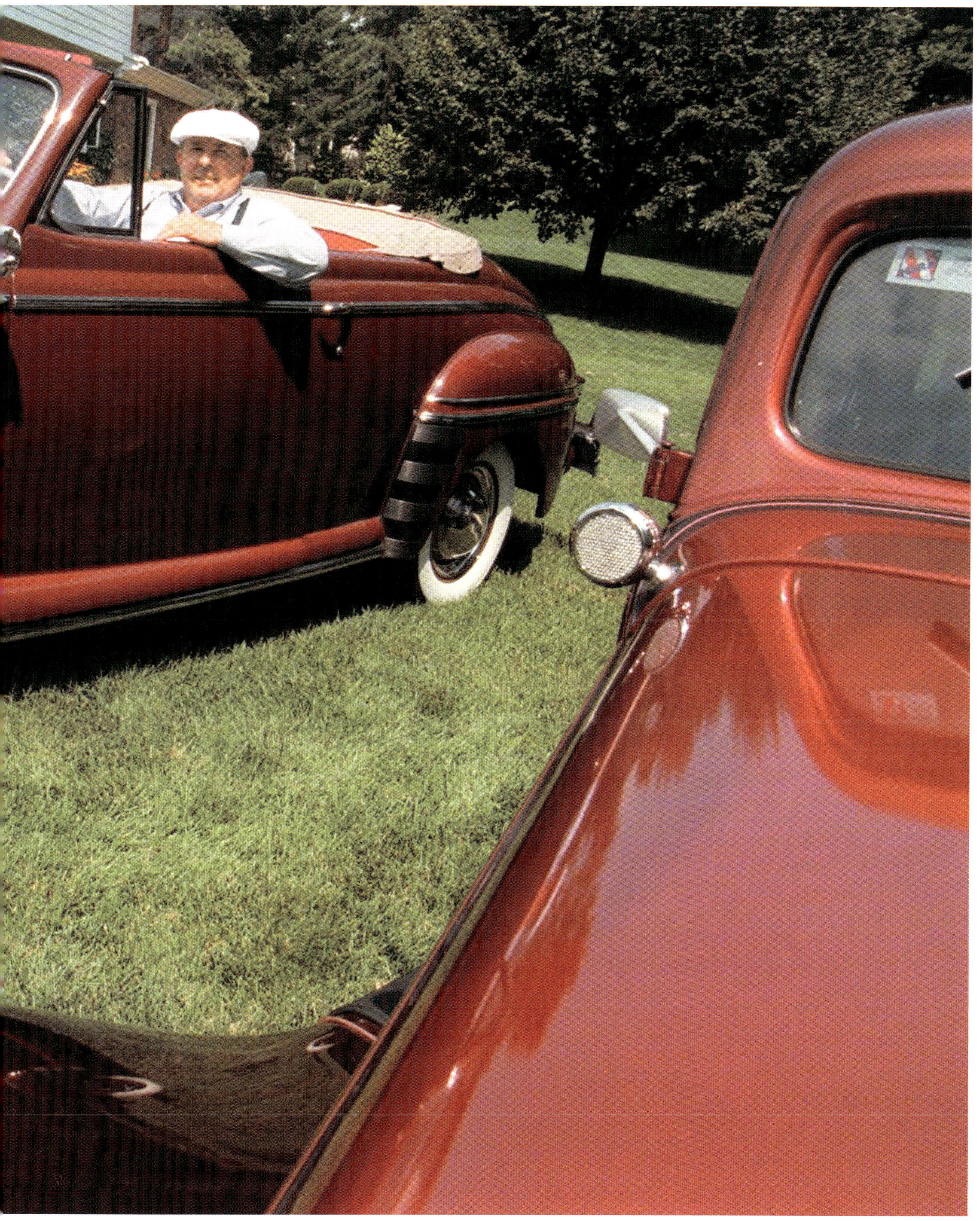

HUGH GRANNUM

PAGE 80: IT'S A LABOR OF LOVE for Bill Large, a retired General Motors Corp. engineer, who spent most of his time restoring cars and driving hot rods. The 1948 Mercury convertible Large drove in the 2000 Dream Cruise was stored for years in someone's east-side garage. During the four years Large worked on it in his own Shelby Township garage, every piece of the car was taken apart.

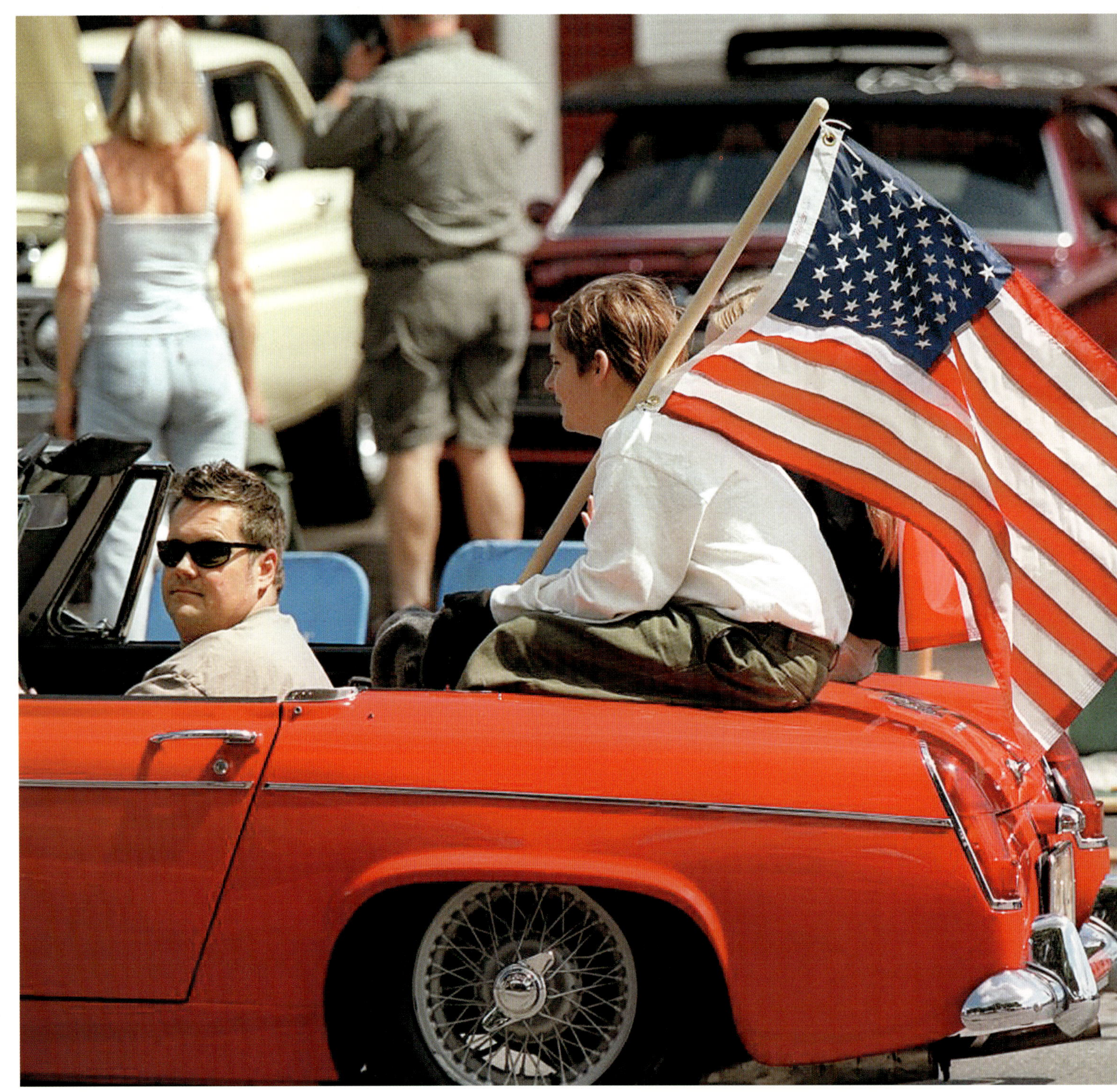

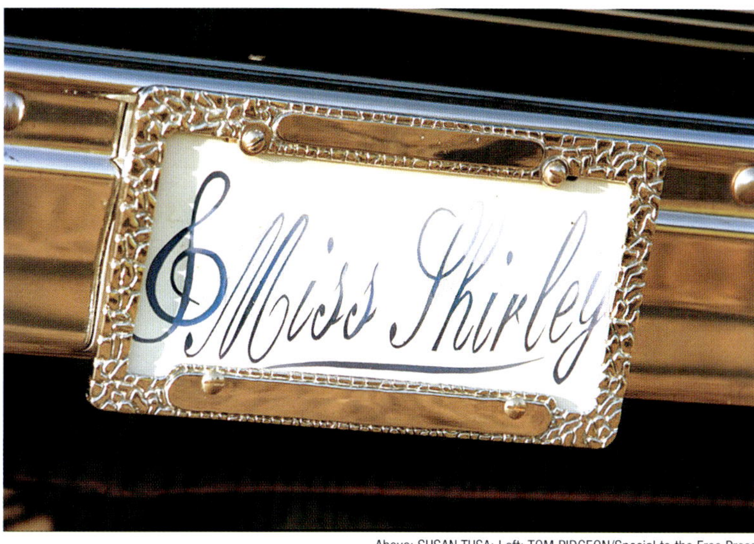

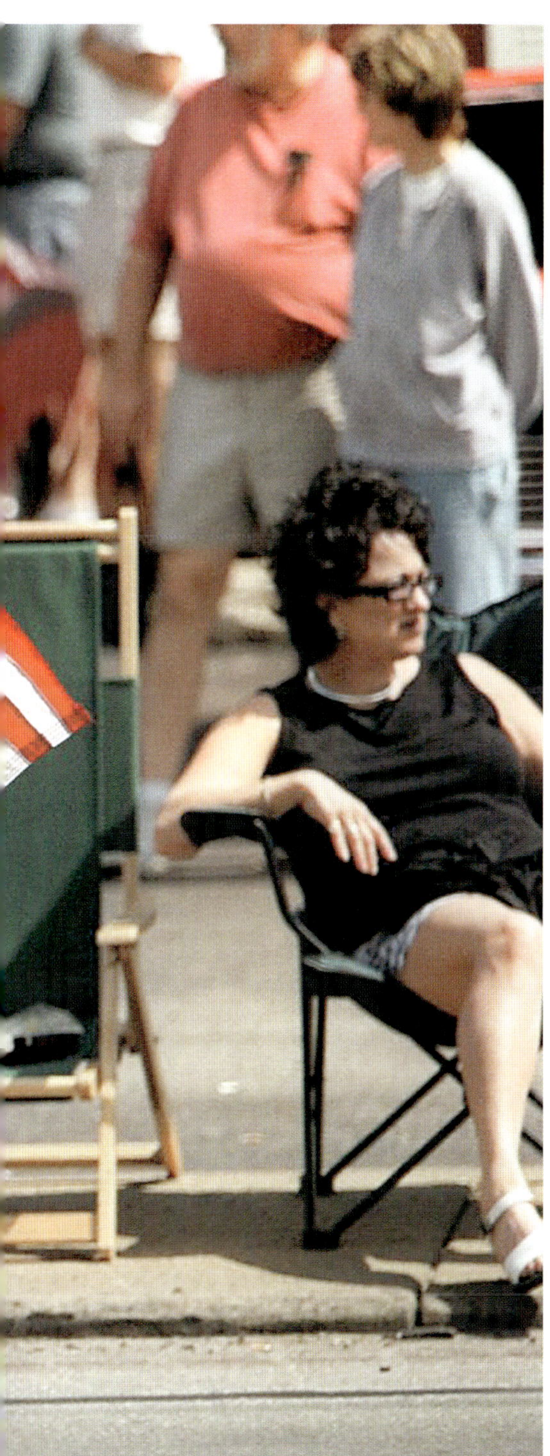

Above: SUSAN TUSA; Left: TOM PIDGEON/Special to the Free Press

ABOVE: NOW THAT'S A LICENSE TO DRIVE. This personalized plate adorned Shirley Farrugia's award-winning blue 1977 AMC Pacer X. Once-reviled, the car now basks in the admiration of fans across the state. The 68-year-old Belleville resident, known as the Pacer Lady on the male-dominated street machine circuit, participates in 10 to 15 car shows a year around Michigan. "The Pacer was a car way ahead of its time. It came out about 30 years too soon," Farrugia said. Now, "every time I turn around, somebody wants to buy it," she said.

LEFT: THE PATRIOTISM of these cruisers ran high during an event that has come to symbolize a slice of Americana.

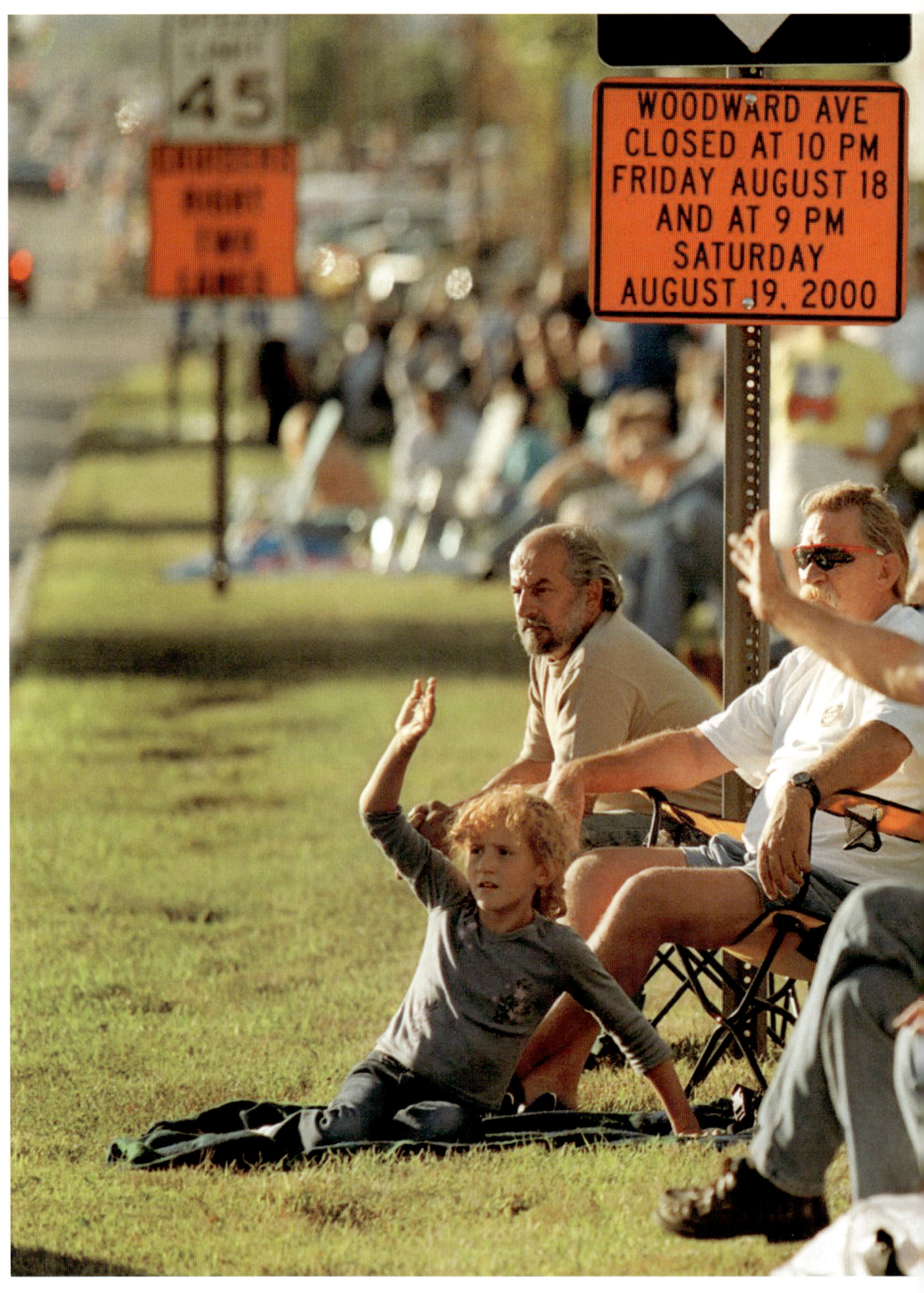
45
WOODWARD AVE
CLOSED AT 10 PM
FRIDAY AUGUST 18
AND AT 9 PM
SATURDAY
AUGUST 19, 2000

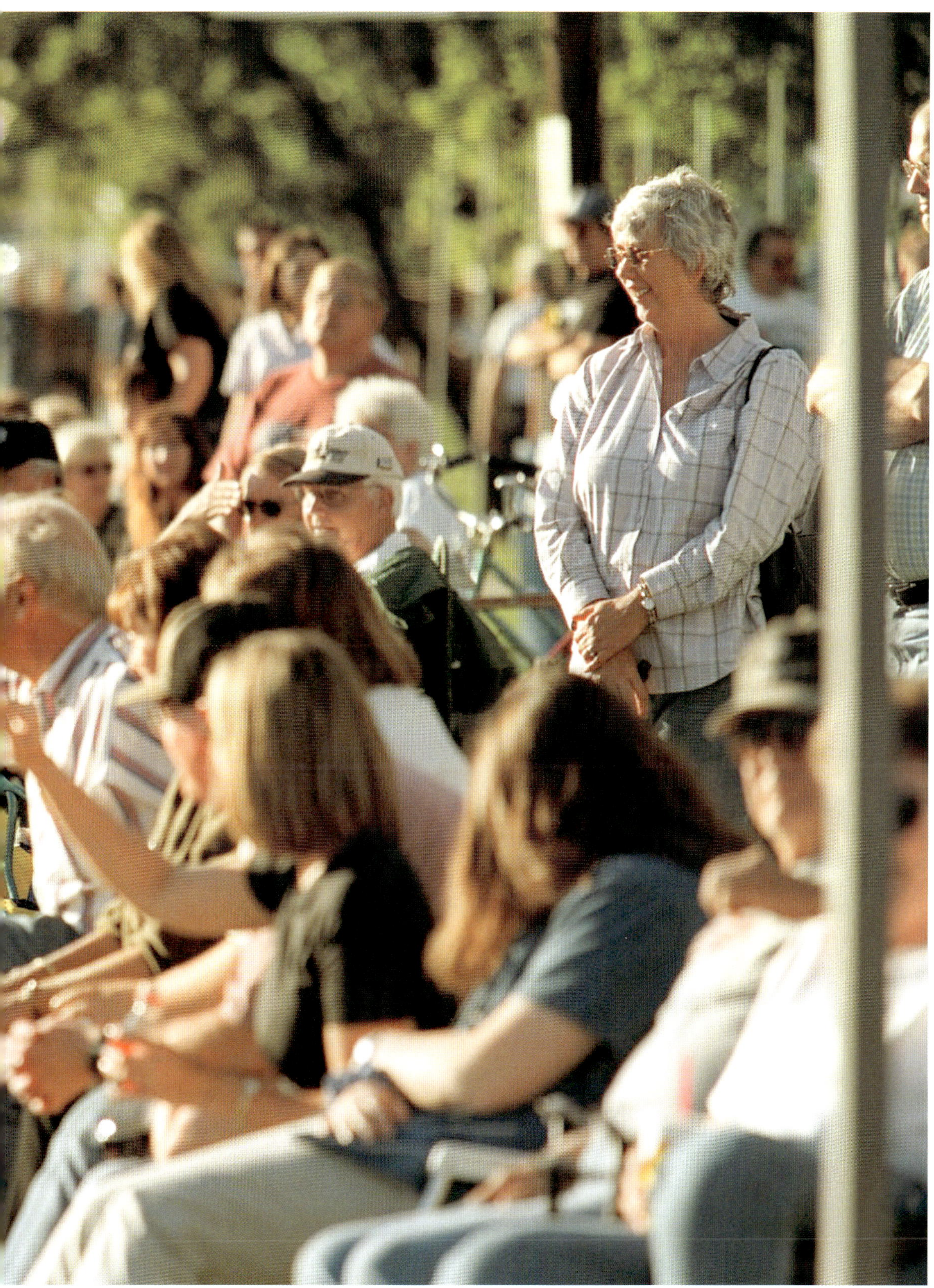

TOM PIDGEON/Special to the Free Press;

CURBSIDE SPECTATORS lined Woodward at 13 Mile in Royal Oak. An estimated 1.3 million people attended this year's event.

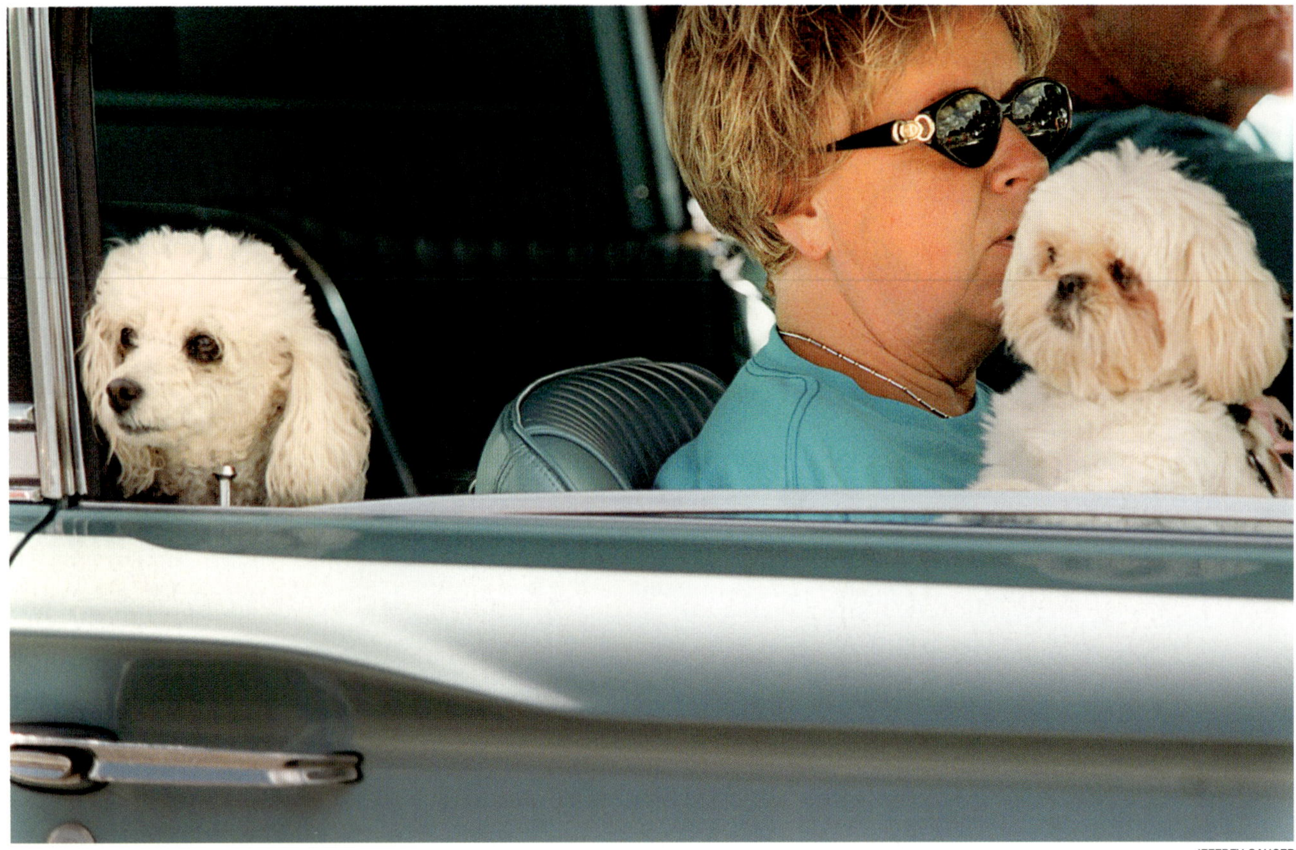

JEFFREY SAUGER

ABOVE: IN THE DOG DAYS OF SUMMER, Sylvia Ebaugh of Royal Oak cruised in a 1966 Ford Thunderbird with her dogs Ginger, left, and Jewell. Ebaugh and her dogs went along for the ride with car owner Tom Schweigel of Mancelona. “I think this is a great community builder,” she said.

RIGHT: DRESSED FOR THE OCCASION was McKenna Lynch, 4, of Royal Oak, who pointed to a car that caught her eye while crossing 13 Mile at Woodward in Royal Oak. Holding her hand was her mother, Janie, who made the skirts for her daughters.

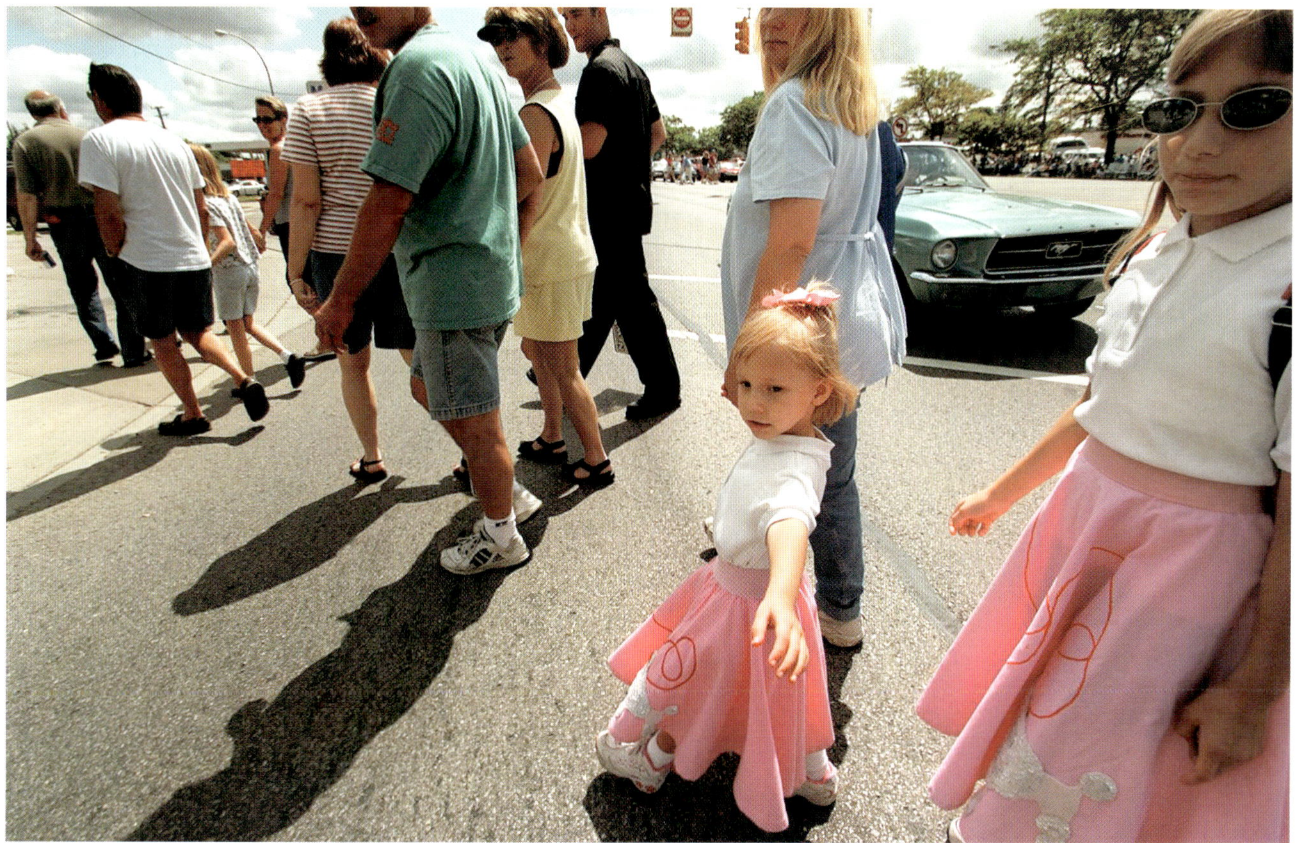

TOM PIDGEON/Special to the Free Press

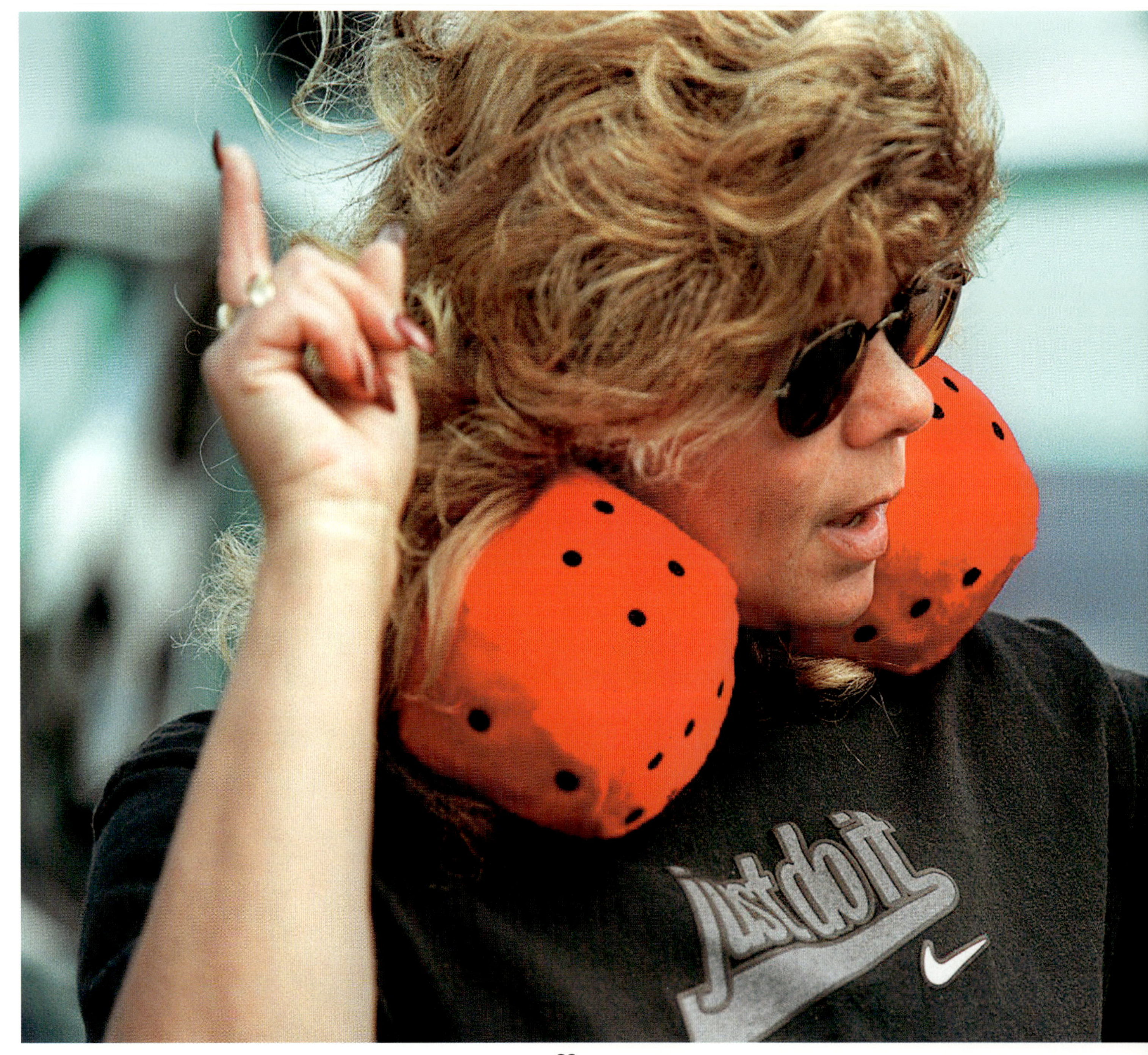
Just do it

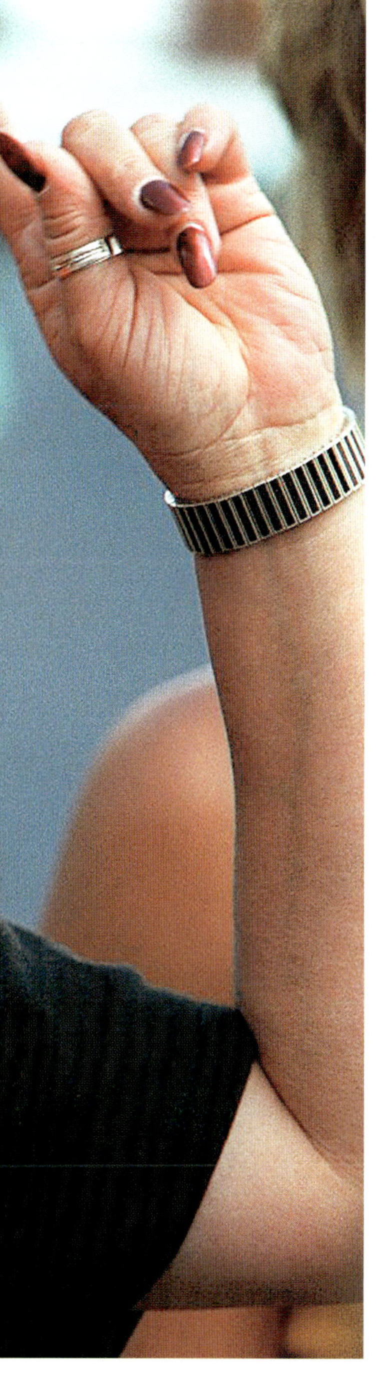

FOR SOME, THE CRUISE IS SERIOUS BUSINESS. Jean Baker showed off her fuzzy dice earrings during the cruise. Fans wishing to display their cruise spirit or take home a souvenir kept cash registers ringing at tents and kiosks in the seven cities selling licensed Dream Cruise merchandise.

PAGE 90: A CLASSIC THUNDERBIRD cruised Woodward. About 30,000 vehicles hit the strip.

Left and following page: TOM PIDGEON/Special to the Free Press

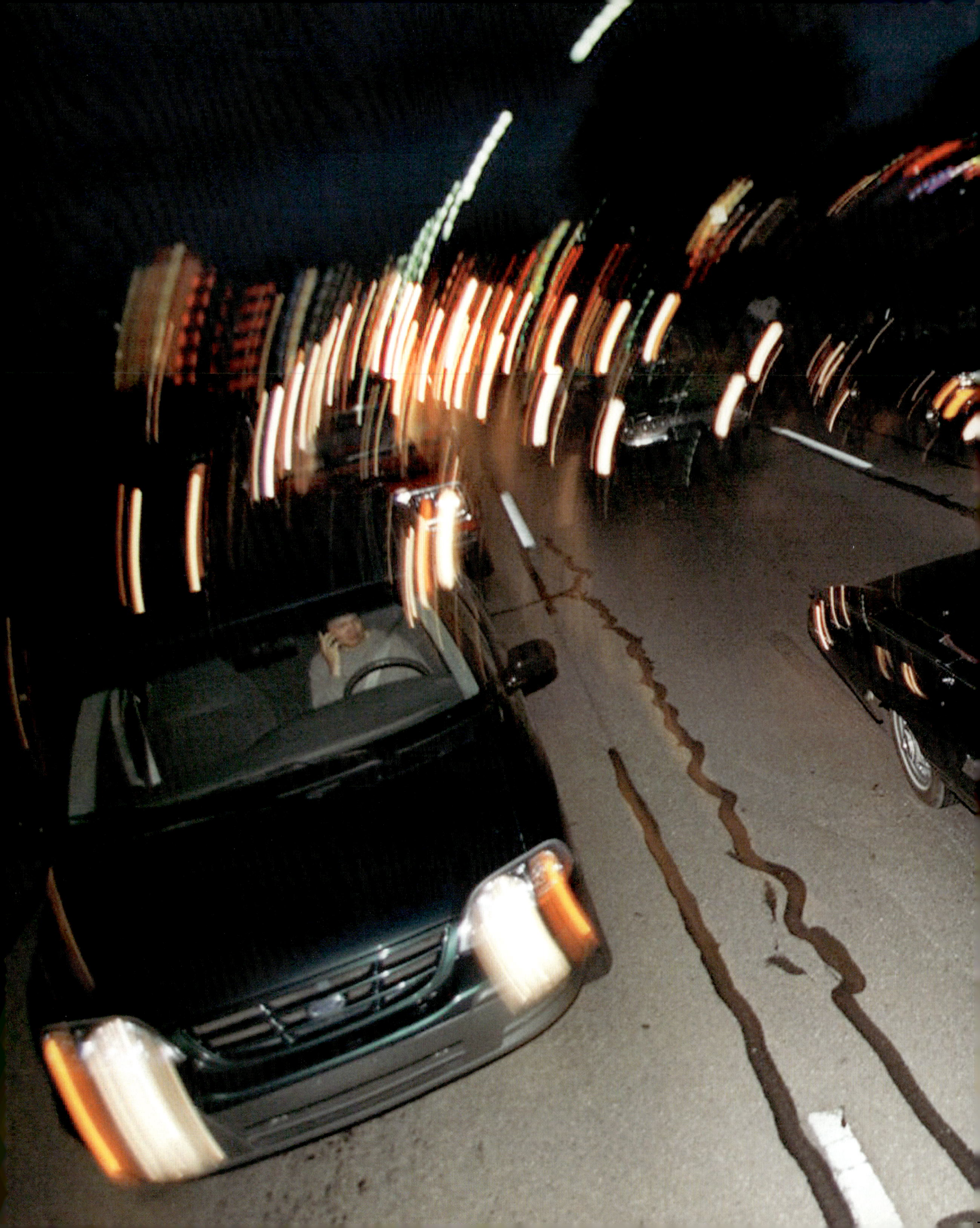

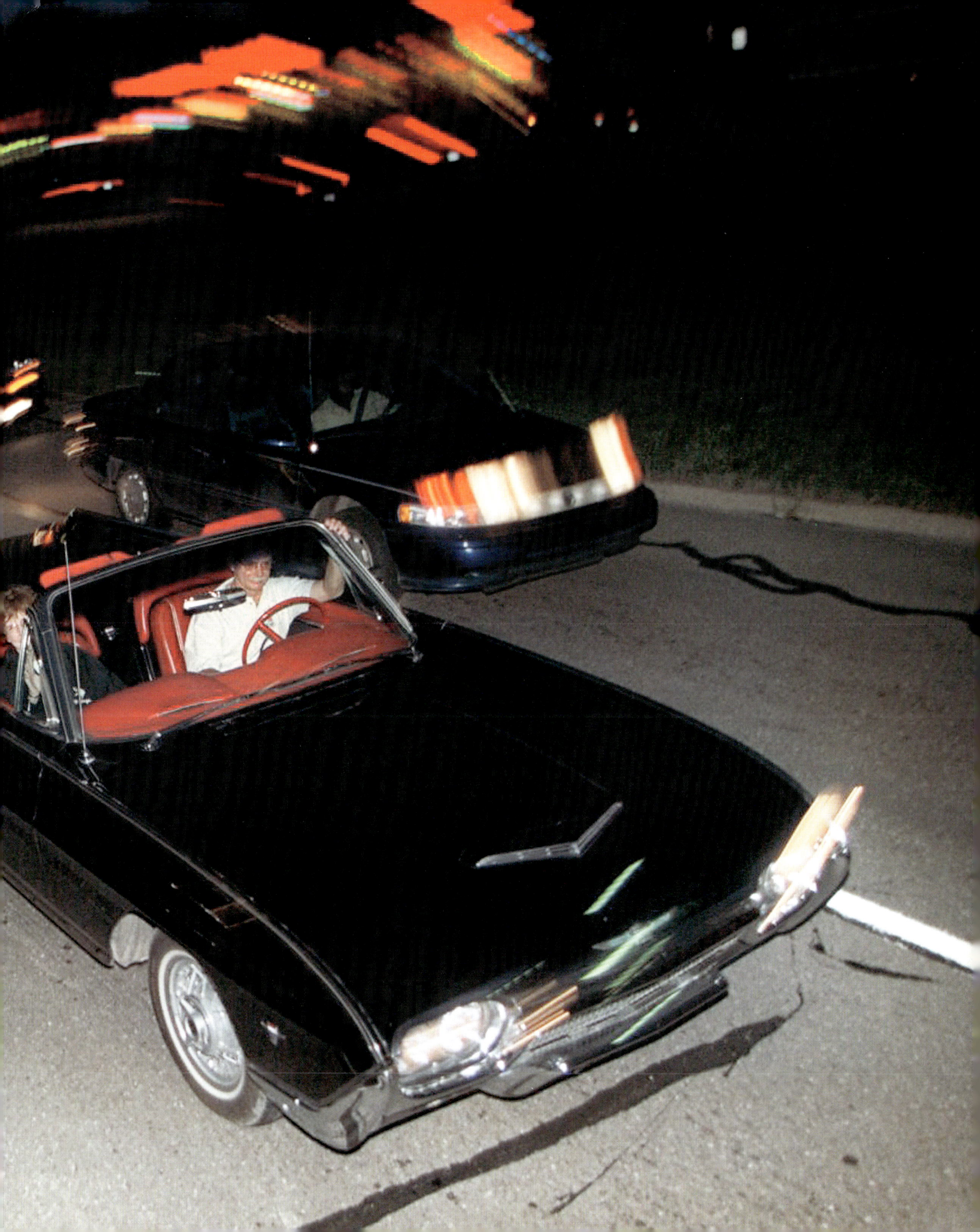

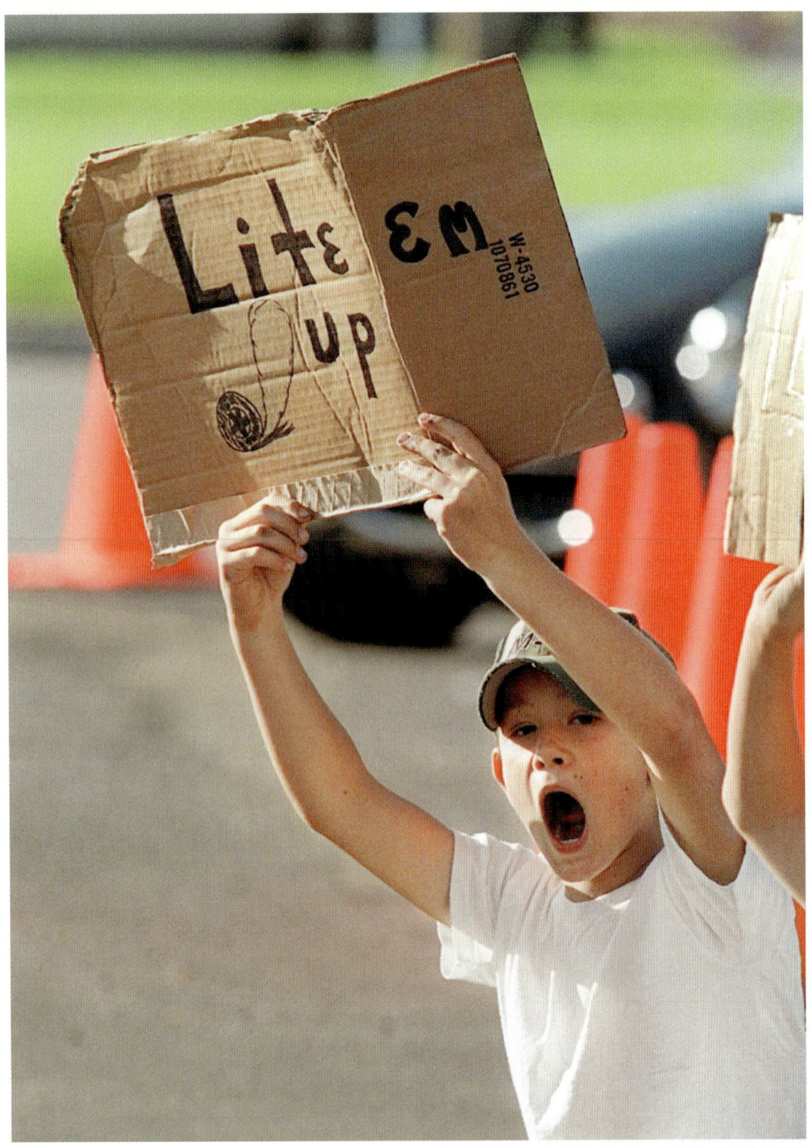

Above: TOM PIDGEON/Special to the Free Press; Right: JEFFREY SAUGER

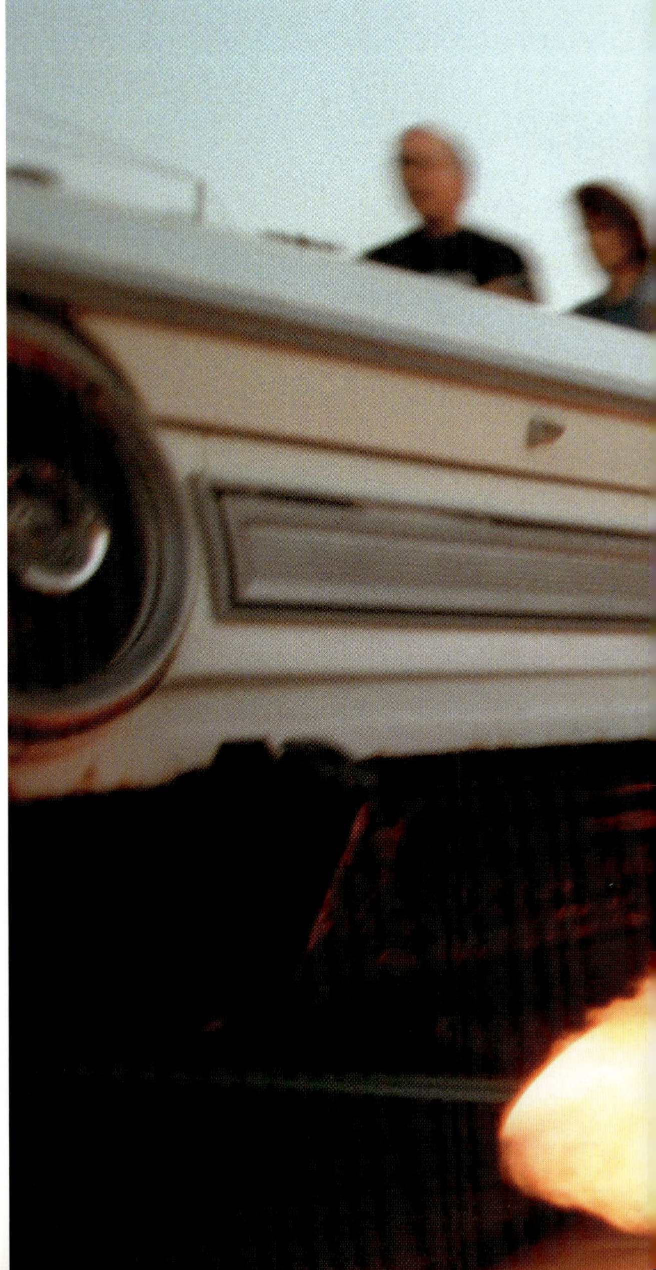

ALL FIRED UP, Luke Barnes, 10, of Clawson, left, held a sign urging classic-car drivers on Woodward to "Lite em up." Cruisers Bernie and Lisa Parsons did just that as flames shot from their 1964 Galaxy 500. The Detroiters controlled the blaze from a flamethrower kit in the trunk of the car.

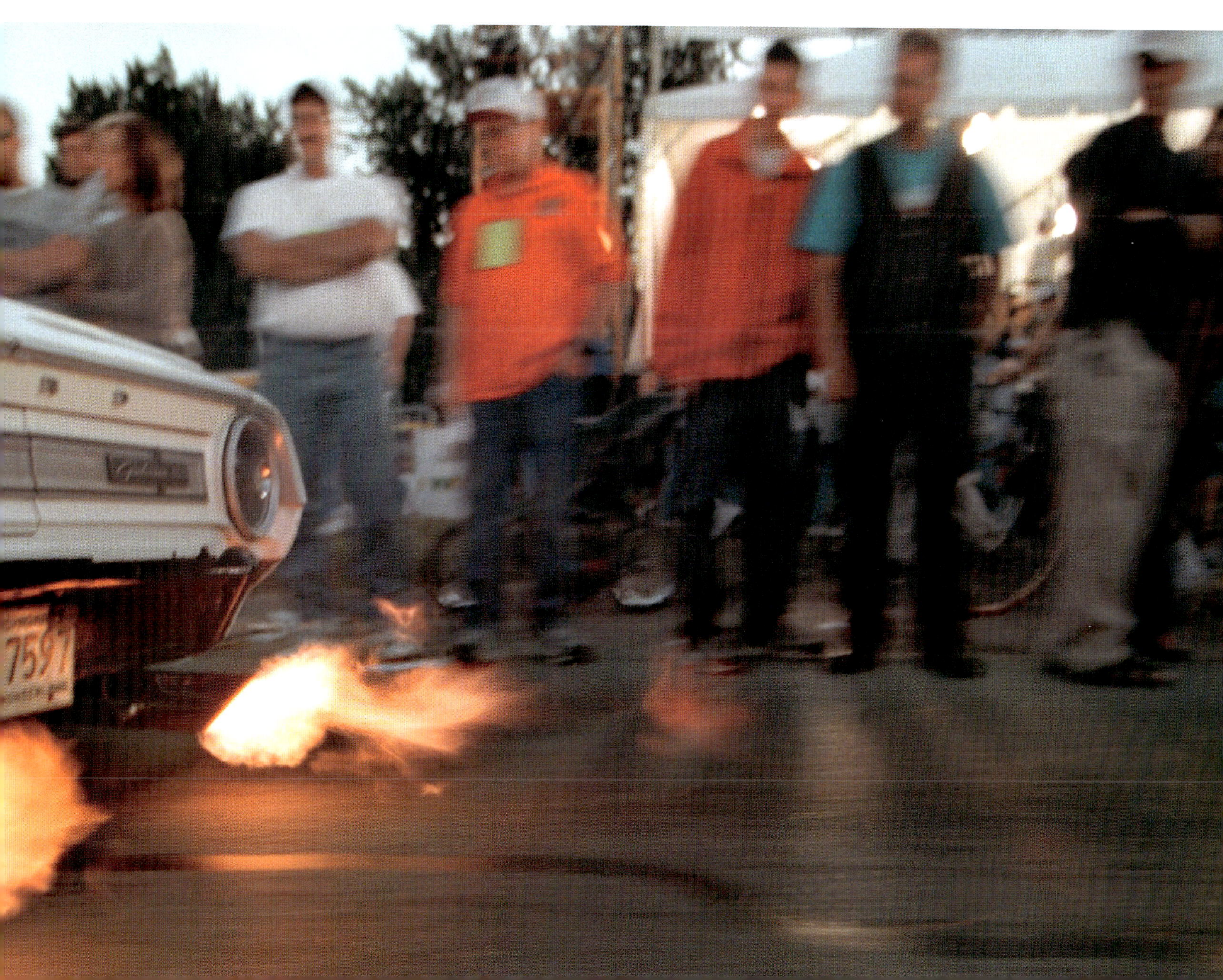

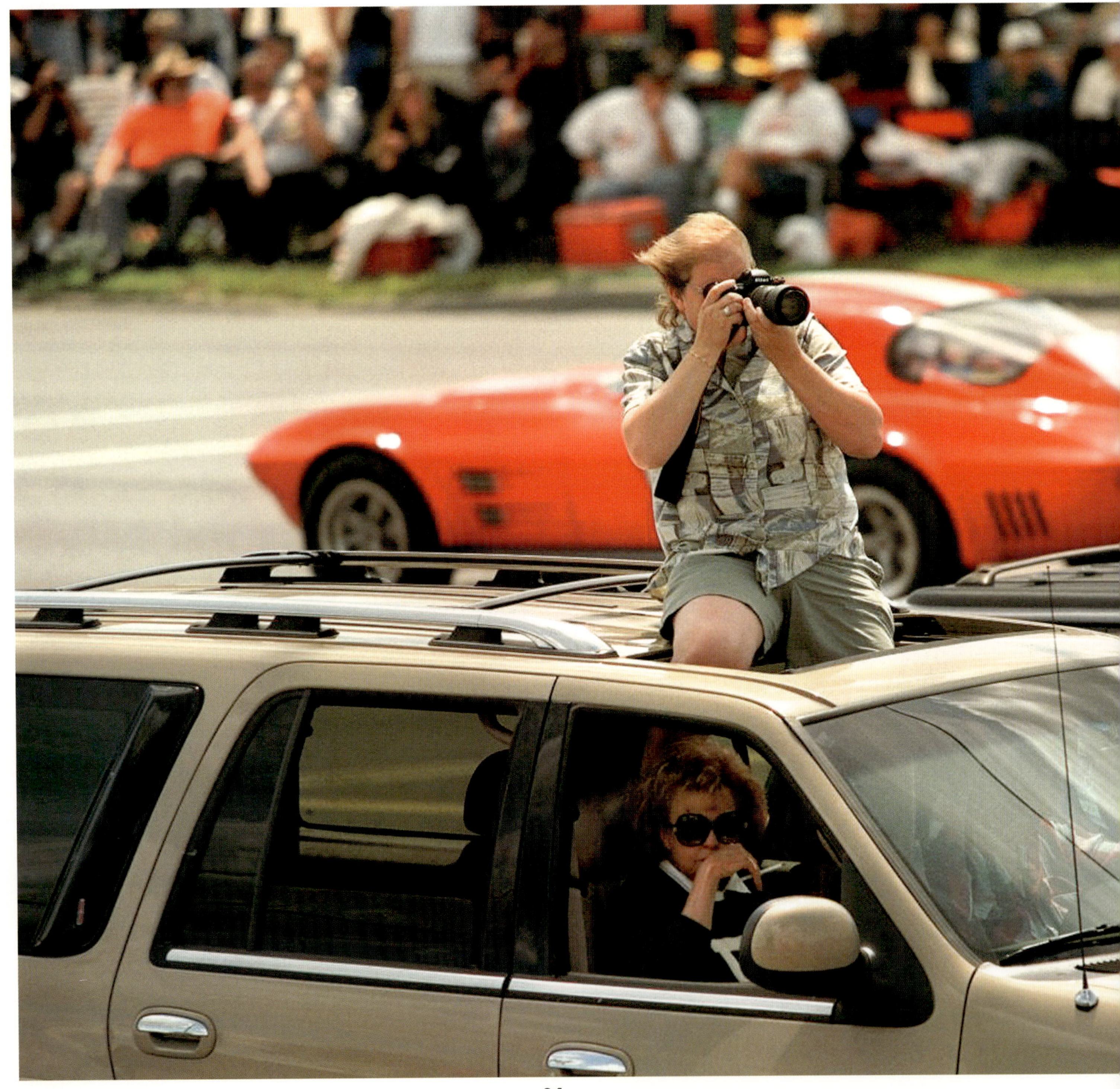

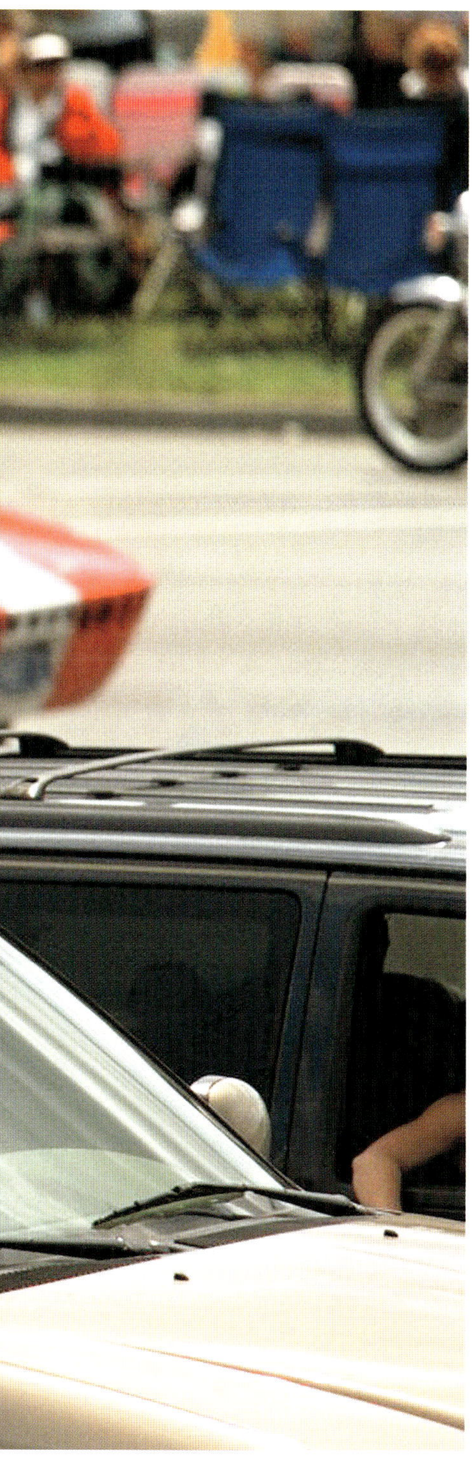

FROM THE MIDDLE OF THE ACTION, a Dream Cruise fan shoots pictures from the sun roof of a sport-utility vehicle on Woodward at 13 Mile in Royal Oak.

PAGE 96: IN A COSTUME FIT FOR A KING, Craig MacIntosh addressed spectators as he and his brother made their way down Woodward. The 41-year-old Bloomfield Hills resident, who spent a couple thousand dollars on his outfit, performs once a year for charity. They cruised in 45-year-old Todd MacIntosh's 1976 Cadillac Eldorado. This was the second Dream Cruise in which Craig MacIntosh dressed as Elvis.

Left: TOM PIDGEON/Special to the Free Press; Next pages: JEFFREY SAUGER

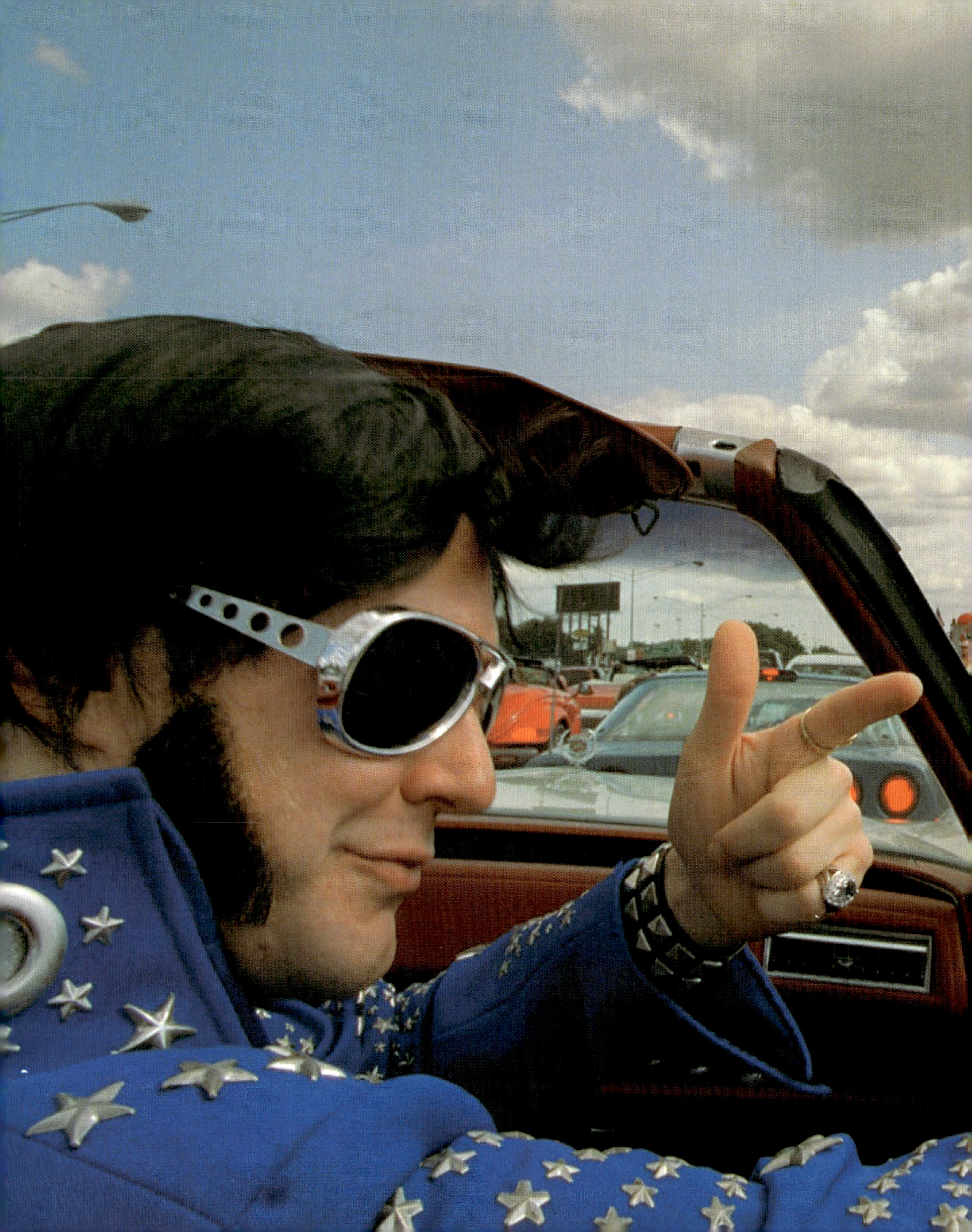

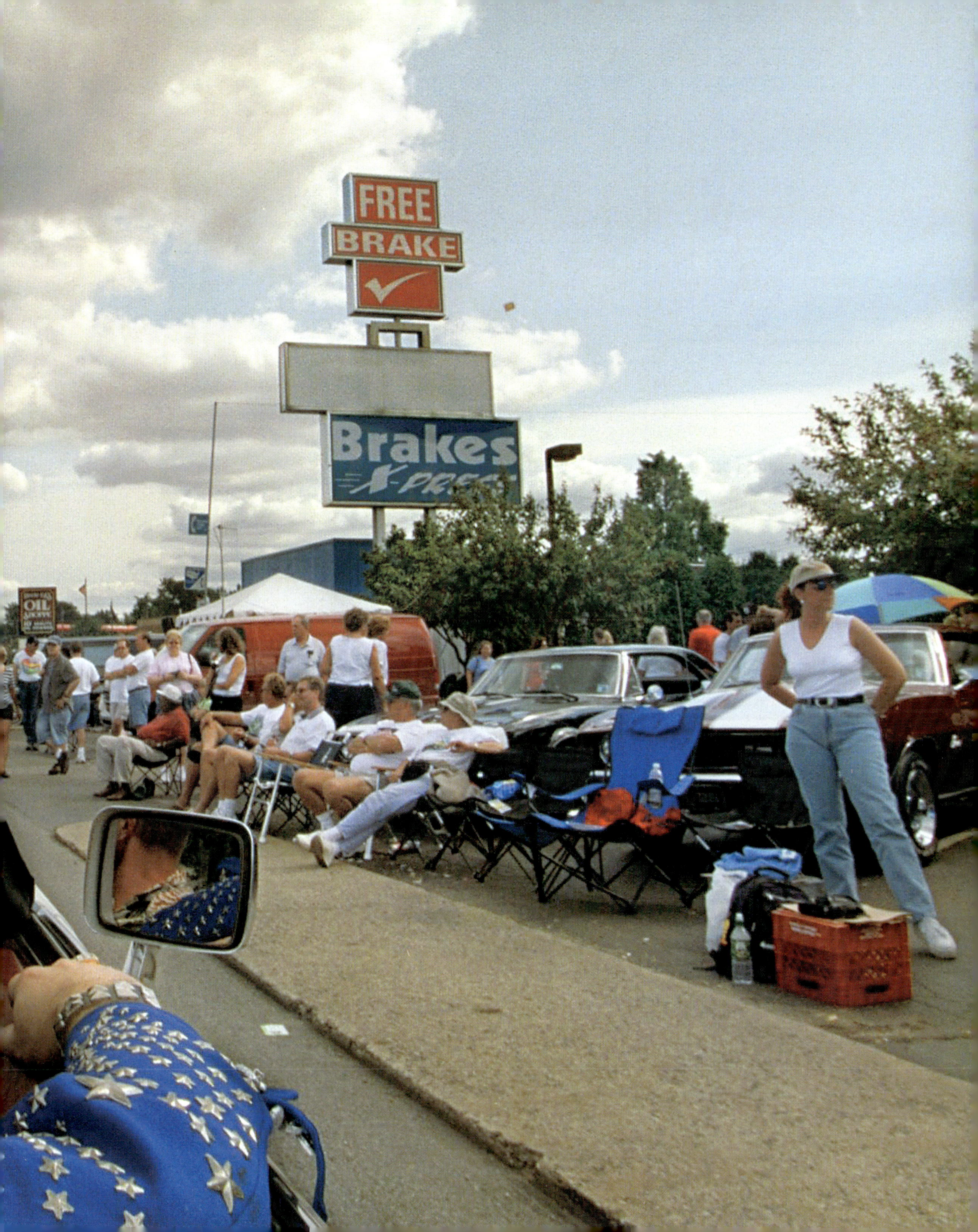
FREE
BRAKE
Brakes
OIL

Date: Aug. 18

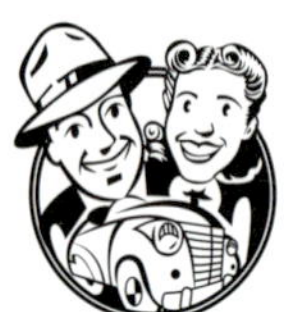

Attendance: 1.6 million

Special moment: The cruise goes south! The route extended to the Michigan State Fairgrounds, which timed its run to include cruise day. Elephant ears to go, anyone?

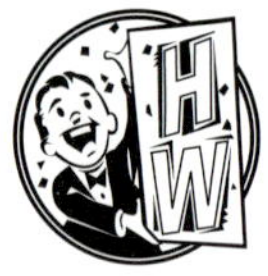

Dream theme: Huntington Woods' theme was "Beatle/Beetle," celebrating the classic band and the classic VW. "The Love Bug" is shown in the park.

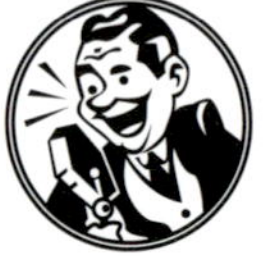

Party time: New this year was the official pre-cruise party and car show at MotorCity Casino in Detroit.

High-tech first: Car buffs got interactive at www.woodward dreamcruise.com with a guest book and discussion groups. One posting, from Carl Johnson in Harlingen, Texas: "My biggest dream is to do a Dream Cruise someday. It's got to wait till after a lung transplant next year. Thanks for this Web site; it's almost like being there."

2001

THIS WAS THE YEAR THAT THE DREAM CRUISE OFFICIALLY grew south to the Michigan State Fairgrounds in Detroit, at 8 Mile and Woodward.

The fairgrounds offered a big show of classic cars, acres of parking and shuttle-bus access to the cruise route via free SMART buses that made the fairgrounds their transit hub. Plus, it had a demolition derby and rock concerts.

This also was the year organizers battled complaints that the Dream Cruise had become a weeklong headache for businesses, residents and police along Woodward.

Police began shooing out of parks and parking lots those cruisers trying to create a Dream Cruise week.

This also was the year that delegates from Bloomfield Hills and Bloomfield Township began attending Dream Cruise board meetings. The two communities, longtime holdouts from the big event, officially joined in 2002. That came after residents of Bloomfield Hills told their mayor that many of them were auto executives and engineers — so their city belonged in the event.

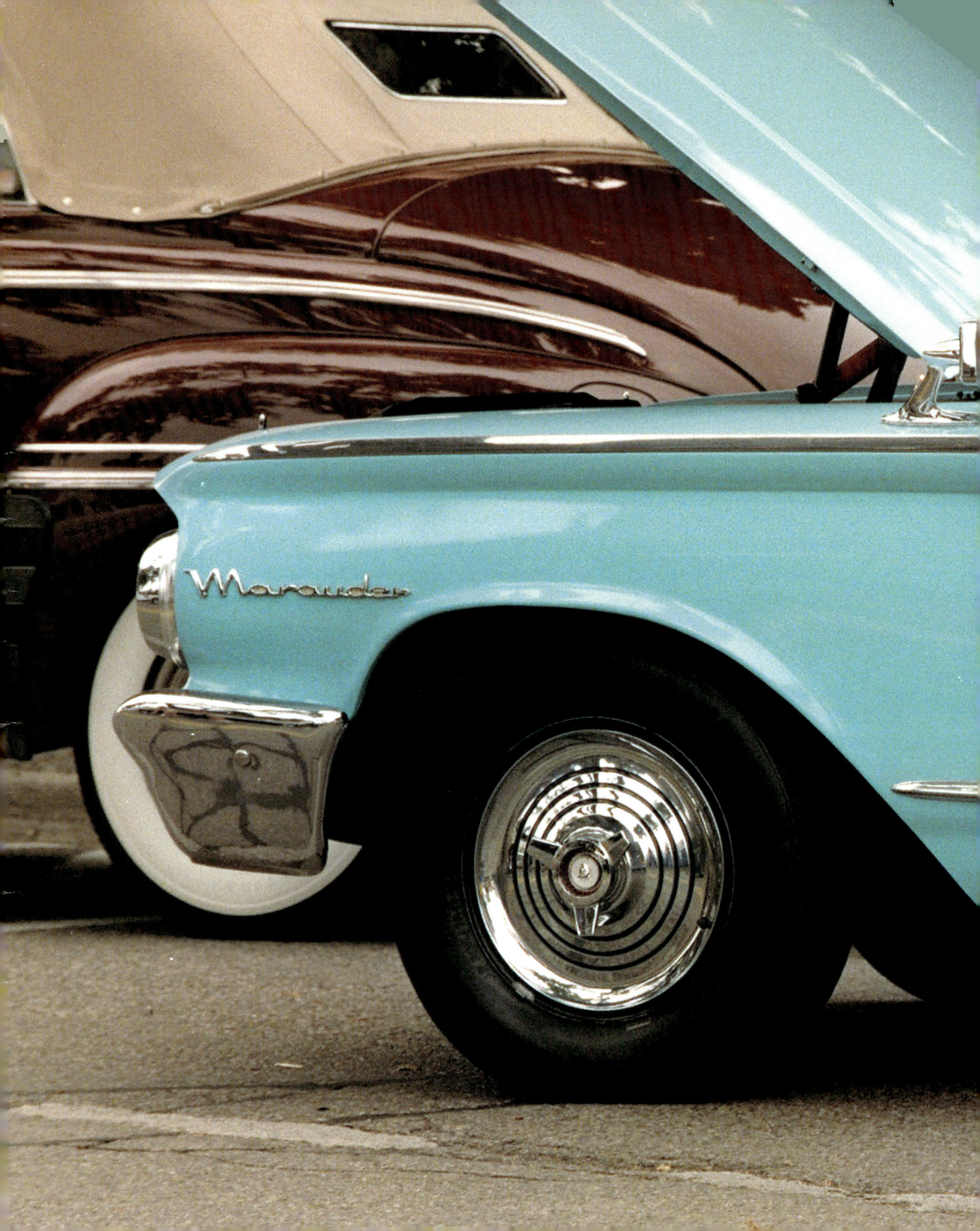
Marauder

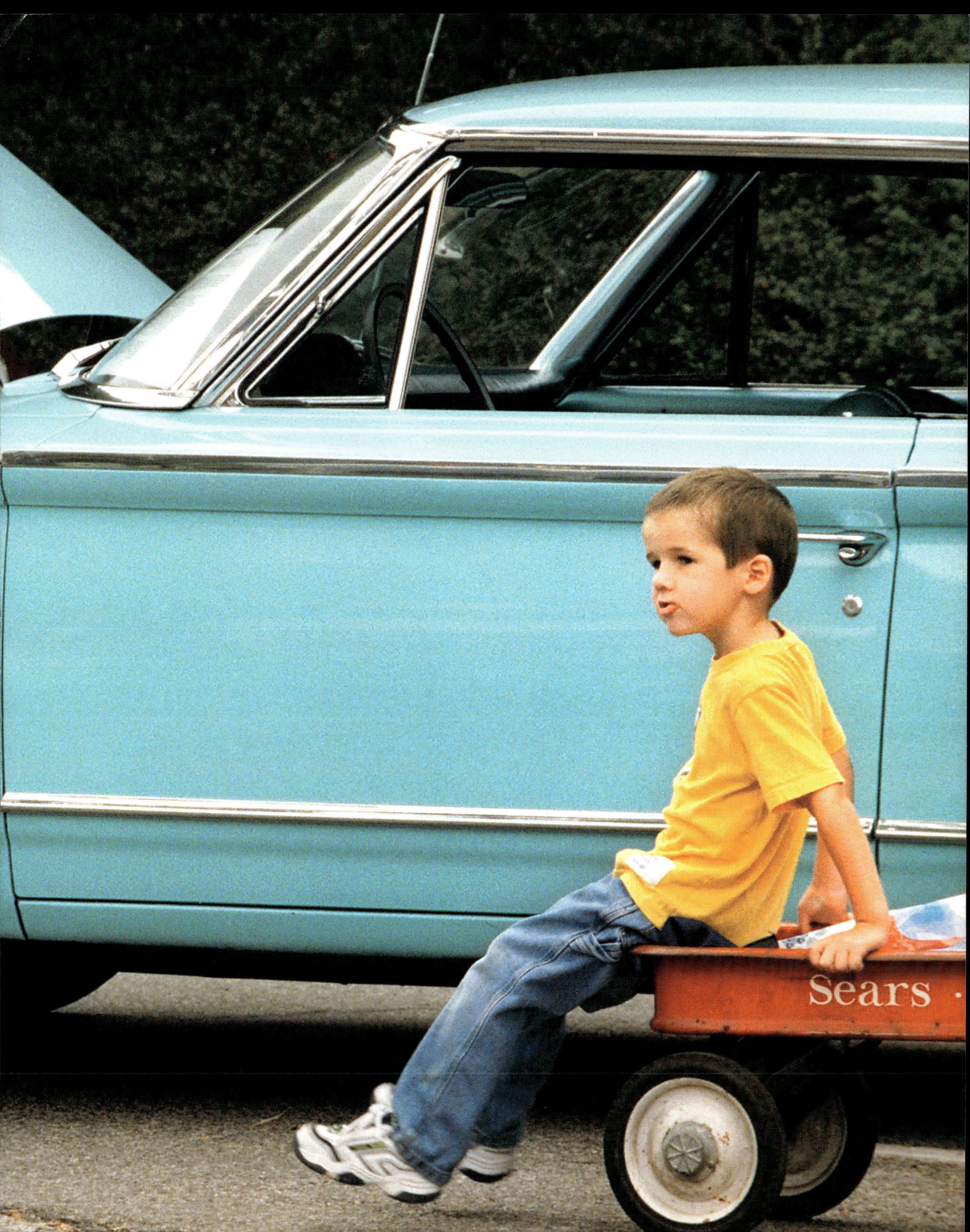
Sears

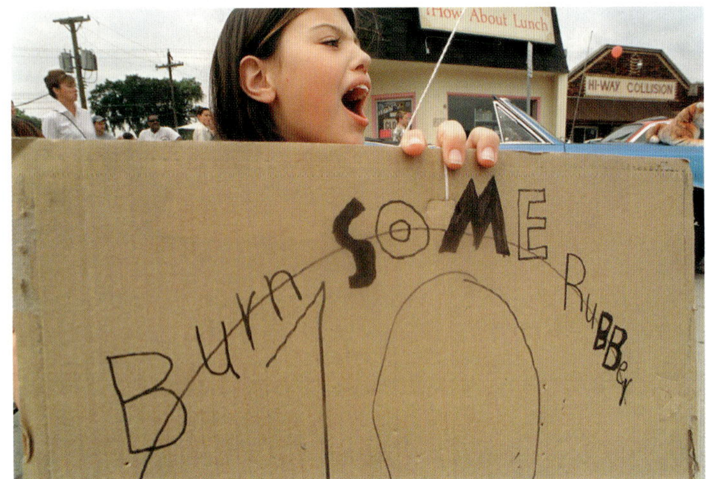

Previous page, above and right: KENT PHILLIPS

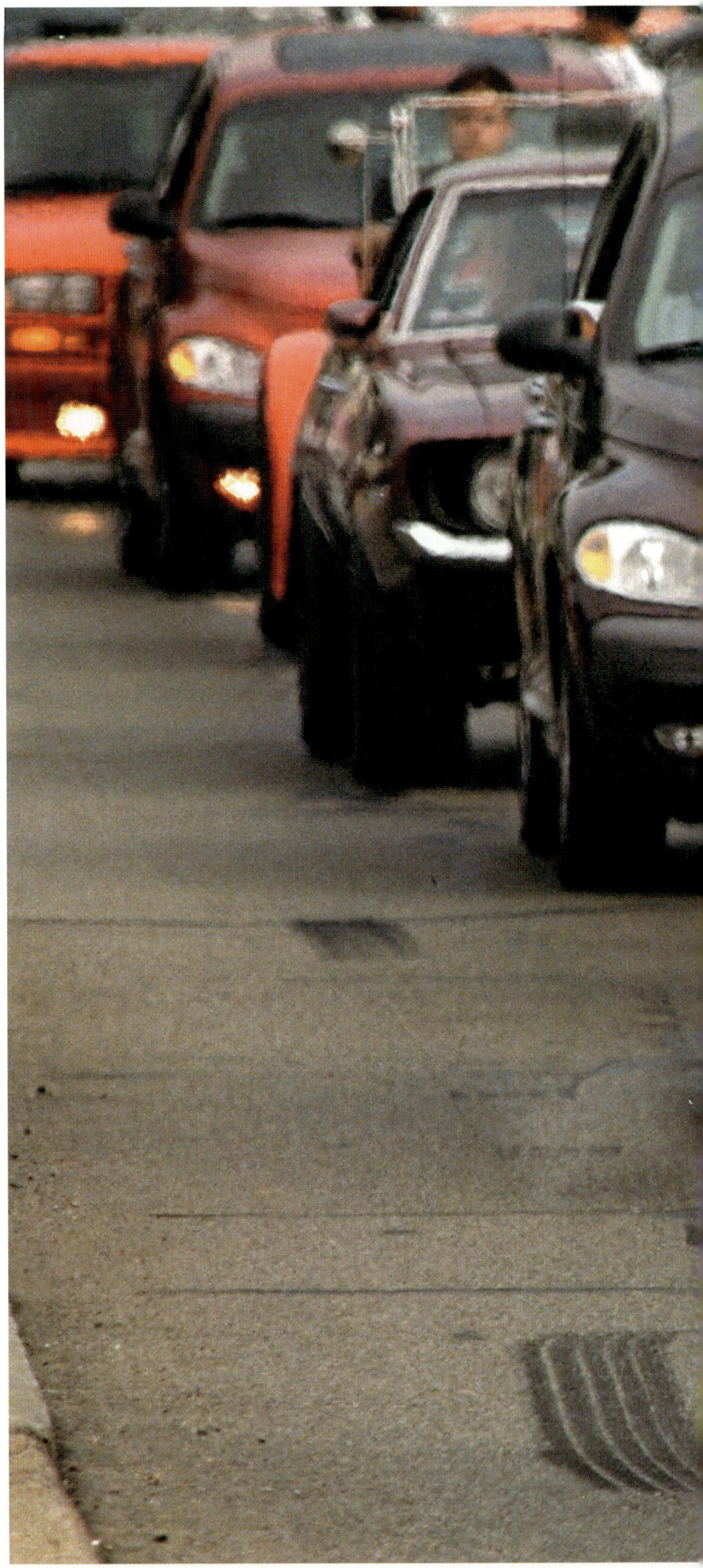

IT JUST KEEPS GETTING BIGGER and bigger and bigger and bigger. The parade of creeping classics started early Saturday, flooding Woodward from 9 a.m. to at least 9 p.m. with 1.6 million people. Early birds anticipating the seventh year of the world's largest one-day car event couldn't wait until the weekend: They started jamming the avenue and joy riding Tuesday, underscoring a trend to make The Big Day last a whole week. To disperse the traffic, which could have hindered emergency vehicles getting to Beaumont Hospital off Woodward in Royal Oak, police closed the road for up to an hour on some nights leading up to the cruise, starting at 10. Far more of a worry to police than these cruisers made their way south near 14 Mile were fans like Hillary Hall, above, for whom the cars weren't enough. Hall, 10, who lived in Waterford, wanted to see some action: "Burn em!" she yelled, in case drivers didn't see her sign. Judging from the marks on the road at right, some of them listened.

PAGE 100: THE 1963 MERCURY MARAUDER was cool, but to Quinn Rathgeber, 4, of Livonia, the musicians providing Dream Cruise entertainment were cooler. Quinn checked out the action from his wagon in Birmingham while waiting to be pulled to the next classic.

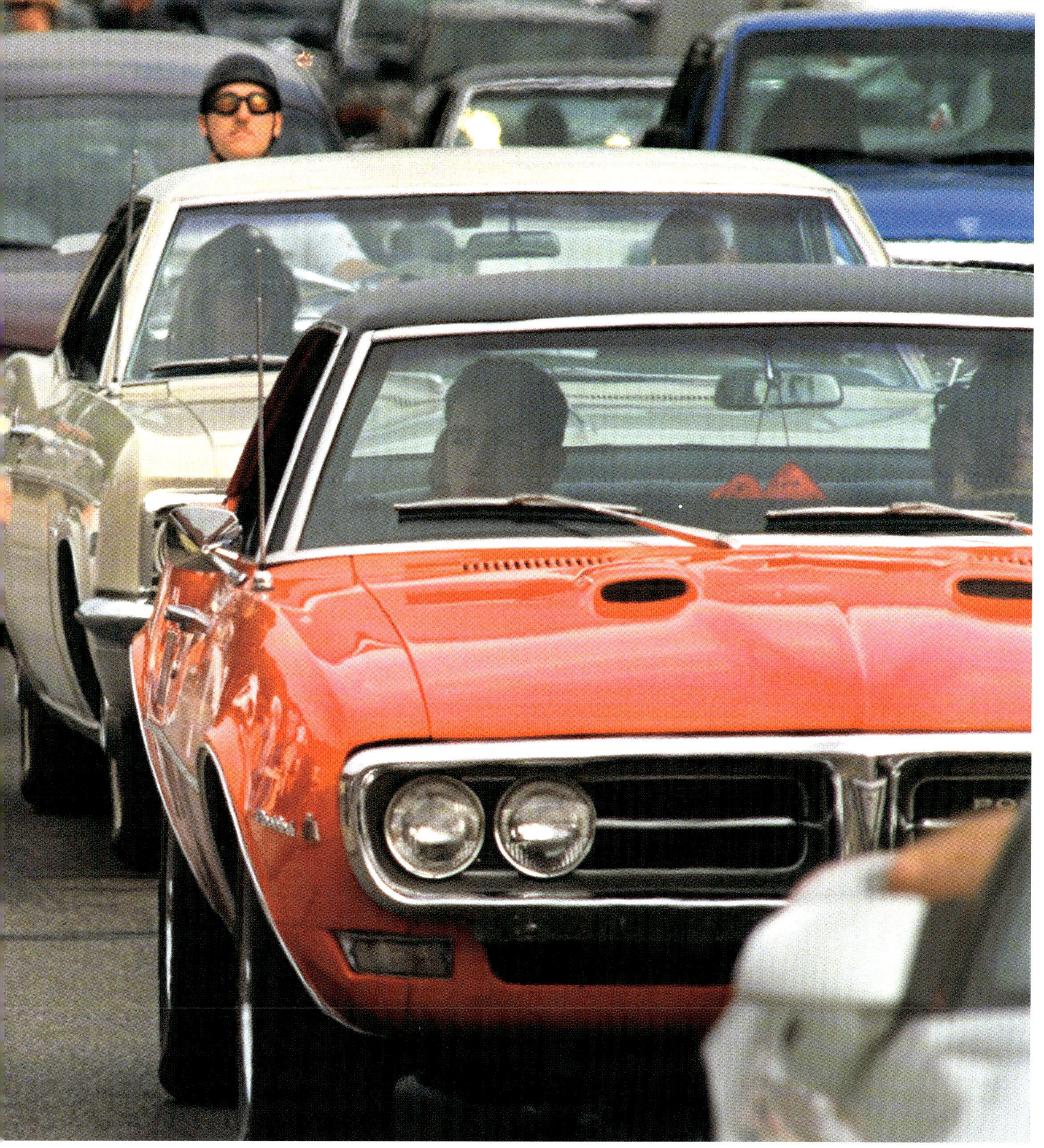

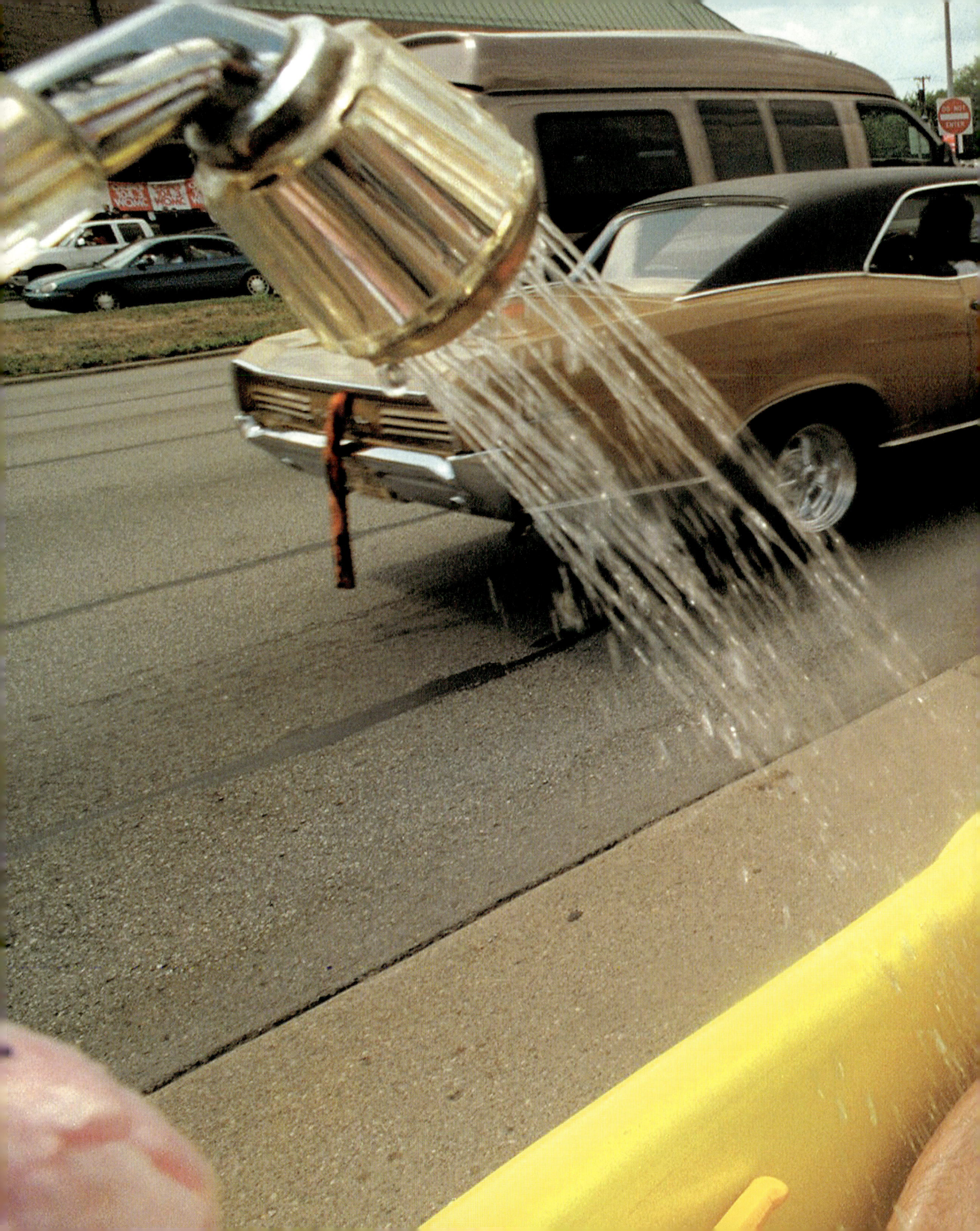

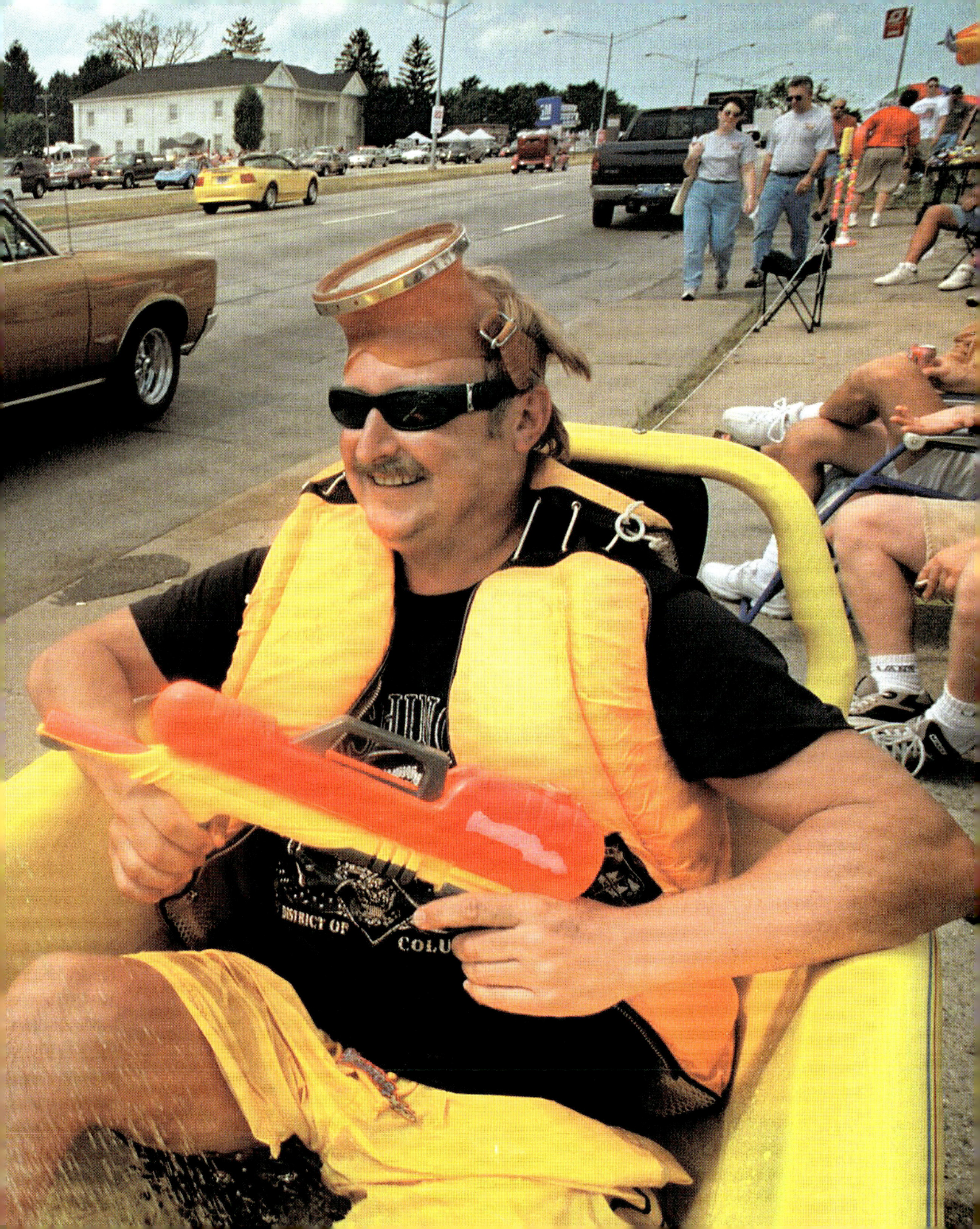
DISTRICT OF
COLU

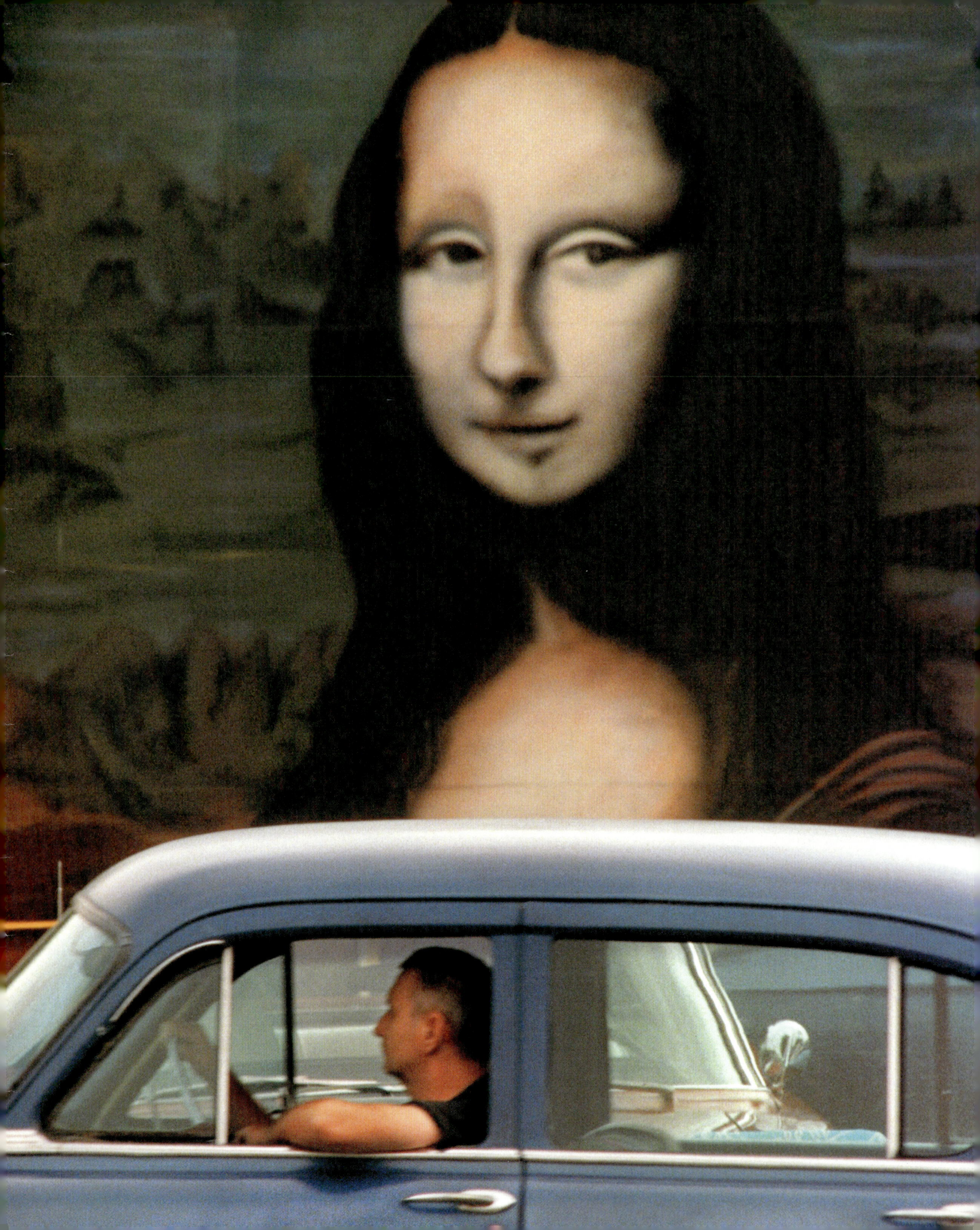

THIS MURAL OF MONA LISA, on the side of the ArtCraft art supply store in Royal Oak, provides the perfect backdrop for the works of art rolling along Woodward. Business at stores like the art supply started falling early in the week and dropped by half during the Dream Cruise; many owners along the route — which runs from Ferndale through Pleasant Ridge, Royal Oak, Huntington Woods, Berkley and Birmingham and then into Pontiac — decided to close for the day, ceding their parking areas to crowds of car lovers.

PAGE 104: SPLISH SPLASH! While Rick Peterson sat along the highway in his custom trailer tub, neverminding the crowd, he wet those who passed by with his little squirt gun.

PAGE 108: GETTING COMFY in the backseat of a '62 Chevy Impala are Natalie Mercurio, 29, of Dearborn and Tom Petrere, 24, of Westland. Their friend Tony Alfonsi of Livonia is in the driver's seat, adjusting the hydraulics for some tilting and thumping down Woodward. Riding beside him is Rebecca Chessor of Dearborn, 19.

Previous page and left: KENT PHILLIPS

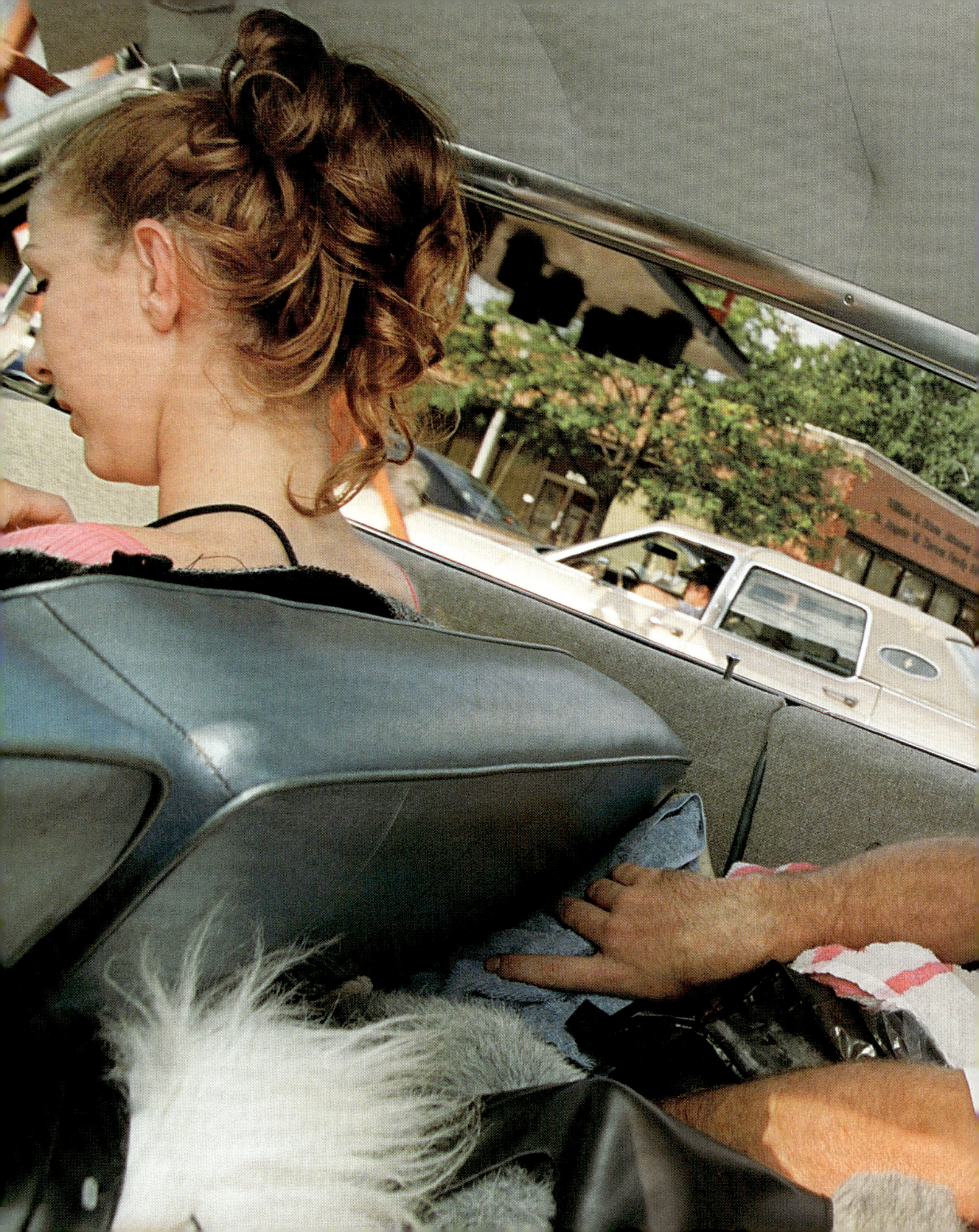

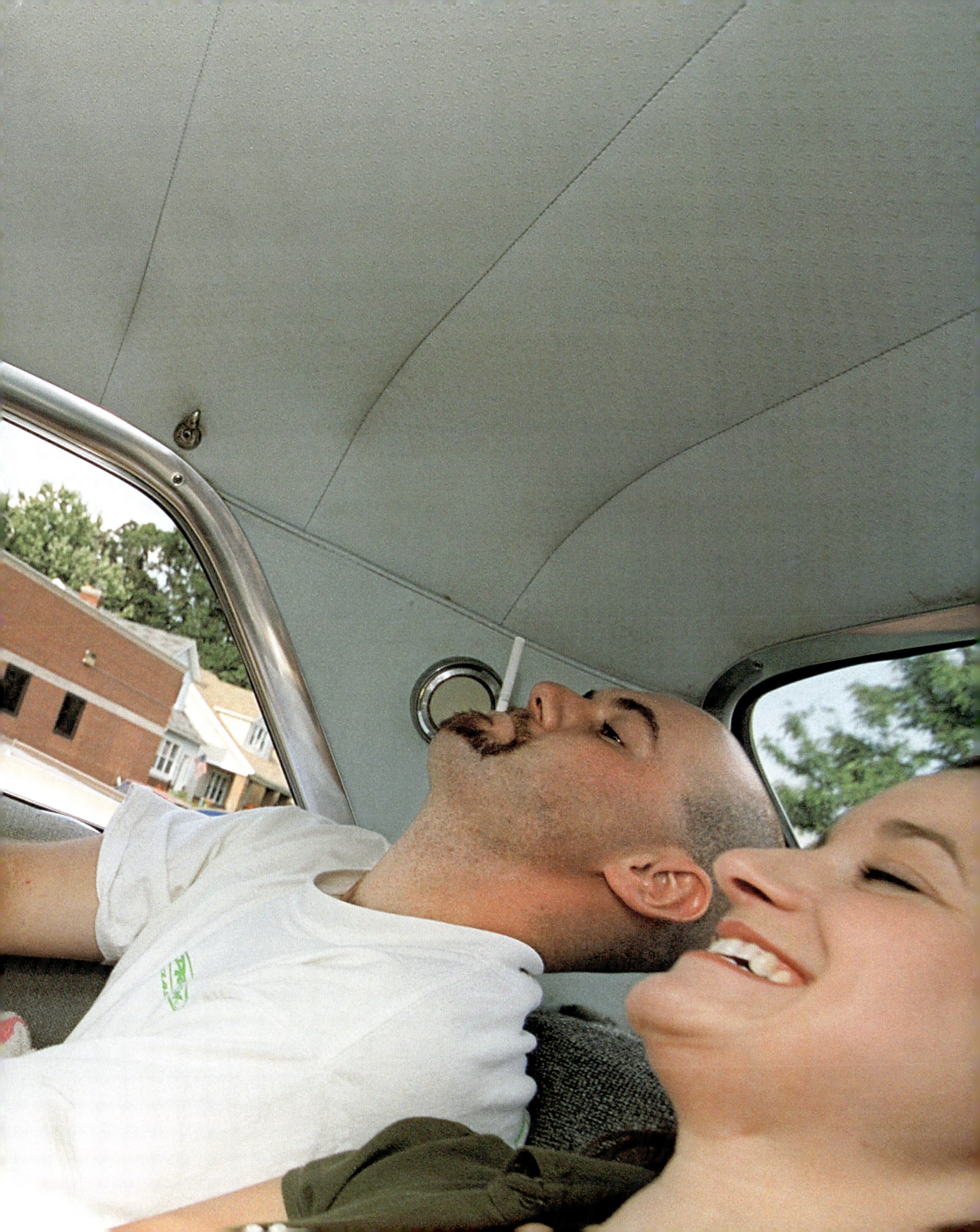

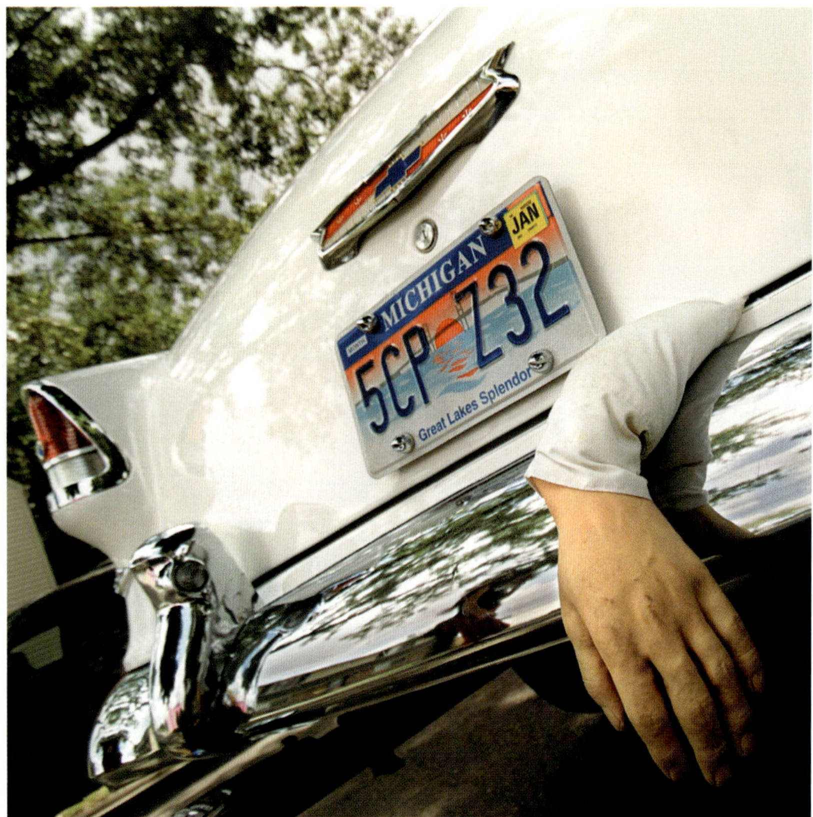

Previous page and above: PAUL GONZALEZ VIDELA; Right: KENT PHILLIPS

WITH SUCH A LARGE AUDIENCE, cruisers like to show off their sense of style and humor. This mid-'50s Chevy is an example of both. For people like these, right, looking at cars on Merrill between Pierce and Old Woodward in Birmingham, a hot rod equals a good time. Cruise-era machines are easier to tinker with, compared with the electronics found under the hood these days. "You can open up an old car and say, 'This is the electrical system; this is the fuel system,' " said Don Platz, a member of the Mott Rodders, a group of about 50 current and former auto shop and power mechanics students at Warren Mott High School who have, with the help of teacher Richard King, restored cars for the last 20 years. King met his wife while cruising Woodward in a '57 Pontiac. Platz, the oldest active Mott Rodder, graduated in '68. "This has always been a rite of passage, teaching kids what cars are really about." The group has restored several GTOs, a 1959 fuel-injected Corvette, a '65 Plymouth Belvedere and many more. After it was all fixed up, each car was sold to pay for the next project.

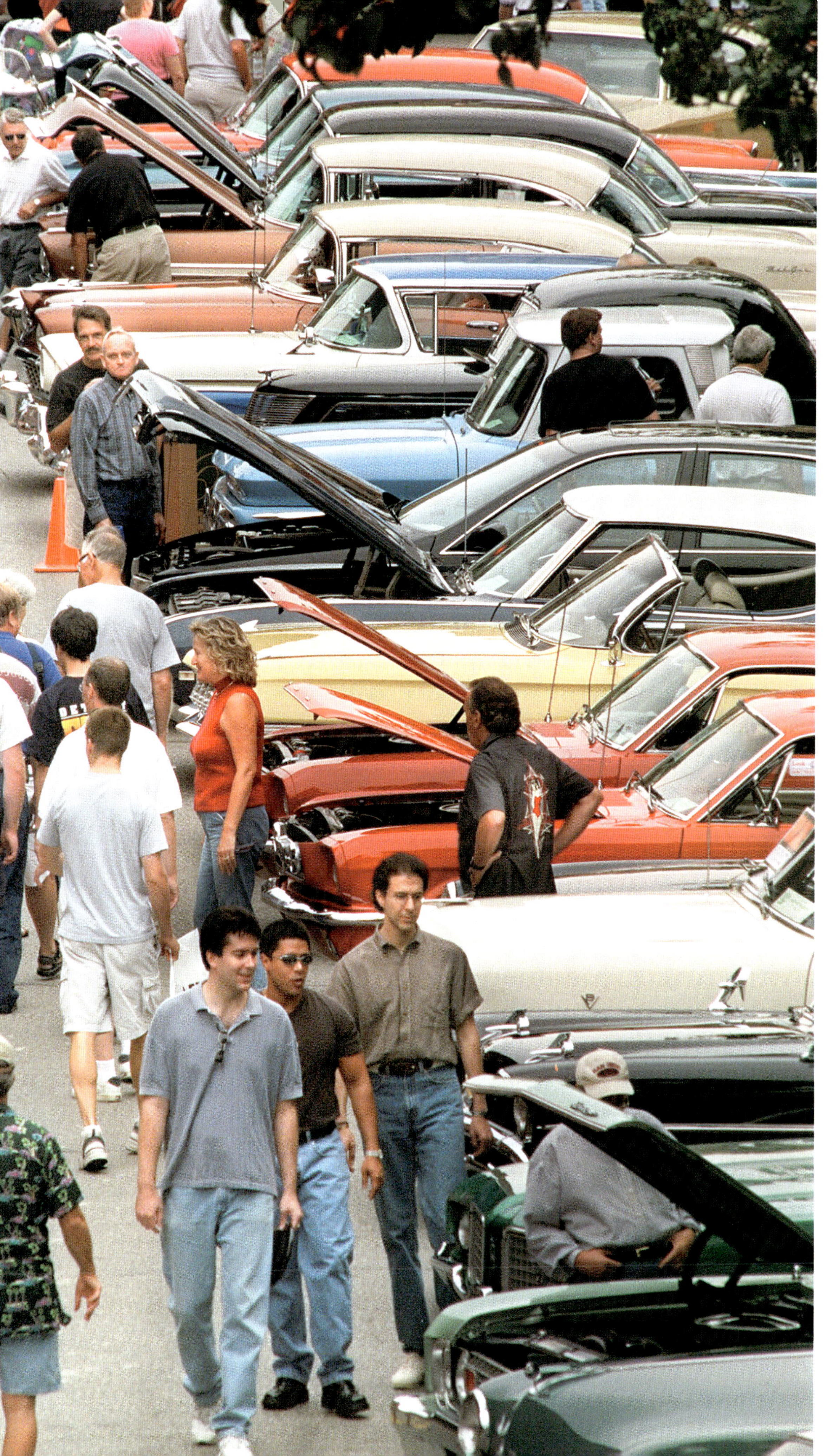

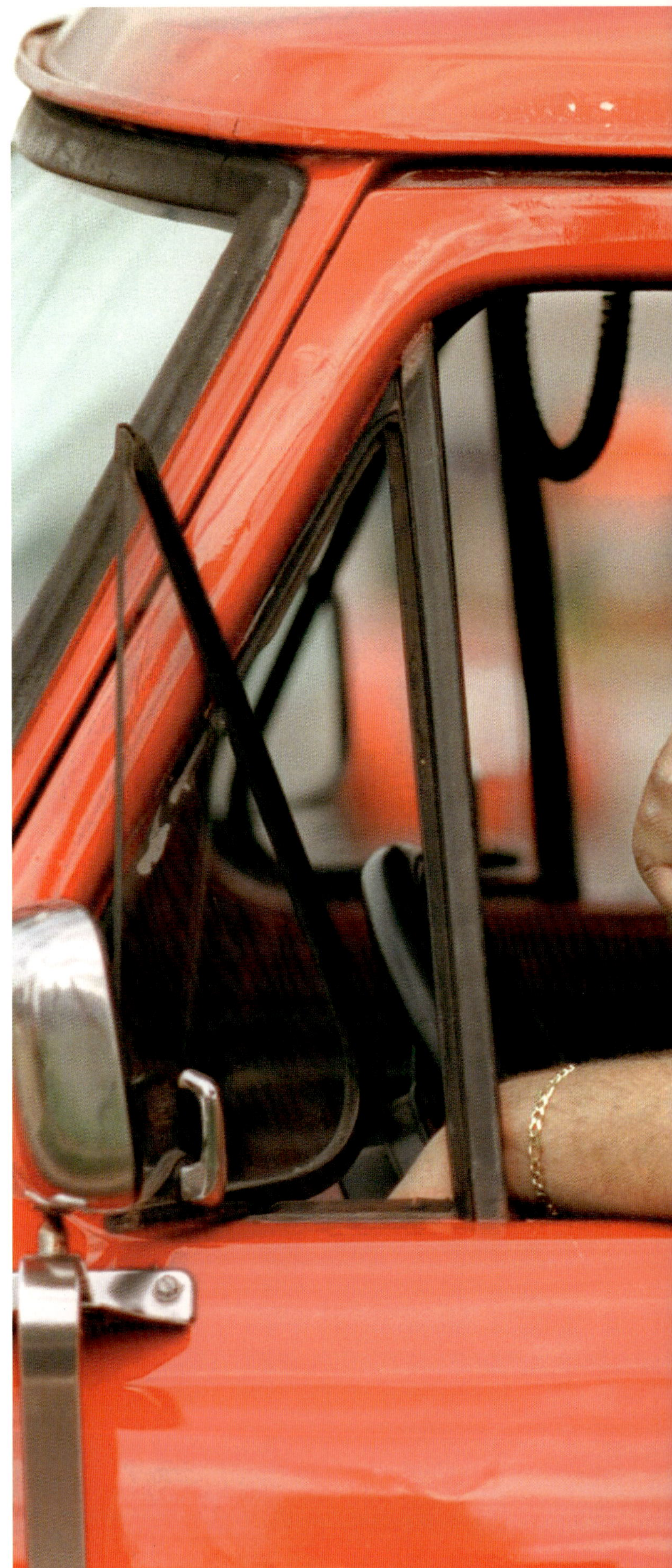

JUST OFF WORK, Ryan Prouse, 33, of Ferndale took his 1968 F-100 truck out for a spin on Woodward. The cruise began as a grassroots affair for people like Prouse who enjoy the simple pleasures of driving. But this year, everybody wanted a piece of the action. Politicians cruised the strip, stumped for votes and picked constituents' brains on issues. Cindy Williams (Shirley) and Eddie Mekka (Carmine) from "Laverne and Shirley" and Donny Most (Ralph) and Erin Moran (Joanie) from "Happy Days" came to sign autographs at Murray's auto parts store. A General Motors president drove a Buick Bengal concept car down Woodward, and Ford packed 3,000 people into a fund-raiser charging $175 a head. There were news conferences and billboards and photo opportunities and commercials. The cruise even got its own car: The PT Dream Cruiser, modeled on the 2001 North American Car of the Year. The list price was $23,170 for a manual transmission; $23,995 for an automatic. For a little more — $499 — would-be cruisers could get flame accents on the side.

PAUL GONZALEZ VIDELA

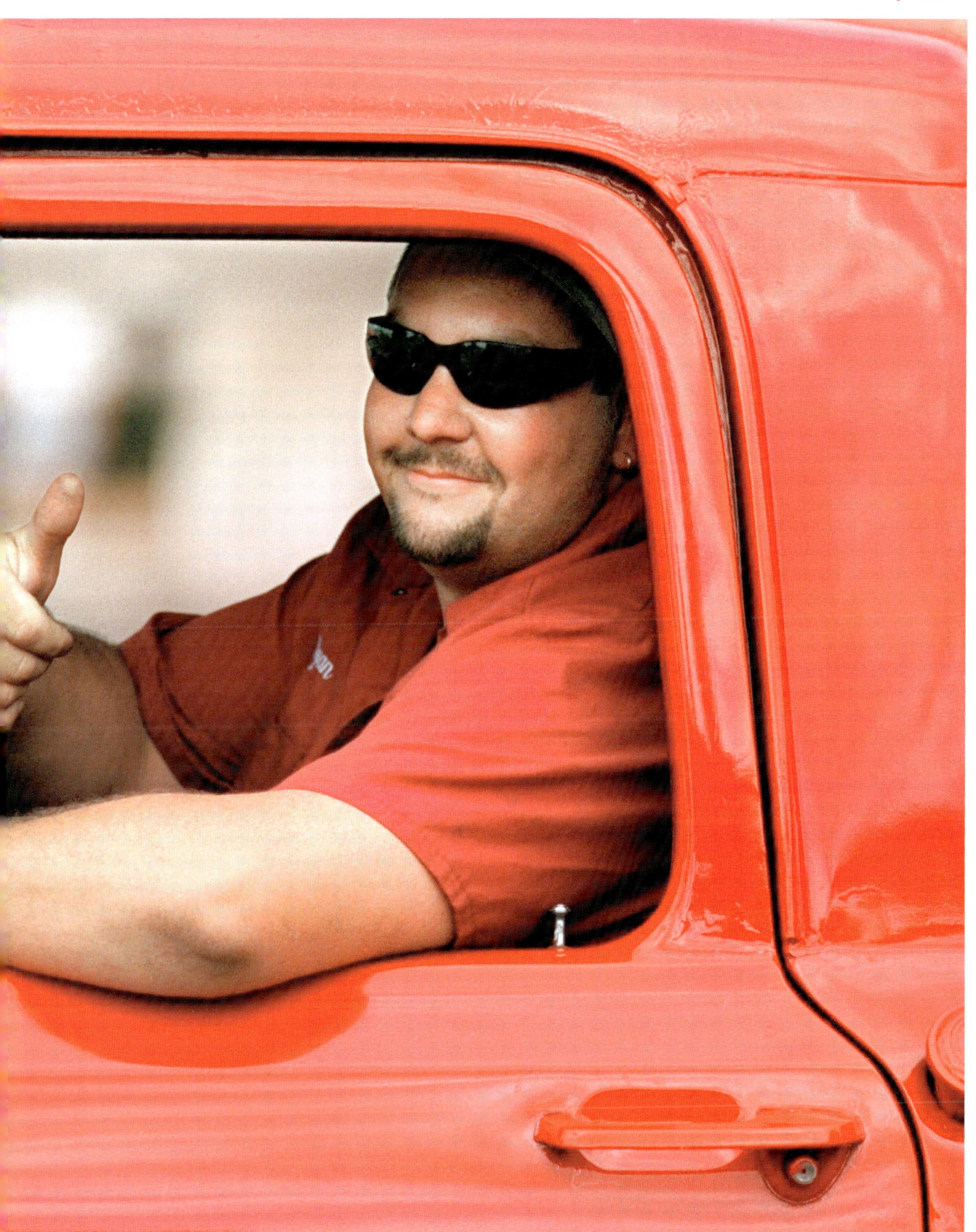

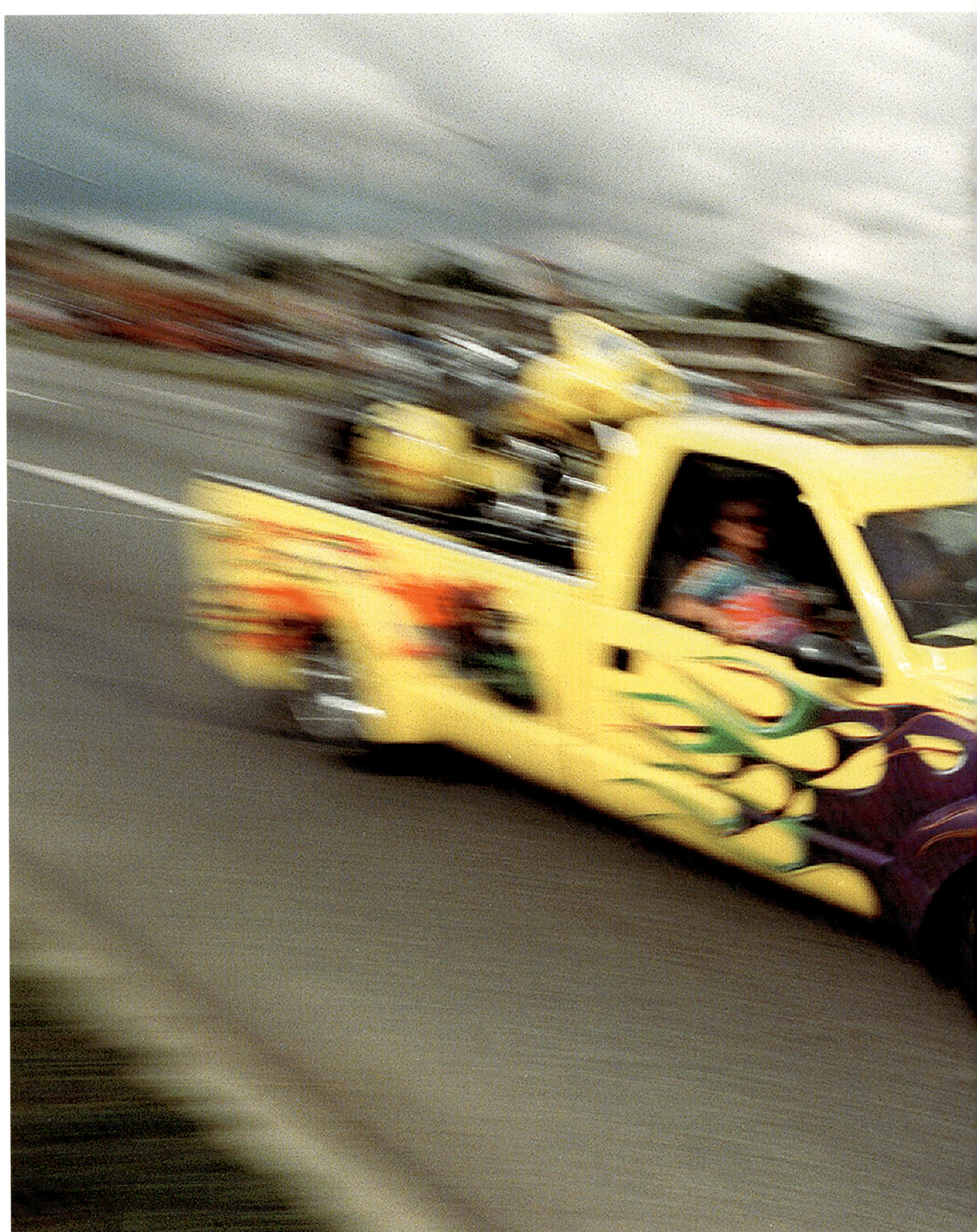

WILLIAM ARCHIE

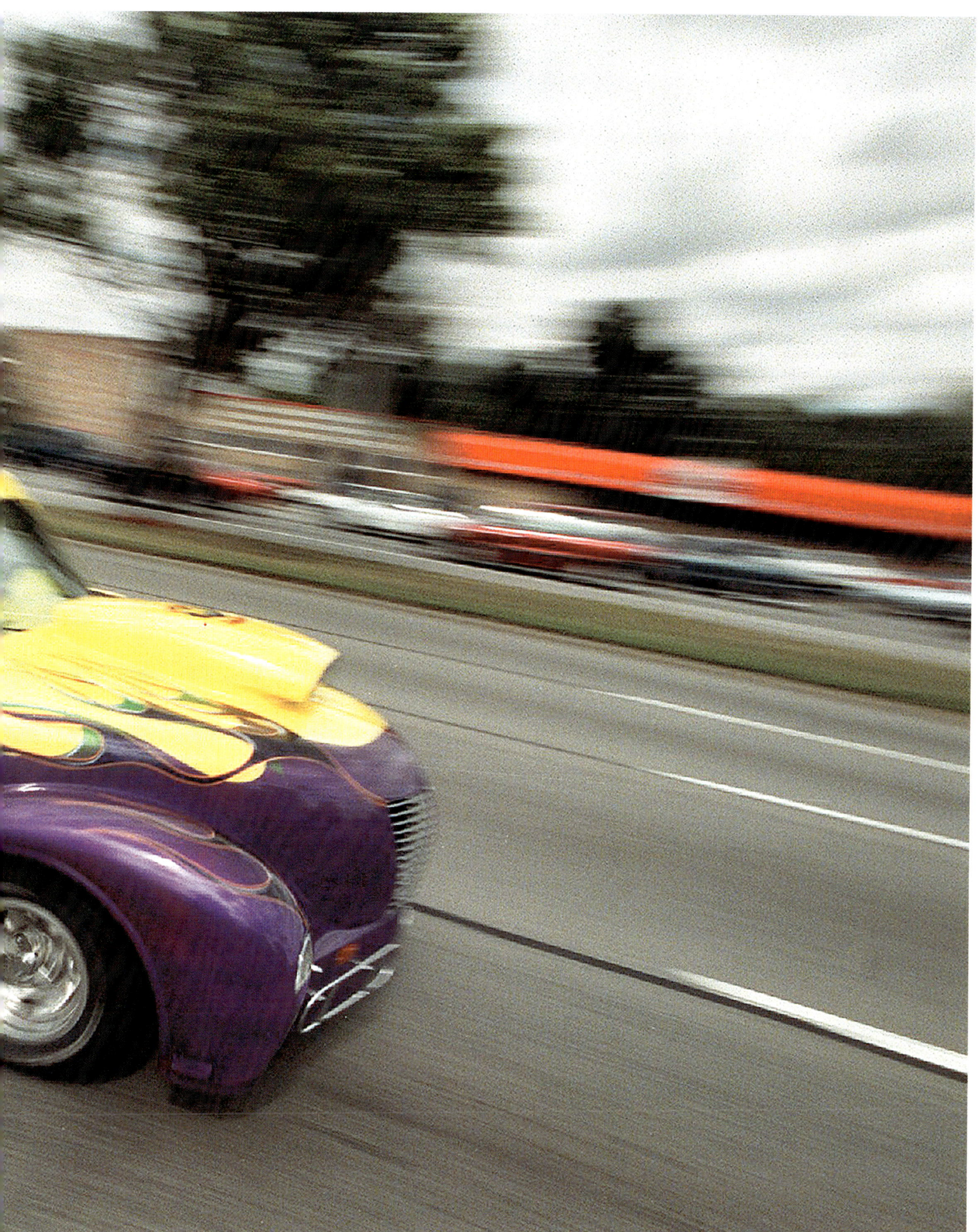

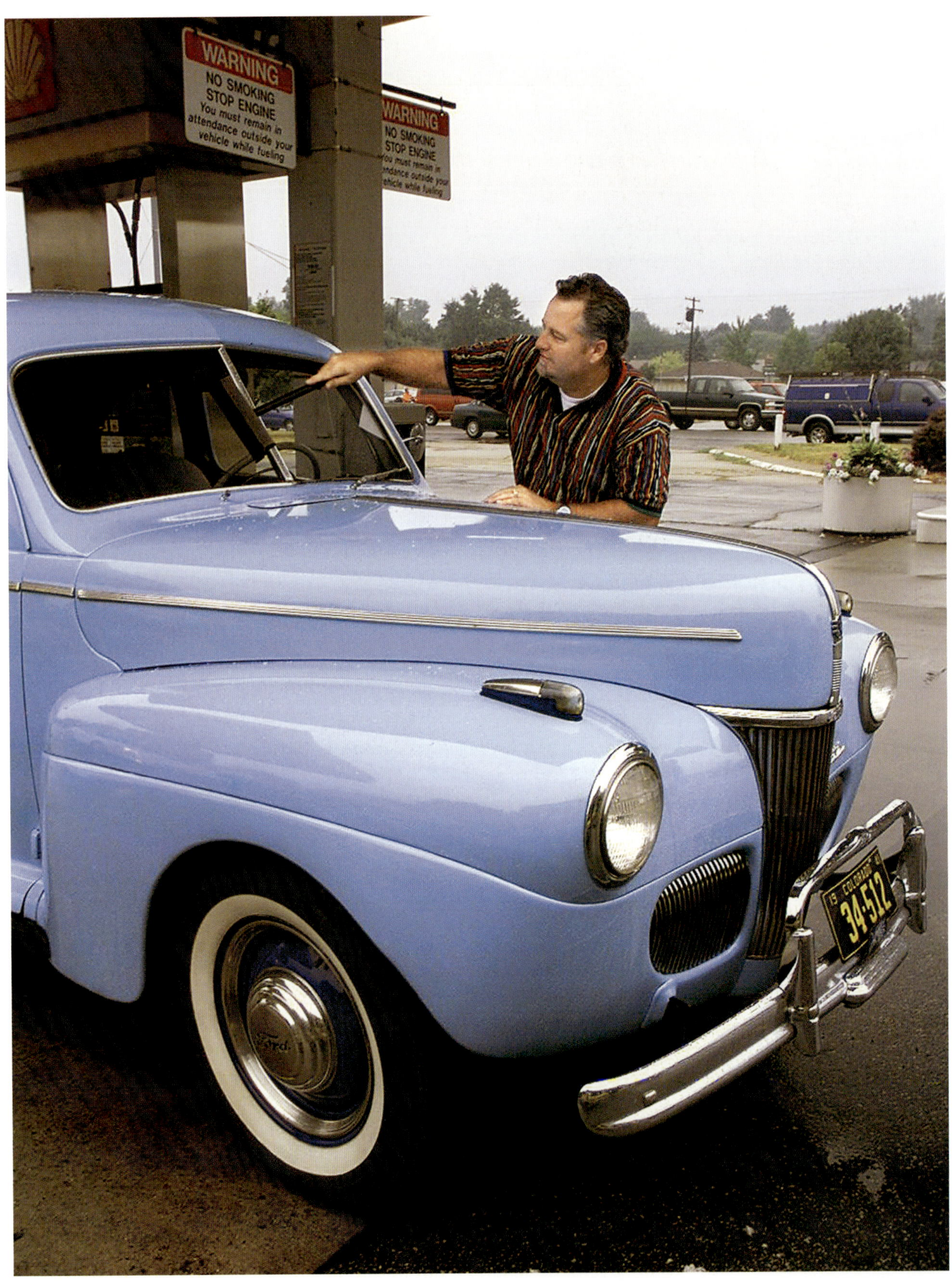

TWO THOUSAND ONE

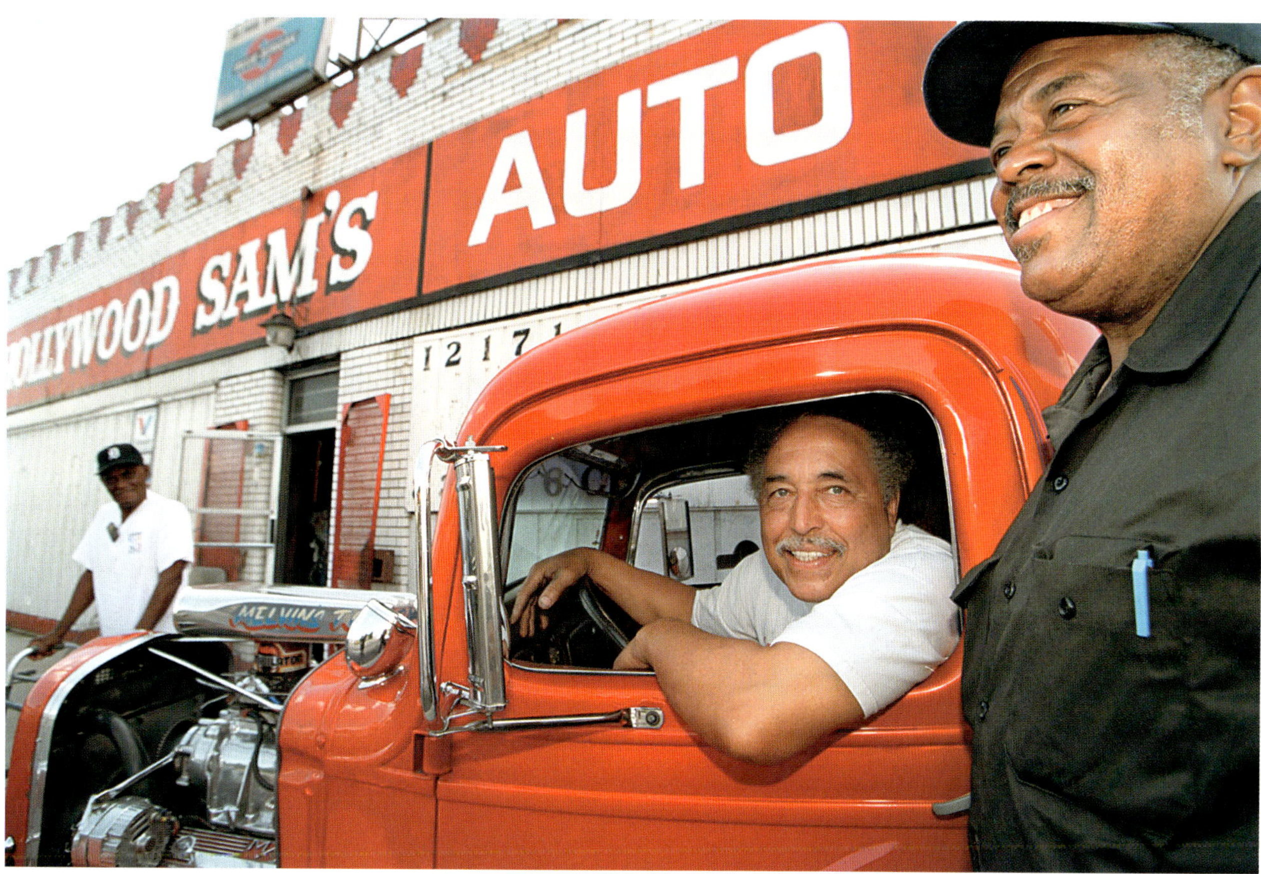

Left: WILLIAM ARCHIE; Above: PAUL GONZALEZ VIDELA

IT'S ALL ABOUT THE MEMORIES. The cruise used to mainly be about paying homage to the '50s and '60s. But after all those years of the Dream Cruise, people were beginning to develop memories of the actual event. One of those people was Sam Gurley, above right, a 58-year-old Detroiter. His business was cars; he owned Hollywood Sam's Auto Parts in Detroit and had been involved with cars since he was a high schooler in the '60s. But in 1995, when he and the buddy with him, Melvin Howard, set off to cruise in Howard's 1936 Chevy pickup — named Miss Melvina — he was shocked. "Some of these cars, I've never seen before in my life," he said. "Every time we came to a turnoff, I swear I was going to get off and go home," he continued, "but then I'd see another car or another group of people ahead. I was so geeked, I just couldn't stop." Tim Grisham, far left, was so geeked about cars, he came all the way from Houston, Texas, to participate in the cruise. He made a pit stop near 13 Mile in Royal Oak to clean the windshield of his '41 Ford.

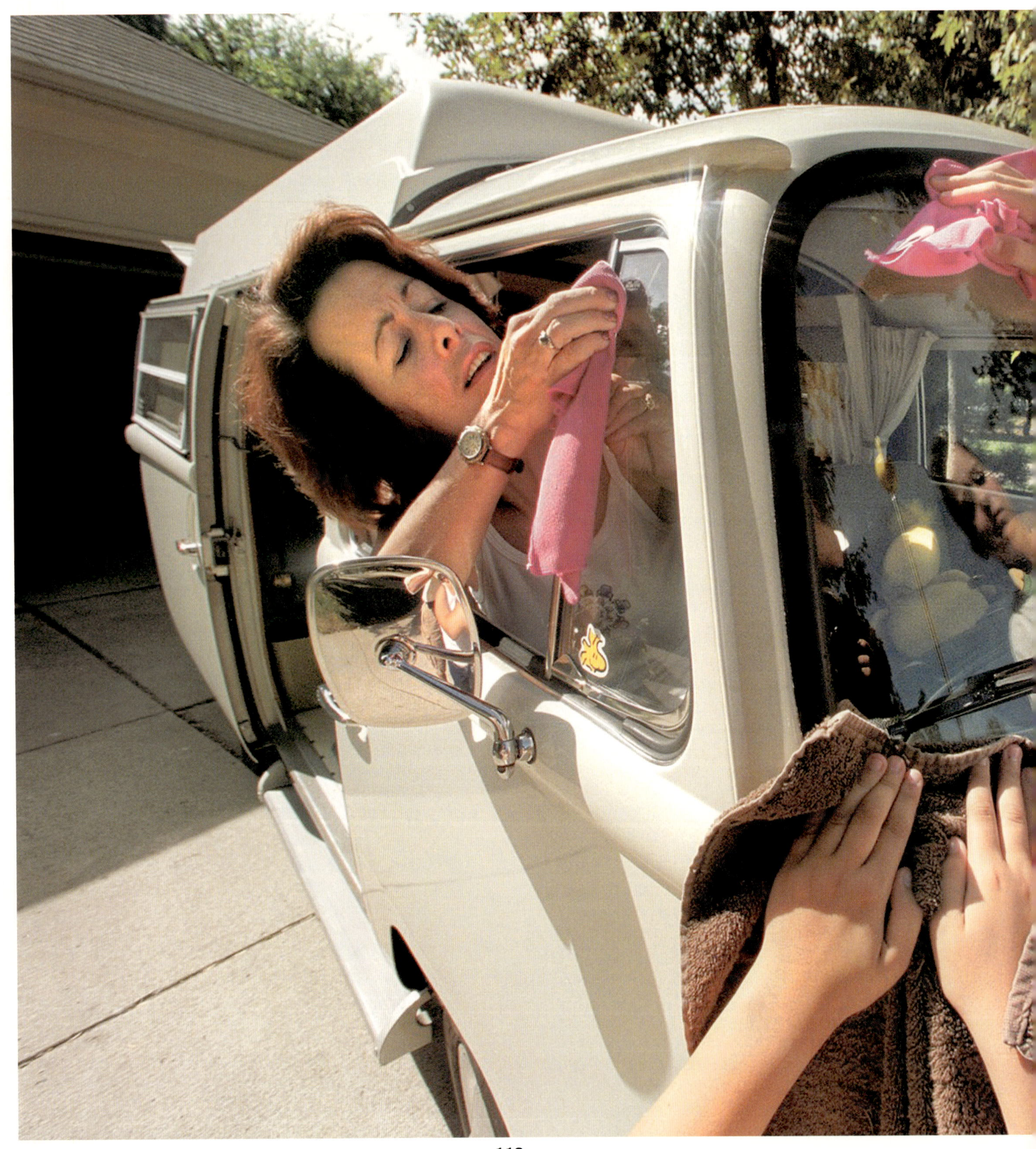

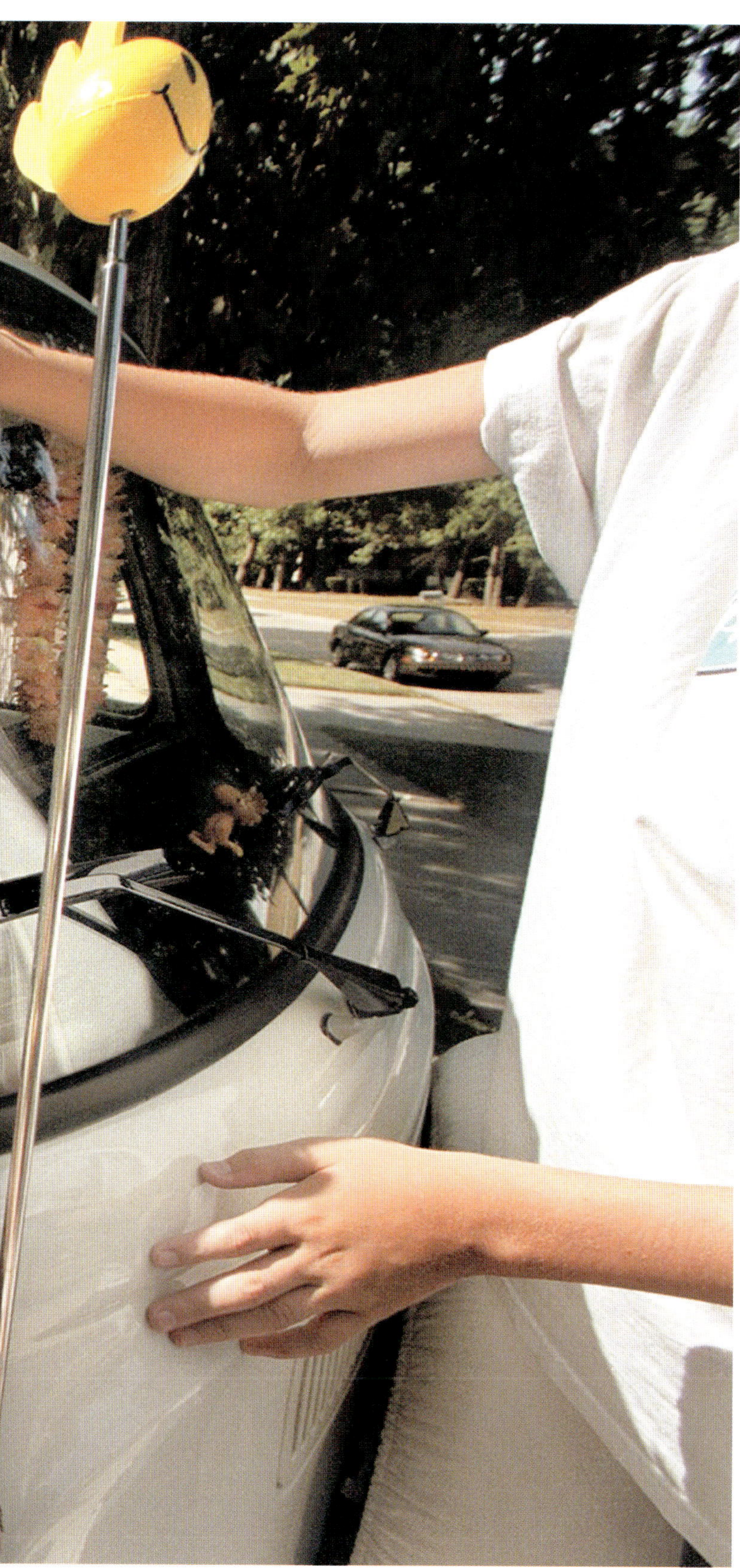

GETTING READY FOR THE CRUISE meant getting the car all spiffed up. The Andersons of Clinton Township — Lynn and her children Laura, 11, and Paul, 12 — polished the family's VW camper van.

PAGE 120: HEY, WANT TO BUY A DICE? Jesse Magee is the person to see. Magee wiggled the fuzzy cubes at drivers making their way south on Woodward Avenue at Ravenna in Royal Oak, hoping to entice them into spending $2 to benefit the Oakland County Food Bank.

Left: DAVID P. GILKEY; Next page: KENT PHILLIPS

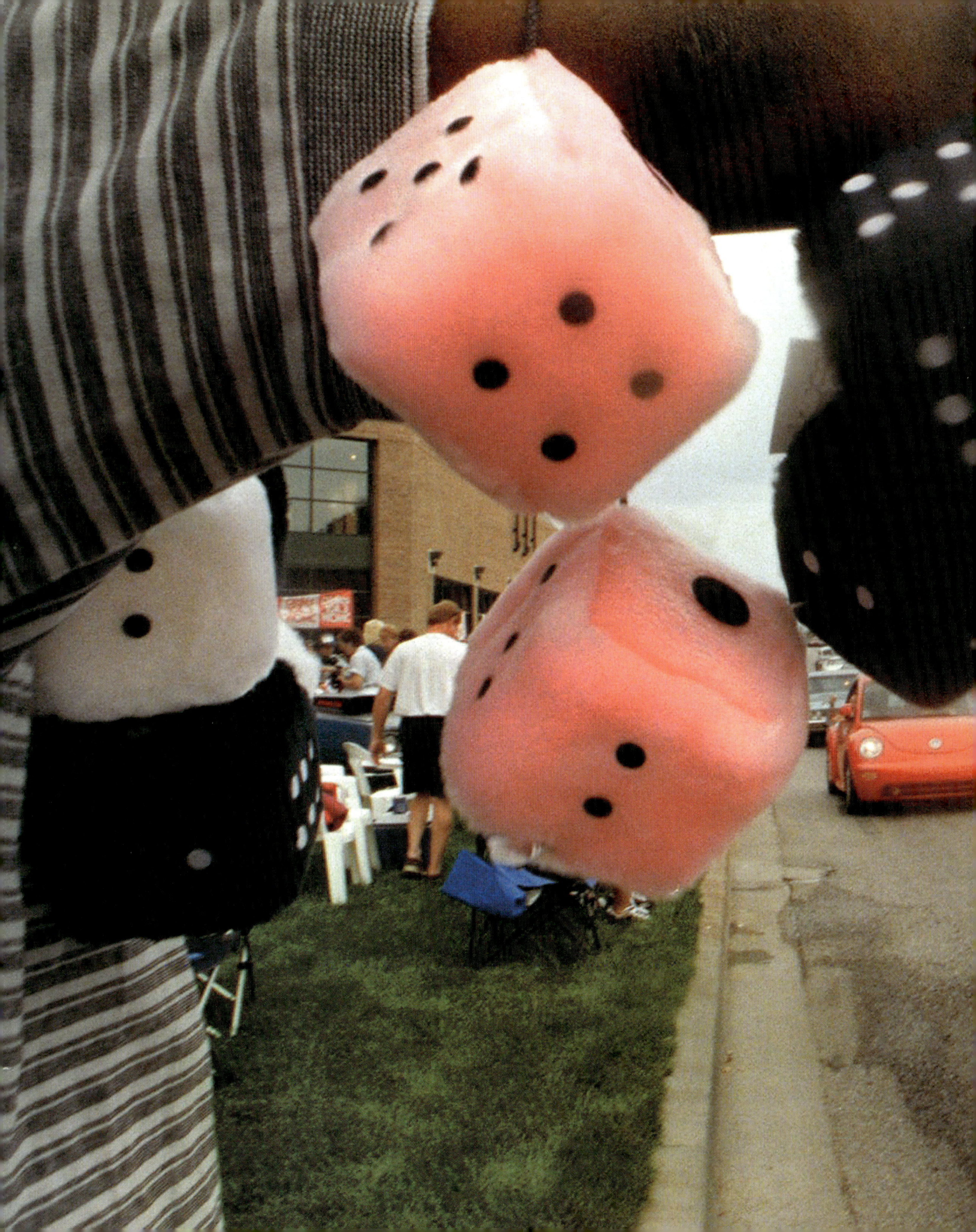

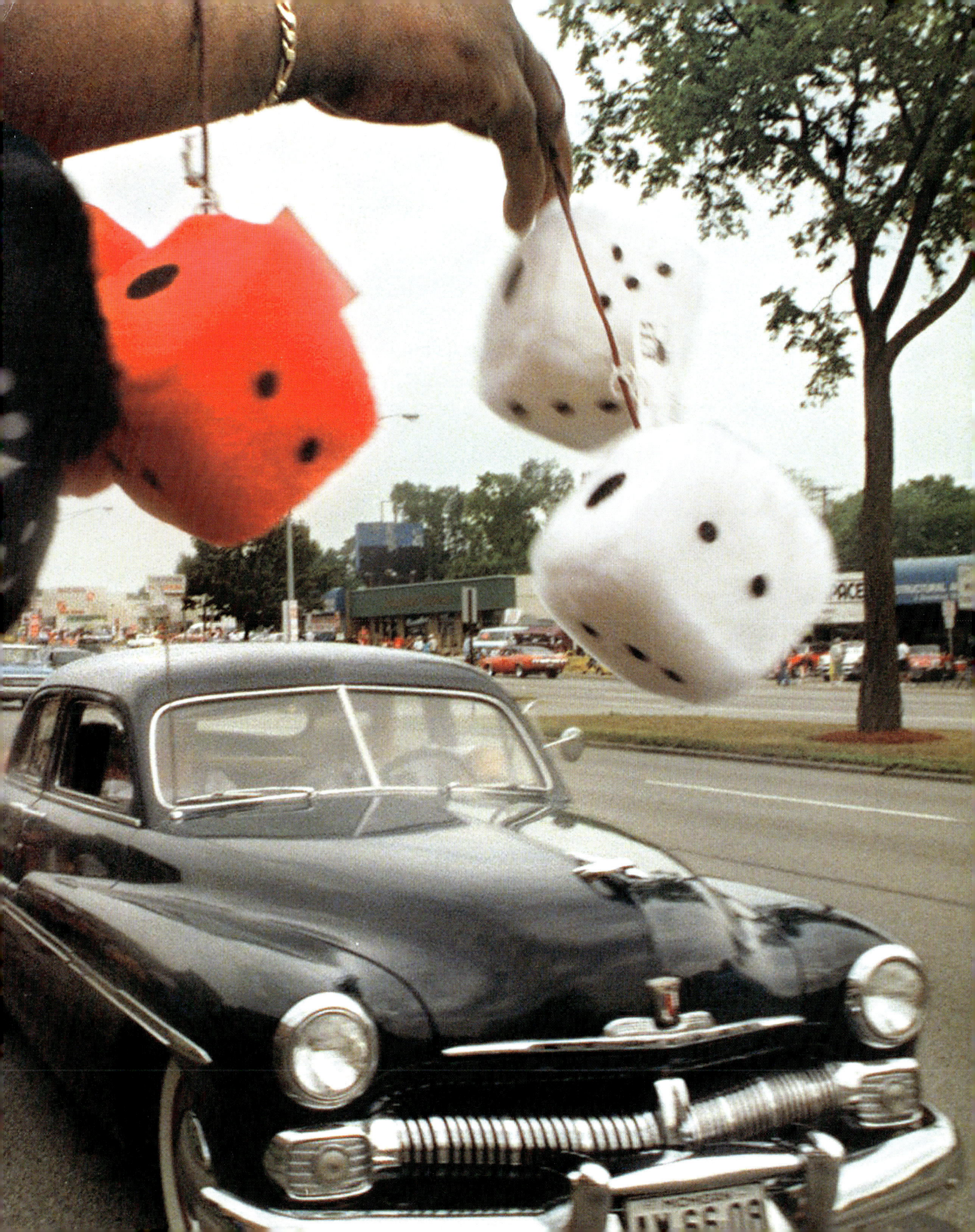

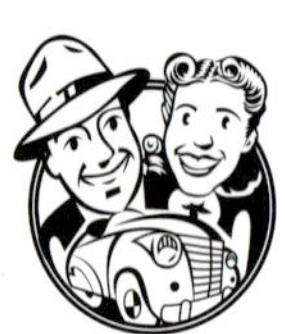

Date: Aug. 17

Attendance: 1.7 million; another milestone.

Special moment: Bloomfield Hills and Bloomfield Township joined the fun and completed the entire length of Woodward Avenue in the route from the Michigan State Fairgrounds to Pontiac.

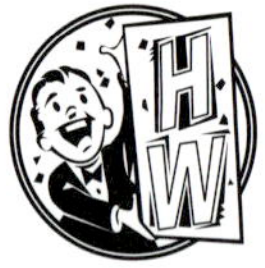

Elvis sighting: Huntington Woods showed "Jailhouse Rock" in the park. Impersonators paraded down Woodward in Royal Oak.

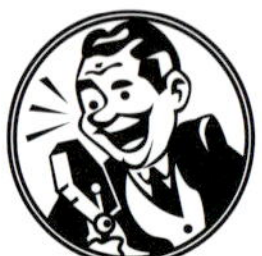

Summer sounds: Ferndale hosted Junior Walker and the All-Star Band.

Real winners: Sales of refreshments and official merchandise benefited about 100 charities.

2002

THE HEAT WAS STIFLING. CONGESTION WAS AWFUL.

Yet the world's biggest one-day car event surged through another blissful year with a record unmarred by serious injuries. Attendance hit a record 1.7 million.

The heat got to vintage DJ Lee Alan, whose broadcasts in the '60s were synonymous with Detroit cruisin'.

In the 2002 cruise, Alan rode in a GTO convertible as a guest of honor. In Royal Oak, he became a man of auto action. Leaping from the smoking GTO — owned by an unmechanically inclined member of the Kontinentals car club — Alan splashed water on the steaming radiator of the 389-cubic-inch engine, with its three Rochester three-barrel carburetors.

"It takes an hour to go a mile out there, and these cars just can't take it," Alan said.

Not far away, a 1982 Chevrolet Monte Carlo had begun smoking, then caught fire on Woodward just north of I-696. Owner Calvin Pruitt of Flint fled with his wife and passengers to the curb while his car burned and tires exploded in just seconds.

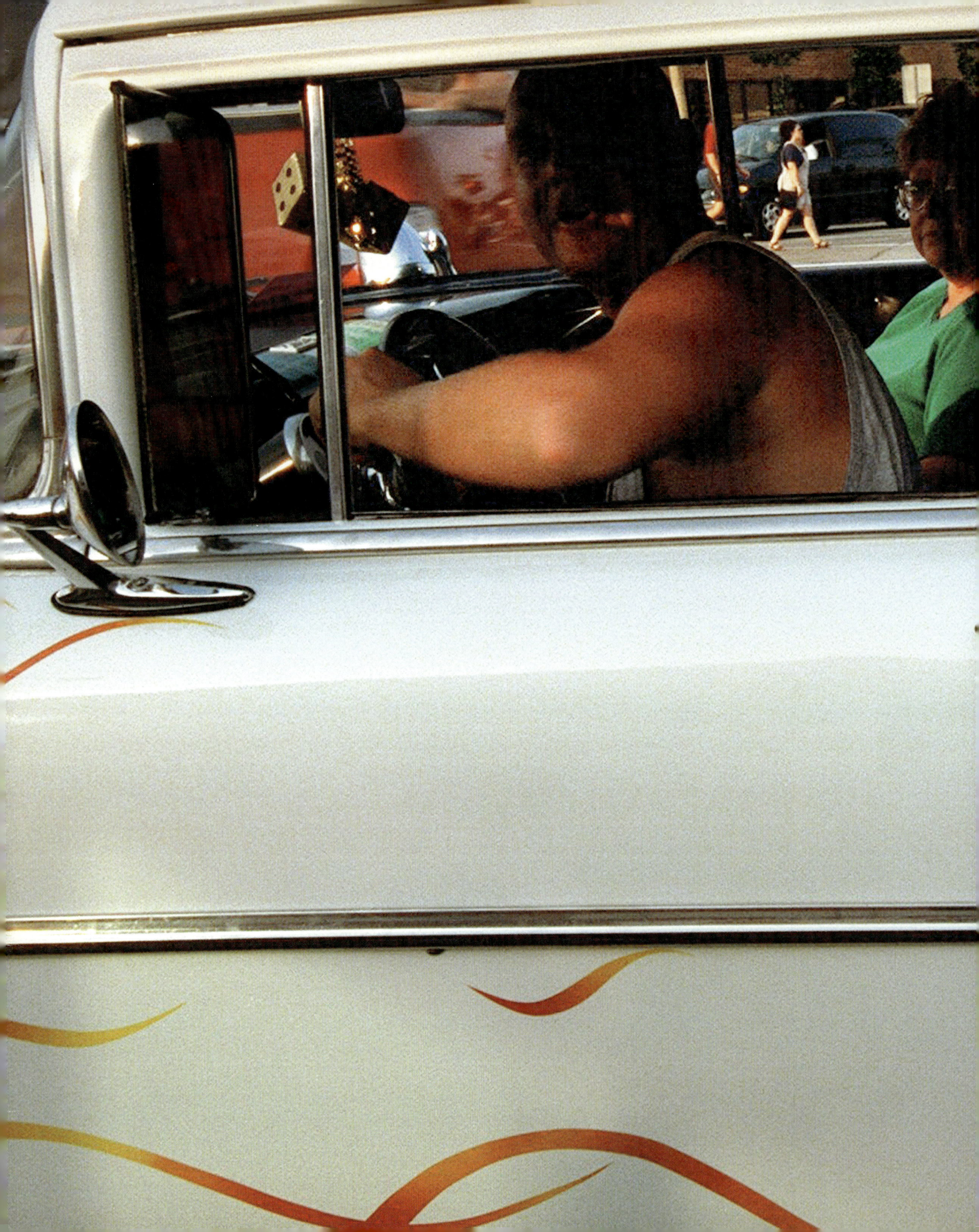

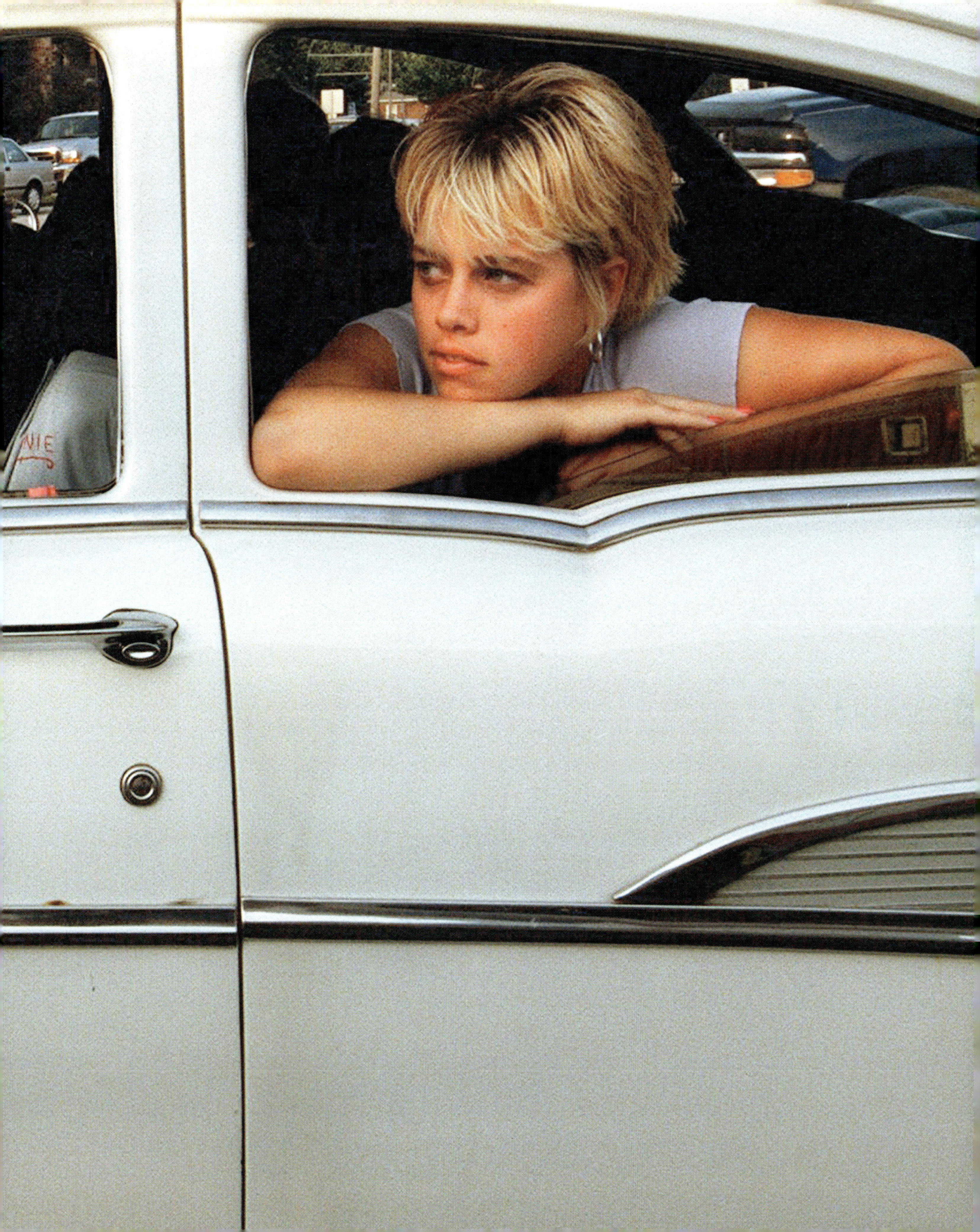
NIE

CELEBRITY SIGHTINGS WERE PLENTY. Detroiters Matthew Agee, left, Nikoe Harris, Chris Brown and Nakia Carter got a kick out of the Elvis impersonators parading down Woodward in Royal Oak. This year, Elvis impersonators had to share the spotlight with other famous faces. Rock 'n' roller Chubby Checker, who recorded the 1960 smash hit "The Twist," was scheduled to make special appearances at several Birmingham locations during the cruise. Checker, born Ernest Evans, was joined by look-alikes of Lucille Ball, Marilyn Monroe, Judy Garland, Ed Sullivan and Sammy Davis Jr.

PAGE 124: AS DUSK FELL, Shelby Township resident Lisa Porada checked out the Dream Cruise action along Woodward Avenue from the backseat of a 1957 Chevrolet. Despite heat, congestion, parking hassles and hordes of non-classic cruisers clogging the strip, the crowds kept coming and the Dream Cruise kept growing. A record crowd flocked to Woodward for the eighth annual event, which stretched from Ferndale to Pontiac. This year, Bloomfield Hills joined the party, teaming up with the seven cities to host the cruise: Berkley, Birmingham, Ferndale, Huntington Woods, Pleasant Ridge, Pontiac and Royal Oak. It was a big step in neighborliness. In the event's early years, Bloomfield Hills turned a cold shoulder to the spectacle of muscle and classic Detroit iron.

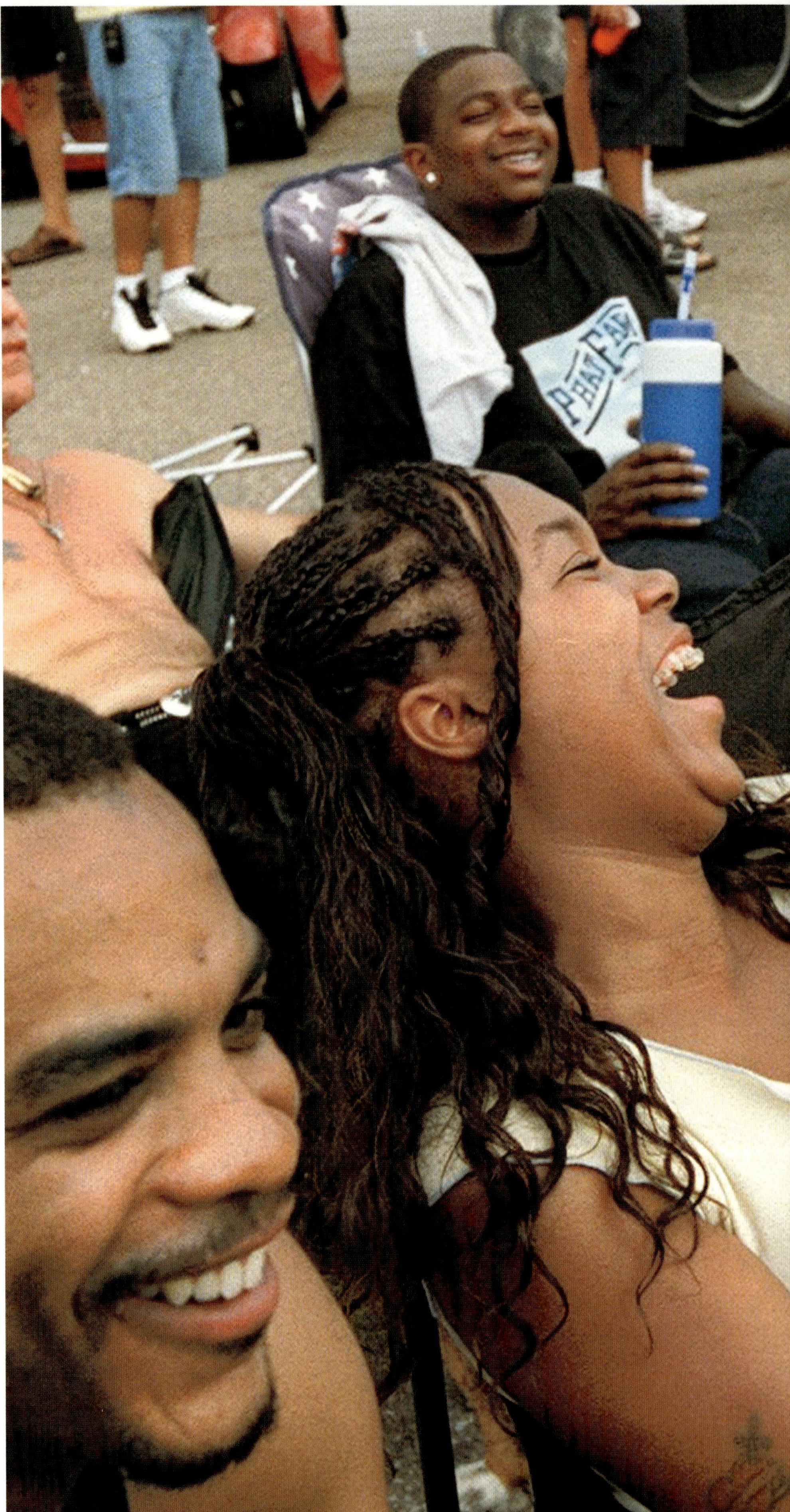

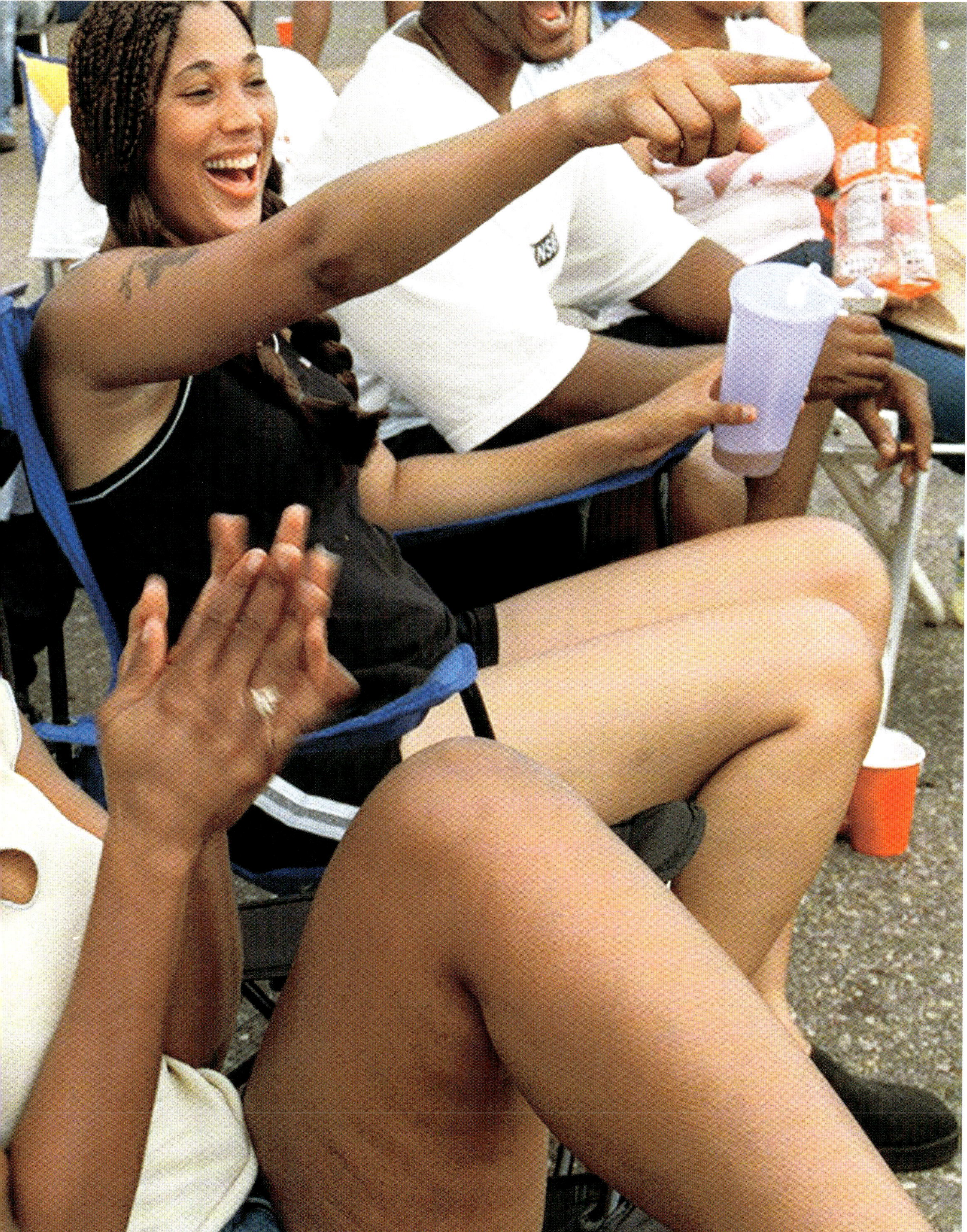

Previous page and right: AMY LEANG

"NICE COCONUTS!" That's what a passing motorist shouted as Steve Fisk of Georgetown, Ky., told cruisers to burn some rubber in Royal Oak. "I've loved cars ever since I was 15 years old," said Fisk, who owned 30 cars — and a hula outfit.

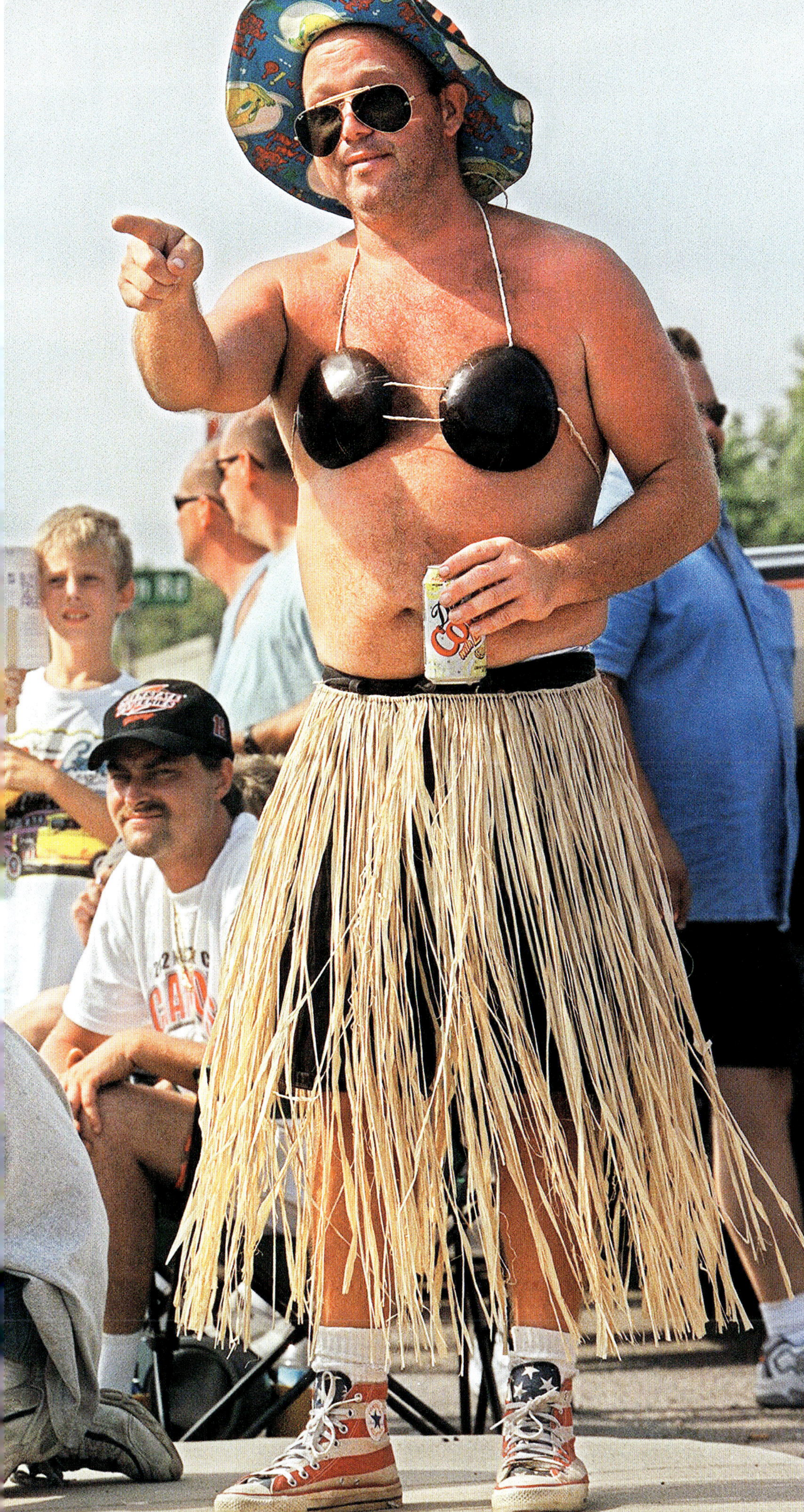

AMY LEANG

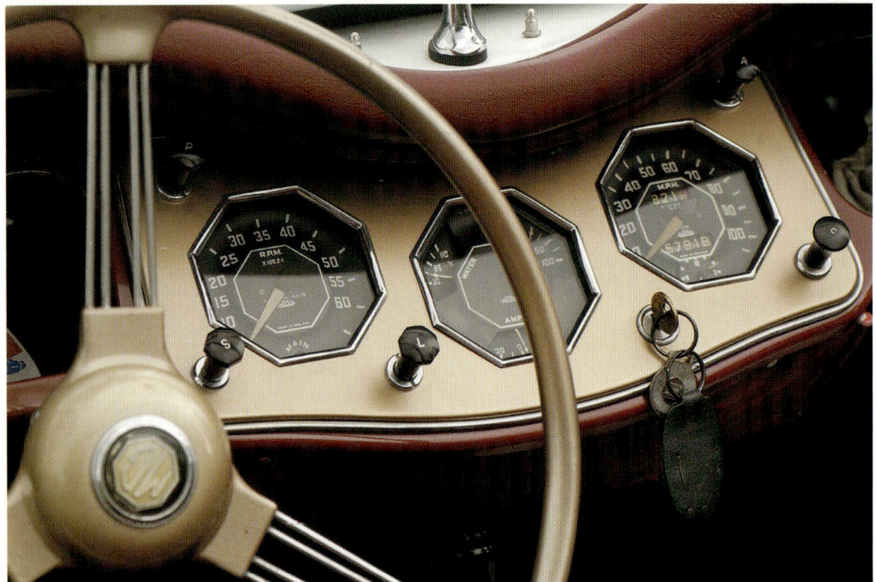

Above: WILLIAM ARCHIE; Right: AMY LEANG

ABOVE: A CLOSE-UP of the dashboard of a restored 1955 MG TF owned by Canadian Bernie Lajoie.

RIGHT: THE CLOUDS LOOKED OMINOUS Saturday morning, but the rains held off and cruisers kept their hoods up and tops down as they flooded the streets and parking lots in Royal Oak.

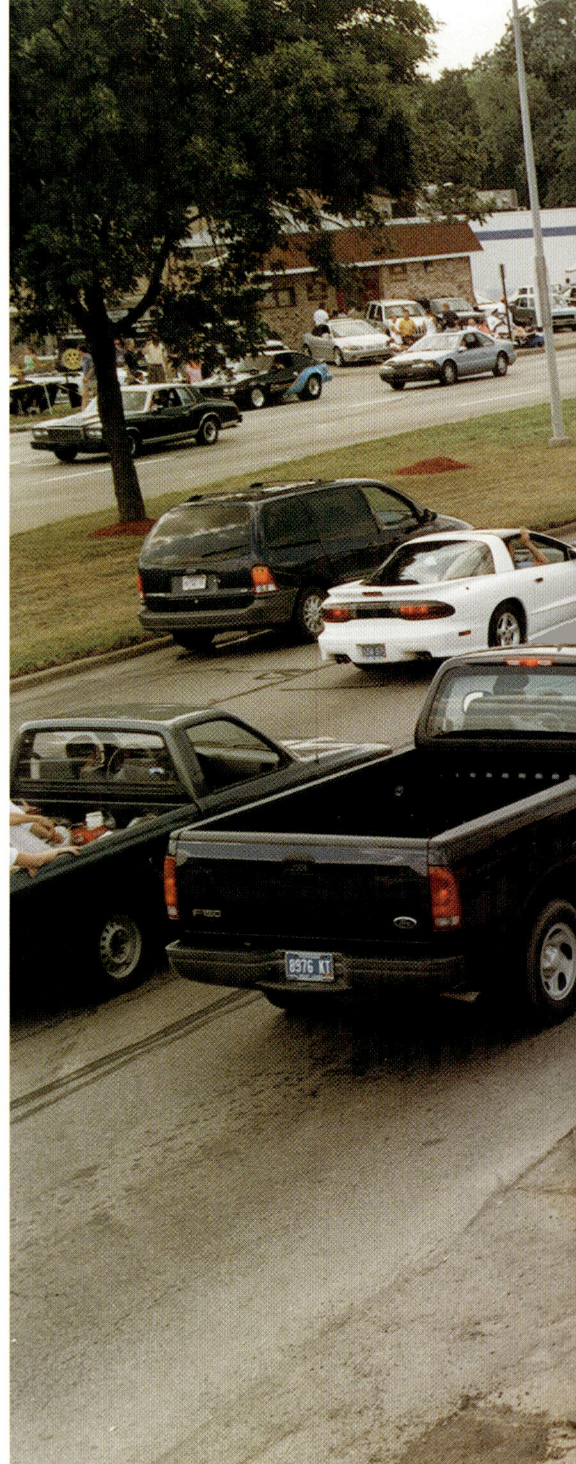

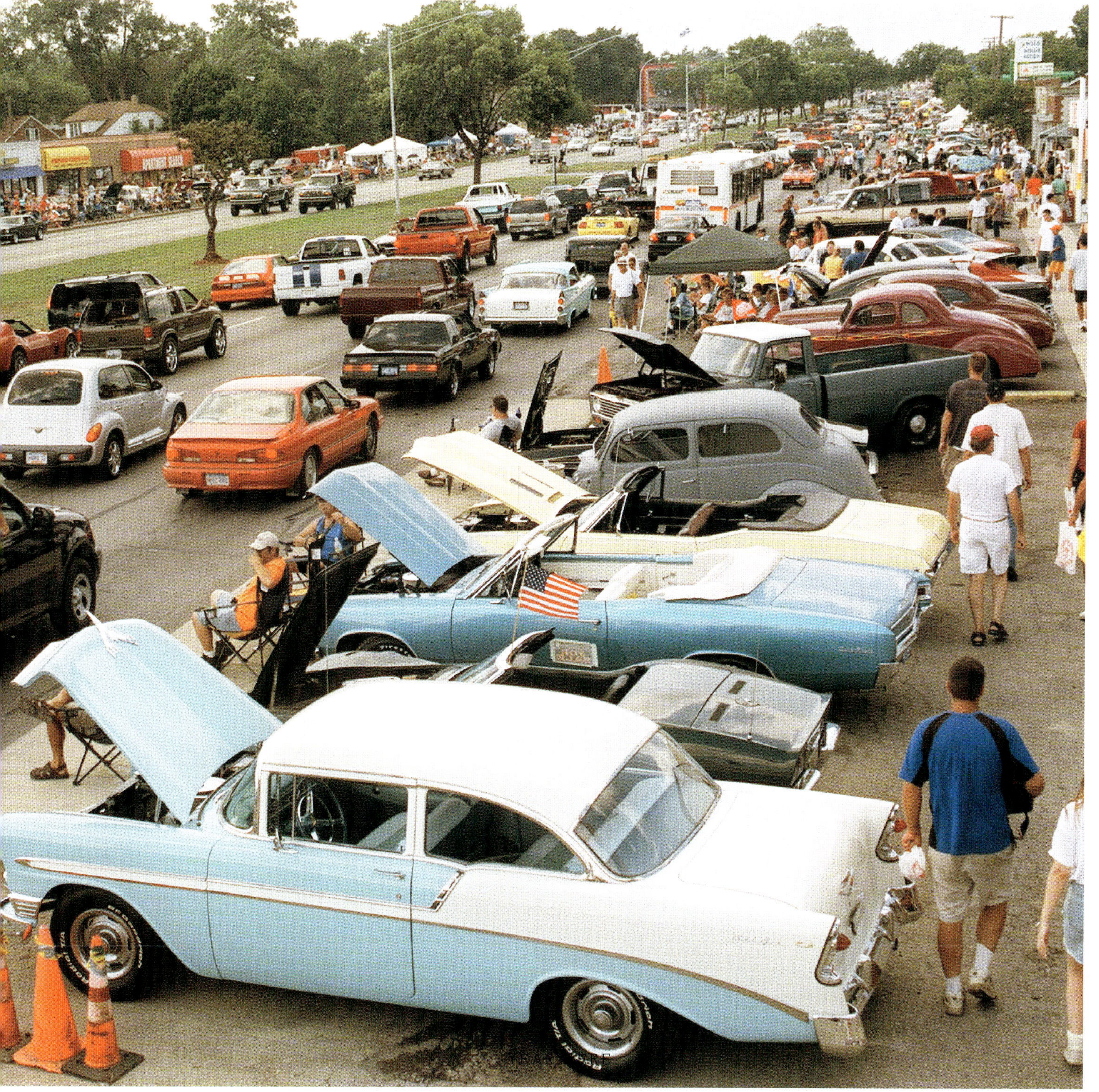
APARTMENT SEARCH
WILD BIRDS

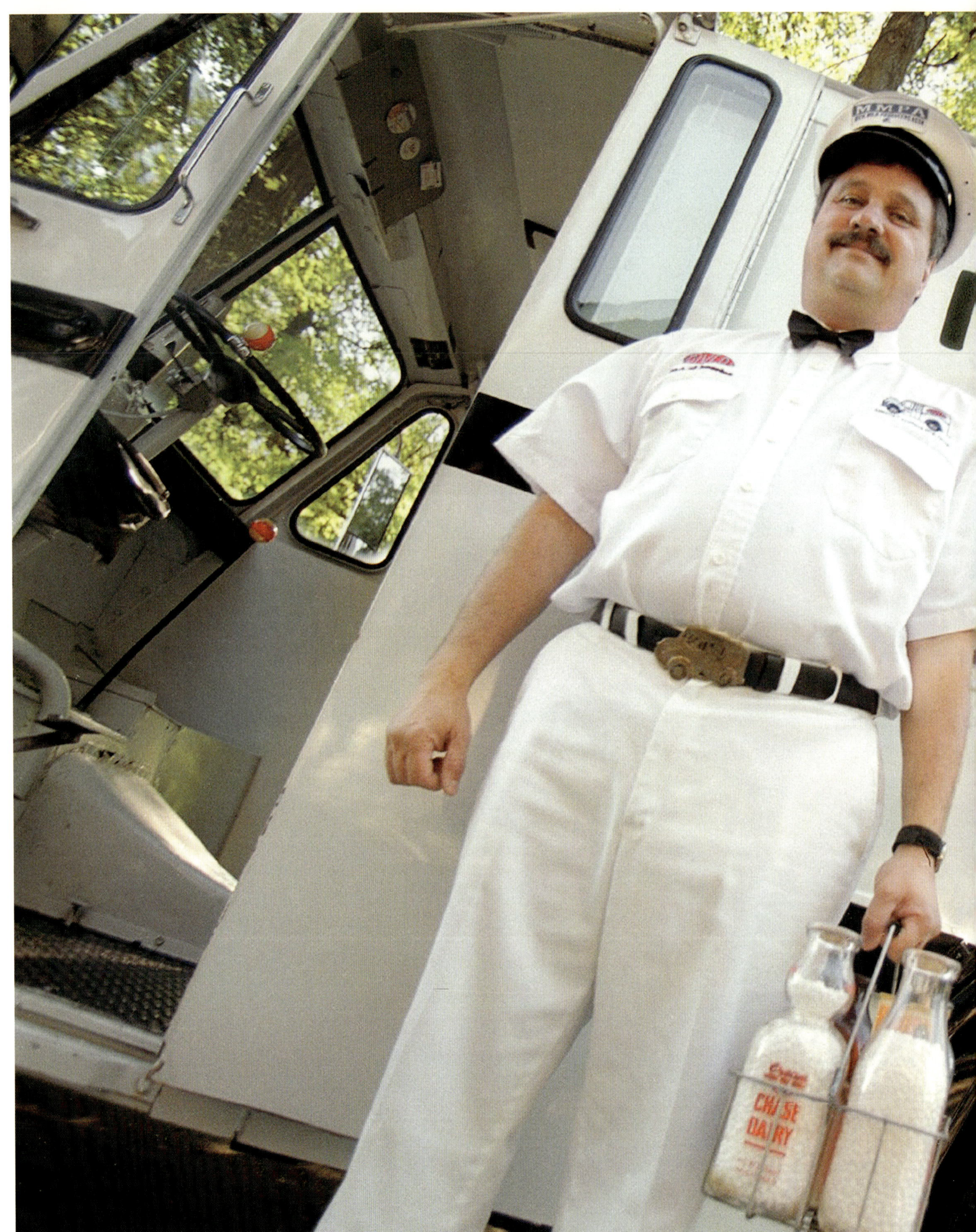
MMPA

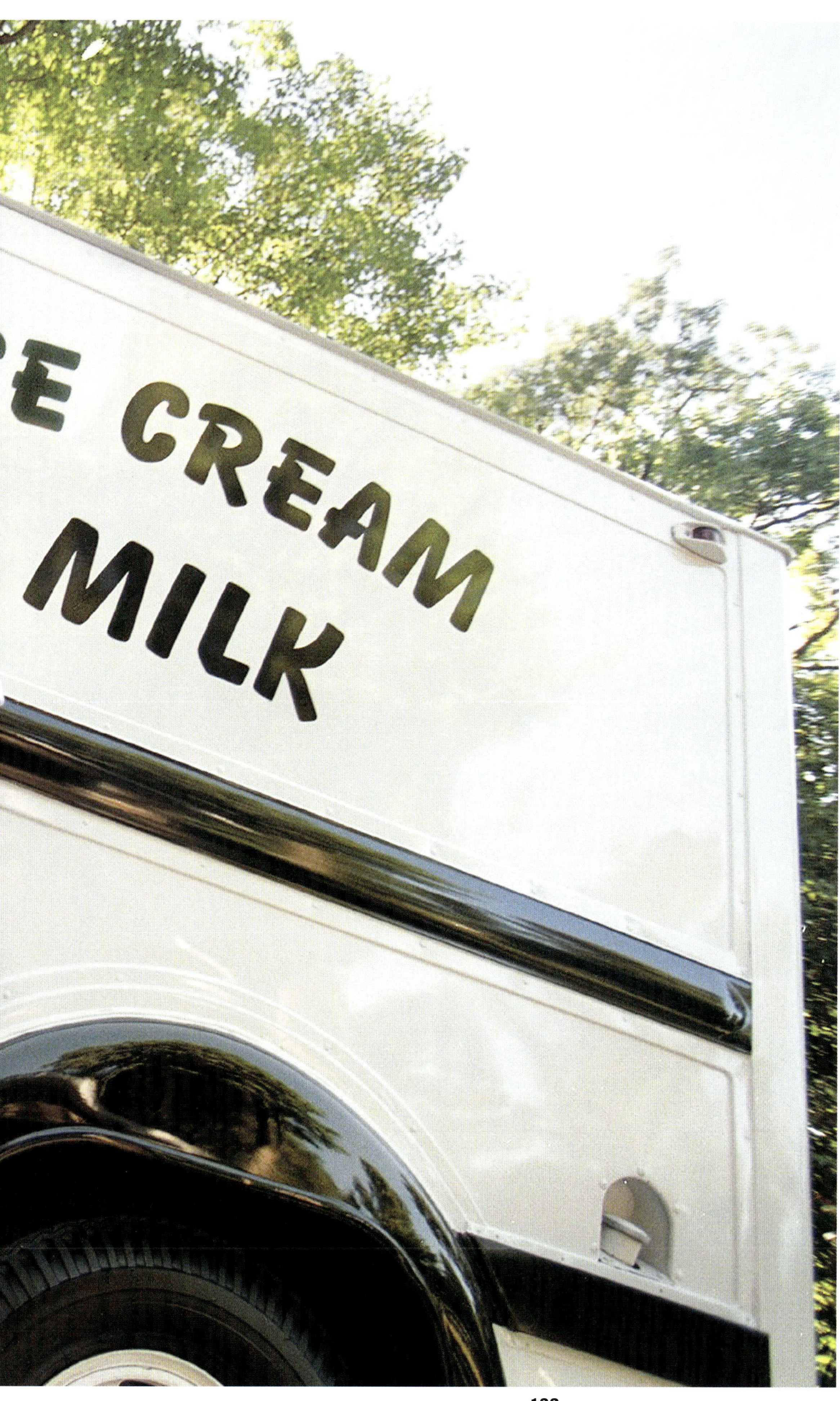

GOT MILK? Like homogenized milk, it is short on excitement. But, thank goodness, the Dream Cruise has no stuffy panel of judges to turn away this cool gulp of nostalgia. John Straight, 53, of Mt. Pleasant was ready to roll in Saturday's event. Dressing the part, he planned to cruise in his 38-year-old milk truck, crates of old glass bottles clinking behind him. This isn't just any old milk truck, he would tell you. It's a DIVCO, whose cult following included an owners club of 1,200 members and a Web site that proclaimed: "DIVCO trucks were once as much a part of the American way of life as baseball and Mom's apple pie." Straight's DIVCO was built in 1964. Tens of thousands of DIVCOs were manufactured in Warren from the late 1930s to 1960s by the Detroit Industrial Vehicle Co. In 1989, Straight rescued the milk truck when a Saginaw dairy was soon to scrap it. He paid $500, then invested $11,000 in its restoration.

TONY CEPAK/Special to the Free Press

WITH FRONT-ROW SEATS, from left, Leon Horne, 22, of Shelby Township; Steve Gott, 22, of Rochester Hills; Cathy Meyers, 19, of Shelby Township, and Susan Corbin of Royal Oak checked out Ohioan Tony Sablar's 1967 Chevy Super Sport Nova as it crept along Woodward.

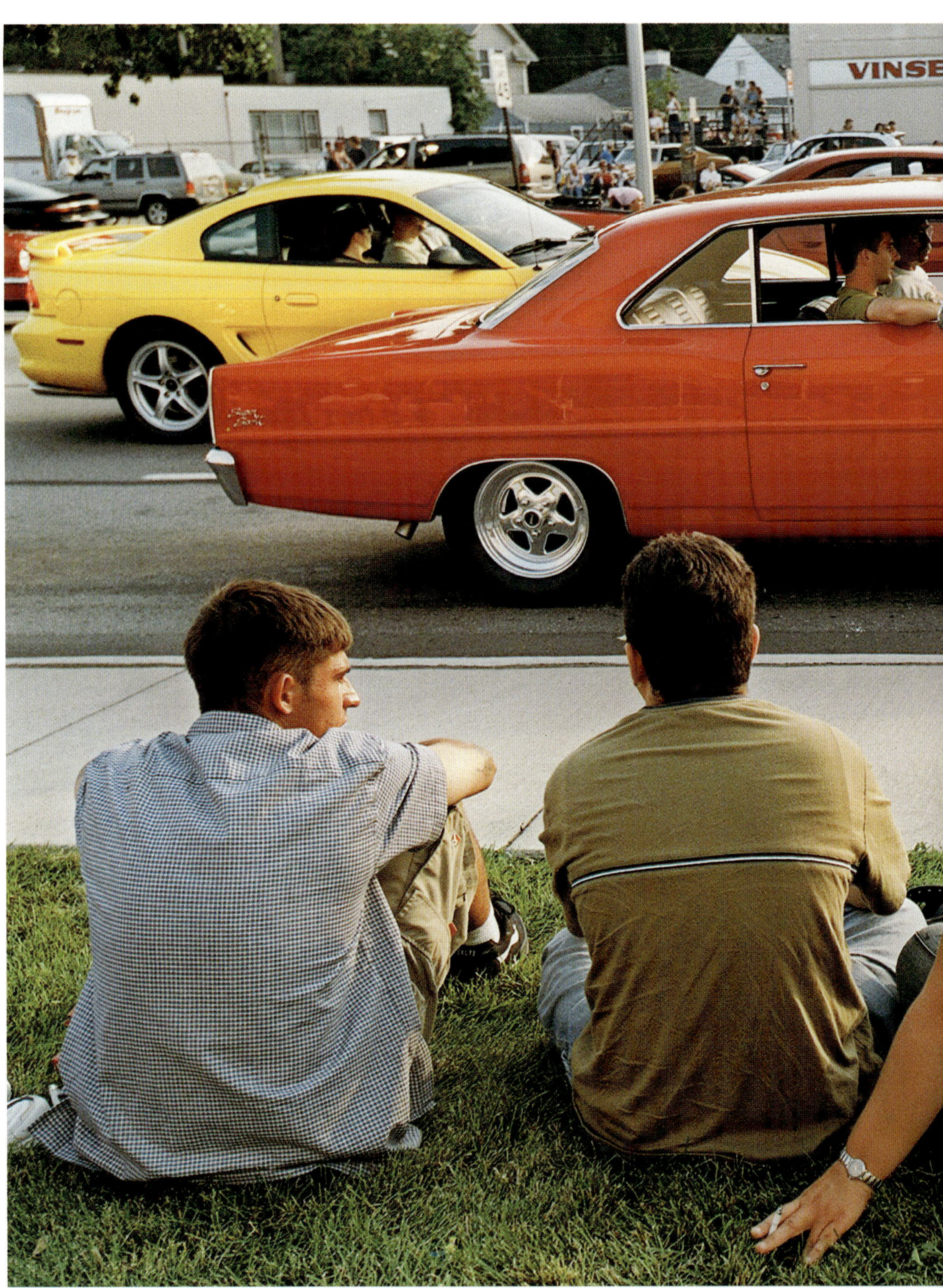

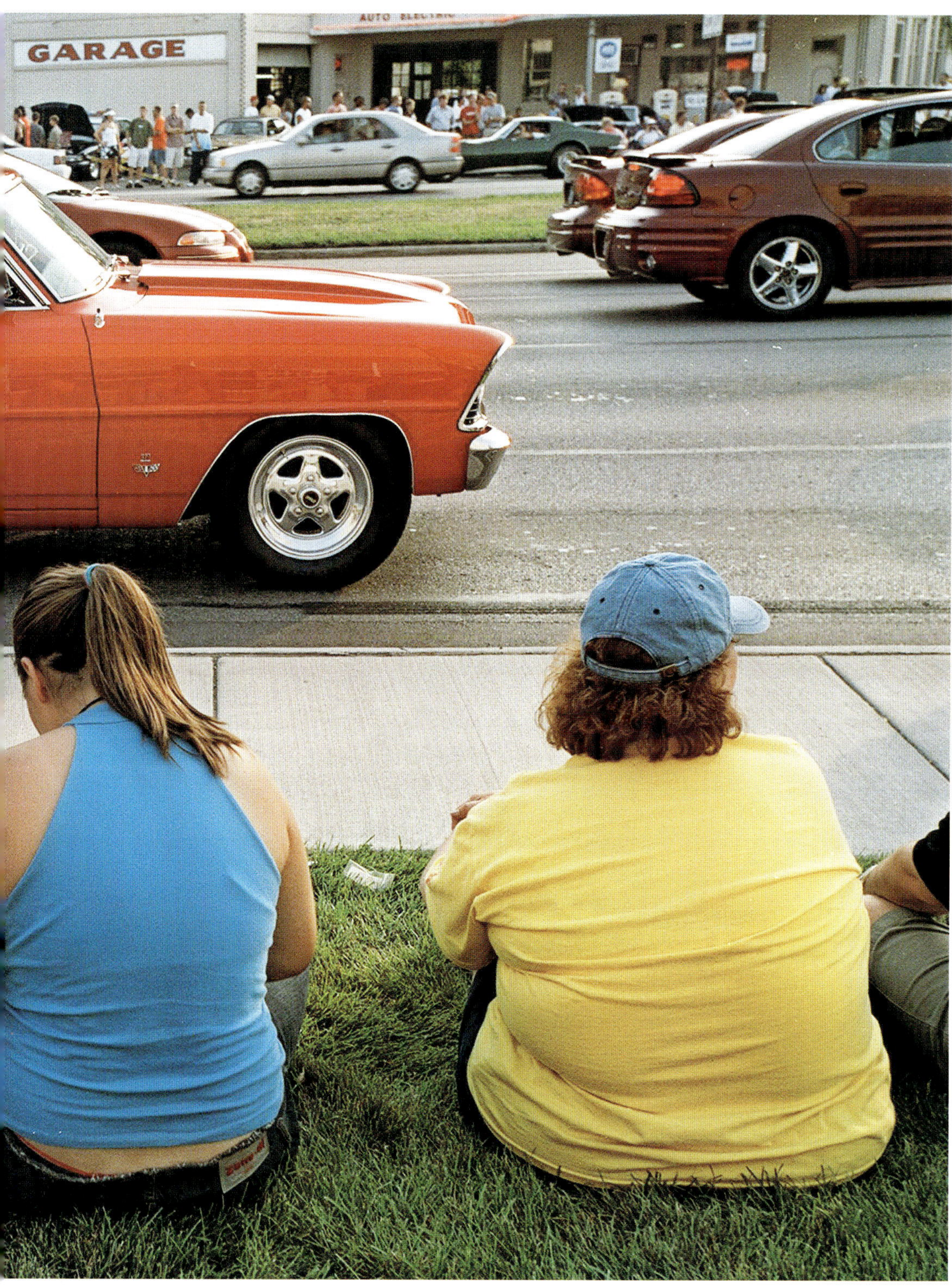

AMY LEANG

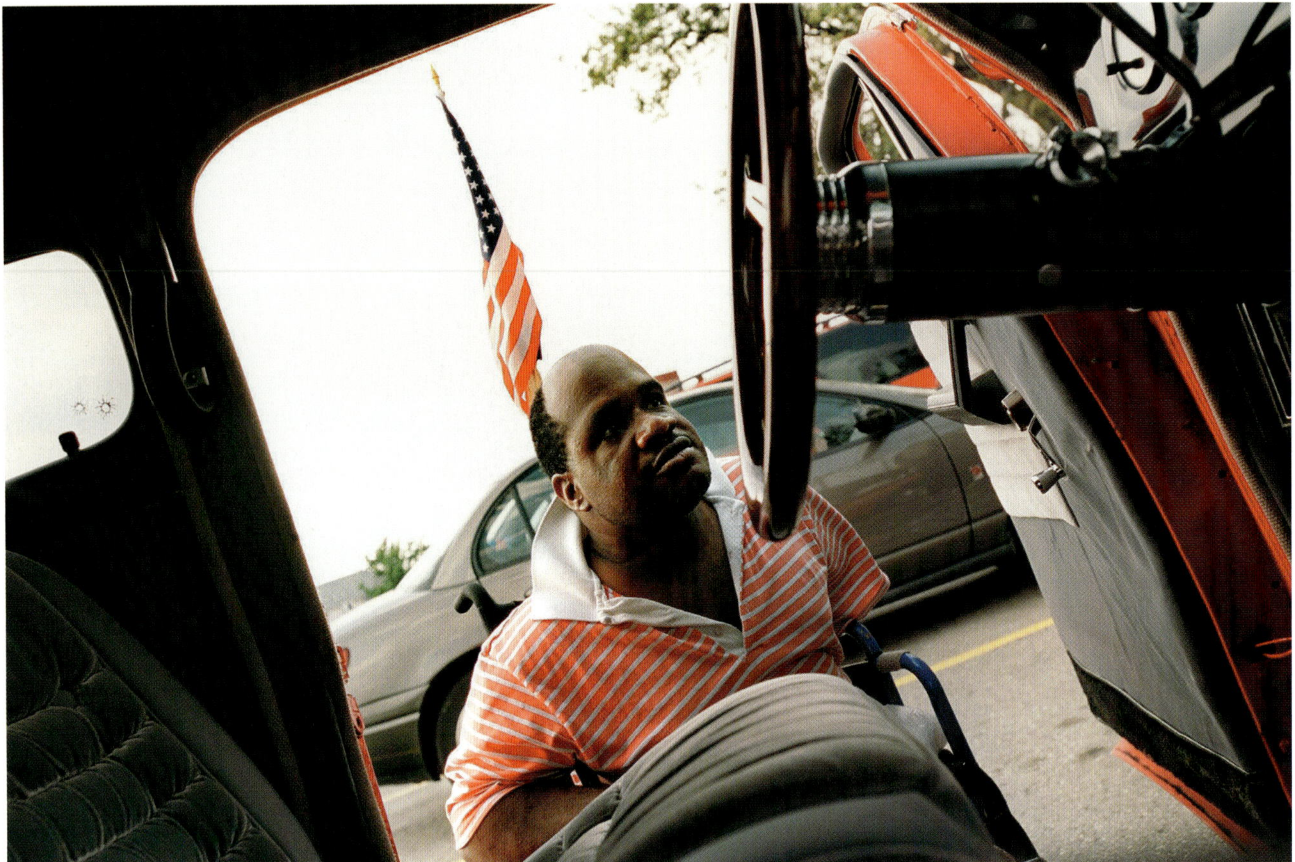

AMY LEANG

ABOVE: SOMETHING SPECIAL caught the attention of Beverly Hills resident Rodney Perry, who admired Richard Lang's 1938 Buick Special, which was on display in the Northwood Shopping Center parking lot at the southwest corner of 13 Mile and Woodward. It was the Tuesday before the cruise, and already, car enthusiasts had hit the strip to ogle the classics, talk engines and peek under someone else's hood. Lang began driving in from Chesterfield Township the previous Thursday, setting up early — popping the hood, shining the silver dice stem valves and dusting off the dash. As he sat back in his lawn chair, Lang, 52, explained what it's all about: "Sitting out here is like going back in time, when life was simple and relaxing. It's the highlight of my year, the one week I don't wear a watch — and let the time just breeze by."

RGHT: A CRUISE FAN PEEKED in the window of a 1939 Ford V8, which was powered by the company's historic flathead V8.

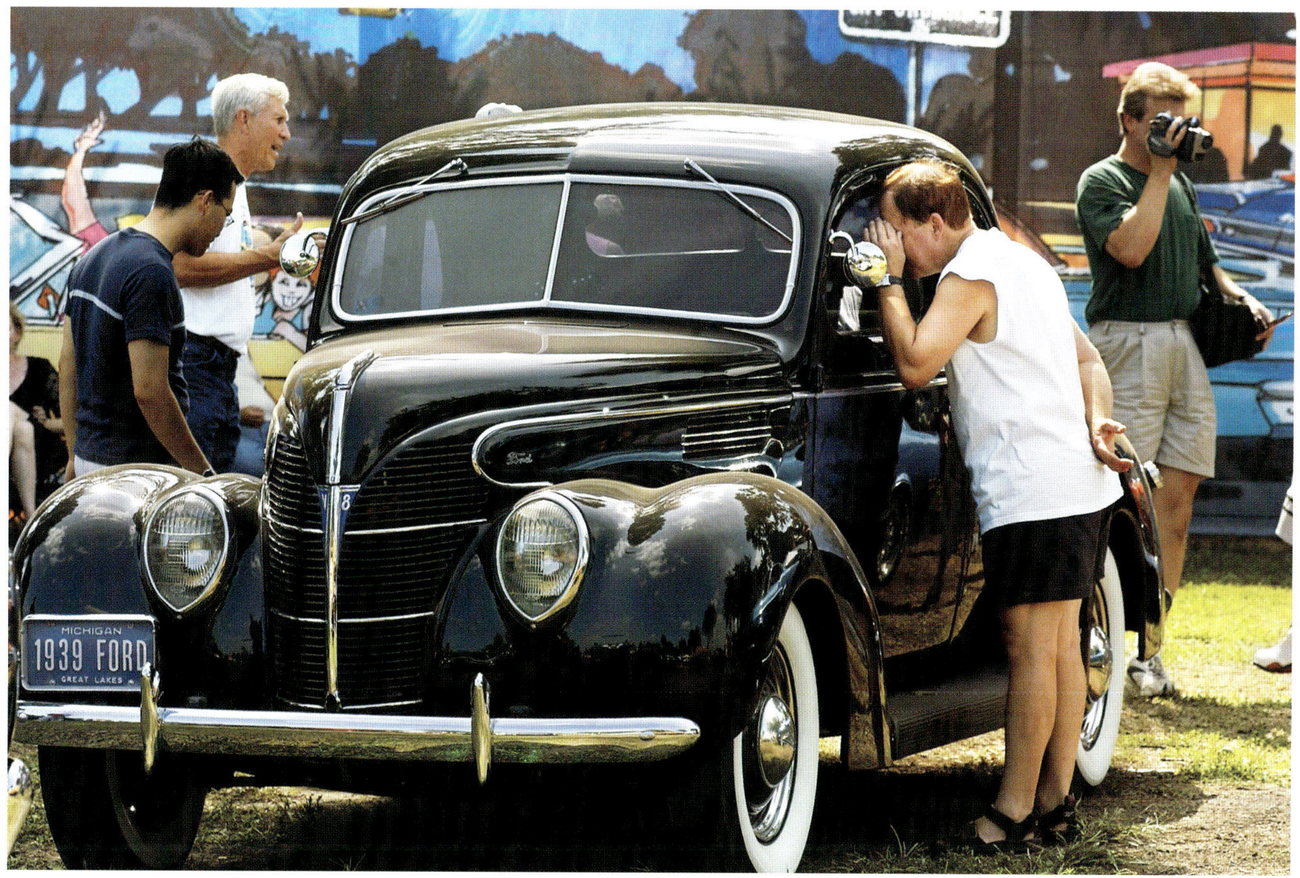

Above: WILLIAM ARCHIE; Next page: PAUL GONZALEZ VIDELA

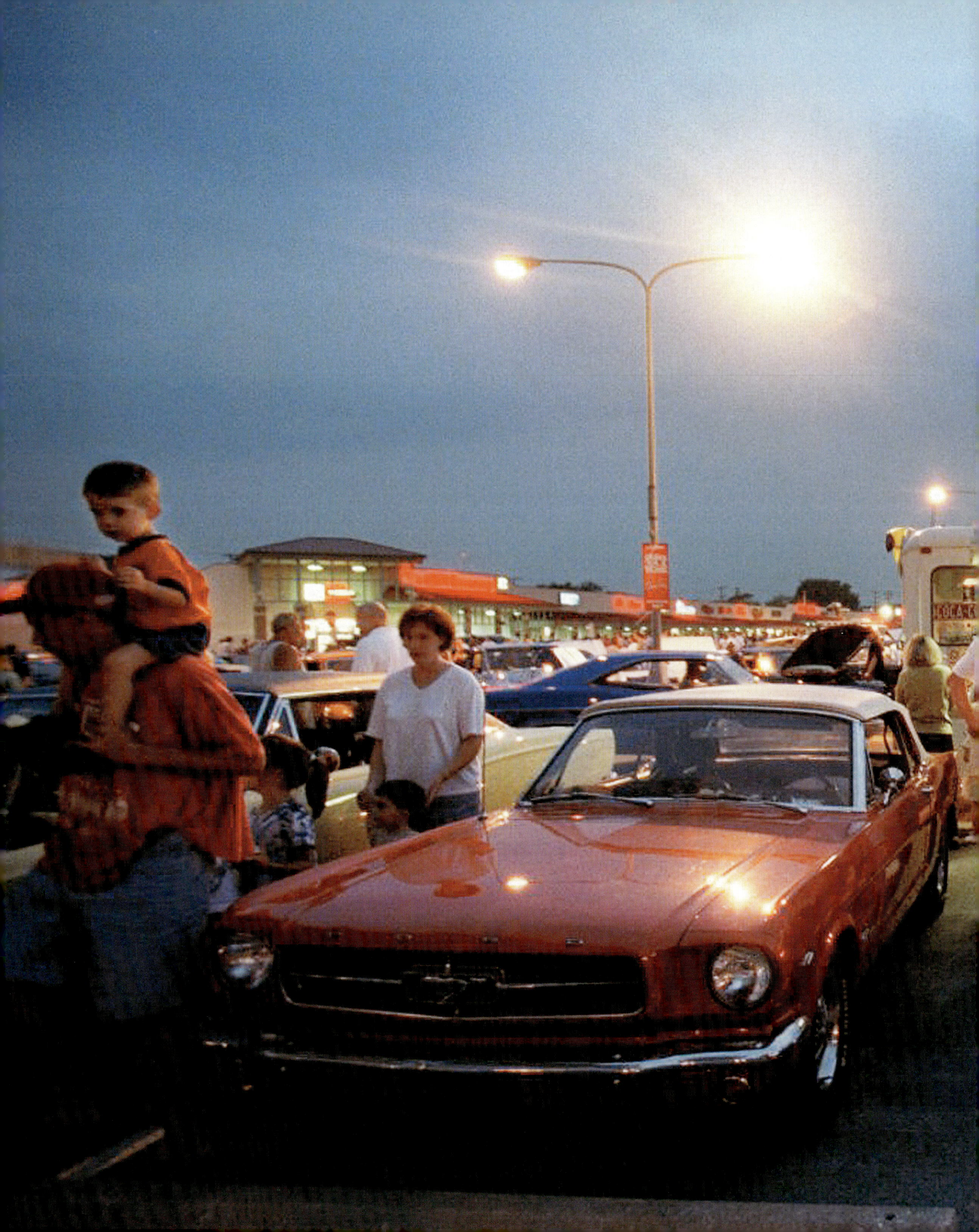

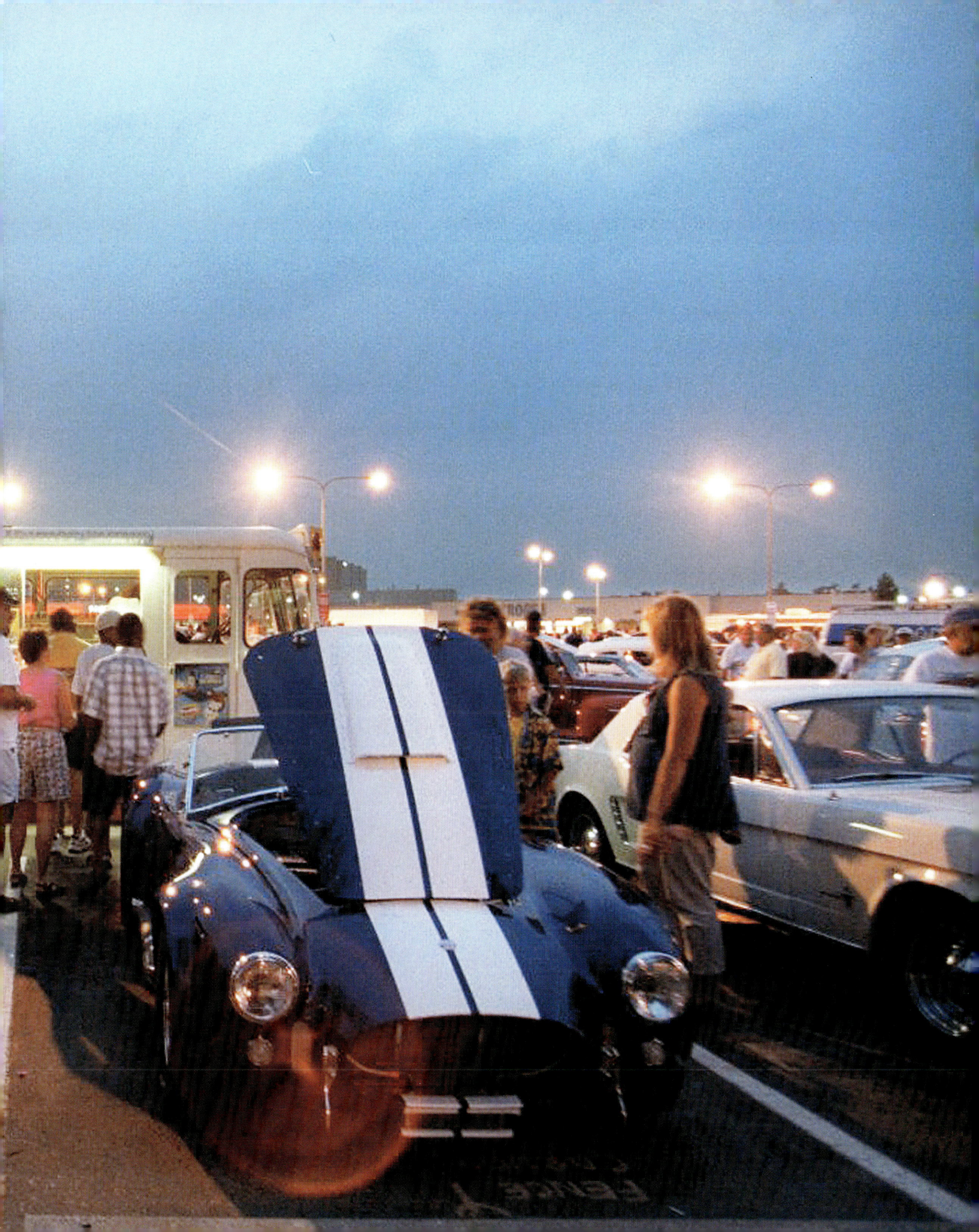

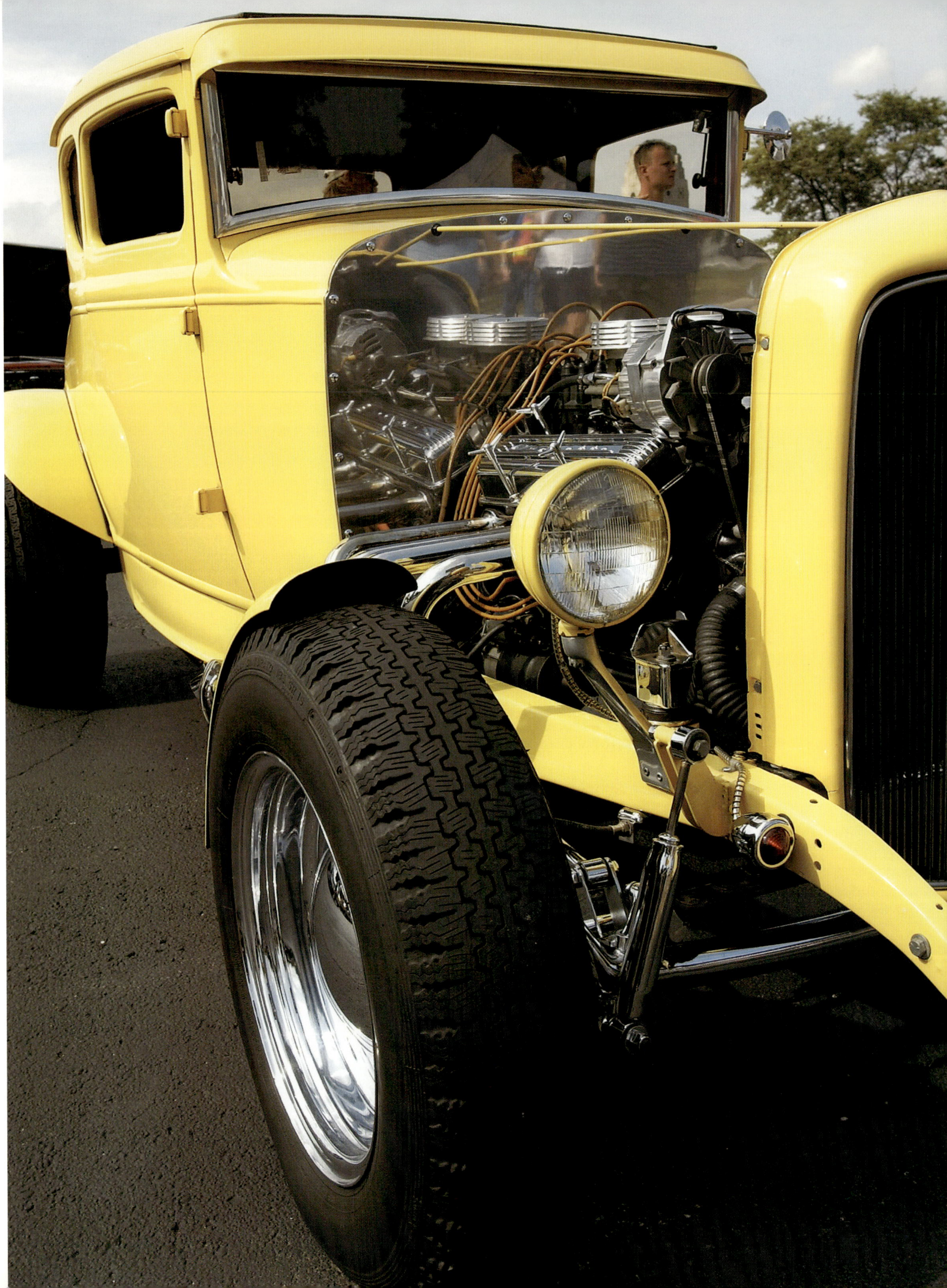

LEFT: HAND-BUILT, CHROME-TRIMMED engines like this one often elicit as much admiration as the hot rods they power.

PAGE 138: THE NORTHWOOD SHOPPING CENTER parking lot, packed on the Tuesday night before the cruise, was a favorite gathering spot this year, with early cruisers congregating there more than a month before the cruise, said Rod Dotten, a retired auto-body shop owner in Madison Heights. "Three or four hundred cars were showing up" at the shopping area's parking lot several nights each week. After police dispersed the impromptu cruise-ins, cruisers began limiting their gatherings, which revved up again in the pre-cruise week. "The bees are swarming early, so to speak." Still, the trend is clear for dream cruising to become a summer-long auto fling, said Dotten, who often cruised in his customized 1964 Buick Riviera.

PAGE 142: CAPTURING FORDS ON FILM, Frank Allen of Waterford videotaped Mustangs at a replica of a drive-in Saturday afternoon in Berkley. The big new draw at the eighth annual Woodward Dream Cruise might be the next best thing to the cars of yesteryear: old-fashioned drive-in food. And serving up the scads of snow cones, hot dogs and ice cream were the pioneers of mass production, Ford Motor Co. Ford, in a 3-year deal to be Berkley's major Dream Cruise sponsor, agreed to place a retro-looking drive-in eatery on Woodward, evoking classic Woodward burger shrines like the Wig Wam in Pleasant Ridge and Ted's in Bloomfield Township. Surrounding the Ford drive-in were a collection of classic Ford Mustangs, hot rods and other cars.

Left: WILLIAM ARCHIE; Next page: AMY LEANG

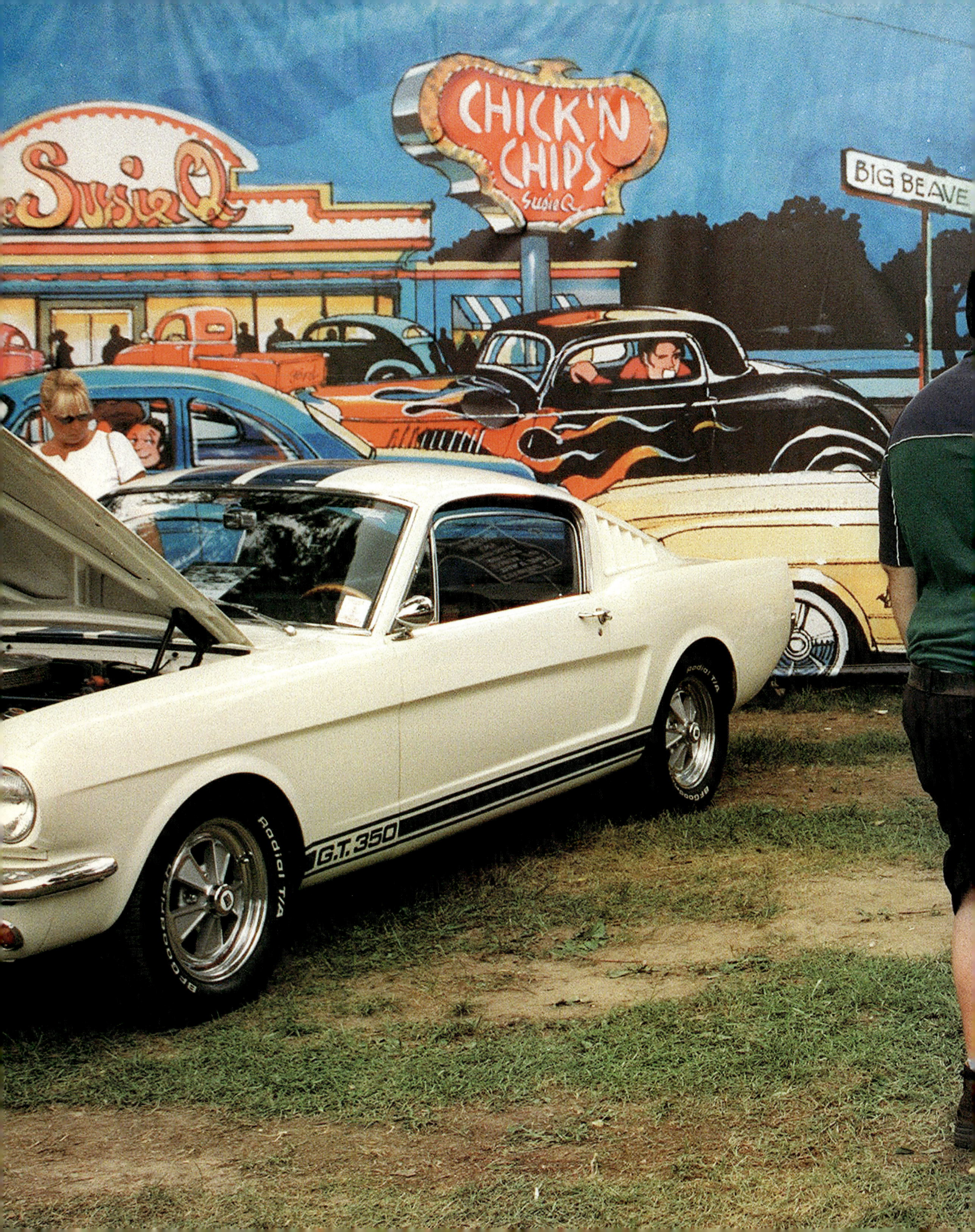

Susie Q
CHICK'N CHIPS
Susie Q
BIG BEAVE
G.T. 350
Radial T/A
BFGoodrich

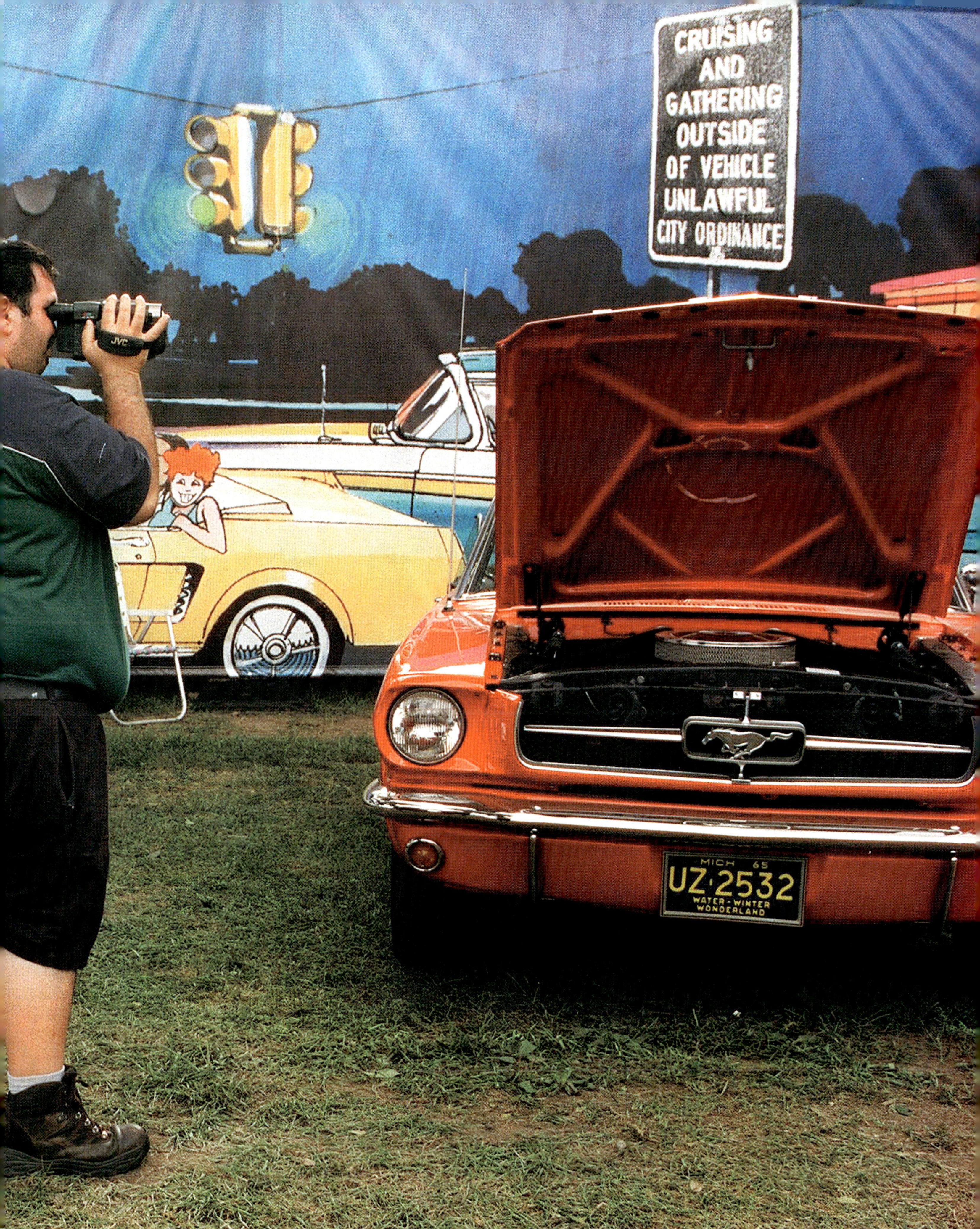
CRUISING
AND
GATHERING
OUTSIDE
OF VEHICLE
UNLAWFUL
CITY ORDINANCE
JVC
MICH 65
UZ·2532
WATER-WINTER
WONDERLAND

Date: Aug. 16

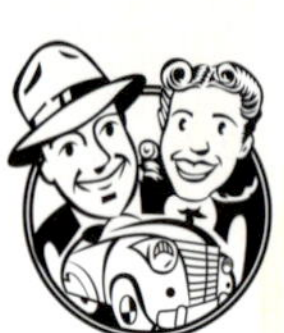

Attendance: 1.1 million and 40,000 classic cars — a dip partly caused by the first-ever downpours.

Special moment: Despite the Blackout of 2003, the cruise went on as planned.

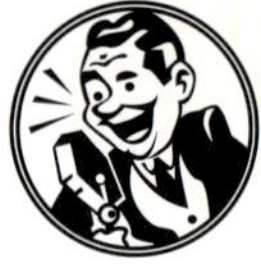

Making history: Woodward was named a Michigan Heritage Route and National Scenic Byway with the slogan, "Cruisin' the Original — Woodward Avenue."

Looking ahead: A king and queen will be crowned for the first time in 2004, celebrating their participation in the event, their love of cars, their sense of fun and their cruising attitude.

2003

THE BIG BLACKOUT OF 2003 COULDN'T STOP THE CRUISE. Fans dubbed it "Dream Cruise unplugged."

A cascading power failure, the biggest in the nation's history, forced cruisers to drive for hours from Detroit to find gas stations with working pumps, then stock backseat ice chests because most restaurants near Woodward were closed.

Dream Cruise publicist Linda Ashley recalled, "People were calling from Ohio, Ontario, Idaho, all over, and they'd ask, 'Is there going to be a Dream Cruise?' "

The outage "just didn't faze them," she said.

There were torrential rains, too — a first in the history of the event. But owners of the classics merely ran for cover, then emerged as the rain eased to wipe down their cars.

Many said they liked 2003's smaller event, when attendance dropped to a mere 1.1 million. To keep 2004's much-ballyhooed 10th anniversary event that small, better pray for another power outage ... and snow.

And even that might not keep the car lovers away. This is, after all, the greatest one-day car event in the world.

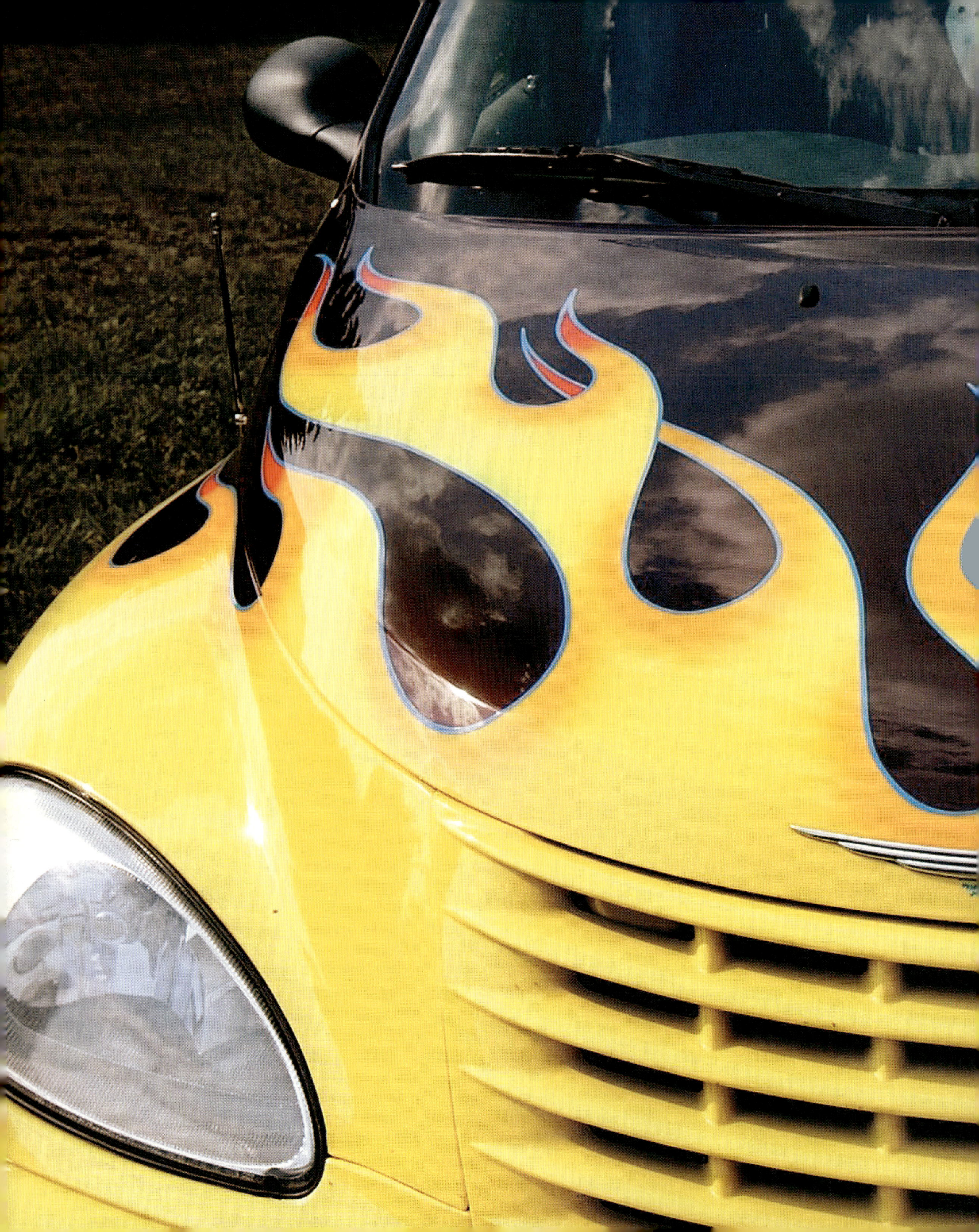

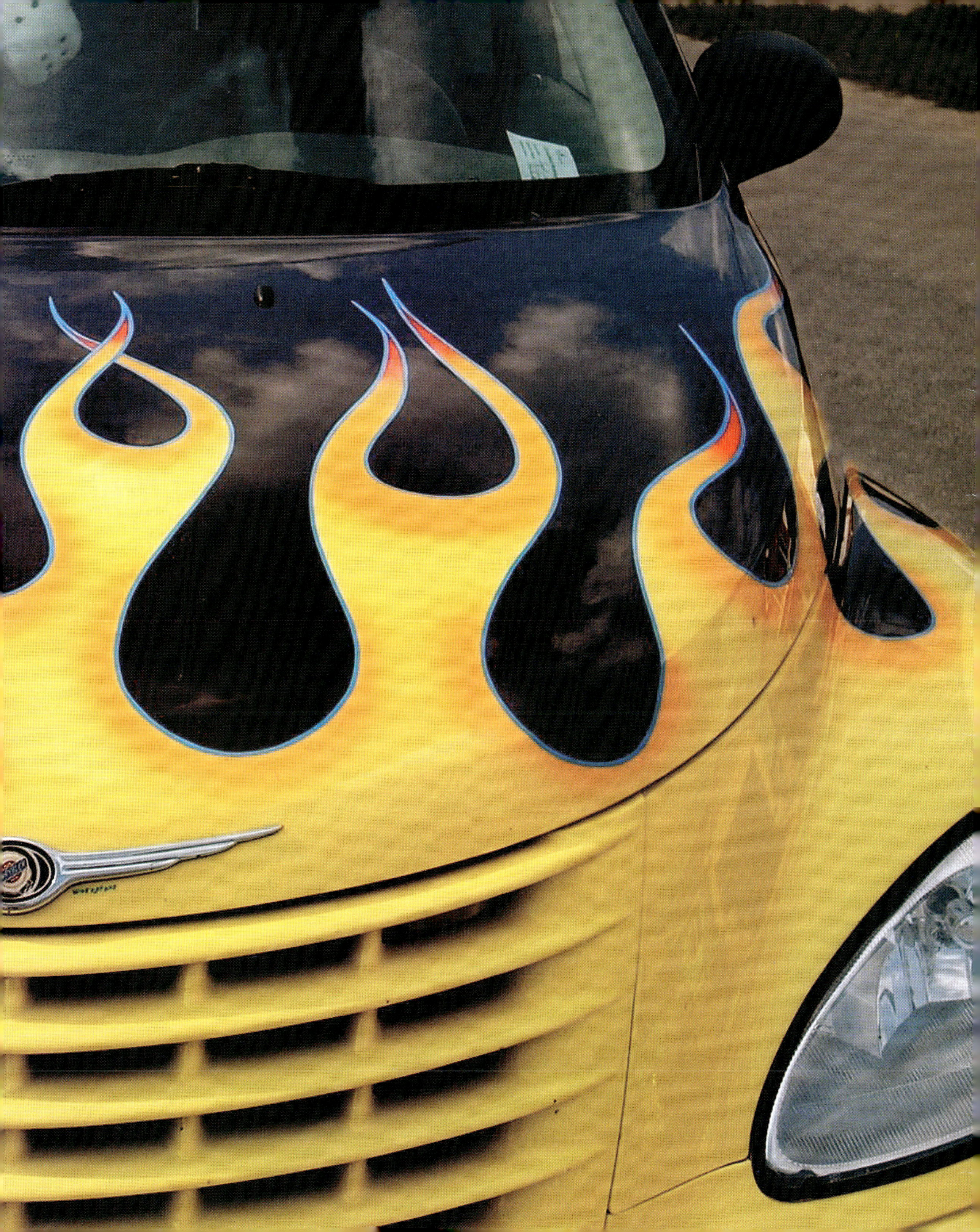

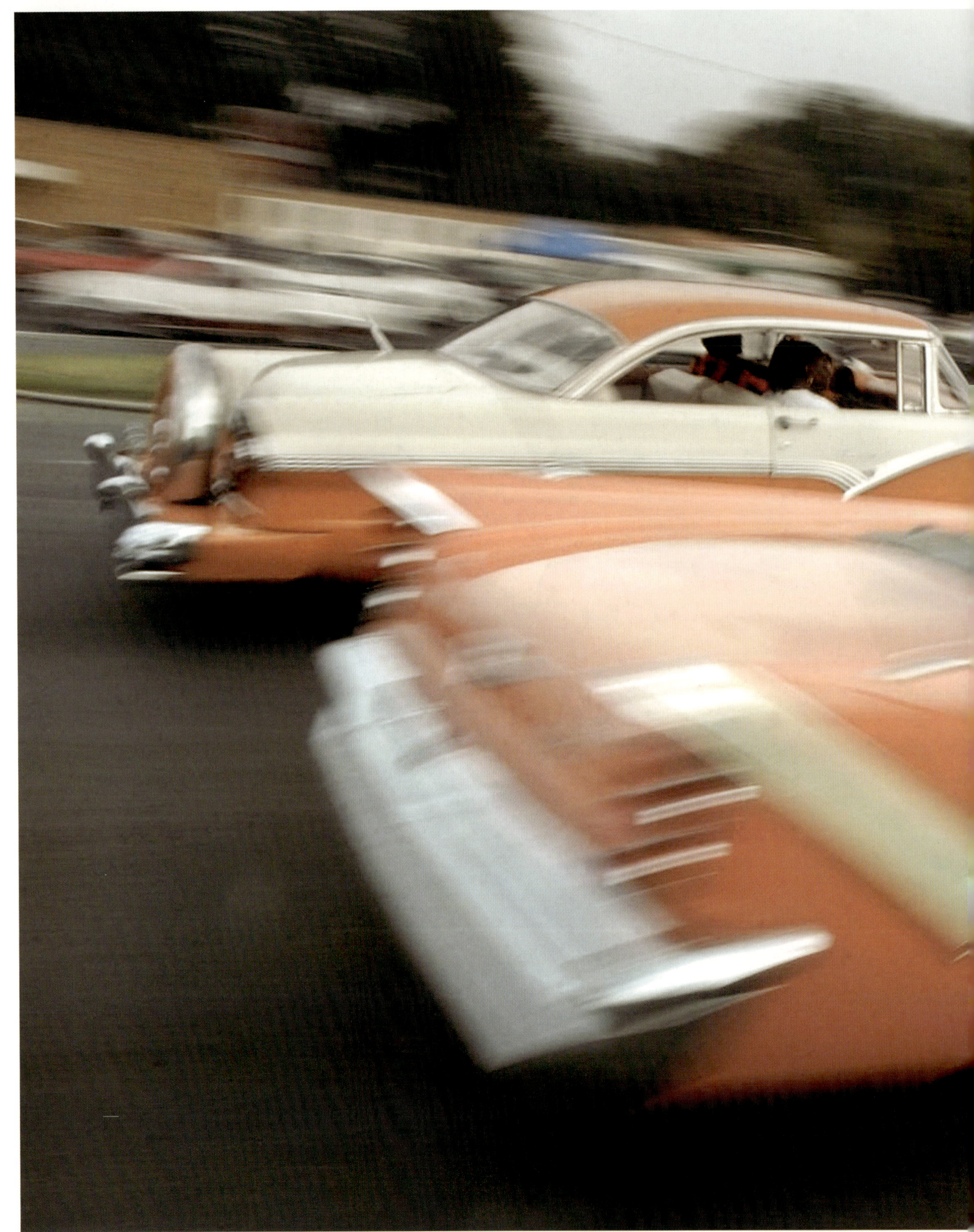

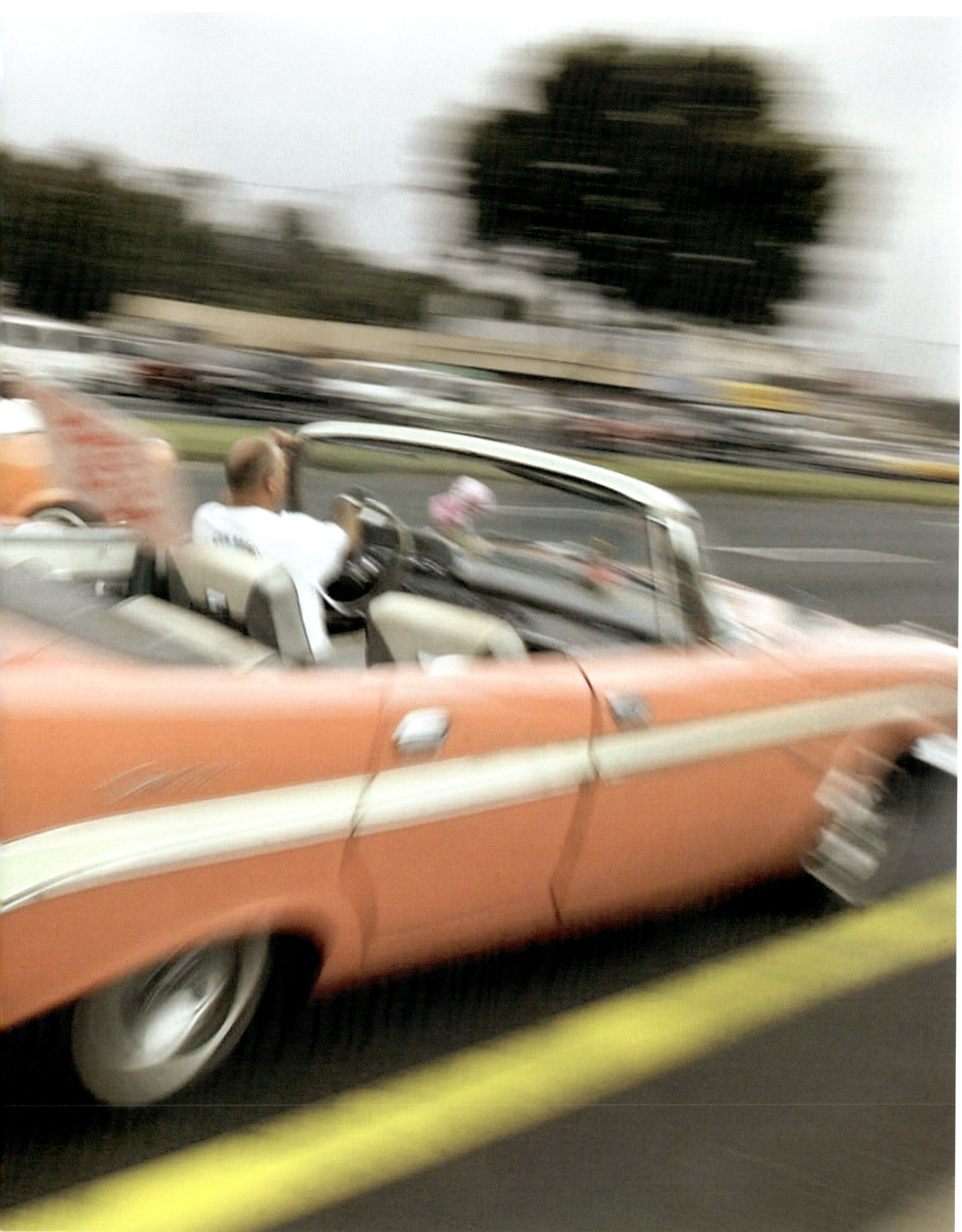

Previous page: SUSAN TUSA; Above: WILLIAM ARCHIE

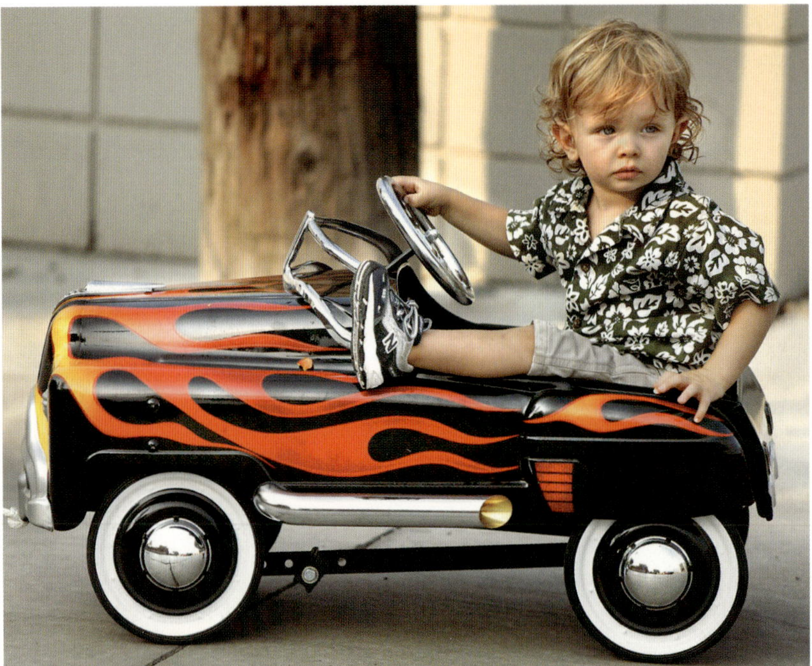

Above and right: J. KYLE KEENER

ABOVE: AFTER WATCHING THE CRUISE with his parents, Henry Stackpoole, 1, steered his little hot rod toward his home. Henry hasn't been cruising long enough to master the pedals, so Mom and Dad — Cristine and Pete Stackpoole of Birmingham — helped by pulling him along.

RIGHT: "EVERYONE JUST LOVES THIS EVENT," the Rev. Doug Jones, a cruise organizer, said — even when there's no power. Not having electricity didn't stop Connie DeKlerk, 38, of Bloomfield Hills, left, and her friends from having fun. Standing in front of her home, they tried to coax muscle cars to stop, hoping the drivers would speed away with squealing tires. With her are, from left, Kristy Williams, 30, of Metamora; Lena DesJardins, 26, of Livonia, and Shannon Dexter, 34, of Davison. Police frown on such antics. But far more of a worry are the cruise watchers and drivers who pour bleach on the road. When hot tires spin on bleach, then Royal Oak Police Chief Theodore Quisenberry said, it turns to smoke, and occasionally flames. Rapidly spinning tires grab the pavement, and a driver can lose control.

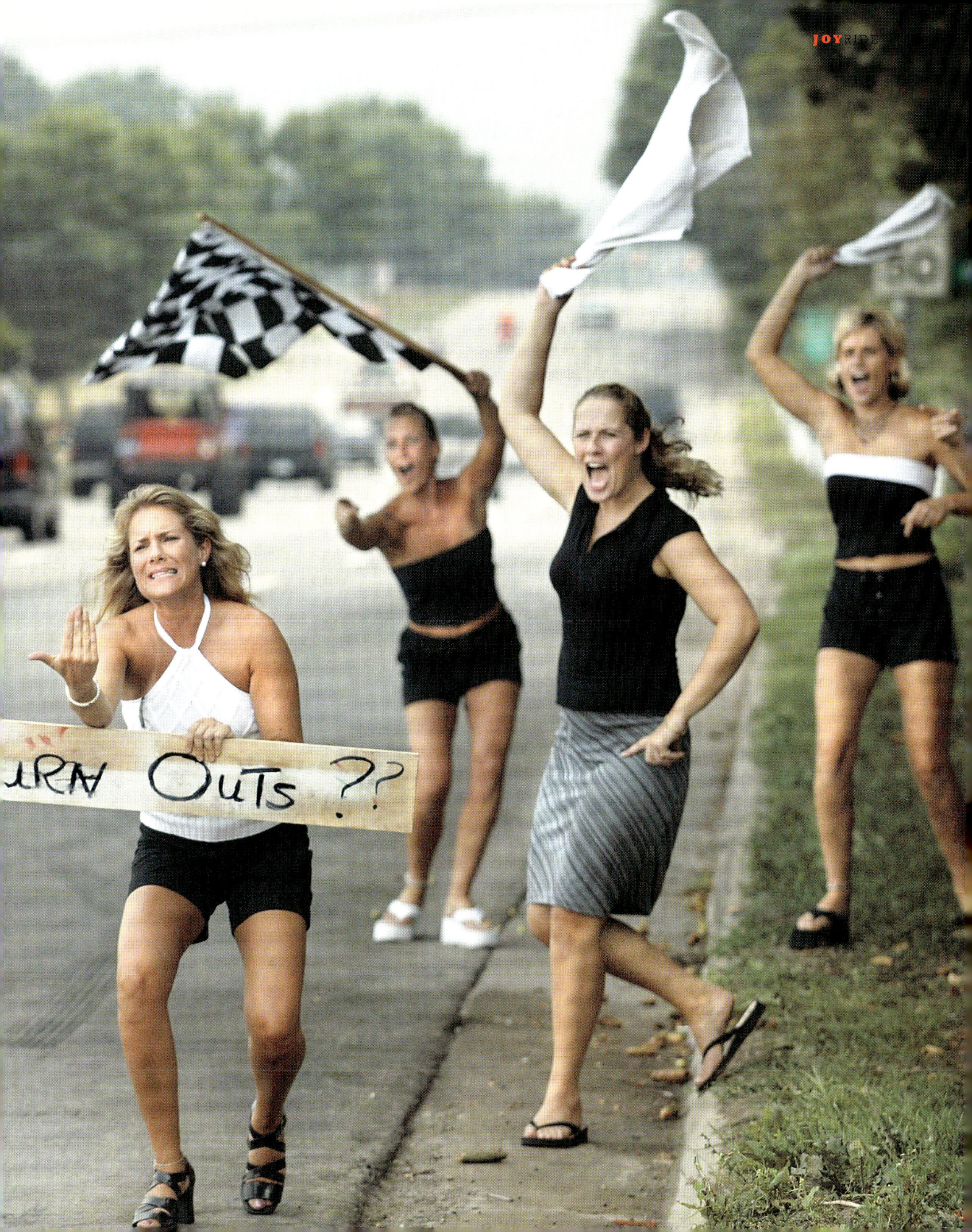
OuTs ??

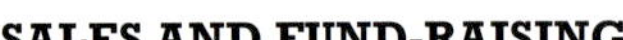

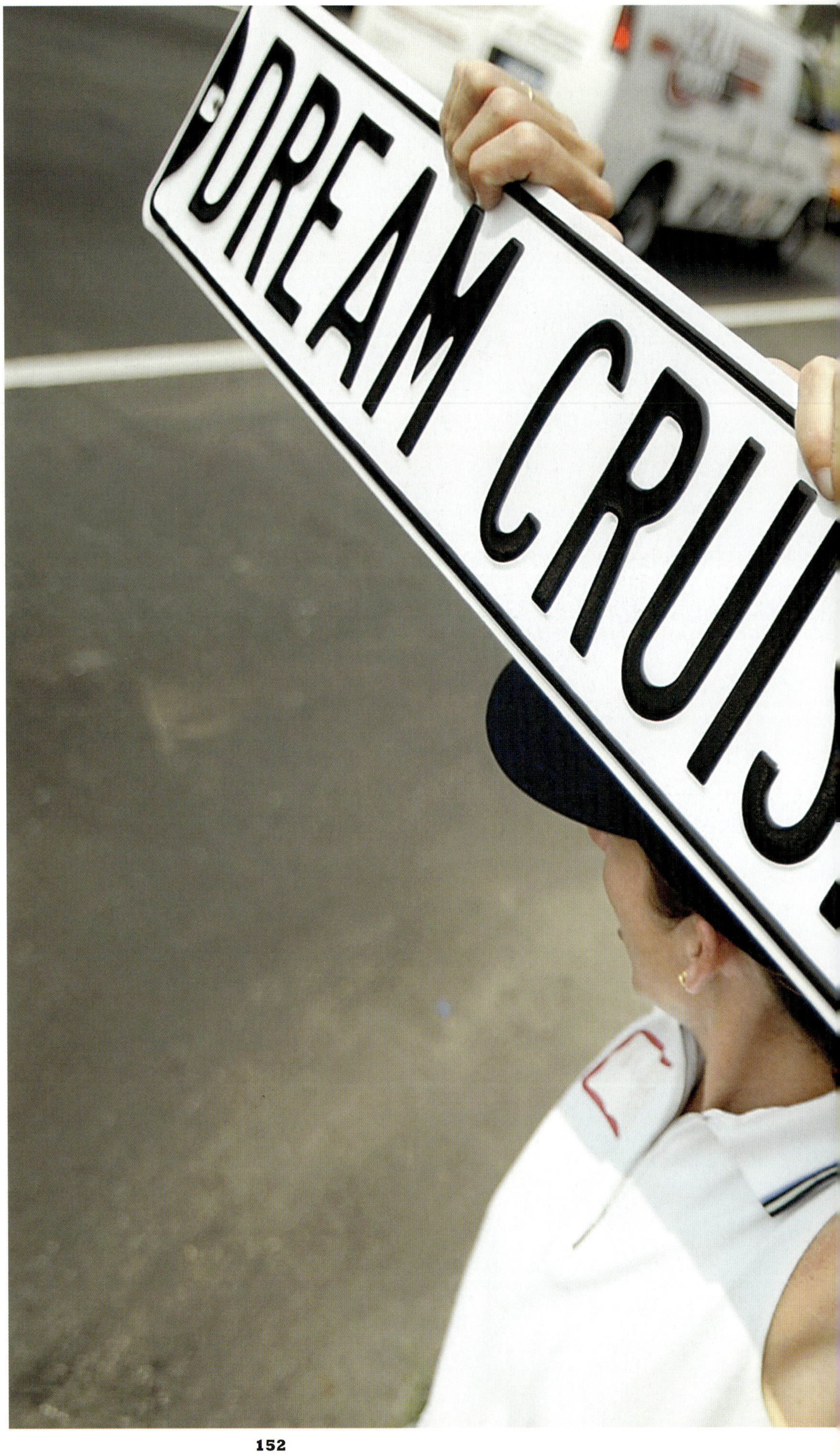

SALES AND FUND-RAISING were slow this year at the Dream Cruise, thanks to thunderstorms, heat and humidity that reduced the crowd for the first time ever. Margaret Steward of Royal Oak was among those selling signs and other merchandise along the route in Royal Oak. Proceeds benefitted schools and other charities. The cruise was a marketing success. A professor at the University of Detroit Mercy started a course on it in the fall, exploring how a modest fund-raiser for a children's soccer field grew into a juggernaut. "It's just been an incredible phenomenon," professor Michael Bernacci said. What's the big draw? The dream, said student Gabriela Hinojosa, 21, of Allen Park. "The whole nostalgia thing . . . basically sells itself."

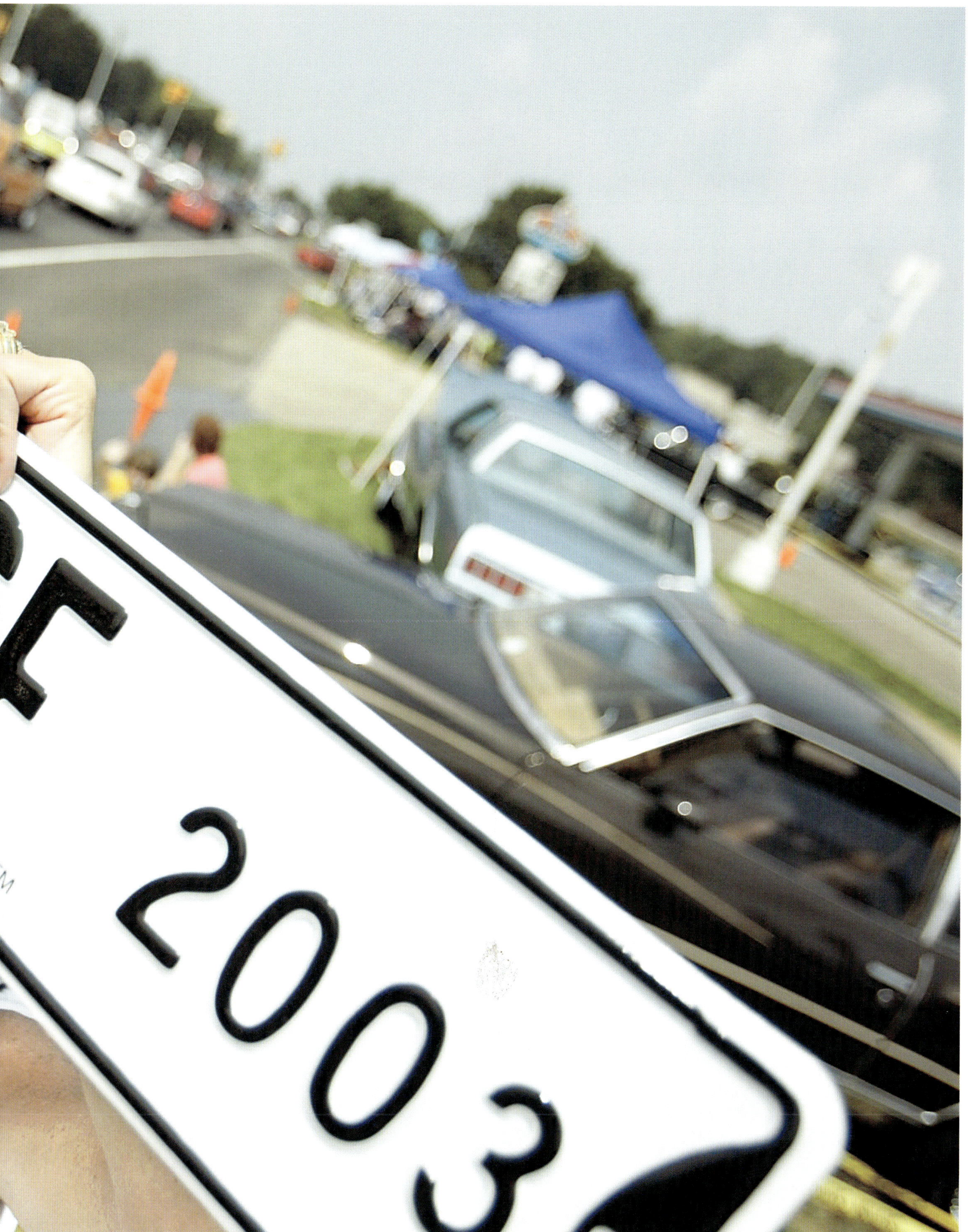

ROMAIN BLANQUART

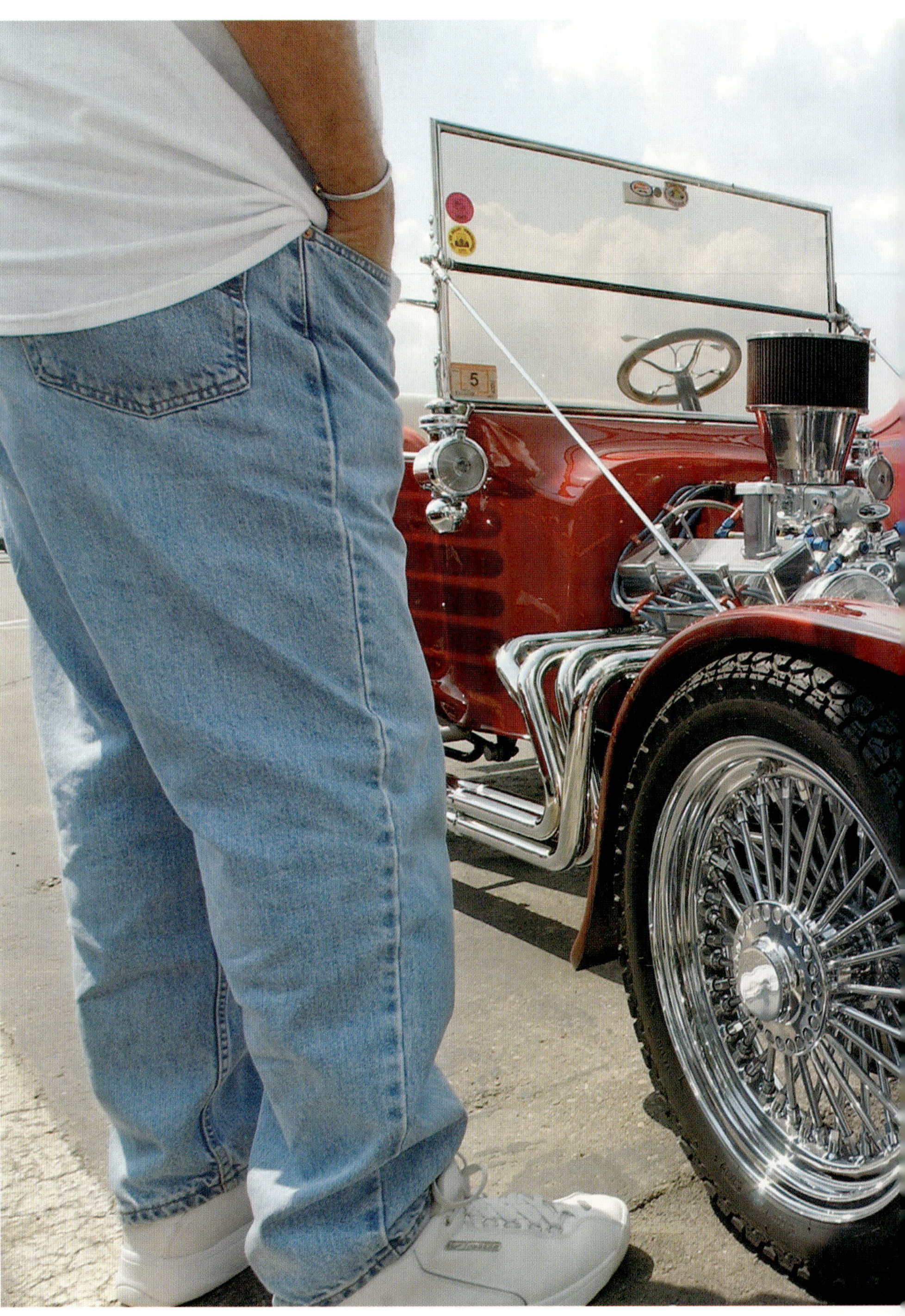

TWO THOUSAND THREE

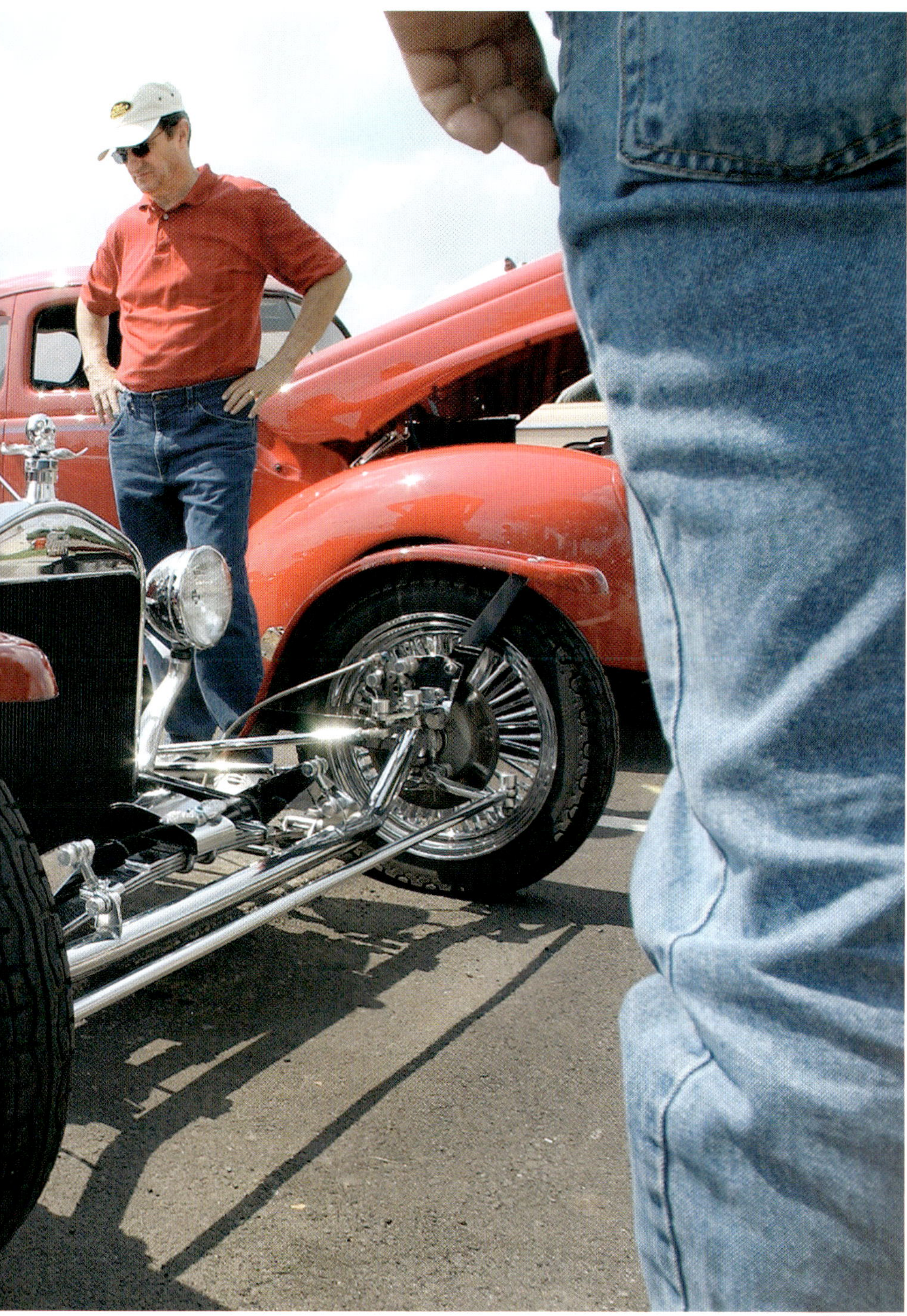

PATRICIA BECK

THREE DAYS BEFORE THE CRUISE, Andy Fontana, 60, of Shelby Township checked out a 23T — a 1923 modified Model T hot rod — at the Northwood Shopping Center at 13 Mile and Woodward.

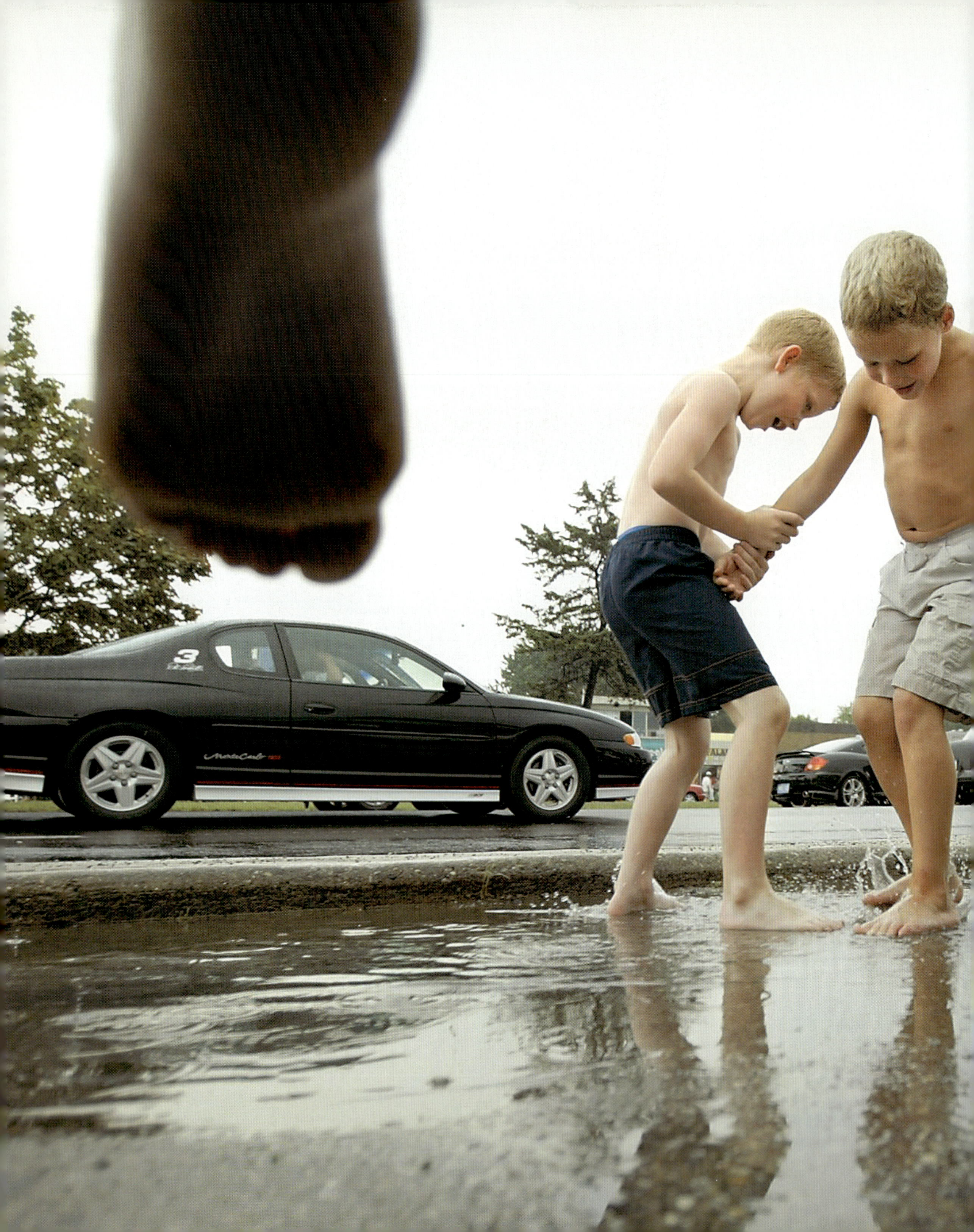
3

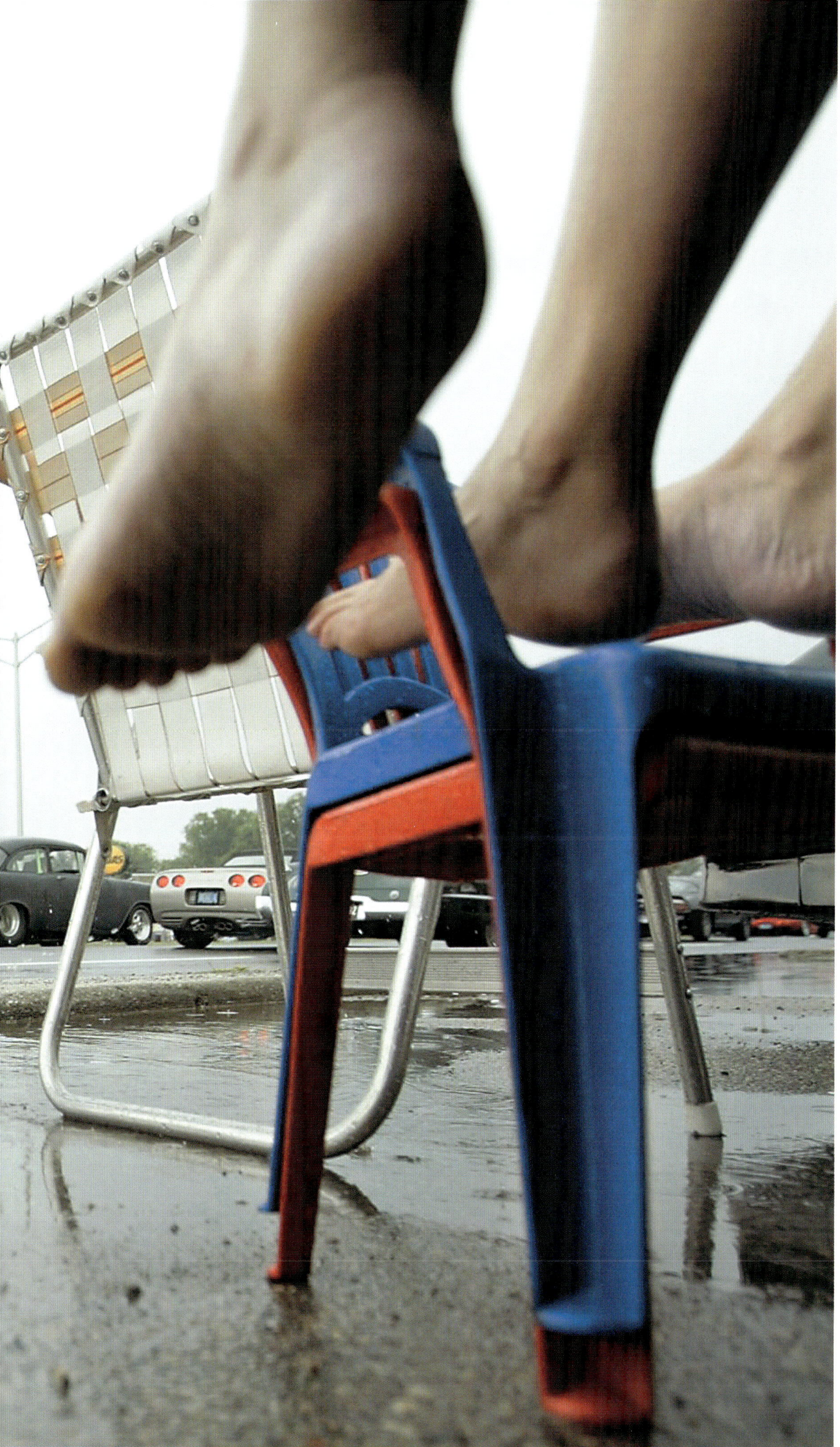

MOST PEOPLE AT THE DREAM CRUISE focused on the cars, but playing in a puddle was more fun for 6-year-olds Gregory Willett, left, and Cameron Gwinn, both from Waterford. About a million people attended the cruise; some lined sidewalks along Woodward from Ferndale to Pontiac to see thousands of classics. Joann Marts, 44, of Ypsilanti appreciated that the event was less crowded this year. "It was a lot less congested," said then Sgt. Michael Bunting of the Pleasant Ridge police force. "There were a lot less cruisers and a lot more average, up-to-date cars."

ROMAIN BLANQUART

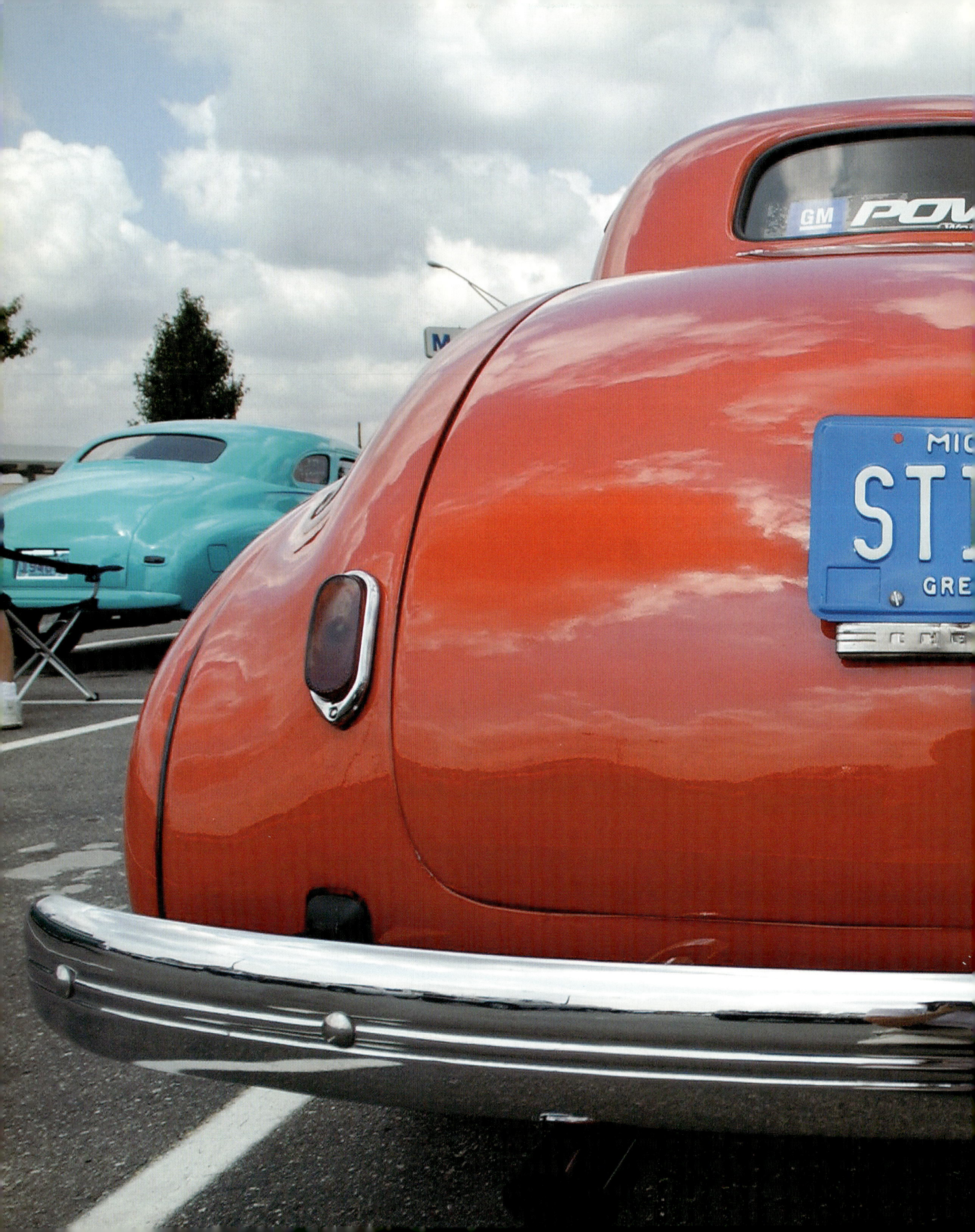
GM

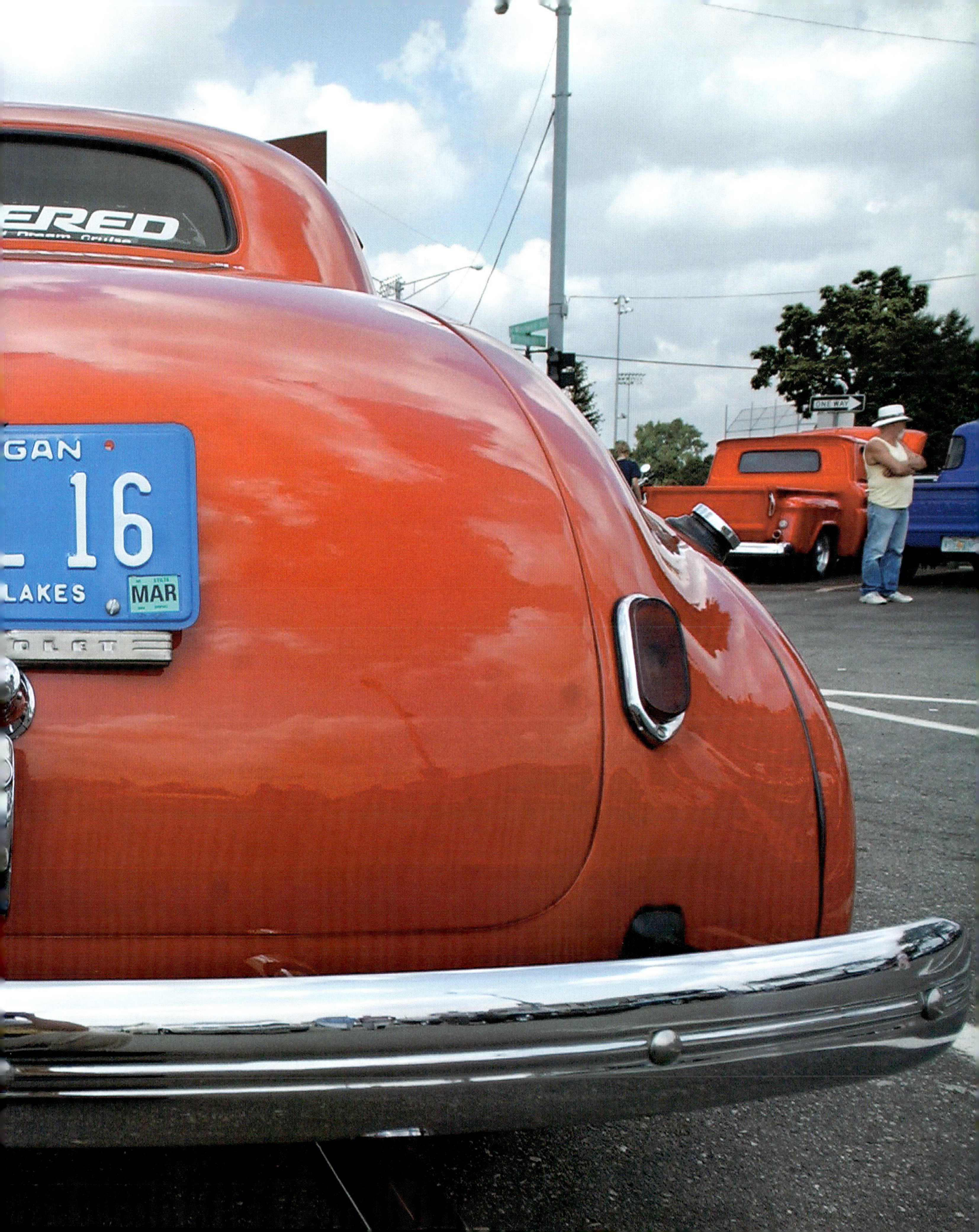
ERED
GAN
16
LAKES
MAR
ONE WAY

STEVE WINKLER OF WARREN rode his 1903 high-wheeled bike next to a 1953 two-door Manhattan Kaiser Fraiser. "I don't have a fancy car, so I ride my bicycle."

Previous page: PATRICIA BECK; Right: ROMAIN BLANQUART

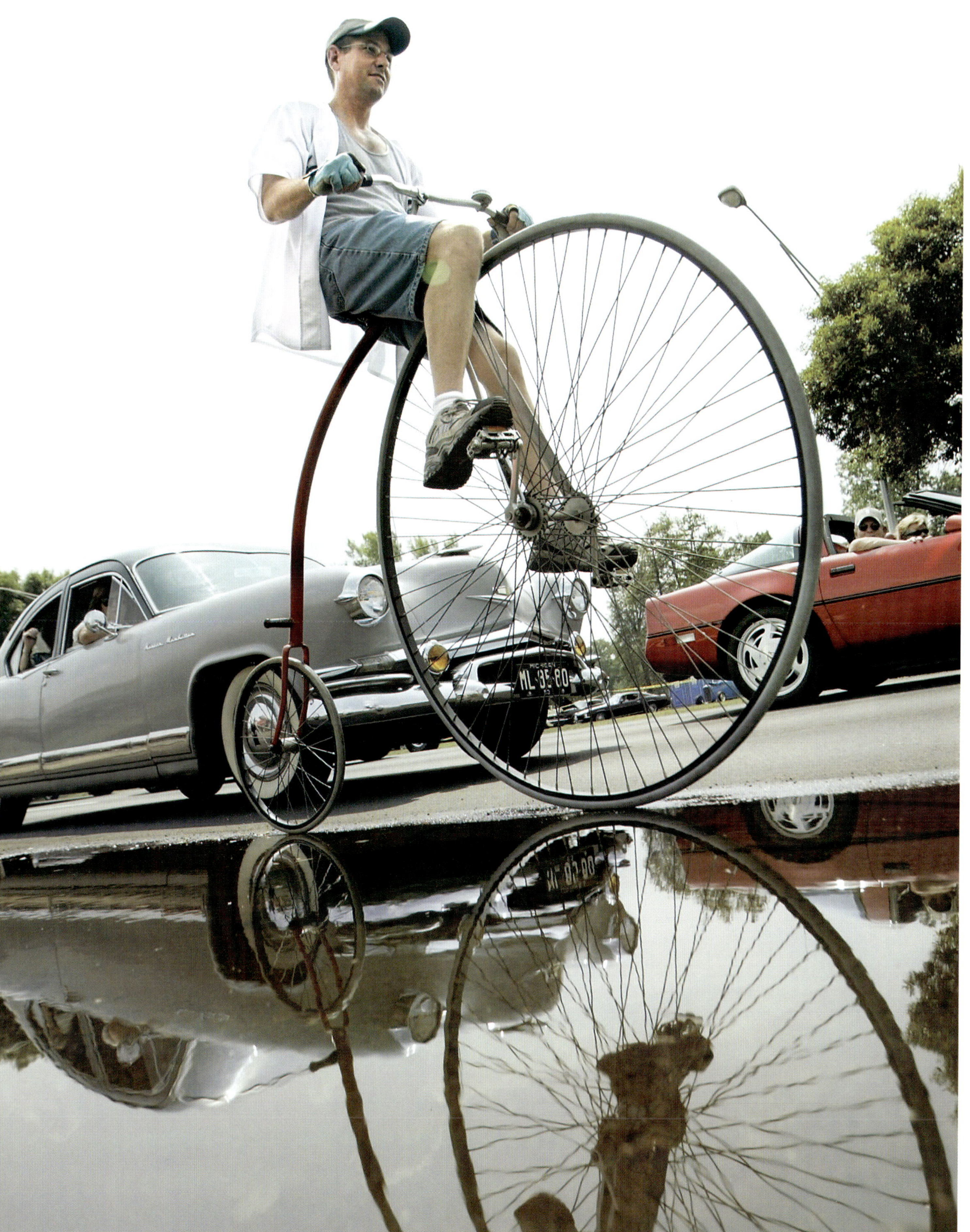

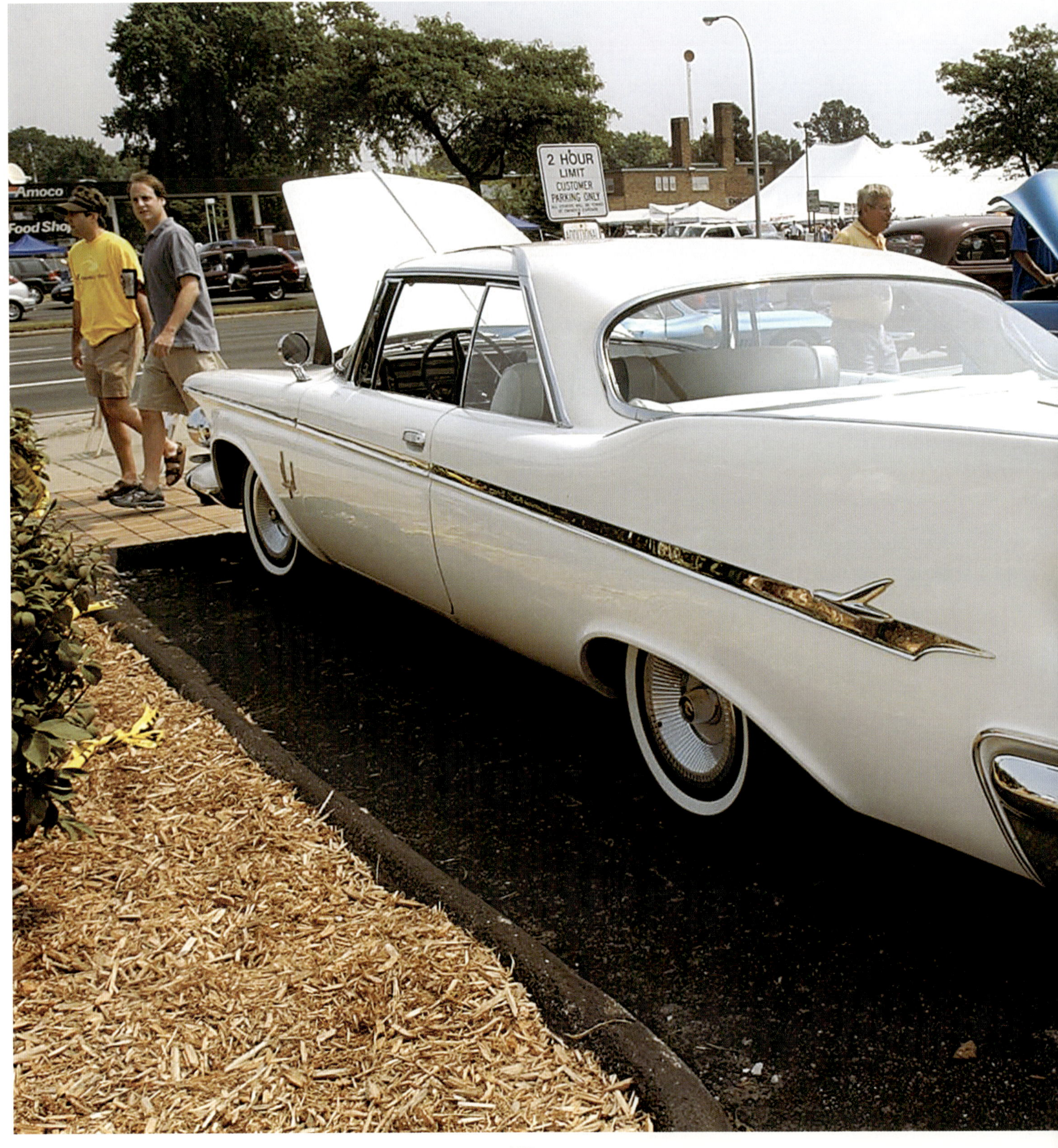
Amoco
2 HOUR
LIMIT
CUSTOMER
PARKING ONLY

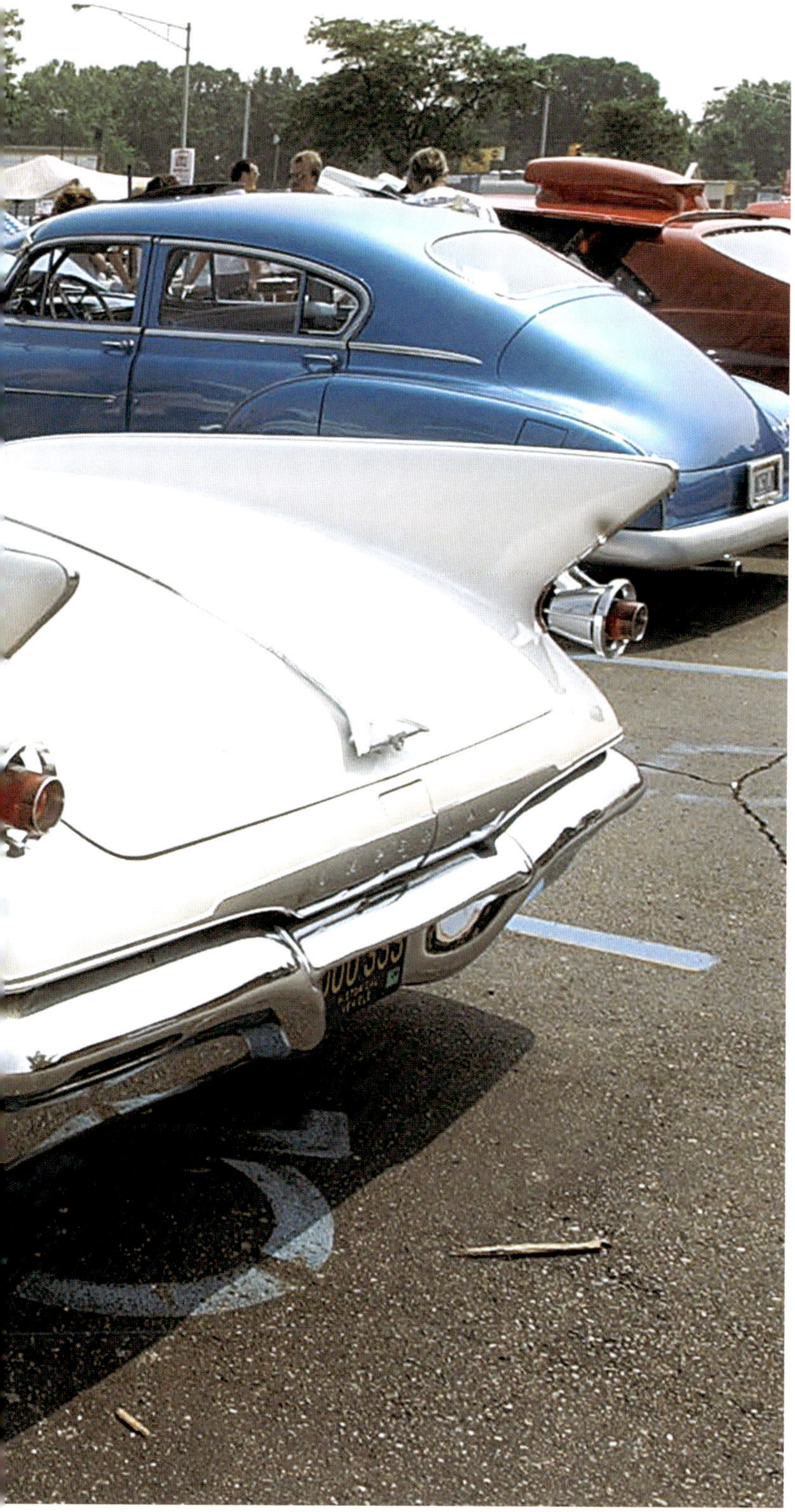

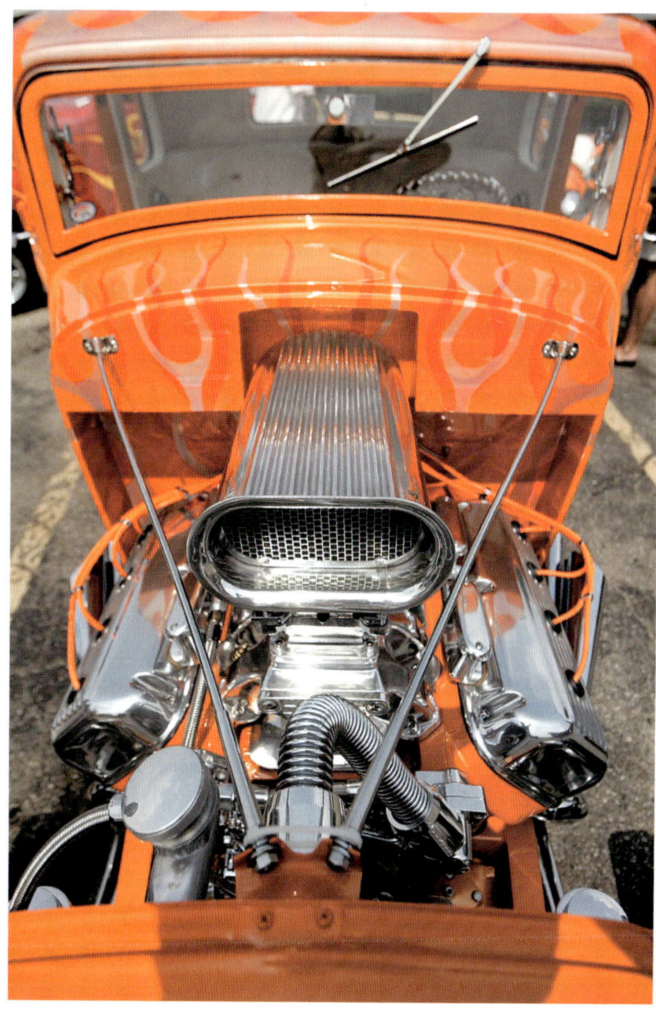

ABOVE: ALONG THE STRIP, Larry Spivey of Milan showed off his 1932 Ford Deuce coupe, which, by the way, is equipped with a 392 Hemi motor.

LEFT: REGAL VEHICLES WERE THE TALK OF THE TOWN. Spectators admired a rare 1961 Chrysler Imperial with its hood popped, just off Woodward near 12 Mile in Royal Oak. Only 880 two-door models were ever built. Classic cars of all types converged on the weekend's ninth annual event. Among the cars at the cruise were a 1967 Rolls Royce Corniche, a 1949 Packard sedan and a 1923 Ford T-bucket.

Left: WILLIAM ARCHIE; Above: ROMAIN BLANQUART

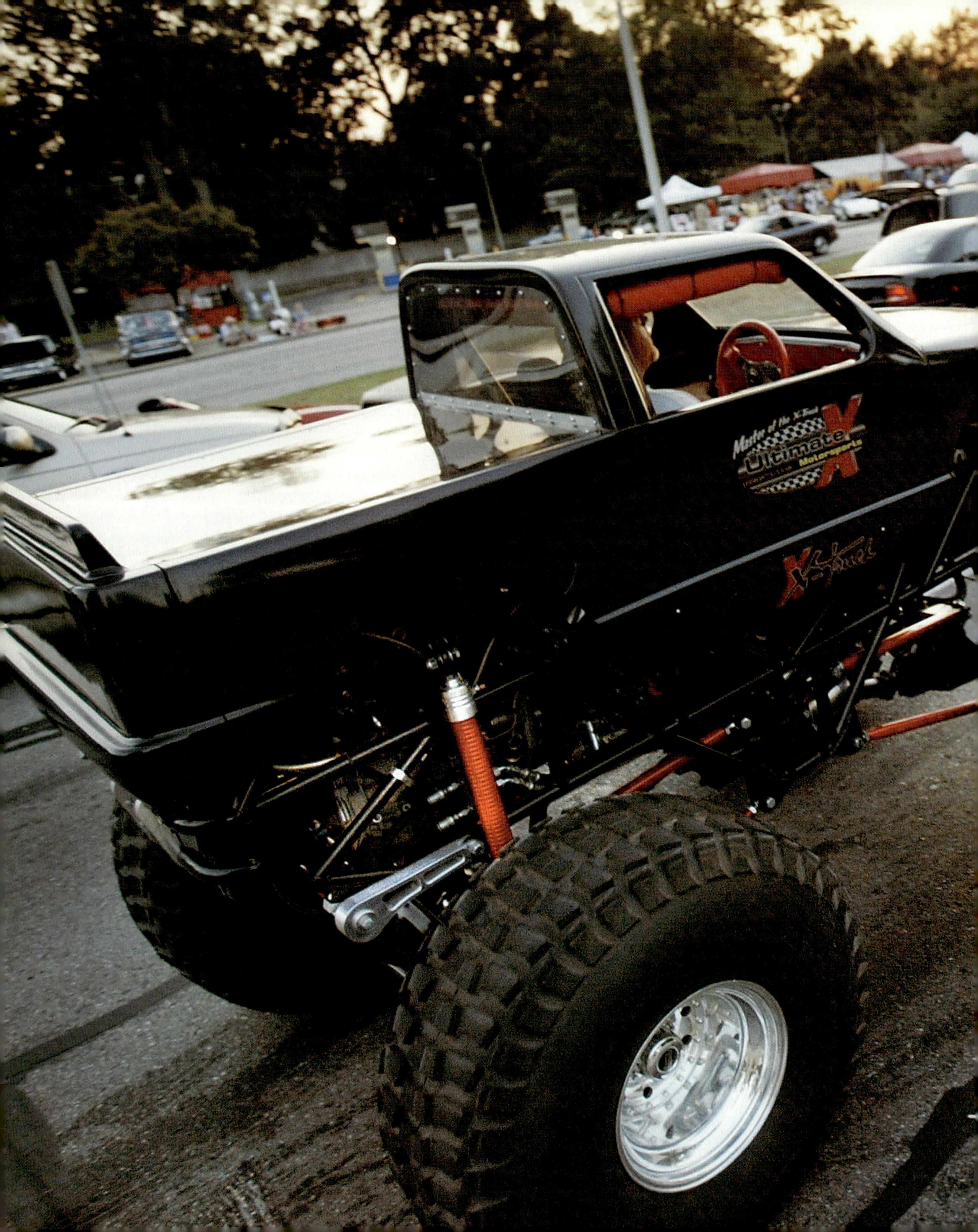
Ultimate
Motorsports

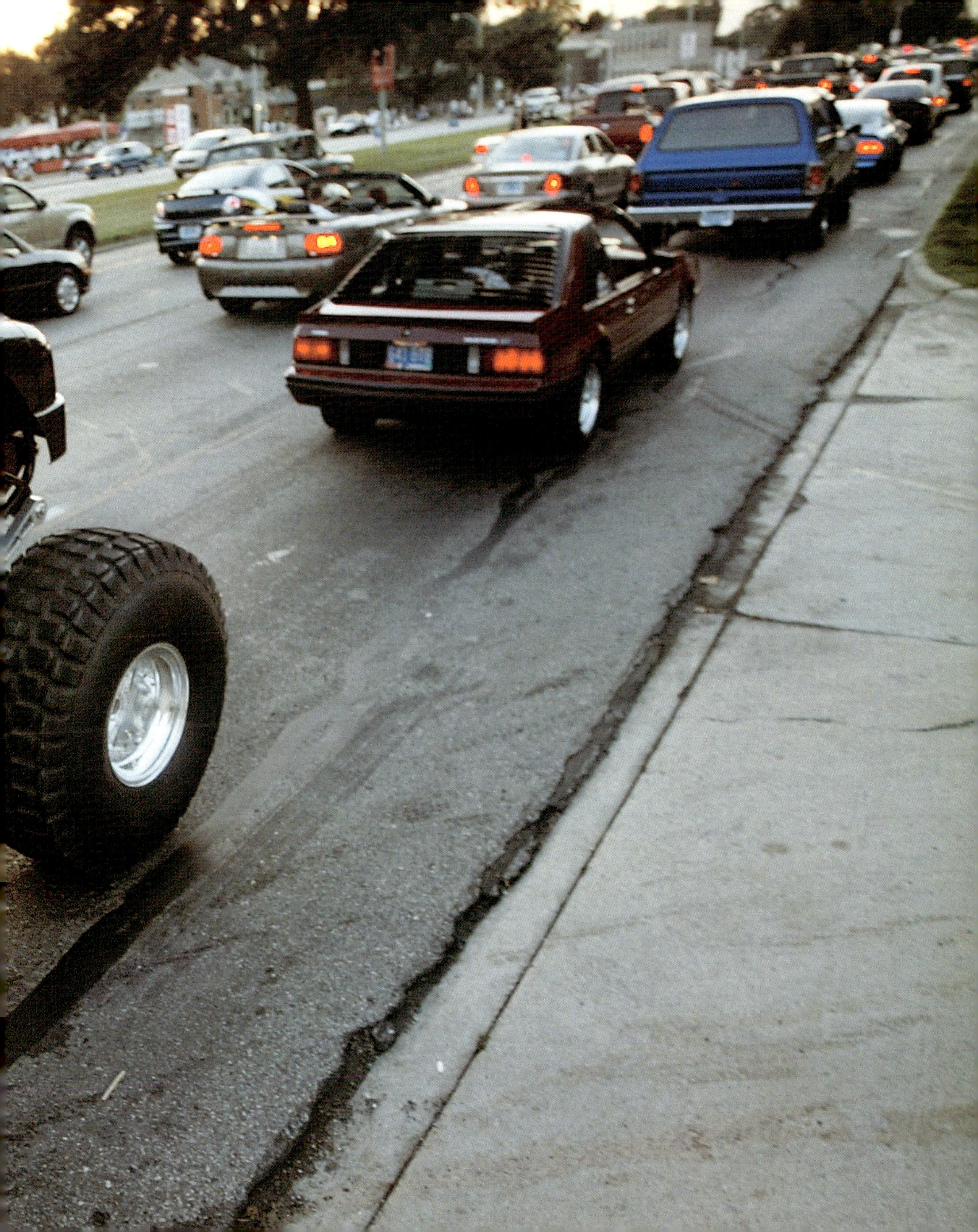

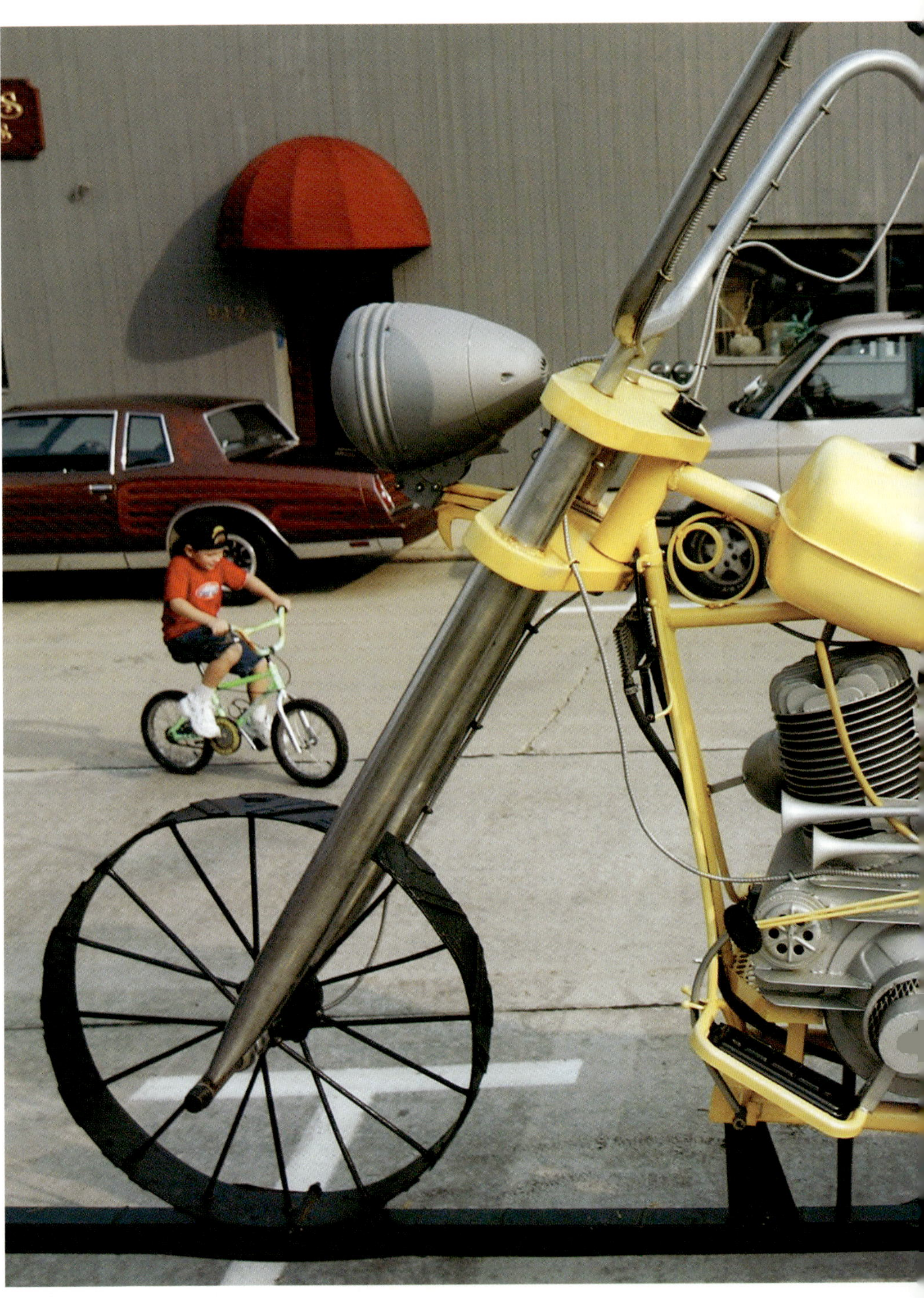

TWO THOUSAND THREE

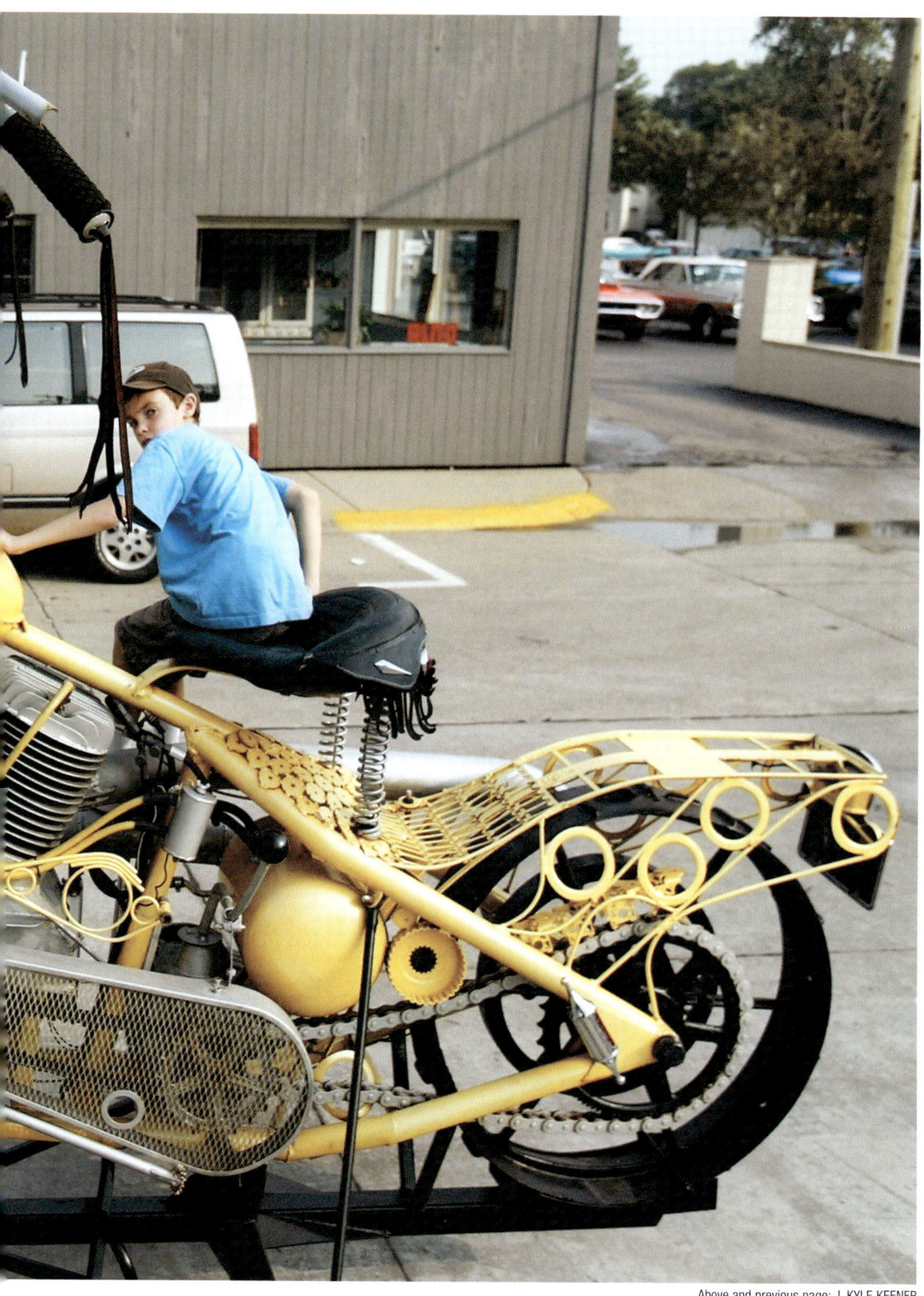

Above and previous page: J. KYLE KEENER

DRAWN TO THE LARGER-THAN-LIFE SCULPTURE, James Creevey, 8, of Lake Orion climbed aboard a massive metal chopper in Birmingham. The big bike was built by legendary chopper designer Ron Finch of Pontiac. He used a hair dryer for a headlight and tractor wheels for tires. His creation is all for show — it didn't run — but it did shoot flames from the tailpipe. In the background is Mason Vires, 6.

PAGE 164: A CUSTOM-BUILT MINI-MONSTER TRUCK crawled north on Woodward in bumper-to-bumper traffic.

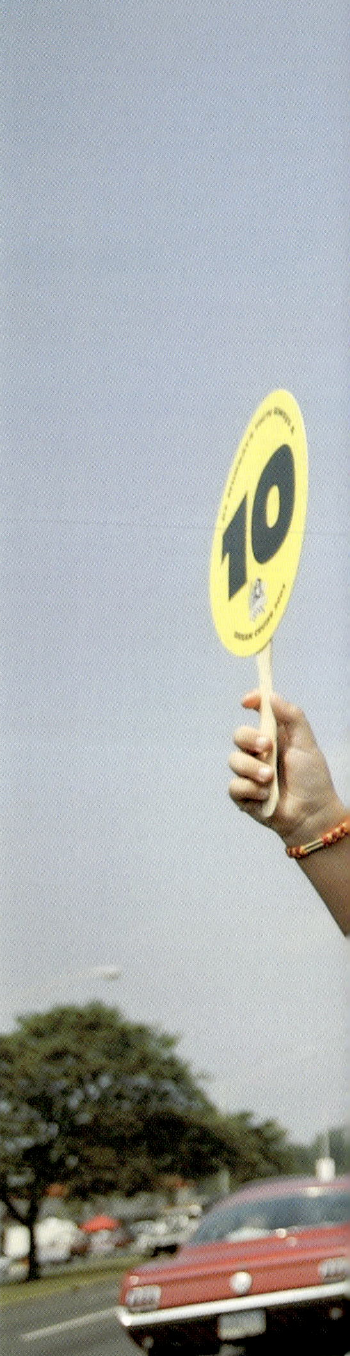

RIGHT: KIDS GOT IN THE ACT, TOO. Sean Cubbler, left, with sisters Erin Cubbler and Haley Cubbler, all 7, and cousins Monica Heymes, 10, and Eric Heymes, 9, waved to cars cruising by.

BELOW: But it was the parked classics that captured the attention of many adults.

PAGE 170: RIDING IN STYLE were Robert Bey, 21, of Lapeer, and Becky Plagens, 18, of Richmond, in a 1991 Ford Diesel 72-passenger bus as Drum Master Mike, back left, and DJ Matt McCorry mixed techno-house music. The van's restoration was done by Jason Harrison of Hadley, who made the vehicle available for party use.

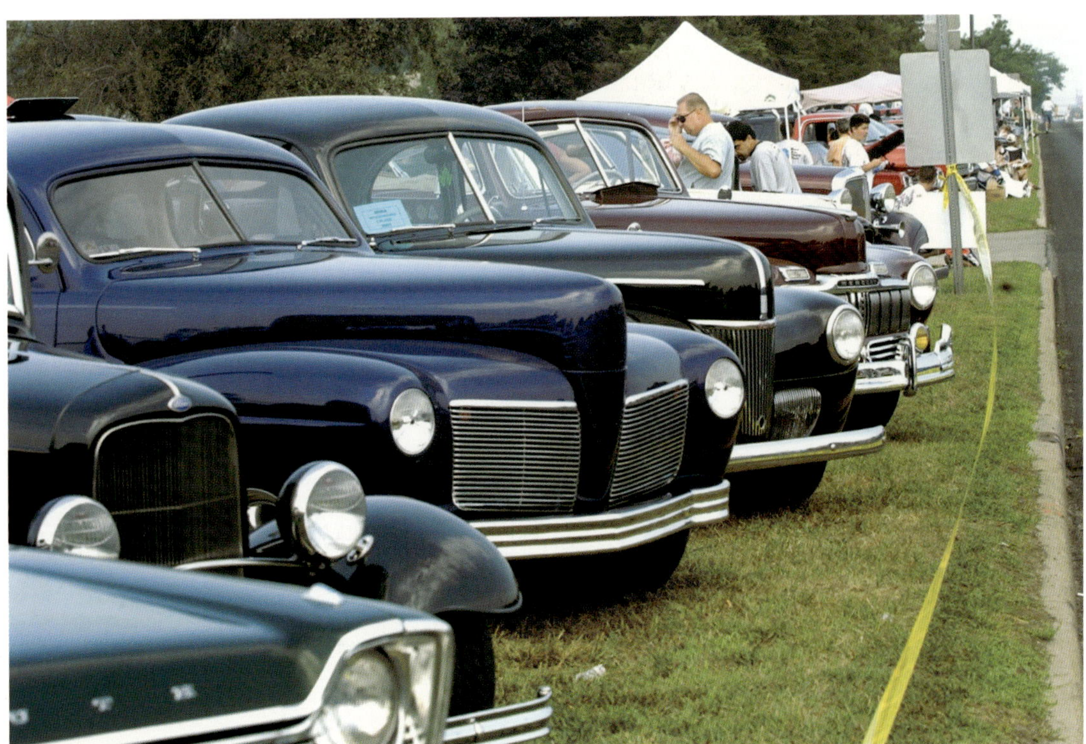

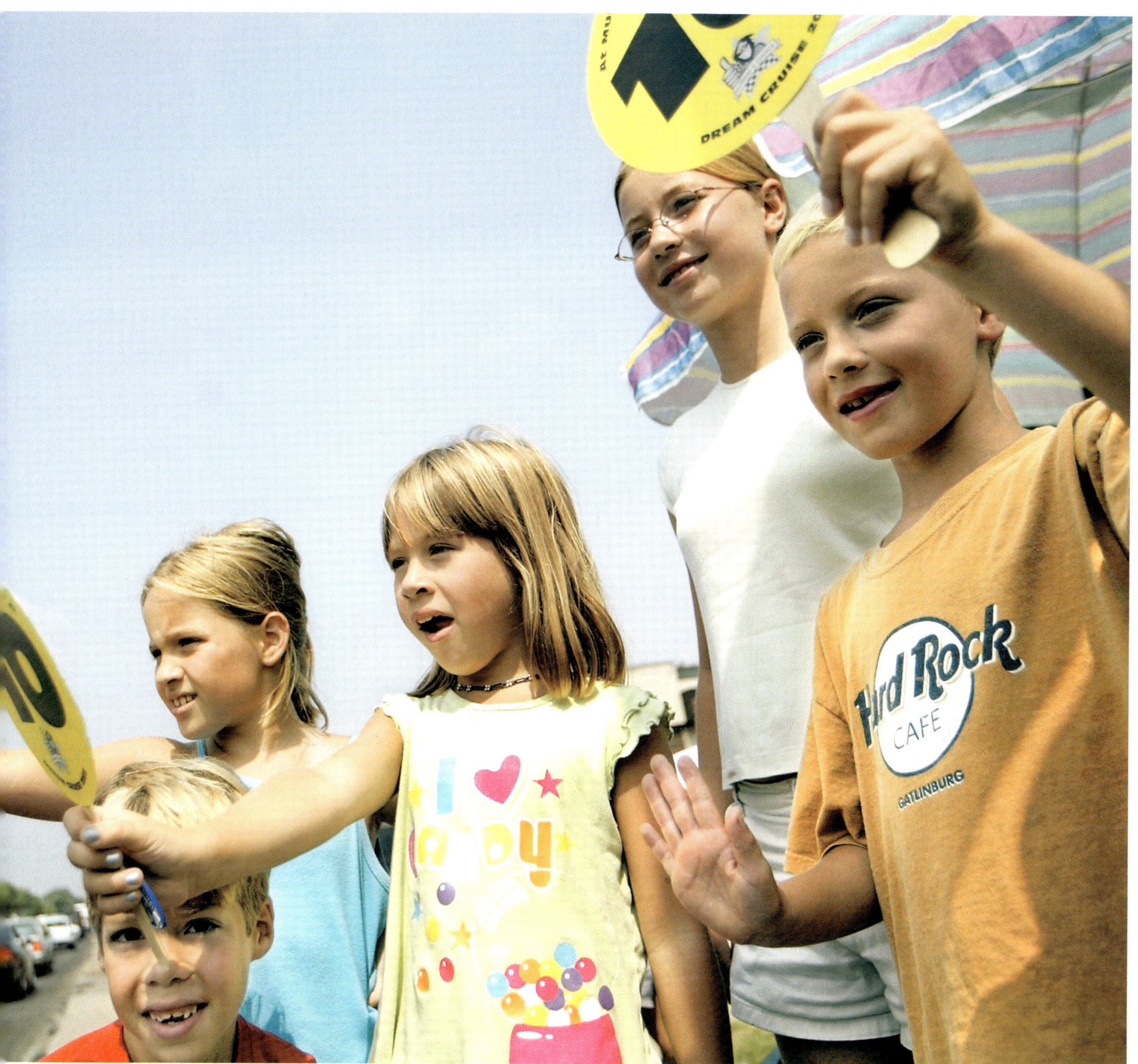

Left: WILLIAM ARCHIE; Above and next pages: ROMAIN BLANQUART

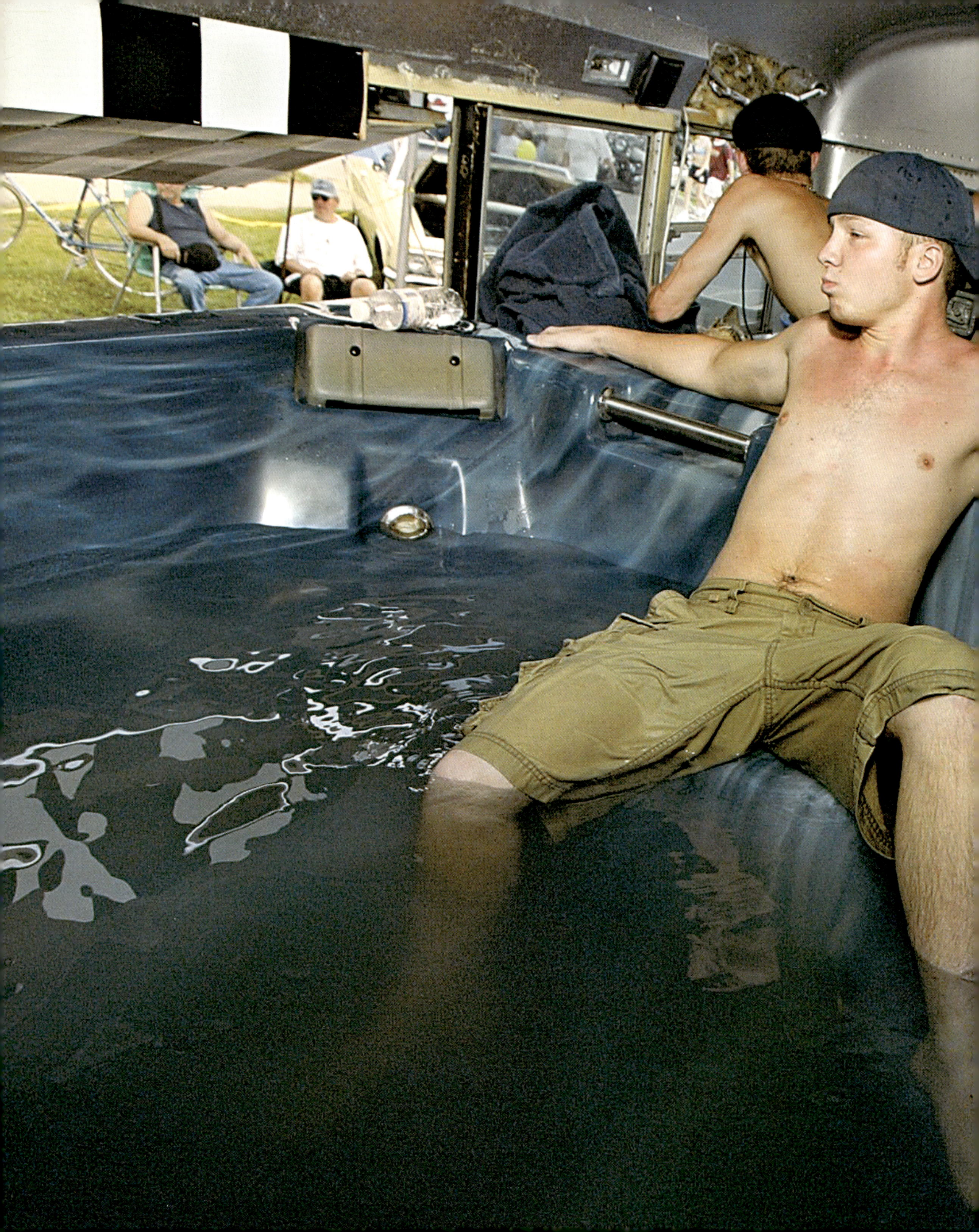

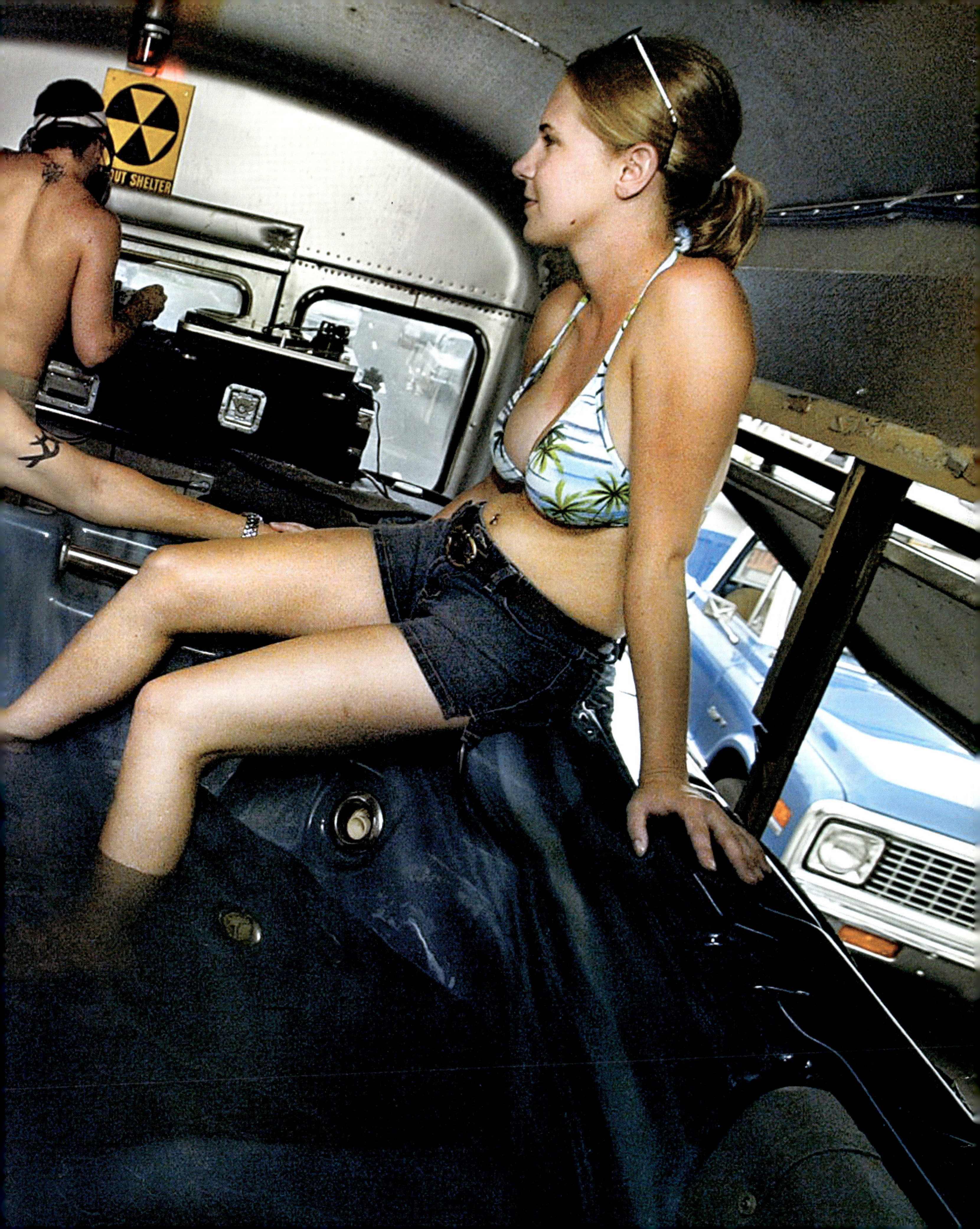
SHELTER

MIRROR IMAGES

Some people look like their pets. Others like their spouses. And a few look like their cars, mirroring an extraordinary relationship between proud car owner and gleaming alter ego on wheels.

In honor of the 2003 Woodward Dream Cruise, Free Press photographer J. Kyle Keener and staff writer Bill Laitner showcased these look-alikes. They are the ultimate proof of Detroit's classic maxim: You are what you drive.

RUSS AND JAMES DUNSKY, WYANDOTTE, 1969 LINCOLN MARK III

Elvis has left the building, and he's getting into a car in Wyandotte.

Shhh! It's really Russ Dunsky, 44, whose consuming passion since he was 13 has been impersonating Elvis Presley.

When Dunsky hit on being the 1969 version of the King — that out-of-fashion balladeer who made a comeback with the hit "Suspicious Minds" — just one car would do. It was a '69 Lincoln Mark III, Elvis' car in his comeback movie of 1970 called "Elvis: That's the Way It Is."

Pinstriped on the trunk is Elvis' silhouette. Hanging from the rearview mirror are Elvis scarves; one is autographed by the King.

If the Mark keeps purring, Dunsky's Elvis-pointin' protege will someday drive it. That would be James Dunsky, 6. He's been impersonating Elvis since he was 3.

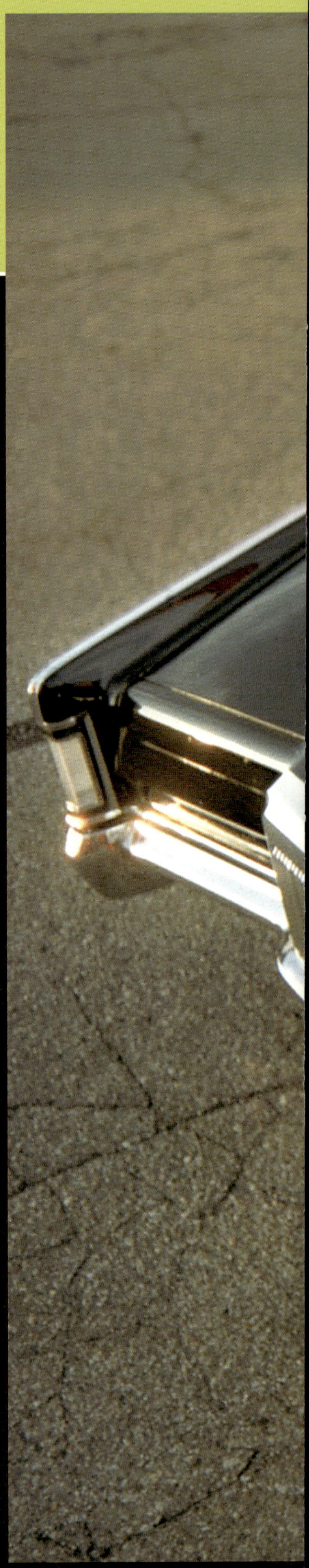

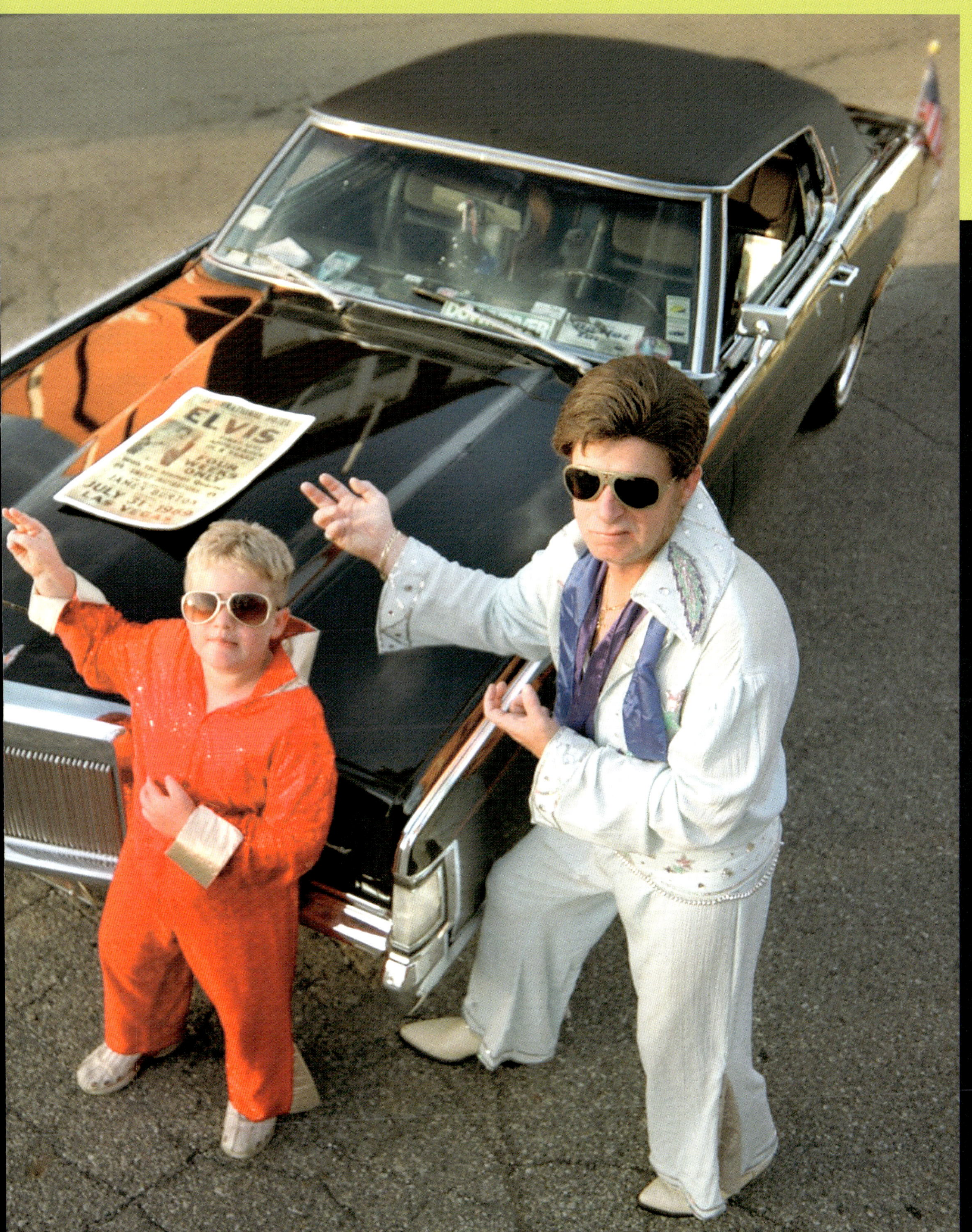
ELVIS
FOUR WEEKS ONLY
JAMES BURTON
JULY 31

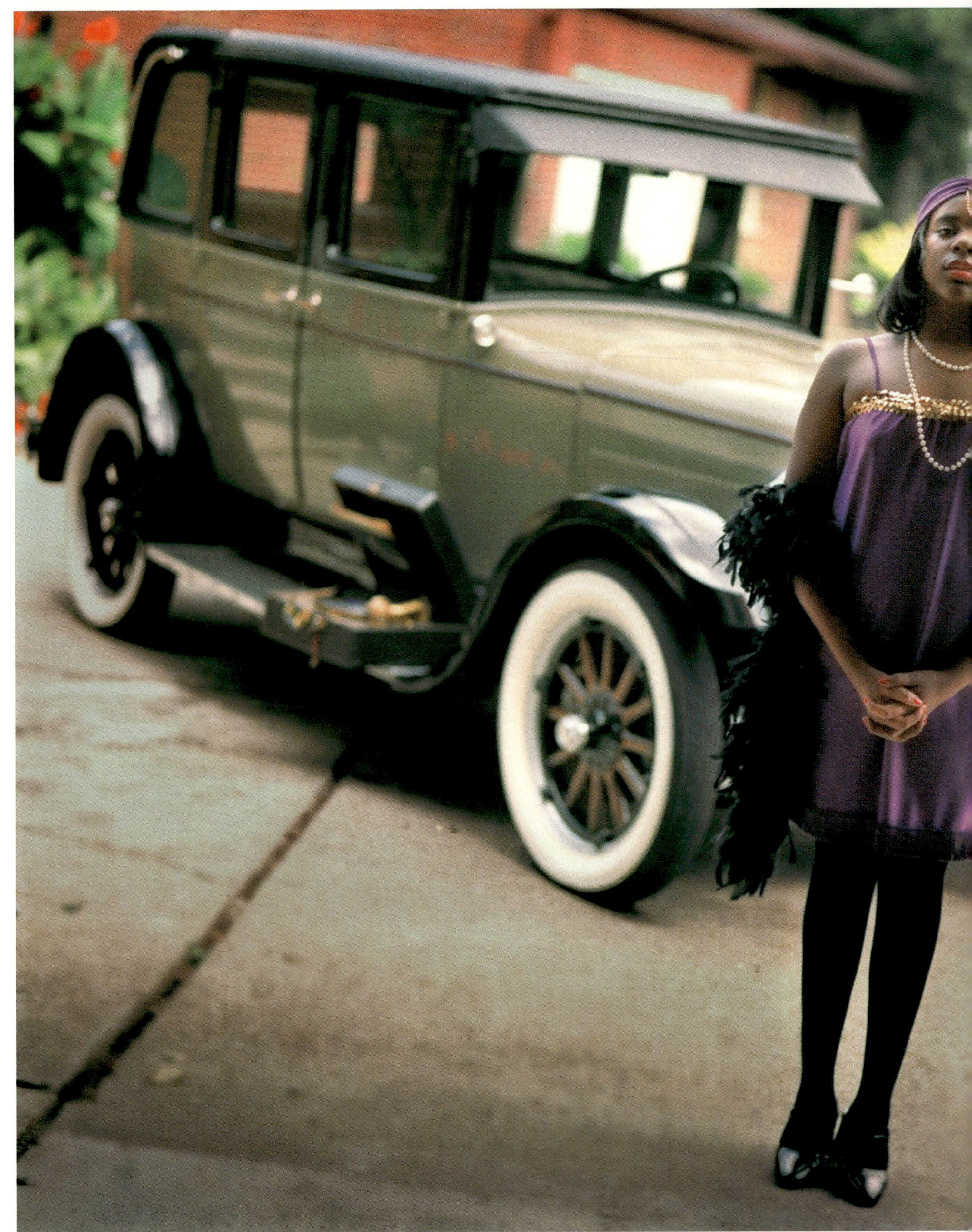

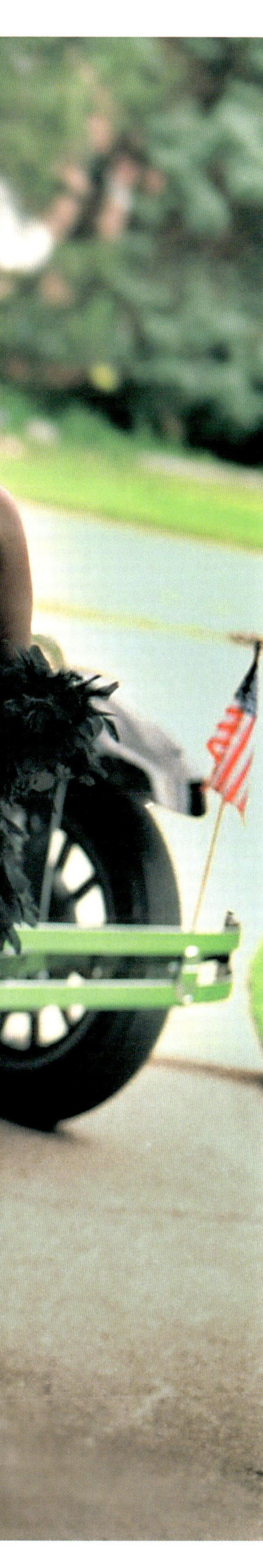

SHANELL HUDSON, DETROIT, 1926 OAKLAND LANDAU SEDAN

A father-and-daughter project led to this two-of-a-kind — a 1926 box elder-green Oakland Landau sedan and a little girl who loves dressing up.

Three years ago, Larry Hudson, 48, of Detroit bought his vintage machine. When new, Oaklands were super-premium autos priced at $1,295 each — triple the cost of most cars. Bank robbers Bonnie and Clyde drove one.

But Hudson's needed serious work. Daughter Shanell, then 8, asked, "What can I do, Daddy?" So the two sanded, scraped and reinstalled parts after having them plated, until the car shone and won awards. Then Shanell asked for a new role.

"We went to a costume place and got her a flapper's outfit. Mom does her hair up ... when she feels like being Bonnie," her father says.

"One day," he adds, "it will be hers."

PEARL WATTS, FERNDALE, 1955 CADILLAC COUPE DEVILLE

"55 PEARL" is on the license plate of a much-loved pearl-white '55 Cadillac Coupe DeVille.

Owner Pearl Watts, 60, is a match — in name, attire and elegance.

With her Caddy, Watts wears white or beige. Only.

"A lady should always look like a lady," Watts declares. "Like my car. She has a custom interior. Air-conditioning. All leather inside. A horn that sounds like a steam liner."

Her car is classy. And doesn't she look just like it? Oh no, she says.

"Honey, I look better than my car!"

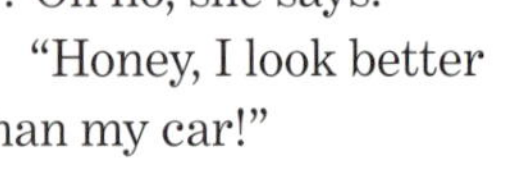

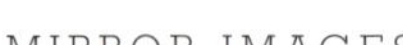

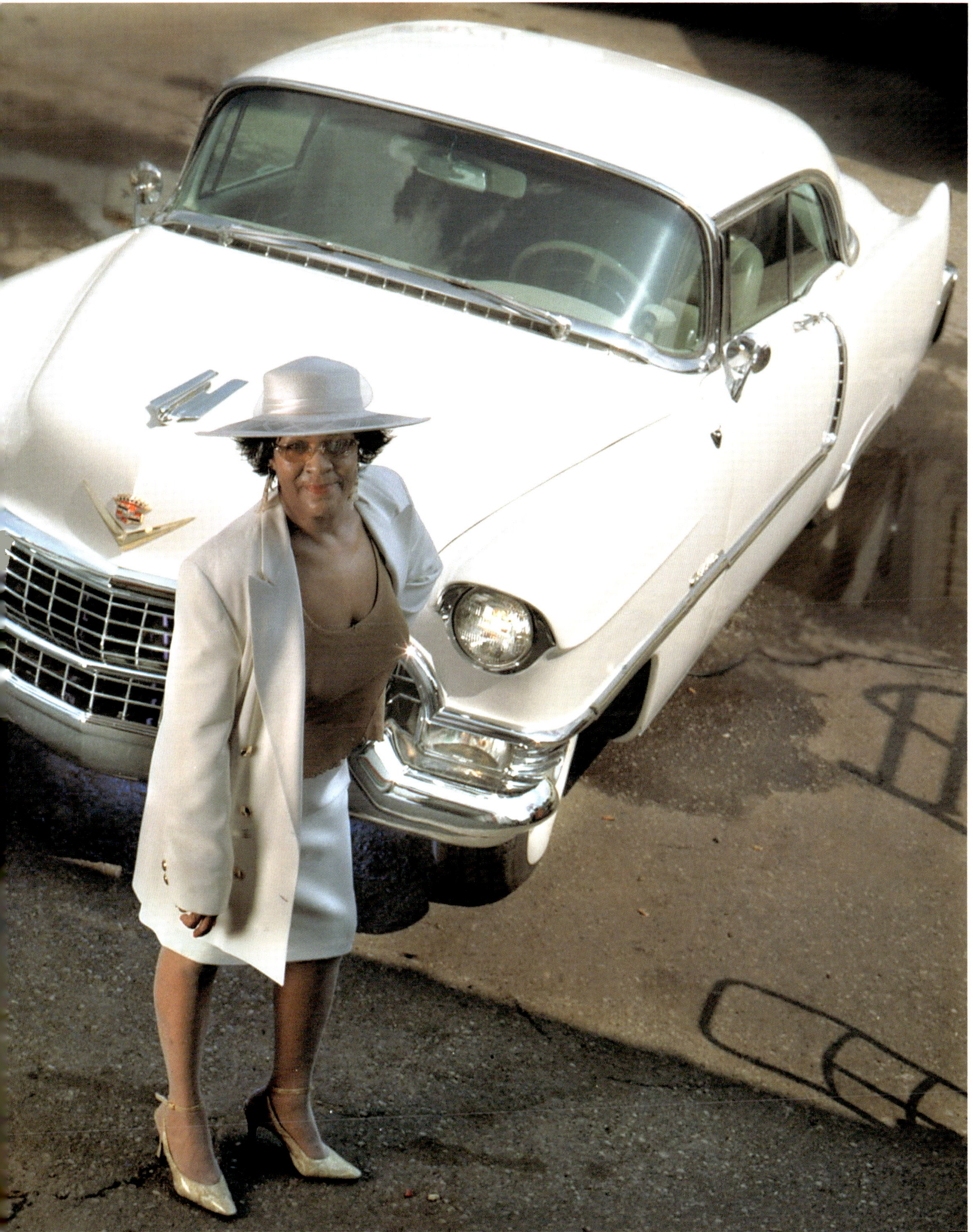

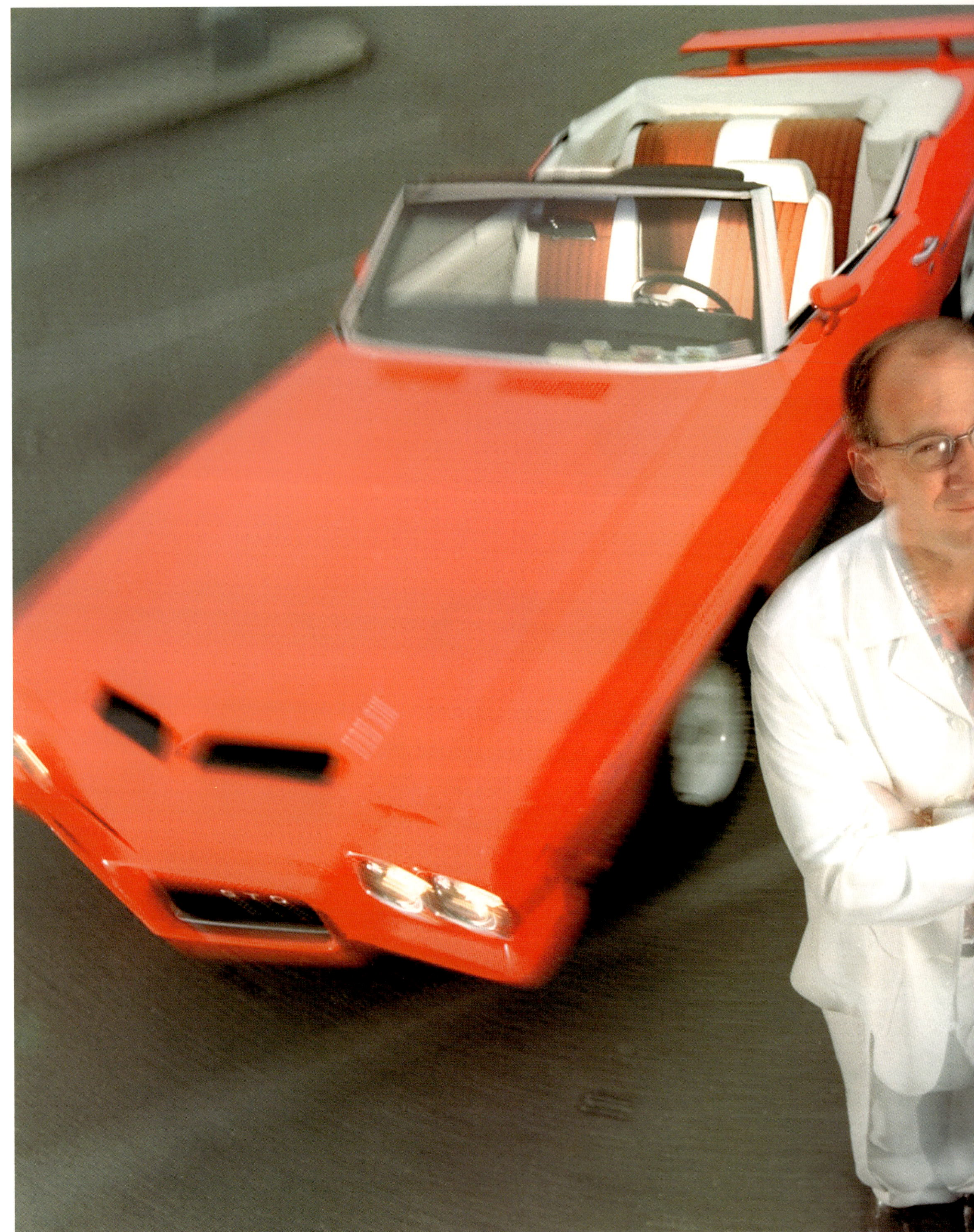
GTO

TODD BAILEY, ANN ARBOR, 1971 PONTIAC GTO

In his white silk suit and orange Hawaiian shirt, who could look more in sync with a '71 bright orange-on-white Pontiac ragtop than Todd Bailey, 36?

After Bailey bought the car, he couldn't help himself. He began spotting clothes that matched. Now, when he displays his car at shows, man and car dress alike.

His car is a trophy winner. So is that suit.

WILLIE GUATERI, EASTPOINTE, 1949 CHEVROLET

Both old, both short and pals for half a century yet still going strong. That's Willie Guateri, 82, and his 1949 royal blue Chevrolet.

In 1952 — when Woodward cruising was no nostalgia trip but a right-now thing — Guateri chopped 5 inches from his car's top, then lowered its chassis more than an inch. Unwittingly, he set up a match with his own diminutive stature, 5 feet 2.

The Chevy now has parts from a dozen other cars.

Both sport classy tops — he, a vintage fedora, his car, a pleated ceiling and removable roof.

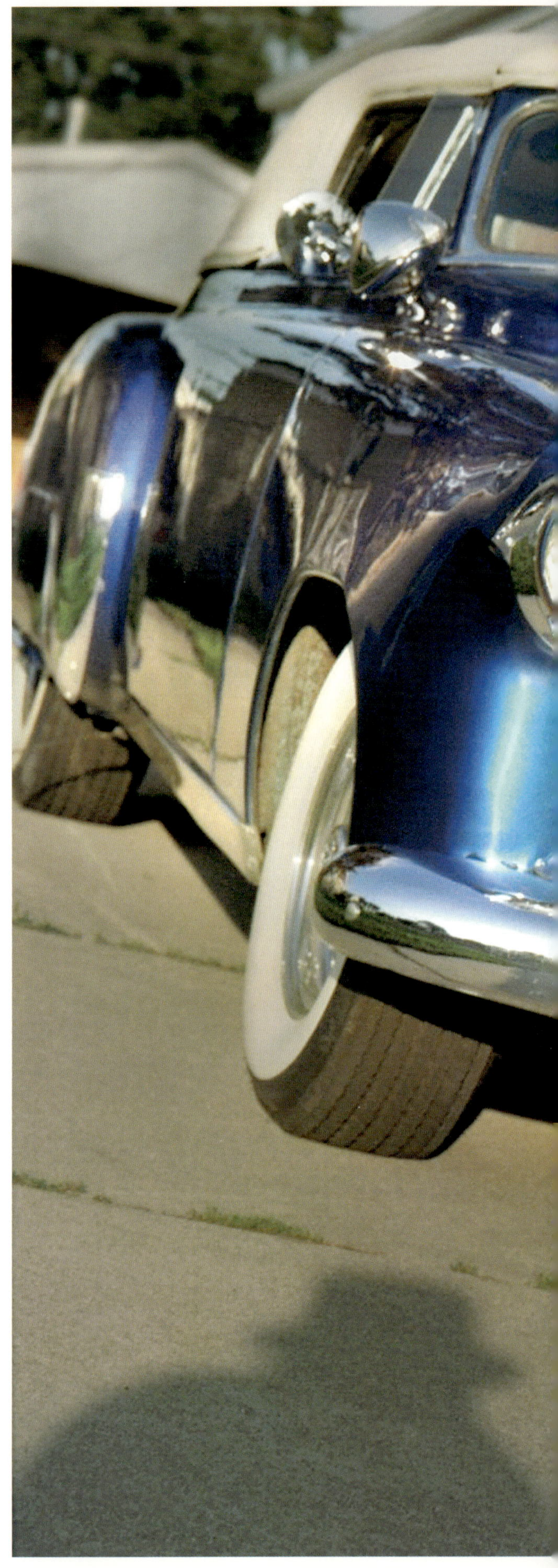

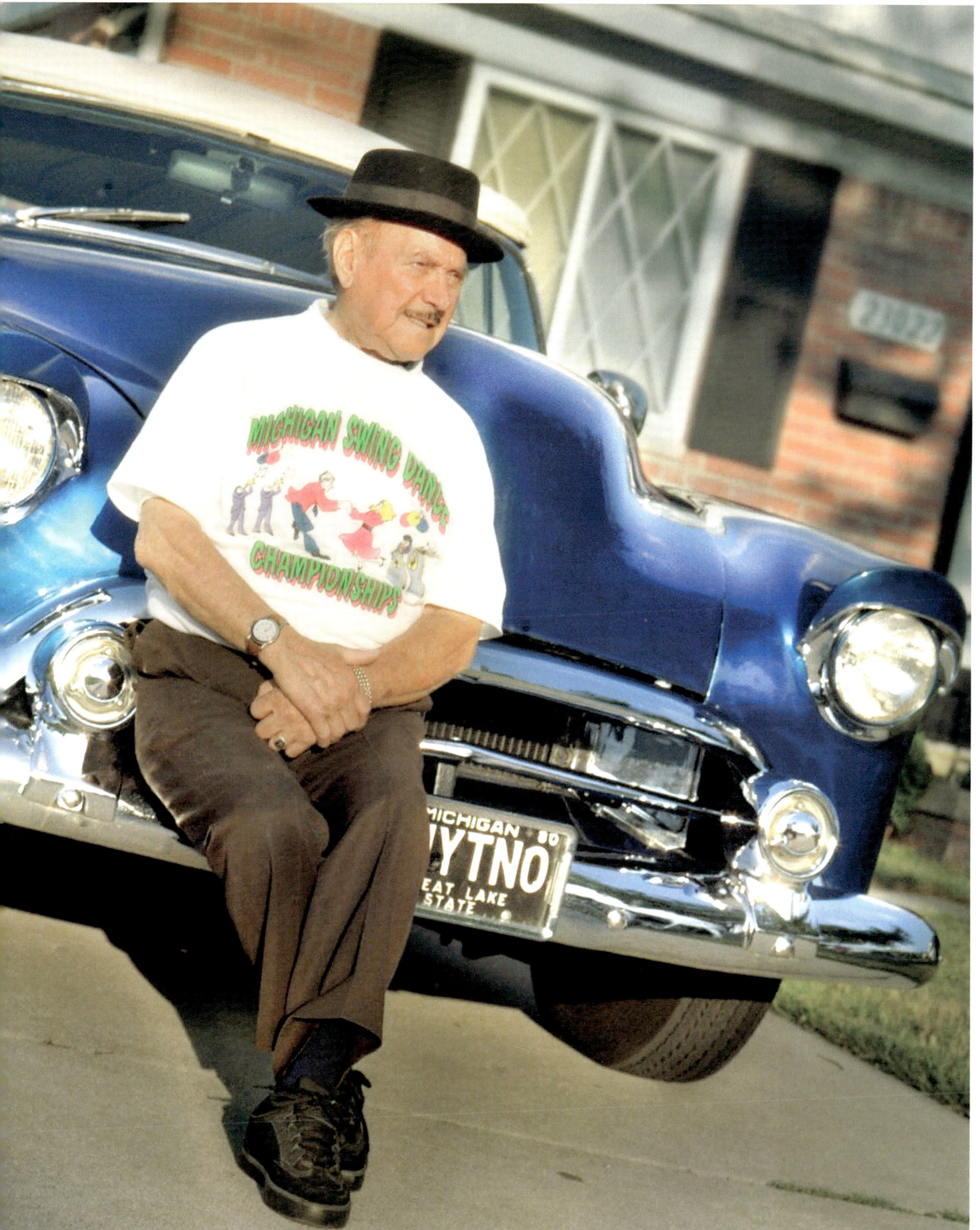
MICHIGAN SWING
CHAMPIONSHIPS
MICHIGAN 80

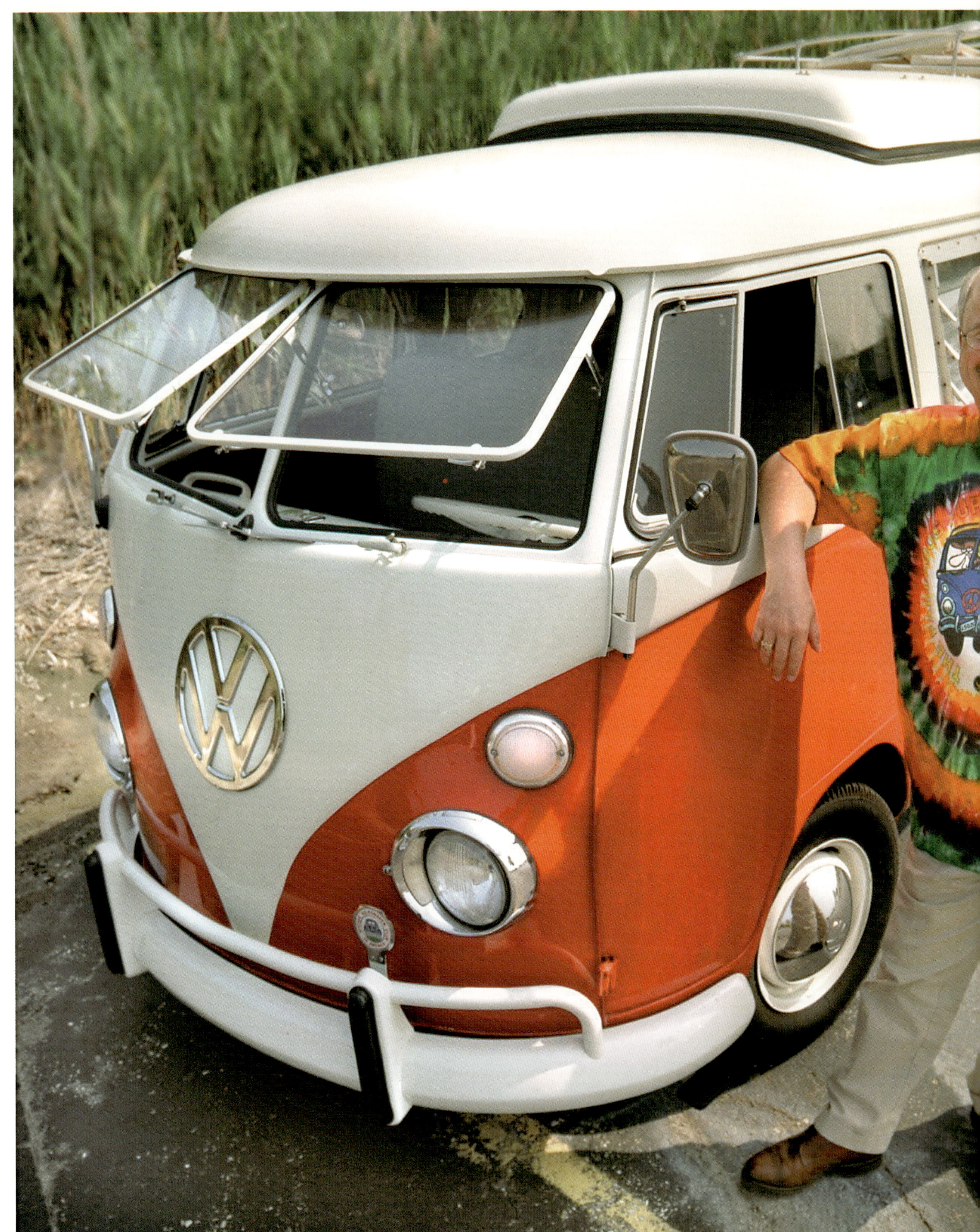

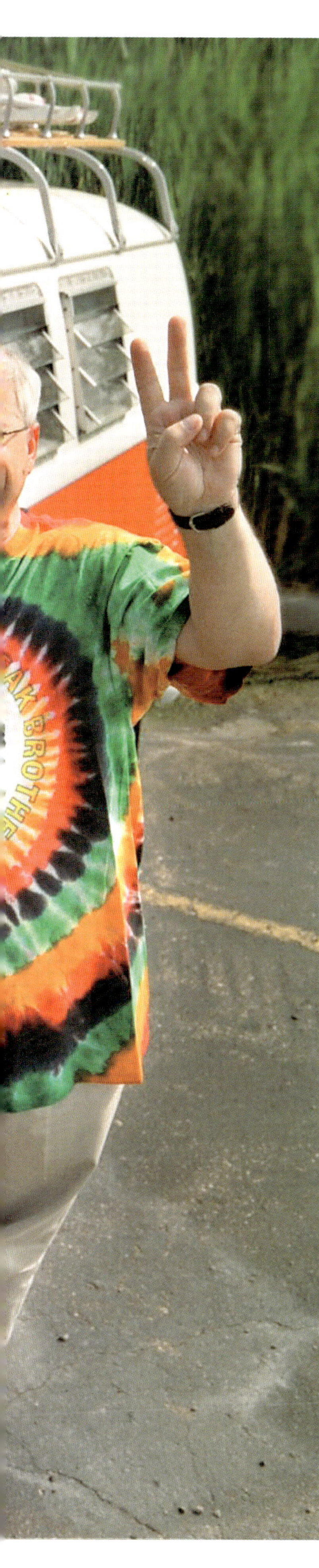

RICHARD HAMANN, FARMINGTON HILLS, 1967 VOLKSWAGEN CAMPMOBILE

He may be an automotive-component salesman now. But Richard Hamann, 50, can't forget his high school days, when he had a VW Microbus.

Nor the years when he attended the University of California at Los Angeles, with hair that fell past his shoulders. Though the long locks have disappeared, "I'm still a hippie at heart," he says.

So is his 1967 Volkswagen Campmobile, perfectly set off by Hamann's tie-dyed shirt.

When he bought it in 1985, the bus came with high miles on the odometer, and it badly needed a makeover. Hamann and his wife, Roberta, spent two years doing much of the work themselves.

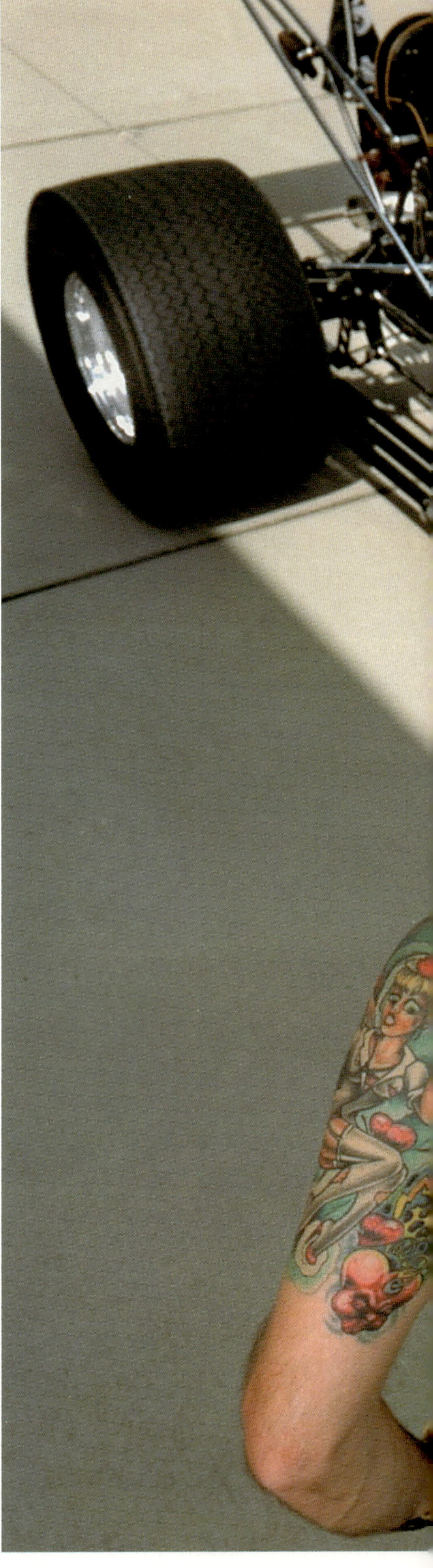

FRANK BIANCO, ROCHESTER HILLS, CUSTOM-BUILT OPEN ROADSTER

Two kinds of body art move in tandem when Frank Bianco, 50, takes a drive.

Bianco's tattoos coordinate beautifully with the air-brushed yellow and red flames on his hand-built, black open roadster. Both are swathed in a patriotic indictment of the Vietnam War.

The car, and the war, too, he calls the Devil's Joke. Bianco's left leg bears the names of six buddies who never came back.

"There's lots of flags, both places. ... All the upper thighs, the back and left leg are in tribute to our Vietnam veterans, men and women. And the vehicle is all that way," Bianco says.

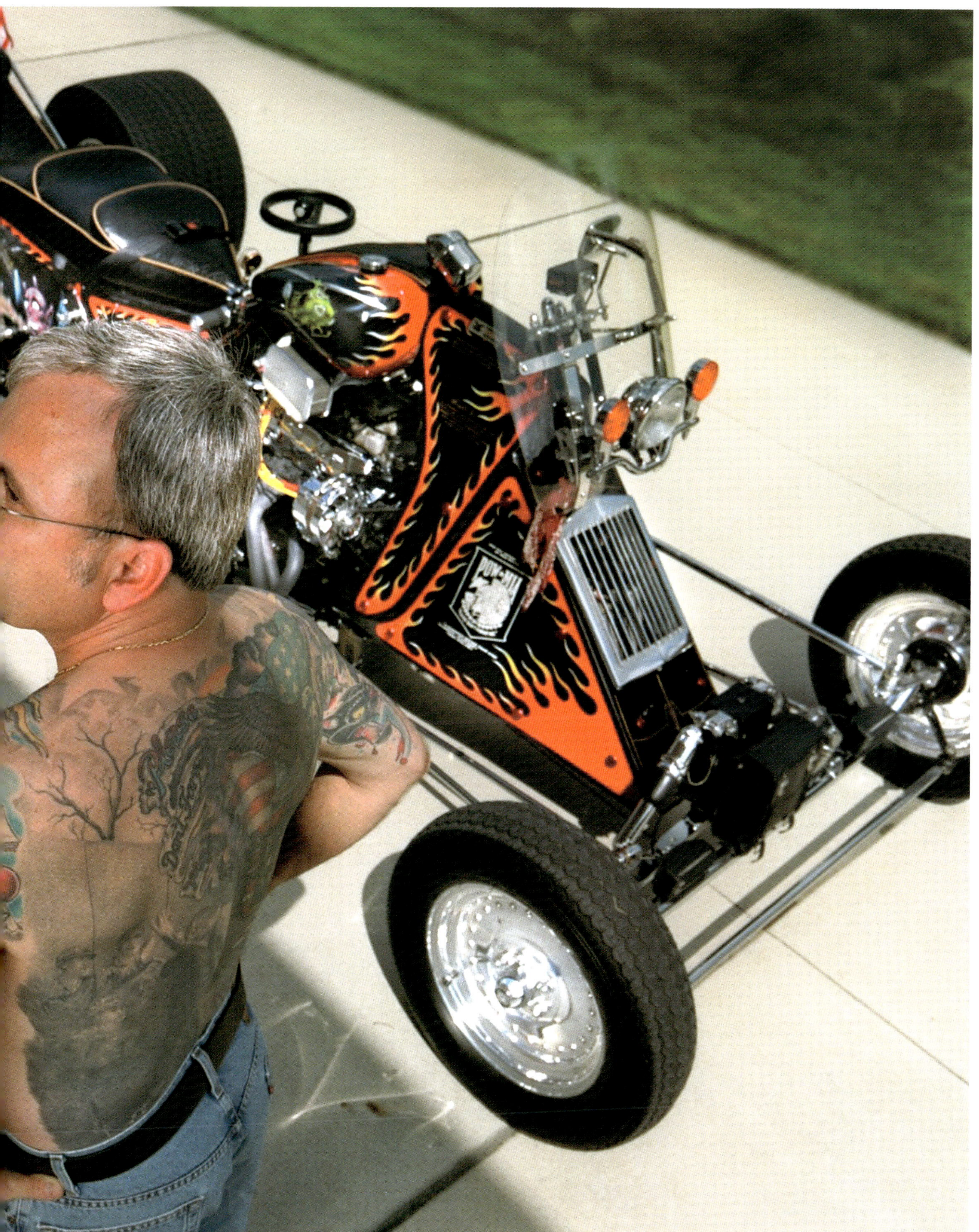

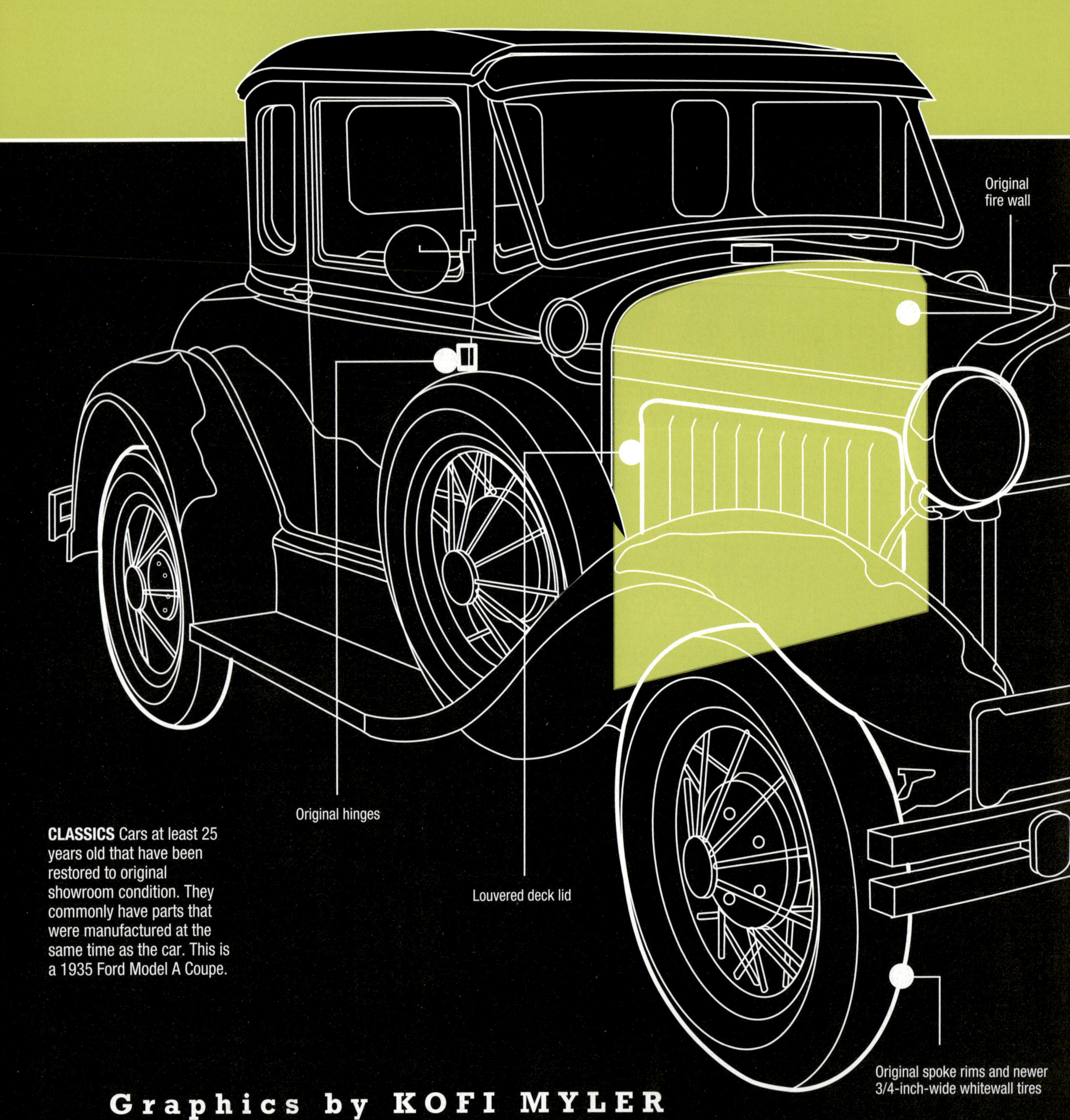

CLASSICS Cars at least 25 years old that have been restored to original showroom condition. They commonly have parts that were manufactured at the same time as the car. This is a 1935 Ford Model A Coupe.

Graphics by KOFI MYLER

INSIDE JOBS

By MARK PHELAN

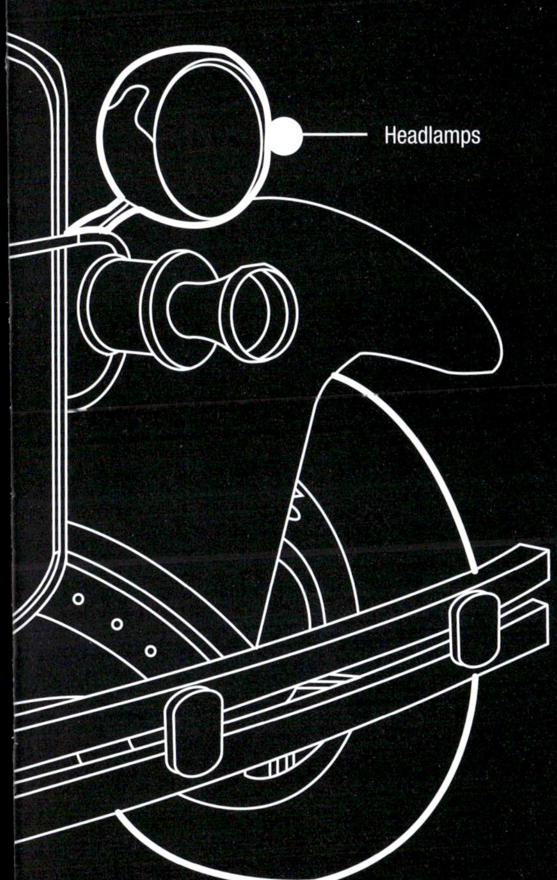

Cruising Woodward became a phenomenon when hotshot auto execs blasted up and down the avenue in their companies' '60s muscle cars, but the wheels you'll see in the Dream Cruise reflect every era and type of vehicle.

Muscle cars from the '60s and '70s predominate. The first muscle cars were born when automakers realized they could drop a huge V8 into a basic family car and make their whole product line more glamorous and desirable by association.

Woodward also echoes with the sound of street rods, which are generally 1930s to 1950s production cars that were reworked to the limits of legality. The modifications often include hood scoops or exposed engines. It's not uncommon for street rods to have both their suspension and roofline lowered — chopped and channeled, they call it — to create a racy and rakish profile.

The cruise also draws many classic cars that have been painstakingly restored to their original condition, often right down to the use of steel-belted whitewall tires and original fabric upholstery. > > >

Strictly speaking, a classic car is 25 years old, according to the Michigan Secretary of State, which issues special license plates for the cars.

Other types of cars likely to hit the road during Dream Cruise:

> Low riders, which use complicated systems to change the cars' height and even bounce them up and down.

> Customs, late-model cars, trucks and SUVs packed with accessories ranging from DVD players to spinner rims and neon underbody lights.

> Tuners, late-model compact and subcompact cars with accessories to boost performance, personalize their appearance or upgrade their stereos to window-rattling power. ■

LOW RIDERS This car, which began at the same time as the hot rod, originated with Latino culture in East Los Angeles. Famous for going slow and riding low, contemporary low riders are given tinted windows, custom paint jobs, hydraulic systems and heightened horsepower. This is a 1985 Oldsmobile Cutlass Supreme.

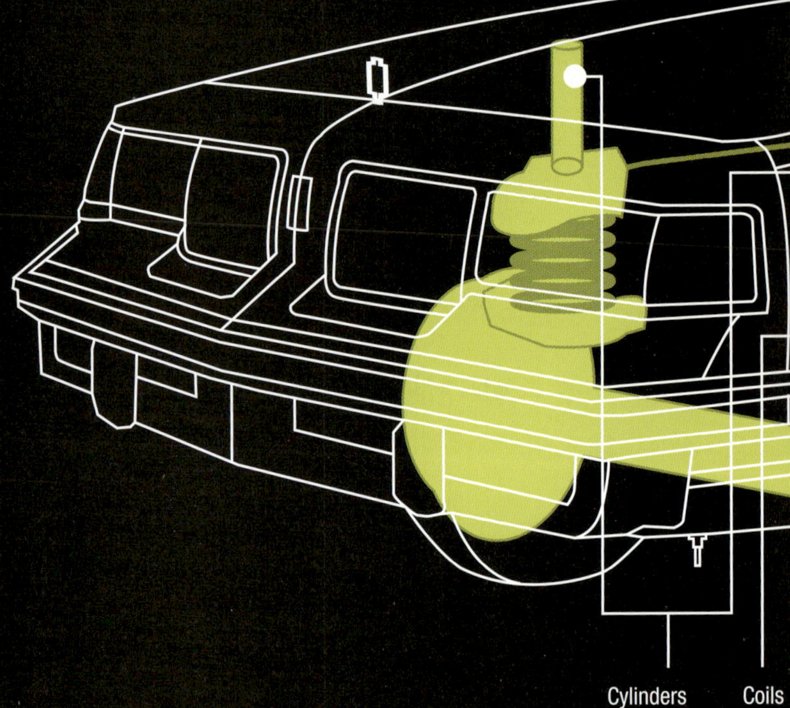

HOT RODS OR STREET RODS Cars from the 1930s to 1950s that have modified engines and appearances. Common modifications include custom paint jobs, lowered roof and ride heights and flamethrower systems that emit fire from the exhaust pipes. This is a 1932 Ford Roadster.

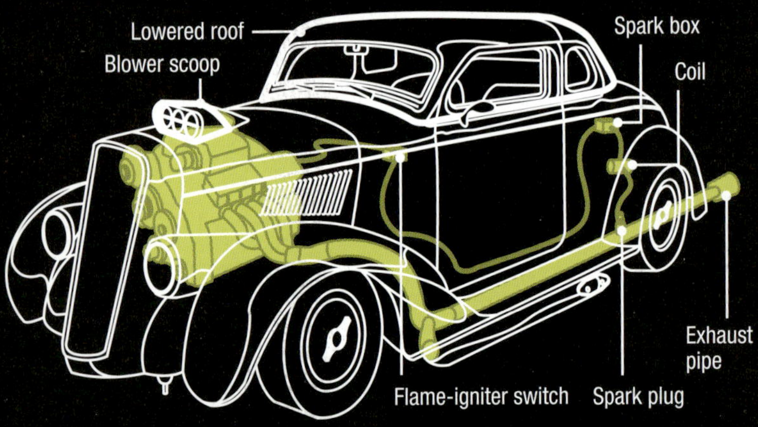

MUSCLE CARS These cars are commonly restored to original showroom condition, and their engines are decorated with chrome or gold parts. This is a 1965 Pontiac GTO.

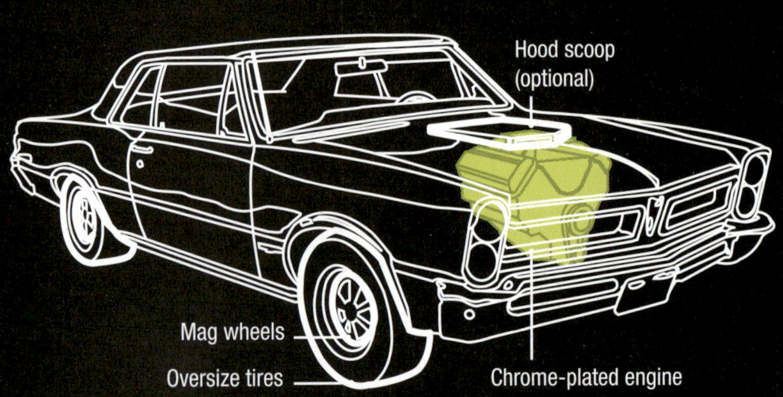

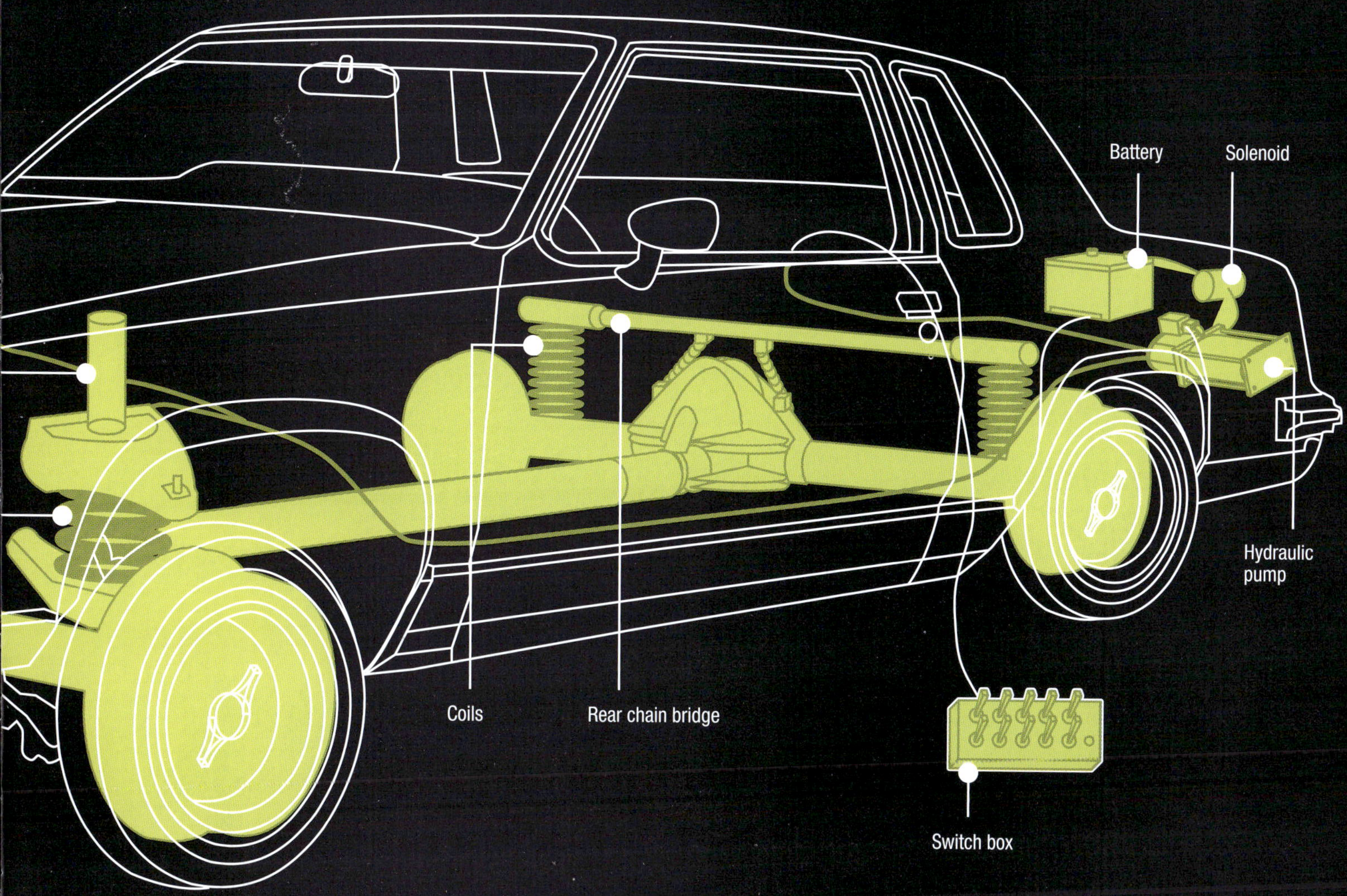

Battery

Solenoid

Hydraulic pump

Coils

Rear chain bridge

Switch box

TUNERS Tuners are ordinary street or sports cars, mostly Japanese brands, modified for high performance and appearance. Common modifications include nitrous oxide to increase horsepower, advanced intake systems, stereo upgrades and neon trim. This is a 1999 Honda Civic SI.

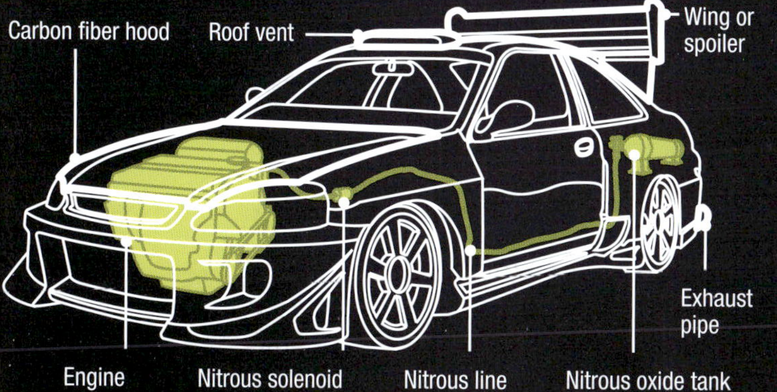

CUSTOMS Revered in hip-hop culture. The arrival of SUVs has ushered in a trend of customized and luxury riding that include stereo upgrades, entertainment stations, designer upholstery such as Louis Vuitton or Gucci, extra-large tires and expensive rims. This is a 1998 Lincoln Navigator.

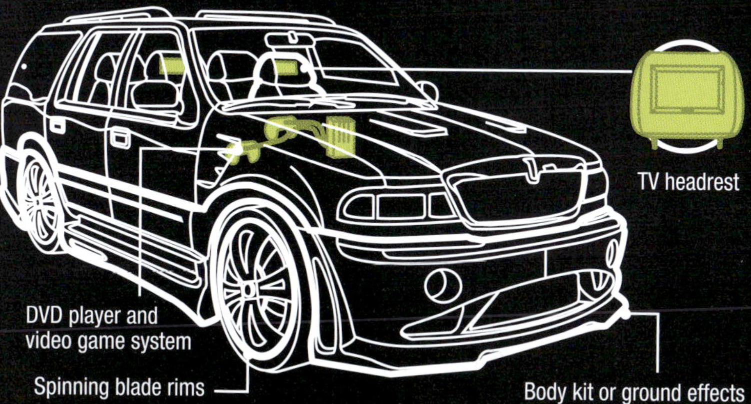

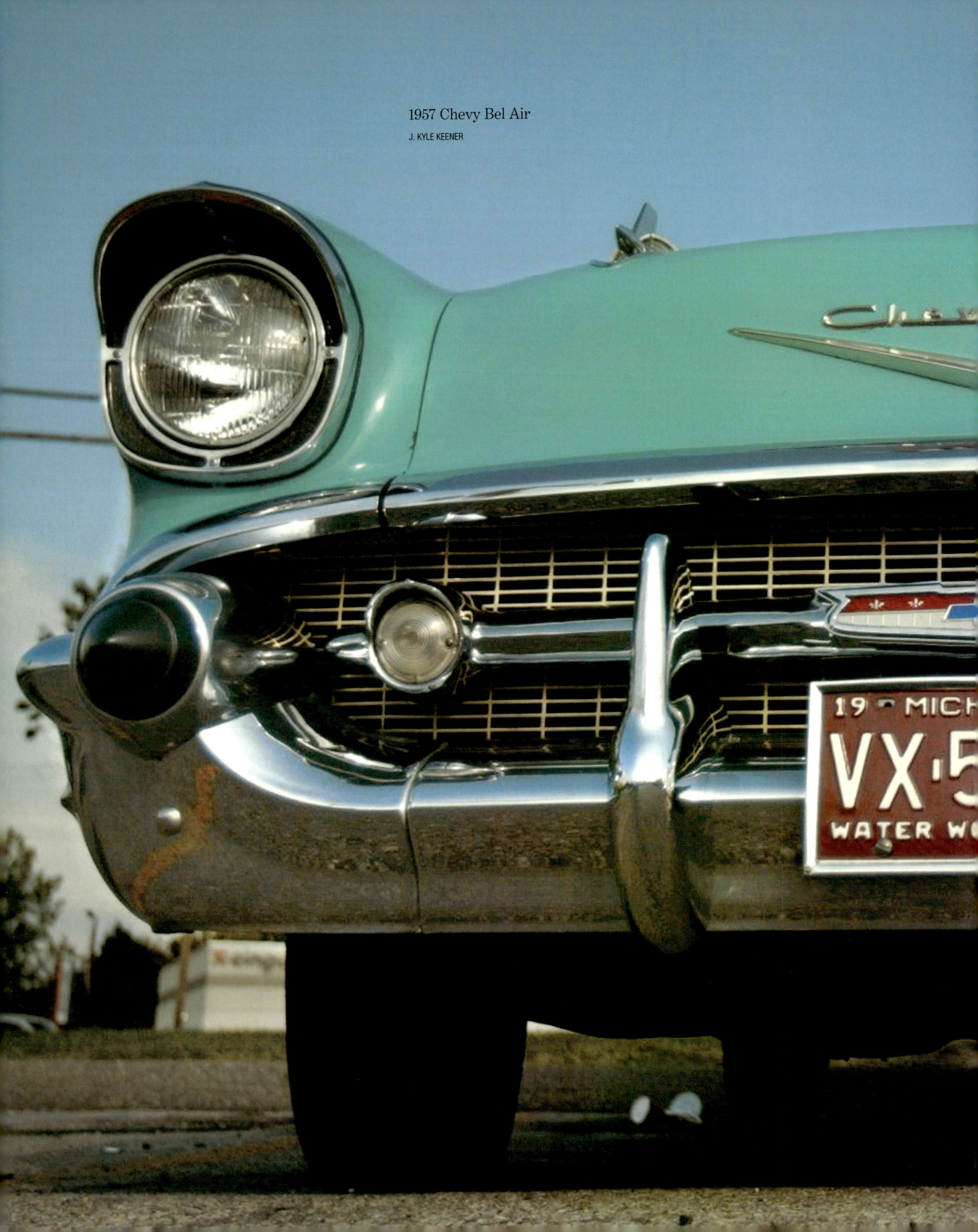

1957 Chevy Bel Air

J. KYLE KEENER

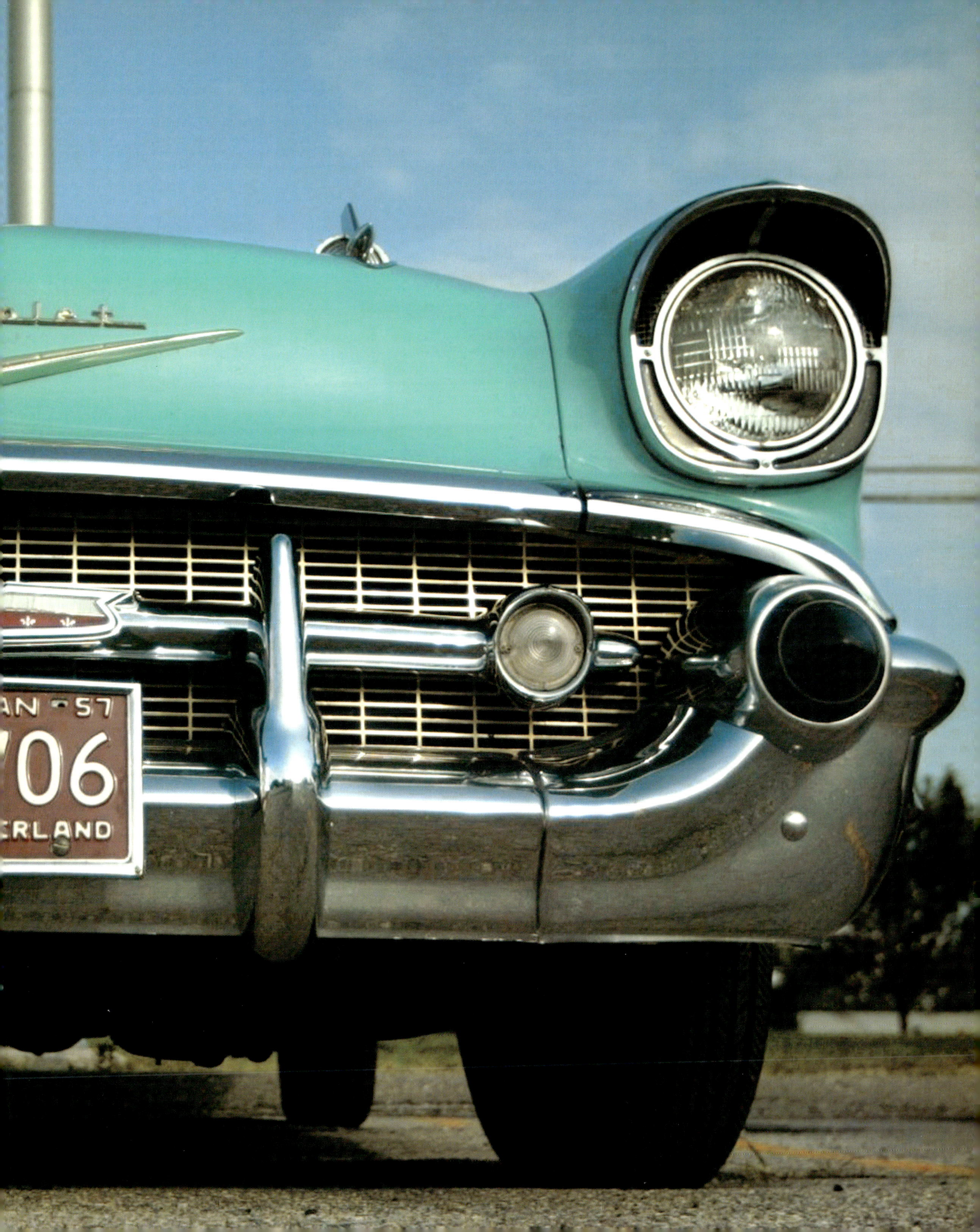
AN 57
706
ERLAND